Lecture Notes in Artificial Intelligen

Edited by J. G. Carbonell and J. Siekmann

Subseries of Lecture Notes in Computer Science

Yang Cai (Ed.)

Ambient Intelligence for Scientific Discovery

Foundations, Theories, and Systems

Series Editors

Jaime G. Carbonell, Carnegie Mellon University, Pittsburgh, PA, USA
Jörg Siekmann, University of Saarland, Saarbrücken, Germany

Volume Editor

Yang Cai
Carnegie Mellon University, School of Computer Science
5000 Forbes Avenue, Pittsburgh, PA 15213, USA
E-mail: ycai@cmu.edu

Library of Congress Control Number: 2004117781

CR Subject Classification (1998): I.2, H.2.8, H.4, H.5, I.3, C.2

ISSN 0302-9743
ISBN 3-540-24466-2 Springer Berlin Heidelberg New York

Springer is a part of Springer Science+Business Media

springeronline.com

© Springer-Verlag Berlin Heidelberg 2005
Printed in Germany

Typesetting: Camera-ready by author, data conversion by Olgun Computergrafik
Printed on acid-free paper   SPIN: 11382027   06/3142   5 4 3 2 1 0

Preface

For half a century, computer scientists have been working on systems for discovering lawful patterns in letters, numbers, words and images. The research has expanded into the computational study of the process of scientific discovery, producing such well-known AI programs as BACON and DENDRAL. However, *autonomous* discovery systems have been rarely used in the real world. While many factors have contributed to this, the most chronic difficulties seem always to fall into two categories: (1) the representation of the prior knowledge that people bring to their tasks, and (2) the awareness of new context.

Many difficult scientific discovery tasks can only be solved in *interactive* ways, by combining intelligent computing techniques with intuitive and adaptive user interfaces. It is inevitable that human intelligence is used in scientific discovery systems. For example, the human eyes can capture complex patterns and relationships, along with detecting the exceptional cases in a data set. The human brain can easily manipulate perceptions (shape, color, balance, time, distance, direction, speed, force, similarity, likelihood, intent and well-being) to make decisions. This process consists of *perception* and *communication* and it is often ubiquitous and autonomous. We refer to this kind of intelligence as ambient intelligence (AmI).

Ambient intelligence is about human interaction with information in a way that permits humans to spot interesting signs in massive data sources – building tools that capitalize on human strengths and compensate for human weaknesses to enhance and extend discovery capabilities. For example, people are much better than machines at detecting patterns in a visual scene, while machines are better at manipulating streams of numbers.

Scientific discovery is a process of creative perception and communication. With growing data streams and the complexity of discovery tasks, we see a demand for integrating novel digital media and communications (e.g., body media, capsule cameras, WiFi, etc.) and opportunities for ambient intelligence to use interaction methods that are usually taken for granted, such as perception, insight and analogy. We want to search for solutions to interesting questions such as: How do we significantly reduce information while maintaining meaning? How do we extract patterns from massive and growing data resources?

This volume represents the outcome of the SIGCHI Workshop on "Ambient Intelligence for Scientific Discovery," held in Vienna, on April 25, 2004. The chapters in this volume were selected from the revised papers submitted to the workshop and contributions from leading researchers in this area. The objective of this volume is to present a state-of-the-art survey of studies in ambient intelligence for scientific discovery, including novel ideas, insightful findings and ambient intelligence systems across multiple disciplines and applications. The volume is published for graduate students, senior undergraduate students, researchers and professionals. Therefore, extended references are provided in each chapter.

The contents in this volume are organized into three tracks: Part I, New Paradigms in Scientific Discovery; Part II, Ambient Cognition; and Part III, Ambient Intelligence Systems. Many chapters share common features such as interaction, vision, language, and biomedicine, which reflects the interdisciplinary nature of this volume.

I. New Paradigms in Scientific Discovery. Processing massive data has been a bottleneck to modern sciences. In Chap. 1, "Science at the Speed of Thought," Devaney et al. describe a virtual laboratory that is designed to accelerate scientific exploration and discovery by minimizing the time between the generation of a scientific hypothesis and the test of that idea, and thereby enabling science at the speed of thought. In Chap. 2, "Computational Biology and Language," Ganapathiraju et al. present a breakthrough approach that enables exploitation of an analogy between natural language and speech processing techniques in computational biology. In Chap. 3, "Interactive Comprehensible Data Mining," Pryke and Beale present their interactive data mining system that helps users gain insight from the dynamically created virtual data space. In Chap. 4, "Scientific Discovery Within Data Streams," Cowell et al. present the architecture of a next-generation analytical environment for scientific discovery within continuous, time-varying data streams.

II. Ambient Cognition. Understanding how people sense, understand and use images and words in everyday work and life can eventually help us design more effective discovery systems. In Chap. 5, Leyton reviews his theory of "Shape as Memory Storage", addressing shape description over time. Leyton's theory has been used in more than 40 fields, such as radiology, metrology, computer vision, chemical engineering, geology, computer-aided design, anatomy, botany, forensic science, software engineering, architecture, linguistics, mechanical engineering, computer graphics, art, semiotics, archaeology, and anthropology, etc. In Chap. 6, Hubona and Shirah investigate how various spatial depth cues, such as motion, stereoscopic vision, shadows and scene background, are utilized to promote the perceptual discovery and interpretation of the presented imagery in 3D scientific visualization. In Chap. 7, "Textual Genre Analysis and Identification," Kaufer et al. present a knowledge-based approach for encoding a large library of English strings used to capture textual impressions and report on a study of a popular textual genre – the technology review. The expert system incorporates contextual information, e.g., culture, emotion, context, and purpose, etc., which is different from many prevailing methods such as machine learning or statistics. In Chap. 8, "Cognitive Artifacts in Complex Work," Jones and Nemeth use acute care and scientific ethnographic field studies to show how cognitive artifacts can be used to grasp the nature of cognitive work in uncertain, complex, technical work settings. This front-end research is aimed at optimizing distributed cognitive work.

III. Ambient Intelligence Systems. Ubiquitous sensors and communication technologies not only can assist scientific discovery, but can also catalyze new sciences. In Chap. 9, "Multi-modal Interaction in Biomedicine," Zudilova and Sloot investigate the practical deployment of virtual reality systems in the medical environment. They explore the multi-modal interaction of virtual reality and desktop computers in Virtual Radiology Explorer. In Chap. 10, "Continuous Body Monitoring," Farringdon and Nashold describe a personal and continuous body monitor that is one of the few examples of ambient intelligence devices commercially available today. This also brings challenges to sciences: for example, how do we extract the interesting patterns from a continuous body monitor? From this example we can see how the research scope has been extended from laboratories to homes and in vivo. In Chap. 11, "Ambient Diagnosis," Cai et al. explore *Ambient Diagnosis* that is based on traditional Chinese medicine (TCM). The case study shows how to map the visual features on the tongue into a vector of numbers. In Chap. 12, Tanz et al. describe methods for location mapping in a wireless local area network (WLAN) and applications in social sciences. The system cmuSKY developed by the authors has become a public online resource for scientific discovery. In Chap. 13, "Behavior-Based Indoor Navigation," Abascal et al. present a method for motor fusion using ambient information from the environment. Indoor robotic navigation has been an active subject because of applications in assisted-living, such as smart wheelchair control, guidance for the visually impaired, or indoor assistance of the elderly. Finally, in Chap. 14, "Ambient Intelligence Through Agile Agents," O'Hare et al. explore agile agents as a key enabler for the realization of the ambient intelligence vision.

We are deeply indebted to all the authors who contributed papers to this volume; without this depth of support and commitment there would have been no meaningful product at all. We acknowledge the members of the program committee, all those involved in the refereeing process, the workshop organizers, and all those in the community who helped to convene a successful workshop. Special thanks go to Judith Klein-Seetharaman, Peter Jones, William Eddy, David Kaufer, Yongxiang Hu, Bin Lin, and Vijayalaxmi Manoharan for their contributions to the workshop and this volume. Thanks to the external reviewers Howard Choset, Lori Levin, Susan Fussell, and Tony Adriaansen for their comments on the manuscripts. Thanks to Teri Mick for assisting the volume editing and Sarah Nashold for assisting the book design. This project is in part sponsored by NASA grant NAG-1-03024 and National Academy of Sciences (NAS) grant T-37.

Pittsburgh, October 2004   Yang Cai

Organization Committee and Reviewers

Yang Cai (Co-chair), Carnegie Mellon University, USA
Judith Klein-Seetharaman (Co-chair), Carnegie Mellon University,
    University of Pittsburgh, USA, and Forschungszentrum Juelich, Germany
Peter Jones, Redesign Research, USA
Elena Zudilova, University of Amsterdam, Netherlands
Yongxiang Hu, NASA Langley Research Center, USA
Bin Lin, NASA Langley Research Center, USA
Lori Levin, Carnegie Mellon University, USA
Gregory O'Hare, University College Dublin, Ireland
Howard Choset, Carnegie Mellon University, USA
Judith Devaney, National Institute of Standards and Technology, USA
Tony Adriaansen, Telecommunications & Industrial Physics, CSIRO, Australia
Susan Fussell, Carnegie Mellon University, USA

Sponsoring Institutions

National Aeronautics and Space Administration (NASA), USA
National Academy of Sciences (NAS), USA

Table of Contents

Science at the Speed of Thought

Judith E. Devaney[1], S.G. Satterfield[1], J.G. Hagedorn[1], J.T. Kelso[1],
A.P. Peskin[1], W.L. George[1], T.J. Griffin[1], H.K. Hung[1], and R.D. Kriz[2]

[1] National Institute of Standards and Technology, USA
judith.devaney@nist.gov
[2] Virginia Tech, USA
rkriz@vt.edu

1 Introduction

Scientific discoveries occur with iterations of theory, experiment, and analysis. But the methods that scientists use to go about their work are changing [1].

Experiment types are changing. Increasingly, experiment means computational experiment [2], as computers increase in speed, memory, and parallel processing capability. Laboratory experiments are becoming parallel as combinatorial experiments become more common.

Acquired datasets are changing. Both computer and laboratory experiments can produce large quantities of data where the time to analyze data can exceed the time to generate it. Data from experiments can come in surges where the analysis of each set determines the direction of the next experiments. The data generated by experiments may also be non-intuitive. For example, nanoscience is the study of materials whose properties may change greatly as their size is reduced [3]. Thus analyses may benefit from new ways to examine and interact with data.

Two factors will accelerate these trends and result in increasing volumes of data:

- CPU speedup: as companies strive to keep Moore's law [4, 5] in effect
- Computer architecture speedup: as all computers benefit from architecture advances in high end computers.

Figure 1 gives an overview of how these impact problems [6]. These factors make computers ever more capable and increase the move to computational experiments and automation.

But a third factor offers a partial solution: graphics speedup. Computer game enthusiasts are funding a fast pace of development of graphics processing units (GPUs) [7, 8]. The use of these GPUs in the support of science makes the future world increasingly computational, visual, and interactive.

We believe that representation and interaction drive discovery, and that bringing the experiments (computer and laboratory) of science into an interactive, immersive, and collaborative environment provides opportunities for speed and synergy. Adding traditional data analysis, machine learning, and data mining tools, with multiple representations and interactions can speed up the rate

Y. Cai (Ed.): Ambient Intelligence for Scientific Discovery, LNAI 3345, pp. 1–24, 2005.

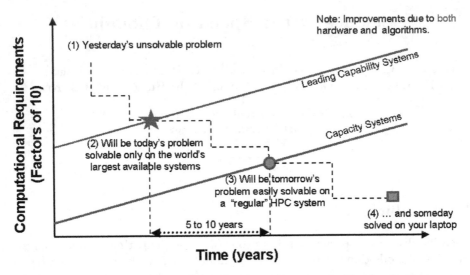

Fig. 1. Transition of solving important problems from unsolvable to solvable on your laptop.

of exploration and lead to new insights and discovery. Creating an environment that is efficient, general and flexible enough to work well across a wide variety of scientific applications is at the heart of our Virtual Laboratory (VL) design.

In section 2, we describe the VL we are building at NIST to address these issues. In section 3, we describe some applications. We present conclusions and future work in section 4.

2   The Virtual Laboratory

The VL needs to be efficient, general, and flexible, but it also needs to be able to get applications into it quickly in order to speed up the process of science and not burden it. Representations and interactions of many types need to be available and easily accessed. To accomplish this, our design consists of the following components:

- A distributed computing environment that provides the communication fabric of the VL,
- An immersive visualization environment that provides representation, interaction, and collaboration capability in the VL,
- A suite of tools for machine learning and analysis.

We will discuss each of these in turn.

2.1   Distributed Computing Environment

An important part of the VL is the capability of users to interact with their data sources, analysis programs, and their experiments, either computer experiments or laboratory experiments, from any of the supported VL access points (see Fig. 2

for a schematic). Examples of access points are the immersive visualization system or a remotely connected workstation. For the purposes of this discussion, data sources and analysis programs will be subsumed under computer experiment. The interactions range from viewing the status of their currently running experiment, or the results of a prior experiment, to providing feedback to the experiment in order to alter or restart the experiment. To provide this range of access requires a framework that enables communication between the user, the experiment, the visualization, and possibly with other collaborators actively interacting with the experiment.

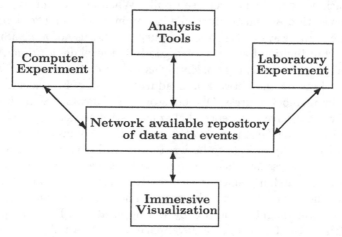

Fig. 2. Schematic of Distributed Computing Environment. Each component may also access other data sources.

The VL uses what is generically referred to as a coordination framework to provide a loose coupling between all participating entities of an experiment. The coupling is loose in that participants, that is, laboratory experiment equipment, computer simulations, visualization systems, user interfaces, and any other connection to the VL, can choose whether or not to utilize this coupling and can connect and disconnect from it at any time without disrupting the system. The VL distributed computing framework is implemented using the Java technology of Jini and JavaSpaces [9] [10]. Both of these packages, Jini and JavaSpaces, are available as pure Java implementations and so are portable to any system that supports a Java virtual machine, which includes systems running Linux, Microsoft Windows, and most Unix based operating systems.

Jini provides support for a form of distributed computing that explicitly handles common issues that arise in a distributed (networked) system, such as intermittent network outages and server crashes. Support includes automatic discovery of services available on the network, active leasing of services to help maintain current service information and to purge services that no longer exist, and distribution of events to remote applications to allow applications to communicate asynchronously and to react to expected or unexpected developments.

JavaSpaces is a specification for a Jini service that provides a coordination framework in the form of a tuple space. The concept of a tuple space was first introduced in the early 1980s by computer scientists David Gelernter and Nick Carriero, within the context of the programming language Linda [11] [12]. This is referred to as a coordination framework since it allows a loose collection of applications, linked over a common network, to communicate asynchronously. This communication is so loosely coupled that the applications do not need to be running, or even exist, at the same time. To take the possibilities to an extreme, application A can send a message that is ultimately to be read by application B (and possibly others) which has not yet been written and will run on a machine that has not yet been built. When application B receives the message, application A, and the machine it ran on, may no longer exist.

There are many ways to describe the purpose and use of a JavaSpace. The concept of a coordination framework is a good high-level description. At a lower level, a JavaSpace can be thought of simply as a shared memory space, accessible from any machine on the network and addressed using an associative lookup rather than by memory address. Objects stored in a JavaSpace are instances of classes in Java that have a few special characteristics needed to support storage and retrieval from the JavaSpace. So the associative lookup uses the Java class type system to identify objects to be written or read from the JavaSpace. This is a very robust addressing scheme, compared to using raw memory addressing or simple string matching, since it ensures that you receive an object of the correct type when you read from the space. These objects can store any type of information that might be needed by the applications. It is also possible to maintain structures of objects in a JavaSpace, such as a linked list of objects, a tree of objects, or an array of objects. Objects can also simply be markers, holding absolutely no data, but giving information simply by their existence or non-existence in the JavaSpace.

In the VL, a JavaSpace is maintained to allow for the coordination of experiments, visualizations, and interacting collaborators accessing the VL through their workstation or other supported interface device. Typical information stored in the VL JavaSpace includes experiment parameters, current status of an experiment such at the latest time-step of a computer simulation, or latest result from a laboratory experiment.

Of course, applications need not be written in Java to participate in the VL. In fact, it is expected that most computer simulations will likely be written in Fortran or C/C++, and most participating laboratory devices will likely not have direct network access. In Jini, applications and devices that are not capable of participating directly, either because of insufficient resources to run a Java virtual machine, or because they are closed systems, can still participate through the use of a surrogate [13]. These surrogates allow the application or device to participate by performing as a communications gateway to the Jini/JavaSpace network and also performing any computation needed in the process. The communication between the surrogate and the Jini/JavaSpace network uses the standard Jini/JavaSpaces protocols. The communication between the surrogate and the application or device uses an appropriate private protocol, unique to each application or device.

Although a JavaSpace is not expected to store objects that include large volumes of data, such as Gigabyte output and input files typically used in large experiments, it can be used to coordinate access to such files. An object in the space can represent such a file, giving status information about the file such as size and time written and allowing for the retrieval of the file contents over the network. A Remote File service (RFS) has been developed to handle this need in the VL. Applications can read and write large files within the VL if they need them to be available, normally for visualization and for feedback in the case of experiment input files.

The looseness of the coordination framework, together with the use of Java-Spaces, Java and Jini provides the communication fabric of the VL robustness and generality. Implementing this way means it is easy to include things. Thus it also provides speed of implementation.

This Jini/JavaSpace based remote file service was developed as part of a related project, Screen Saver Science (SSS) [14], which provides a distributed computing environment for general scientific computing. In SSS, applications utilize otherwise idle processors to complete compute-intensive tasks within a distributed algorithm and use RFS for large remote file input and output. As with the participants in the VL, machines participating in SSS can join in the SSS system to compute tasks at any time and can leave at any time without disrupting the overall operation of SSS. Although this is called Screen Saver Science, there is actually no screen saver application within SSS, but screen savers are sometimes used to help determine when to join SSS and when to leave (other techniques are also used).

2.2 Immersive Visualization Environment

The second component of our VL is an immersive visualization (IV) environment (IVE). IVE is widely used across government, industry, and academia [15]. It is also increasingly used to great advantage in scientific visualization [16, 17, 1].

"By immersive virtual reality we mean technology that gives the user the psychophysical experience of being surrounded by a virtual, that is, computer-generated, environment. This experience is elicited with a combination of hardware, software, and interaction devices. Immersion is typically produced by a stereo 3D visual display, which uses head tracking to create a human-centric rather than a computer-determined point of view [16]." Thus, users interact with "things rather than pictures of things [18]" because the three dimensional data models reside in the same physical space that the user occupies. This enables the user to move around and to view the objects from different angles, to understand physical relationships in an natural way, and to interact directly with the objects in the environment in much the same way that he or she would inspect an apparatus or a sample in the laboratory. Of course, in a virtual environment, the user is not limited to normal physical interactions. Objects in the immersive environment are completely mutable; the user can make objects transparent or invisible, change the scale of objects, move through objects at will, and so on.

IVE provides a true three-dimensional (3D) view of data. But IV provides more than another dimension. Because our natural habitat is 3D, we bring with us into the IV environment all our understanding of relationships in a 3D world. So we do not have to try to understand the relationships we see. We comprehend them naturally.

The IVE is also a scientific instrument like any other. It requires multiple types of calibration and specialized software, for example. But it is also a scientific instrument unlike any other. While it is a finite physical space defined by the physical setup, it is also an infinite virtual space where we can wander indefinitely. It is up to the visualization scientists to decide what to put in the space and how to arrange it. Things at very different scales or types can be placed side by side. For example, a nanostructure can be placed next to a plot of one of its properties. In fact, immersive visualization is where scientific visualization and information visualization [19] can be joined.

Our philosophy for the IVE is similar to the philosophy for the distributed computing environment. It is loosely coupled. In this context, we mean we do not have a single monolithic program but rather a collection of small programs that can be snapped together to create new programs. Each small program is good at doing one thing well. All are designed to work together.

There are three ways we join programs together:

- UNIX [20] pipes and filters for creation and transformation
- Dynamically Shared Objects (DSO's) for functionality
- scenegraph objects for simple placement.

This gives us the generality, flexibility, and speed that we need for the VL.

We have four main categories of tools:

1. IV Infrastructure software
2. IV Representation Software
3. IV Scene Interaction Software
4. IV Collaboration Software

We will discuss each of these in turn.

IV Infrastructure Software. This is software to get visualizations into the IVE and interact with the IVE hardware. We use as our base software the open source software DIVERSE [21] in our IV environment. It uses OpenGL Performer [22] to create a scenegraph that places the objects in the immersive environment. That means that anything that can be loaded into Performer can be immediately loaded into the IVE. It also means that getting a data set into the IVE may require writing a simple filter to convert one file format to another. New file loaders can be written and we have created some for special needs.

IV Representation Software. In the context of an IVE, representation refers to the process of transforming raw data into a visual geometric format that can be viewed and manipulated in the IVE. Representation is an important component for learning. The key to enabling scientists to quickly and easily visualize their scientific data in an immersive environment is to develop useful tools to help convert raw data to immersive data. We have designed our system to use our own representations but also to take advantage of representations computed by other packages. For these tasks, we have created a Glyph Toolbox to easily create our own geometry, and we have built software to convert the output of other packages to a form that can be displayed in the IVE.

Glyph Toolbox: The Glyph Toolbox is a set of programs to create and manipulate three-dimensional objects in a format readable by a variety of visualization programs. Glyphs are visual symbols used to convey information based on appearance or position. Simple glyphs include bars on a bar chart and dots on a statistical plot. The Glyph Toolbox is a set of three-dimensional glyphs both complex and intuitive enough to convey information to a wide audience, while simple enough to generate geometry from scientific data.

The purpose of the Glyph Toolbox Project is to build a collection of individual Unix style command line programs. Each program accomplishes a single task to create or manipulate geometry that can be used to build a polygon based virtual environment. A series of individual UNIX style simple commands can be combined to create objects, and then scale, color, rotate, and/or translate them to a particular specification. The tools (command and filters) output an ASCII based file that is machine and rendering independent. The actual display of the ASCII files is handled by converting the output polygon file into a format suitable for display by a viewing program, such as DIVERSE/diversifly, VRML, Open Inventor [23], etc.

The Glyph Toolbox has a wide range of applications. It has been used to create traditional glyphs for displaying data, such as error bars, menu items, or logos. More complex examples include transforming molecular data, i.e. positions of atoms in a grid, into a three-dimensional display of a crystalline structure, as in Fig. 3. Each atom is represented by a Glyph Toolbox sphere, scaled, colored, and put in its proper place in the crystal.

SAVG Format and Converting Other Package Output: Currently under development is another type of Performer-based file format, called the SAVG format (named after our research group, the Scientific Applications and Visualization Group). Unlike the Glyph Toolbox file format, which was developed to help create original objects for visualization, the SAVG format was initially developed as a conversion format to allow data from a variety of scientific modeling packages to be used in our immersive visualization environment. The SAVG format has been enhanced since its origin with features to solve issues with transparency, lighting, and efficiency, and has grown into a very robust format for our virtual laboratory. Geometry can be defined using polygons, lines, points, and triangle strips. Polygons can be converted into their corresponding wire frame objects, or individually shrunk for better viewing. Examples of visualizations using the SAVG format are shown below in Figs. 4 and 5, which demonstrate SAVG capabilities in transparency, as well as the shrinkage effect.

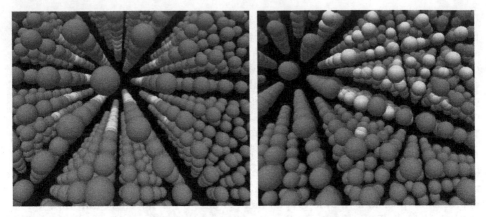

Fig. 3. A nano-structure of gold and copper atoms. Visualization is created with the Glyph Toolbox.

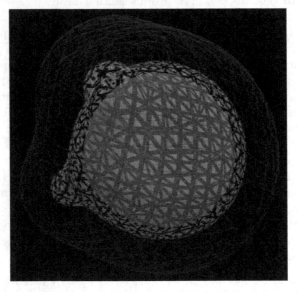

Fig. 4. Use of transparency and shrinkage in the SAVG file format to display isosurfaces of electron density of a water molecule.

In order to visualize data as quickly as possible, it is important to use what has already been done. To this end we use other software to create a variety of representations. For example visualization packages such as openDX [24] and VTK [25] easily generate representations such as isosurfaces. Output from these packages is converted to our own format and loaded into the IVE via DIVERSE. See Fig. 6 for an example of a set of isosurfaces visualized this way.

We can get data into the IVE quickly, once we have created converters from the format of outside software packages to a format that our environment recognizes. But the software packages providing the data need not be visualization

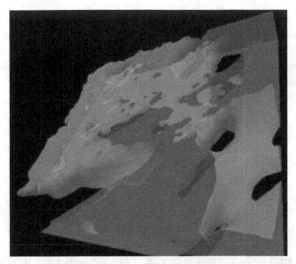

Fig. 5. Use of transparency to display polymer scaffolding.

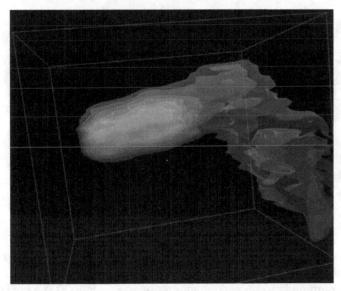

Fig. 6. Bayesian reconstruction of a circuit with an electromigration void. Visualization is via nested transparent isosurfaces.

packages. Representation is key to learning and any way to convert a data set to another representation may increase our insight. See section 2.3 on Machine Learning.

IV Scene Interaction Software. For efficient scientific exploration, it is important to have user interaction that is both easy to set up and easy to modify. It is also important that the software work on a wide variety of platforms.

A variety of different graphic displays and input devices can be used with the DIVERSE graphics interface by the use of separately compiled and loaded Dynamic Software Objects (DSOs). By plugging in one of many DSOs for graphics display, for example, the same visualization programs can be used on desktop, laptop, or full three-dimensional immersive systems.

Individual DSOs are also used to add new functionality to our visualization software system. Our group has developed a wide range of DSOs that allow a user to interact with the objects he or she is viewing. This includes functionality to move objects around, select individual objects or sets of objects and assign functionality to the selected objects, interact with outside software programs, bring data into the system, send data out of the system, and load or unload objects during a visualization.

Individual DSOs can be loaded to add simple functionality to a scenegraph, such as adding a particular light source or an object to represent a pointer for the user to select objects. Our **wandPointer** DSO for example, is loaded with the **objectMover** DSO, as shown in Fig. 7, to allow a user to select an object and then move it with the movement of the wand.

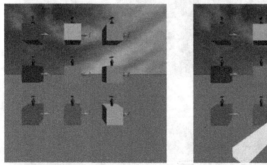

Fig. 7. Demonstration of the **objectMover** and **wandPointer** DSOs.

Another set of DSOs that allow a user to take a look inside an object is particularly useful for viewing large sets of volume data. Figure 8 below demonstrates the **clipWand** DSO. Through the use of shared memory, a user can enter shell script commands to an accompanying program, `hev-clipwand`, to specify up to 6 different clipping planes that are defined with respect to the direction and position of the wand. The wand is a hand-held device and its position is continually tracked by this system. This enables the user to interactively position the clipping planes in real time in order to reveal the interior detail of three-dimensional data sets. These clipping planes can be turned on and off interactively during a visualization. Volume data can also be manipulated with DSOs that edit lookup tables, making only objects within certain color ranges visible, for example.

A DSO known as **objSwitchExec** has evolved to give functionality to the objects of a scenegraph. When selected, an object can be assigned the function

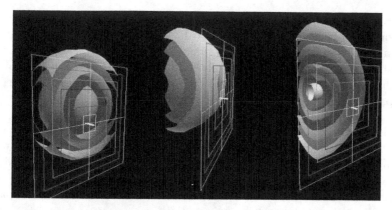

Fig. 8. Layered spheres demonstrate the capabilities of the **clipWand** DSO.

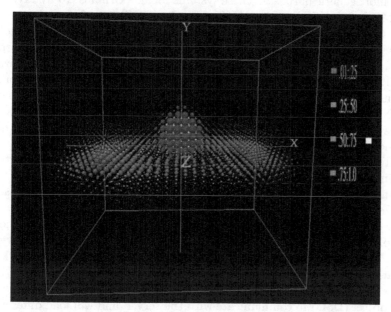

Fig. 9. Use of menuing objects to turn on and off visibility of data, using the **objSwitchExec** and **desktopWandHPR** DSOs.

of turning on or off another object or itself, or executing a shell command to interact with another DSO or an outside program. In this way, an internal menu structure can be assembled, as in Fig. 9. Menu items can be selected which make objects visible, initiate time simulations, define clipping planes, etc. Different DSOs can be loaded to allow a user to select objects differently depending on whether they are using desktop mode or are in a three-dimensional immersive environment. For example, the **desktopWandHPR** DSO can be loaded to use simple keyboard controls for object selection at the desktop.

The objects themselves can be loaded or unloaded from a scenegraph during a visualization with the use of the DSO, **blink**. Using an accompanying program, a user can issue shell commands to load or unload objects, or make them visible or not visible in the scene. By individually loading pre-compiled dynamic objects, a user has access to a wide variety of combinations of functionality useful for desktop, laptop, and full immersive systems.

IV Collaboration Software. Scientists rarely work alone today. A glance at any current scientific journal shows the extent of collaboration as well as how geographically distributed scientific collaborators are. Scientists need to be able to enter and leave the VL at will and discuss results in the VL regardless of distance. Collaboration in virtual environments (VEs) occurs when spatially separated participants interact in the same VE.

A variety of collaborative VE's have been built both for specific applications and for more generic purposes. These systems include Crumbs [26–28], NICE [29, 30], LIMBO [31], Collaborative CAVE Console (CCC) [32,33], and D Atomview [34]. In the future, it is hoped that participation in device-independent collaborative VEs will become as simple and commonplace as today's web browsers and networked multi-user games. Challenges remain in the areas of standardization, especially in the area of interface design, to minimize the learning curve for using different VEs, and provide support for a plethora of hardware configurations.

At NIST we are building a framework for collaborative VE applications which we hope will be a step towards this goal. Our work uses the DIVERSE VE library and a modified and extended version of the collaborative tools currently available with DIVERSE. DIVERSE was chosen because our group already has extensive experience with this package, and DIVERSE's open source license allows us to build on prior work on collaborative VEs. Our system will also be open-source, available for free download from our web site.

Our collaborative VE system will support both synchronous and asynchronous applications, using a central server to provide persistence. The server will keep track of the state of the VE, but not the application itself. Network communications will be based on the Jini/JavaSpace distributed computing infrastructure described earlier. Each participant will load a collaborative dynamically shared object (DSO) to communicate with the server, and will load different sets of DSOs for the application based upon whether they are using a stereo head-tracked immersive CAVE, a workstation, or a standard desktop Linux system.

Our system will use SGI's OpenGL Performer as its graphics engine. Performer is designed to provide optimal graphics performance in a platform independent manner. It uses a scenegraph data structure to represent its graphical elements, easily allowing modeling transformations which affect an entire subtree. Since Performer and DIVERSE are written in C++, new classes have been built to provide a data-driven graphical capability. For example, a node in a scenegraph might contain a transformation matrix. A DIVERSE class can read shared memory every graphics frame and update the matrix in the node based on changes to the shared memory. In this way a simulation, or the collaborative server, can directly modify the VE by merely updating data in memory. In fact, the simulation needn't be written as a graphical collaboration. All it needs to do is update shared memory.

Our system is designed to use as little network bandwidth as possible. For example, the position of an object is given by six floating point numbers representing its location (X,Y,Z) and orientation (H, P, R Euler angles), and these six numbers are updated only if the object actually moves. Six numbers can also be used to specify the orientation of a node in a scenegraph (seven if a uniform scale factor is needed), so complex animations can be achieved with minimal data transfer.

Simulations also use shared memory as a data-passing mechanism, and multiple simulations can read and write between themselves and the VE. Participants in the VE will communicate with the simulations using shared memory too, so the difference between modifications from a participant and from a simulation is completely transparent.

Permissions and file loading/unloading will be handled using the Jini/Java-Space distributed computing environment. This system will keep track of who is allowed to do what, transfer and update data as needed, and handle problems of resource allocations and conflicts. This functionality will be incorporated into a DSO that will work in conjunction with the central server.

Additional DSOs will implement awareness tools that reflect the status of the collaborative VE. For example, one DSO can display the relative position of all participants in the VE on a two-dimensional radar display. DSOs can be written to work best in an immersive environment or on a desktop, and users can choose the DSOs that best suit their needs.

2.3 Machine Learning Tools

Representation is critical to understanding and learning. This is true for immersive visualization, where productivity is dependent upon how well the data is represented in the 3D world. Representation is also important for machine learning. In that context, representation means the feature space of the data, and the formalism for describing the data [35].

Finding the appropriate representation is important, but more than one representation may be beneficial. A scientific paper uses multiple representations: equations, plots, images, tables, diagrams, charts, drawings, and text. A scientific presentation may also contain movies or animations of various types. All of these are in support of communication of ideas. But these are also used by scientists as they work towards their own understanding.

With the VL, different representations of data can exist side by side. They can also be created interactively. Whatever aids understanding can be placed in the virtual space.

Very large data sets present a challenge, even for visualization. Data sets can be large in terms of the number of dimensions or the size of the dataset, or both. While there exist techniques for viewing high dimensional data sets, such as parallel coordinate plots [36], this may not be the best way to acquire knowledge from the data. A different approach is to look for those dimensions that are most relevant and discard the rest. One recent winner of the Knowledge Discovery in Databases competition reduced the number of features from the original 139,351 down to 4 features in his final model [37]. An alternate approach is summarizing. For example, data can be clustered and the individual components can be studied in various ways.

Machine learning tools can help with both dimension reduction and summarizing. We use the Weka [38] implementations of many machine learning algorithms. We also use the autoclass [39] clustering software. In addition we have developed our own genetic programming software package, GPP [40]. We also have our own equation discovery software [41]. This provides us with many avenues for displaying, interacting, and gaining insight into our results.

Our visualization of the Iris data set [42] contains multiple representations. Figure 10-a shows part of our visualization. On the near side of the left wall is a parallel coordinate plot [36] of the cluster identified with the transparent envelope. On the far side of the left wall is a plot of the probability density distribution of each of the attributes in the data set. The right wall shows how the attributes rank with Information Gain [38]. In the foreground is a set of statistics that have been computed on the fly in response to a user command. The points of the data set are represented as glyphs where the attributes have been mapped to glyph attributes using our glyph toolbox. The points are plotted in the central cube. A user can also interact with this visualization by turning the transparent envelops of the clusters on and off individually, and the parallel coordinate plots with them. Figure 10-b shows the same dataset visualized in three different ways, shown in three separate rooms.

Figure 10 helps to bring together all of the main components of our VL. The visualization is run through a distributed computing environment, in which multiple users can interact with the data. The figure demonstrates the interactive IVE, in which users can move, hide, and select objects in the system to control the display the data and the movement of the data into and out of the visualization. Figure 10 also displays results of our machine learning tools, used to analyze the data and select which components to study. With all three of these components, we can speed up concept development.

3   Applications

We speed up insight into our data through representation of the data in the IVE and through interactions with the data. One representation may not be sufficient, so the ability to switch between and interact with representations is important. We describe a set of applications that highlight our approach.

3.1   Multi-modal Imaging and Visualization

In this project we are developing methods for combining related three-dimensional data sets from a variety of sources into visualizations that enable exploration and understanding of the data at a variety of scales and with a variety of techniques. The data is produced by OCM (Optical Coherence Microscopy) and CFM (Confocal Fluorescence Microscopy) techniques being developed at NIST.

These data are being used to investigate structural and functional properties of tissue engineering scaffolds. The scaffolds are porous polymers that act as support structures for the growth of cells. Our visualization techniques are being used in an effort to characterize properties such as mechanical performance and induction of tissue development.

The data are produced at differing scales and data from different instruments show different structures. Our task is to combine these data sets into coherent immersive visualizations. Challenges include registration, segmentation, and exposure of volume structures. We use several important visual and geometric representations of the data, including derived surfaces, two-dimensional slices, and three-dimensional volume renderings. In all cases, we visualize the data in a three-dimensional space that is analogous to the physical dimensions of the

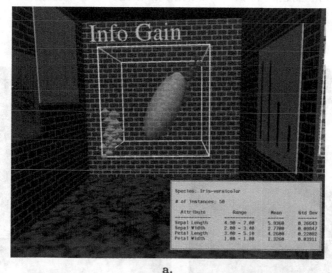

a.

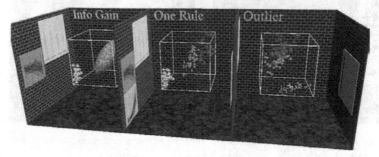

b.

Fig. 10. An immersive visualization of the Iris data set. Image **a** shows one of the rooms of the multiple-view visualization shown in image **b**.

sample. We combine these representations with various rendering techniques and with user interactions to enable exploration of the data.

The most useful information is generated by deriving surfaces from the data. Figure 11-a shows a polygonal surface representing the polymer scaffold. This data was produced by NIST's OCM instrument. The surfaces are derived using simple isosurface algorithms as well as more elaborate level-set approaches.

We enhance the depiction of these surfaces with lighting effects and the use of transparency. Simulated lighting effects help to expose the shape of three dimensional surfaces. Transparency enables the user to see the internal structure of three dimensional data sets. For example, Fig. 11-b shows the same scaffold surface as Fig. 11-a, but the surface is transparent and it is combined with surfaces that represent cells growing on the scaffold. The cell data was produced by CFM techniques and is combined with the OCM data in this scene.

We also make use of two-dimensional representations, but we embed them as appropriate into the three-dimensional scene. For example, in Fig. 11-c, we show a two-dimensional cross section through the three dimensional volume of OCM/CFM data. The scaffold surface has been removed to enable the user to see the cross section.

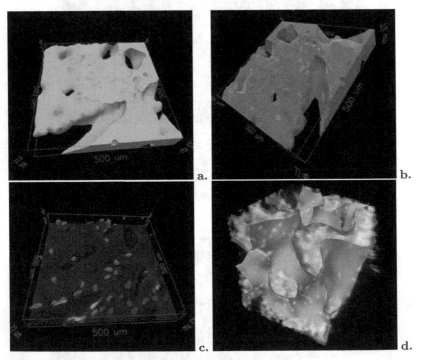

Fig. 11. a. Polymer scaffold material represented as a polygon surface. **b.** Polymer scaffold material with cells. Scaffold surface is represented as a transparent surface. **c.** A two-dimensional cross section of scaffold and cell data embedded within a three-dimensional scene. **d.** Combined volume and polygon representation of OCM scaffold data.

Finally, we use three-dimensional volume renderings to produce views of the data that show more complete structural information throughout the volume. We find that volume rendering techniques must be used judiciously and are often most useful when combined with other techniques. In Fig. 11-d, we combine a volume rendering of OCM scaffold data with a surface rendering of the same data. This visualization provides useful verification of the surface derivation technique.

The user interaction techniques are an extremely important aspect of enabling exploration of the data sets. Our approach to user interactions is based on direct manipulation and navigation of the three-dimensional scene, and on menus that are presented visually within the immersive environment. Navigation through the scene is accomplished through user movement within the immersive environment as well as translations and rotations of a track ball that is part of a hand-held device (the *wand*), which is position-tracked within the immersive environment. The on-screen menus enable the user to turn on and off various components of the scene and change transparency/opacity, and to use our interactive DSOs, such as the **clipWand** DSO described above. Figure 12 shows an example of clipping the data used in previous examples.

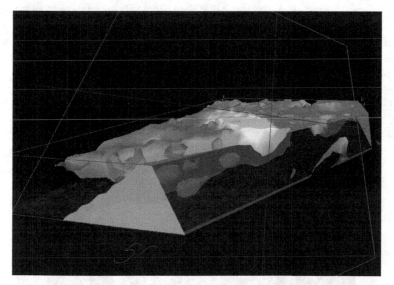

Fig. 12. Interactive clipping of scaffold and cell data visualization. A three-dimensional plane under user control cut data away to expose interior features.

Another interaction technique that is useful during collaborative sessions is the use of a three-dimensional hand-tracked pointer. This pointer is depicted as a three-dimensional geometric object in the virtual scene. It is attached to the position-tracked wand so that it moves with the user's hand. This type of pointer has proved to be very useful because in the immersive environment, non-tracked users have slightly different views, so it is difficult to point accurately at an object with one's hand. But with a geometric pointer embedded in the three-dimensional scene, there is not such ambiguity. This pointer technique will also be very useful when collaborative sessions are being run at multiple sites. It will enable researchers to indicate points of interest to collaborators who are at different sites.

3.2   3D Chemical Imaging at the Nanoscale

The goal of this project is to develop methods for measuring the distribution of chemical species in three-dimensional samples at nanoscale resolution. This work is important for a variety of industrial applications, such as semiconductors, optoelectronics, and biotechnology. Our role in this project is to develop methods for visualizing and interacting with datasets of nanoscale phenomena that enable researchers to investigate three-dimensional structure and interfaces. The data sets will be produced by different instruments at a variety of scales. In some respects these data present challenges similar to those in the MMIV project; we address similar problems of registration and data fusion.

Derived surfaces are a primary means of representing these data sets. For example, Fig. 13 shows a surface representing a three-dimensional scan of photonic band gap material. As in the MMIV project, these surfaces are generated using techniques such as isosurface and level set segmentation methods. As we get data from more and diverse instruments, we expect that the segmentation of the data into different chemical species will prove to be a particularly challenging aspect of the project.

User interaction techniques are a critical component in the exploration of these data sets. As in the MMIV project, we provide to the user a variety of

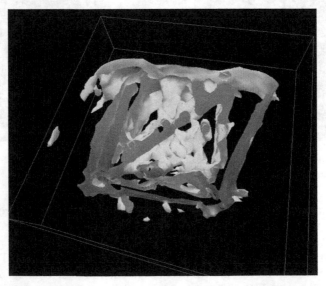

Fig. 13. A surface representing a three-dimensional scan of photonic band gap material.

navigation and menu-based interaction techniques. Particularly useful is the interactive clipping described above. Transparency and lighting remain very important elements of visualization methods used in this project.

3.3   Smart Gel

NIST scientists and collaborators are using the Virtual Laboratory to study *smart gels*, which might someday be used to make exotic foods, cosmetics, medicines, sensors, and other technological devices. Smart gels are inexpensive materials that expand or contract in response to external stimuli. This property could be useful in applications such as an artificial pancreas that releases insulin inside the body in response to high sugar levels. Scientists need to understand how the molecules in these materials behave in order to utilize them in new products.

For this project NIST scientists are studying a subclass of these materials called *shake gels*. Through some complex and as yet unknown process, these watery mixtures of clays and polymers firm up into gels when shaken, and then relax again to the liquid phase after some time has passed. A shake gel might be used, for example, in shock absorbers for cars. The material would generally be a liquid but would form a gel when the car drove over a pothole; the gel thickness would adjust automatically to the weight of the car and the size of the pothole.

The VL helped the scientists see that it is the polymer's oxygen atoms, instead of the hydrogen atoms as previously thought, that attach to the clay. The team has also made theoretical calculations that may help to explain why and how the components of the liquid mixture bind together into a semisolid form. Electrical charges affect the binding process, resulting in water binding to clay surfaces in a perpendicular arrangement, which is believed to help create the firmness of the gel. Theoretical aspects of the smart gels research are discussed in [43]. The work is sponsored by Kraft Foods and involves scientists from NIST, Los Alamos National Laboratory, and Harvard University.

The data provided by the researcher consisted of position data for a collection of atoms over a series of time steps. We created two visual representations from these data. The first depicts stick figure representations of the molecules. Bonds between atoms are derived from proximity of the atoms and the atoms are colored by element. The time series is shown by animating the motion of the atoms and bonds. Figure 14 shows a still frame from this representation.

The second representation draws paths for the atoms as they move over the course of the time series. Each path is shown as connected line segments. The color of the each path indicates the element. In this representation, the movement of atoms over time is represented within a static scene rather than by an animation. Figure 15 shows the path representation of the data.

Note that the two different representations can be used together. When both representations are turned on, the immersive display provides both an atom's motion and its history.

User interactions consist largely of menu interactions; these were implemented within our existing general purpose immersive display utility with menu

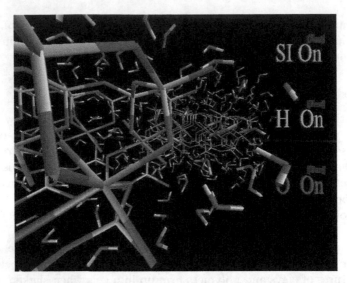

Fig. 14. Animated stick-figure representation of the *smart gel* simulation.

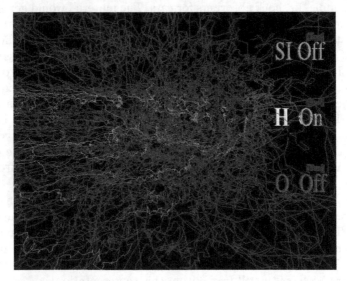

Fig. 15. Atom path representation of the *smart gel* simulation.

enhancements. The added menus were easily implemented using the techniques previously described. Menu items allow the different visual representations of the data to be turned on and off, the animation to be stopped and started, and paths to be made visible based on identity.

The implementation of the immersive visualization for this project was well served by our philosophy used in the IVE (loosely coupled programs that work well together). A new data filter was created using a scripting language to convert the time series data produced by the numerical simulation program into a form suitable for loading into the immersive environment. In this case, an existing file loader implements a *flip book* style animation. The input pipe line thus quickly converts the data of atomic positions at each time step into an visual stick figure representation of the each atom, which animates for the duration of the simulation time frame. Since only a small part of the input pipeline needed new software, the project implementation time was short. The newly created software filter focuses on producing the stick figure representations for the atoms, while the existing file loader handles the task of animating the atoms.

As mentioned above, within minutes of being immersed in the animation, the primary scientists involved realized their previously conceived ideas about which molecules attached to the clay were reversed.

The wide range of our current scientific collaborations has led to an enhanced set of VL tools in the areas of surface and volume rendering and display, creative data representations, animation, and time series data analysis.

3.4 Nanostructures

In the nano-optics project we are working with NIST scientists to understand atomic scale variation in the calculated properties of nano-scale structures.

The data that we receive consists of atom positions and values for s and p orbitals. We represent each atom with a sphere that corresponds to the s orbital and appropriate shapes for the x, y, and z p orbitals. The size of these geometric forms correspond to the calculated values. The colors of the atoms correspond to the element.

As in the other applications, we use our approach of loosely coupled tools to convert the incoming data to the desired geometric representation. In this case, our primary set of tools is the Glyph ToolBox (GTB). These tools facilitate the creation, sizing, and coloration of the orbital shapes.

As part of the creation of these geometric representations, we segment the data into subsets of atoms based on orbital size and symmetry (s or p) and on the spatial location of the atoms. User interactions were implemented using our standard menu tools within the immersive environment. These interactions enable the user to turn on and off the different subsets of atoms. This lets the user explore various features of the nano-scale structures. A sample image from this project is shown in Fig. 9.

4   Conclusions and Future Work

According to Louis Pasteur "In the field of observation, chance favors only the prepared mind" [44]. Scientists are prepared, but can we increase chance? We believe **representation and interaction drive discovery**, and when applied in the most general sense with the tools of immersive visualization, data mining and other analysis, it is possible to accelerate concept development.

In our current scientific world of increasing computing power, parallel laboratory experiments and enormous data sets to explore, a Virtual Laboratory becomes a powerful tool to ferret out important scientific results from otherwise incomprehensible volumes of data. Each component is essential to create a productive environment. Software and hardware capabilities must handle issues of networking and communicating over distances and times. They must take into account the varying resources of the scientists using them, and be capable of growing with new technology as it emerges. The software must be easily available on user-accessible systems. Software tools must handle all types of needs in terms of making scientific data available for viewing in a visualization system, and then making it accessible for user interaction. Limits of scientific resolution lie in how well data can be represented in a visualization system. Tools must be available for studying a wide range of different types of data, on all different size scales, and in a wide range of incoming formats.

The challenges lie in creating a foundation for the Virtual Laboratory that can be built upon as technology changes, and as computational tools improve. Assembling packages of individual tools that can be put together in a variety of useful ways, our current Virtual Laboratory is the beginning of a robust, encompassing scientific laboratory of the future.

5   Disclaimer

Certain commercial equipment, instruments, or materials are identified in this paper to foster understanding. Such identification does not imply recommendation or endorsement by the National Institute of Standards and Technology, nor does it imply that the materials or equipment identified are necessarily the best available for the purpose.

References

1. Sims, J.S., George, W.L., Satterfield, S.G., Hung, H.K., Hagedorn, J.G., Ketcham, P.M., Griffin, T.J., Hagstrom, S.A., Franiatte, J.C., Bryant, G.W., Jaskolski, W., Martys, N.S., Bouldin, C.E., Simmons, V., Nicolas, O.P., Warren, J.A., am Ende, B.A., Koontz, J.E., Filla, B.J., Pourprix, V.G., Copley, S.R., Bohn, R.B., Peskin, A.P., Parker, Y.M., Devaney, J.E.: Accelerating scientific discovery through computation and visualization II. Journal of Research of the National Institute of Standards and Technology **107** (2002) 223–245 May-June issue. http://nvl.nist.gov/pub/nistpubs/jres/107/3/cnt107-3.htm.
2. Westmoreland, P.R., Kollman, P.A., Chaka, A.M., Cummings, P.T., Morokuma, K., Neurock, M., Stechel, E.B., Vashishta, P.: Application of Molecular and Materials Modeling. Technology Research Institute, World Technology Division, Kluwer Academic Publishers (2002)
3. Alivisatos, A.P.: Semiconductor clusters, nanocrystals, and quantum dots. Science **271** (1996) 933–937
4. Moore, G.E.: Cramming more components onto integrated circuits. Electronics **38** (1965) http://www.intel.com/research/silicon/mooreslaw.htm.
5. Moore, G.E.: No exponential is forever ... but we can delay 'forever'. presented at: Int'l Solid State Circuits Conf. (ISSCC) (2003) http://www.intel.com/research/silicon/mooreslaw.htm.

6. Grosh, J., Kaluzniacki, R., Dongarra, J.: Transition of solving important problems. unpublished (2004)
7. Salvator, D.: GPU wars heat up again. PC Magazine (2004) 34–35
   http://www.extremetech.com/6800.
8. Salvator, D.: Nvidia readies geforce 6800. Ziff-Davis online magazine: Extreme-Tech.com (2004)
   http://www.extremetech.com/article2/0,1558,1624009,00.asp.
9. Edwards, W.K.: Core Jini. 2nd edn. Prentice Hall PTR (2000)
10. Freeman, E., Hupfer, S., Arnold, K.: JavaSpaces Principles, Patterns, and Practice. Addison-Wesley (1999)
11. Gelernter, D.: Linda in context. Comm. of ACM **32** (1984) 444–458
12. Gelernter, D.: Generative communication in Linda. ACM Trans. Prog. Lang. and Sys. **7** (1985) 80–112
13. Sun Microsystems, Jini Community: Surrogate project.
    http://surrogate.jini.org (2004)
14. George, W.L., Scott, J.: Screen saver science: Realizing distributed parallel computing with Jini and Javaspaces. In: Conf. on Parallel Architectures and Compilation Techniques (PACT2002). (2002)
    http://math.nist.gov/mcsd/savg/papers/SSS_PACT2002.ps.gz.
15. Sherman, W.R., Craig, A.B.: Understanding Virtual Reality. Morgan Kaufmann (2003)
16. van Dam, A., Forsberg, A.S., Laidlaw, D.H., LaViola, Jr., J.J., Simpson, R.M.: Immersive VR for scientific visualization: A progress report. IEEE Computer Graphics and Applications **20** (2000) 26–52
17. van Dam, A., Laidlaw, D.H., Simpson, R.M.: Experiments in immersive virtual reality for scientific visualization. Computers and Graphics **26** (2002) 535–555
18. Bryson, S.: Virtual reality in scientific visualization. Comm. ACM **39** (1996) 62–71
19. Card, S.K., Mackinley, J.D., Shneiderman, B.: Readings in Information Visualization. Morgan Kaufmann (1999)
20. Kerighan, B.W., Pike, R.: The UNIX Programming Environment. Prentice Hall, Inc. (1984)
21. Kelso, J., Arsenault, L., Satterfield, S., Kriz, R.: DIVERSE: A framework for building extensible and reconfigurable device independent virtual environments. In: Proc. IEEE Virtual Reality 2002 Conf. (2002) DIVERSE source code available at http://diverse.sourceforge.net.
22. SGI: OpenGL Performer™. http://www.sgi.com/software/performer (2004)
23. SGI: Open Inventor™. http://oss.sgi.com/projects/inventor (2003)
24. IBM: OpenDX. http://www.opendx.org (2004)
25. Kitware Inc.: VTK: The Visualization Toolkit. http://www.vtk.org (2004)
26. Brady, R., Pixton, J., Baxter, G., Moran, P., Potter, C.S., Carragher, B., Belmont, A.: Crumbs: a virtual environment tracking tool for biological imaging. In: Proc. 1995 Biomedical Visualization (BioMedVis '95), IEEE Computer Society (1995) 18
27. VRCO: CAVElib user manual. http://www.vrco.com/CAVE_USER/index.html (2003)
28. CAVEav: CAVE audio & video library.
    http://www-fp.mcs.anl.gov/~judson/CAVEav/CAVEav.html (2004)
29. Roussos, M., Johnson, A., Moher, T., Leigh, J., Vasilakis, C., Barnes, C.: Learning and building together in an immersive virtual world. Presence **8** (1999) 247–263
30. Leigh, J., Johnson, A.E., DeFanti, T.A., Brown, M.D.: A review of tele-immersive applications in the CAVE research network. In: VR. (1999) 180

31. Leigh, J., Rajlich, P., Stein, R., Johnson, A.E., DeFanti, T.A.: LIMBO/VTK: A tool for rapid tele-immersive visualization. In: Proc. IEEE Visualizaton '98. (1998) http://www.evl.uic.edu/cavern/cavernpapers/viz98/leigh_j.pdf.
32. Morgan, T., Kriz, R.D., Howard, S., Das-Neves, F., Kelso, J.: Extending the use of collaborative virtual environments for instruction to K-12 schools. In>>sight 1 (2002) 67–82 http://www.sv.vt.edu/future/cave/pub/kriz_ael/insight.pdf.
33. Kriz, R.D., Farkas, D., Ray, A.A., Kelso, J., Jr., R.E.F.: Visual interpretation and analysis of HPC nanostructure models using shared virtual environments. In: Conf. Proc. High Performance Computing: Grand Challenges in Computer Simulations, The Society for Modeling and Simulation International (SCS), San Diego, California (2003) 127–135 http://www.jwave.vt.edu/~rkriz/Pubs/HPC_2003/hpc2003distribute.pdf.
34. Ray, A.A.: The collaborative toolkit for diverse. http://www.sv.vt.edu/future/cave/software/D_collabtools/D_collabtools.html (2003)
35. Rich, E., Knight, K.: Artificial Intelligence. McGraww-Hill (1991)
36. Inselberg, A.: The plane with parallel coordinates. The Visual Computer 1 (1985)
37. Cheng, J., Hatzis, C., Hayashi, H., Krogel, M.A., Morishita, S., Page, D., Sese, J.: KDD Cup 2001 report. SIGKDD Explorations 3 (2002)
38. Witten, I., Frank, E.: Data Mining: Practical Machine Learning Tools and Techniques with Java Implementations. Morgan Kauffann (1999)
39. Cheeseman, P., Kelley, J., Self, M., Taylor, W., Freeman, D.: Autoclass: A Bayesian classification system. In: Proc. 5th Int'l Conf. on Machine Learning. (1988)
40. Hagedorn, J.G., Devaney, J.E.: A genetic programming system with a procedural program representation. In: 2001 Genetic and Evolutionary Computation Conf. Late Breaking Papers. (2001) http://math.nist.gov/mcsd/savg/papers/g2001.ps.gz.
41. Devaney, J.: The role of choice in discovery. Lecture Notes in Computer Science 167 (2000) eds. S. Arikawa and S. Morishita, Springer.
42. Blake, C.L., Merz, C.J.: UCI repository of machine learning databases (1998) http://www.ics.uci.edu/~mlearn/MLRepository.html.
43. Aray, Y., Marquez, M., Rodríguez, J., Coll, S., Simón-Manso, Y., Gonzalez, C., Weitz, D.A.: Electrostatics for exploring the nature of water adsorption on the laponite sheets' surface. J. Phys. Chem. B 107 (2003) 8946–8952
44. Louis Pasteur: Lecture. http://www.quotationspage.com/quotes/Louis_Pasteur/ (1854)

Computational Biology and Language

Madhavi Ganapathiraju[1], N. Balakrishnan[2],
Raj Reddy[3], and Judith Klein-Seetharaman[4]

[1] Carnegie Mellon University, USA
madhavi+@cs.cmu.edu
[2] Indian Inst. of Science, India & Carnegie Mellon Univ, USA
balki@serc.iisc.ernet.in
[3] Carnegie Mellon University, USA
rr+@cmu.edu
[4] Carnegie Mellon University & University of Pittsburgh, USA
judithks@cs.cmu.edu

1 Introduction

Current scientific research is characterized by increasing specialization, accumulating knowledge at a high speed due to parallel advances in a multitude of sub-disciplines. Recent estimates suggest that human knowledge doubles every two to three years – and with the advances in information and communication technologies, this wide body of scientific knowledge is available to anyone, anywhere, anytime. This may also be referred to as ambient intelligence - an environment characterized by plentiful and available knowledge. The bottleneck in utilizing this knowledge for specific applications is not accessing but assimilating the information and transforming it to suit the needs for a specific application. The increasingly specialized areas of scientific research often have the common goal of converting data into insight allowing the identification of solutions to scientific problems. Due to this common goal, there are strong parallels between different areas of applications that can be exploited and used to cross-fertilize different disciplines. For example, the same fundamental statistical methods are used extensively in speech and language processing, in materials science applications, in visual processing and in biomedicine. Each sub-discipline has found its own specialized methodologies making these statistical methods successful to the given application. The unification of specialized areas is possible because many different problems can share strong analogies, making the theories developed for one problem applicable to other areas of research. It is the goal of this paper to demonstrate the utility of merging two disparate areas of applications to advance scientific research. The merging process requires cross-disciplinary collaboration to allow maximal exploitation of advances in one sub-discipline for that of another. We will demonstrate this general concept with the specific example of merging language technologies and computational biology.

Communication between researchers in these disparate fields is facilitated through use of analogies. Specifically, the analogy between words and their meaning in speech and language processing on one hand, and the mapping between

Y. Cai (Ed.): Ambient Intelligence for Scientific Discovery, LNAI 3345, pp. 25–47, 2005.

biological sequences to biological functions on the other, has proven particularly useful. Recent reviews of applications of linguistic approaches to computational biology in general can be found in references [1, 2]. Thus, we will first only briefly explain the analogy between biological sequence and natural language processing in general and then focus the remainder of the review on the use of language technologies to identify the functional building blocks in protein sequences, i.e. the "words" of "protein sequence language". Since it is not known what would be the best word equivalent, we will first describe what types of word equivalents and vocabularies have been explored using the example of one specific area of application, secondary structure prediction and analysis. In some areas of applications of language technologies to language, the words are also not known, for example in speech recognition. In these applications, identifying functional building blocks is a signal processing task and we will describe the analogy to protein sequences from this perspective. This includes first introducing proteins and protein structure in comparison to the terms used in speech processing, followed by a presentation of one specific application of signal processing techniques in computational biology, namely transmembrane helix structure prediction. This will be brought into the broader context of other applications of language technologies to the same task. Finally, we will present a sampling of a few other examples of applying language technologies to the computational biology of proteins. Additional examples can be found referenced on the website of the Center for Biological Language Modeling (BLM) in Pittsburgh, USA [3].

2   Use of Language Technologies in Computational Biology

Most functions in biological systems are carried out by proteins. Typical functions include transmission of information, for example in signaling pathways, enzymatic catalysis and transport of molecules. Proteins also play structural roles such as formation of muscular fiber. Proteins are synthesized from small building blocks, amino acids, of which there are 20 different types (see below). The amino acids are connected to form a linear chain that is arranged into a defined three dimensional structure. The precise interactions between amino acids in the three dimensional structure of a protein are the hallmark of the functions that they are able to carry out. For example, these interactions allow proteins to make contacts with small molecule ligands such as drugs. Figure 1 shows an example protein, lysozyme, to which an inhibitor ligand is bound (shown in magenta). Thus, knowing the three-dimensional shape of proteins has implications not only for the fundamental understanding of protein function, but also for applications such as drug design and discovery.

Obtaining three dimensional structures of proteins experimentally is not straight forward. X-ray crystallography and Nuclear Magnetic Resonance (NMR) spectroscopy can accurately determine protein structures; but these methods are labor intensive, time consuming, and for many proteins are not applicable at all. Therefore, predicting structural features of proteins from a sequence is an im-

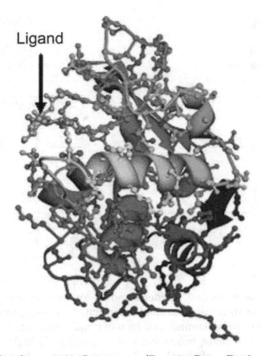

Ligand

Fig. 1. An example of a protein: Lysozyme (Protein Data Bank code 1HEW). The protein is colored in rainbow color from one end to the other end. The main chain is highlighted by ribbons. Side chains extending from the main chain are shown as ball and stick representations. The magenta colored molecule is the inhibitor ligand, tri-N-acetylchitotriose. This figure illustrates how a linear protein chain folds up into a three dimensional structure thereby creating a binding site with which ligand molecules can interact. All protein figures in this paper have been created using Chimera [4].

portant topic in computational biology. Understanding the structure, dynamics and function of proteins strongly parallels the mapping of words to meaning in natural language. This analogy is outlined schematically in Fig. 2. The words in a text document map to a meaning and convey rich information pertaining to the topic of the document. Similarly, protein sequences also represent the "raw text" and carry high-level information about the structures, dynamics and functions of proteins. This information can be extracted to obtain an understanding of the complex interactions of protein within biological systems. Availability of large amounts of text in digital form has led to the convergence of linguistics with computational science, and has resulted in applications such as information retrieval, document summarization and machine translation. Thus, even though computational language understanding is not yet a reality, data availability has allowed us to obtain practical solutions that have a large impact on our lives. In direct analogy, transformation of biology by data availability opened the door to convergence with computer science and information technology.

Many of the hallmarks of statistical analysis of biological sequences are similar to those of human languages. (i) Large data bodies need to be analyzed

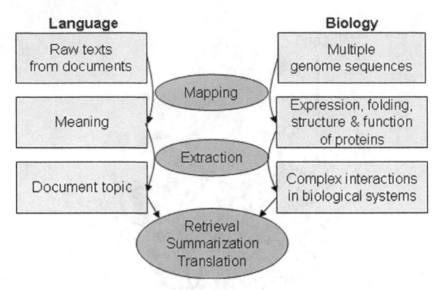

Fig. 2. Analogy between natural language and "protein sequence language". Words combine into sentences to convey meaningful content. Processing words in a document can convey the topic of the document and its meaningful content. Biological sequences are analogous to the raw texts, processing which would yield higher level information on the behavioral properties of the physical entities corresponding to the sequences.

in both cases. (ii) Fundamental units of human languages include higher order structures, paralleled by domains, subunits or functionally linked proteins. (iii) Computer-based derivation of meaning from text is analogous to the prediction of structure and function from primary sequence data. Therefore, the analogy has led to the wide application of methods used in language technologies to the study of biological sequences [1, 5, 6]. Some examples for the use of linguistic approaches for bioinformatics can be found in refs. [1, 5–12]. Recently, proba-bilistic language models have been used to improve protein domain boundary detection [13], to predict transmembrane helix boundaries [14] and in genome comparison [15, 16]. Finally, latent semantic analysis, a technique used in text summarization, has been used for secondary structure prediction [17] and topic segmentation of text or radio speech. The feature prediction methods of Yule's Q-statistic [18] and mutual information [19] have been applied to the membrane protein boundary prediction problem.

2.1   Protein Sequence Language

Like strings of letters and words in a text, protein sequences are linear chains of amino acids. The amino acid is one of the fundamental building blocks in protein sequences. This is illustrated schematically in Fig. 3. Each amino acid has a common component shown in Fig. 3A. In the protein chain, the amino acids are connected through this component forming the backbone of the protein. The side chains, represented by R in Fig. 3A, can be one of 20 different types, corresponding to different chemical structures (labeled as (A, C, D, E, F, G, H, I, K, L, M, N, P, Q, R, S, T, V, W, Y)). The main and side chains in a protein are shown in an example in Fig. 3B. Side-chains themselves have components in common among each other based on their chemical composition. Thus, we could also consider smaller chemical units than the amino acids as the functional building blocks of proteins. This would correspond to the vocabulary shown in Fig. 4. These are in fact more fundamental units than the amino acids themselves, because mutations, i.e. replacements of amino acids in protein sequences, that only exchange one single chemical group, e.g. from phenylalanine to tyrosine (OH group) can have detrimental effects on protein function.

At the other end, there are also cases where a single amino acid is not sufficient to convey a specific "meaning", but a group of amino acids does, generally referred to as a functional motif. For example, the triplet D/E R Y is a conserved motif in a specific protein family (the G-protein coupled receptors) known to encode the ability to interact with another protein (the G-protein). Finally, amino acid sequences can be replaced without loss in function, as individual amino acids or as groups of amino acids. For example, in the above triplet, the first position is not fully defined - it can be either D or E. This is due to the chemical nature of the amino acids: D and E although having different side chains, share a number of properties, most importantly, negative charge in this case. Thus, the biological vocabulary is much more flexible than the human vocabulary, because it is defined through properties with several different chemical meanings and not a single meaning as in the case of the 26 letters. There are hundreds of different scales of properties of amino acids, including size, hydrophobicity, electronic properties, aromaticity, polarity, flexibility, secondary structure propensity and charge to name just a few (see e.g., the online databases PDbase [20] and ProtScale [21]). Thus, although the 20 amino acids are a reasonable starting point to define building blocks in protein sequences, smaller, larger or uniquely encoded units may often be functionally more meaningful.

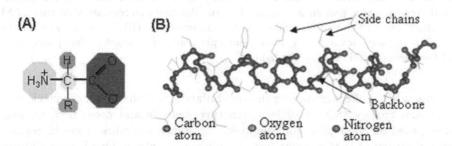

Fig. 3. (A) Chemical composition of amino acids. The composition common to all amino acids consists of a main carbon atom C_α (yellow), NH3+ group (blue), carboxyl group COO- (red), hydrogen atom (green) and a sidechain R (pink). The first three, along with the C_α, are common to all amino acids, where as the side chain R is different for each amino acid [17]. (B) Protein segment. A small protein segment with the composing main chain atoms is shown in ball-and-stick model. Side chains attached to the C_α are shown in grey wire frame.

-Ċ-	=Ċ^{aromatic}	ĊH-	-CH$_2$-
-CH$_2^{\text{riag.}}$	-CH$_3$	=CH^{aromatic}-	ĊH^{ring}
ĊC=O	-COO$^-$	=N-	-NH-
-NH$_2$	=NH$_2^+$	-NH$_3^+$	-NH^{ring}-
-OH	-SH	-Ṡ	

Fig. 4. Chemical Group Vocabulary: The basic chemical groups that form the building blocks of the amino acids are shown. The chemical group in each cell in the figure forms one word in the vocabulary. Thus, the size of chemical group vocabulary is 19. This vocabulary has been studied in the context of secondary structure analysis by Ganapathiraju et al [17].

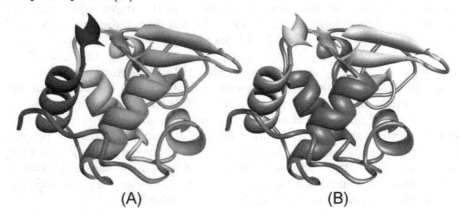

(A)   (B)

Fig. 5. Secondary structure elements in Lysozyme (PDB ID: 1HEW): Three dimensional structure of a protein is composed of smaller units (secondary structure). (A) The chain can be followed by guide of the rainbow colors. (B) The same view of the protein as in A is shown, but repeating elements helix (red), sheet (yellow) and turns and flexible loops (violet) are highlighted.

To study the effect of varying the vocabulary and alphabet on a typical computational biology task, secondary structure analysis and prediction, we first investigated different units for this task. Secondary structure refers to regular units of structure that are stabilized by molecular interactions between atoms within the protein, the most important interaction being the so-called Hydrogen (H) Bond. There are 7 distinct secondary structures, broadly called helix, sheet, turn and loop structures. In helix types, the designating secondary structure is formed due to H-bonds between carbonyl group and amino group of every 3rd, 4th or 5th residues, and these are called 3_{10}−helix, α−helix and π−helix respectively. A strand is a unit that shares long range hydrogen-bond interaction with another strand. Two or more such interacting strands form what is called a sheet. A turn is defined as a short segment that causes the protein to bend. Loop or coil region has no specific secondary structure. Commonly, the 7 groups are reduced to 3 groups, helix, strand and loop (shown in an example in Fig. 5). To study the relevance of different vocabularies for secondary structure formation, we used the following vocabularies: (1) chemical building blocks of amino acids, (2) single amino acids from the 20 amino acid alphabet and (3) reduced alphabets based on similarities between physico-chemical properties of amino acids [17]. Latent Semantic Analysis (LSA) was used to decipher the role of the vocabulary for this task, because it is a natural language processing method that is used to extract hidden relations between words [22]. We should therefore be able to study the effects of different vocabularies on secondary structure without introducing artifacts through the differences in size and geometry in the different units studied. LSA captures semantic relations using global information extracted from a large number of documents and can therefore identify words in a text that are synonymous even when such information is not directly available. LSA was then applied to characterize segments of protein sequences with a given type of secondary structure, helix, strand or loop. Each segment was represented as a bag-of-words vector traditionally used in document processing. The word-document matrix comprising all the protein segment vectors was transformed into Eigenspace through singular value decomposition, and the protein segments were compared to each other in terms of vector representation in singular space. To compare the usefulness of this representation, protein segments were separated into training and test sets and the secondary structure of each segment in the test set was predicted based on the secondary structure of its nearest neighbors in the singular space from among the training set. When representing the amino acid sequences using the three different vocabularies, we observed that different vocabularies are better at characterizing different structure types. Helices and strands are best characterized using amino acid types with LSA, and coils are characterized better with amino acids as vocabulary and using the simple word-document matrix analysis (called VSM [23]) without LSA. Average 3-class prediction (Q_3) was found to be best using chemical groups as vocabulary and using VSM. The results demonstrate that word-document matrix analysis and LSA capture sequence preferences in structural types and can distinguish between the "meanings" of vocabularies for protein secondary structure types. Furthermore, protein sequences represented in terms of chemical groups and amino acid types provide more clues on structure than the classically used amino acids as building blocks [17].

As shown by the above study [17] and many previous studies [24], single amino acid propensities have limited ability to predict secondary structure elements. It was therefore investigated if larger segments composed of several amino acids, so-called k-mers or n-grams of amino acids are more appropriate units of protein sequence language with respect to their meaning for secondary structure [25]. However, this study found that n-grams do not capture secondary structure propensity of protein segments well. This is due to the fact that n-gram features do not encode the types of amino acid substitutions typical for protein sequences exemplified in the motif example above. Therefore, it was investigated if a compact representation of position specific n-grams as $x\{-|+\}N$, where x is the n-gram, $\{-|+\}$ indicates whether it occurs before or after the residue under question, and N is the distance from this residue to the n-gram, may be a better representation of the protein sequence. The analogy to language can be found when classifying documents into possible topics. This task also requires identification of crucial words that can discriminate between possible topics. For example, the word 'ball' can discriminate between "science" and "sports" topics but cannot distinguish between "cricket" and "football" topics. Advances in topic detection methods for text documents have resulted in some reliable methods to identify such discriminating words. In the context of protein secondary structure prediction, there are also position specific propensities of amino acids in different secondary structure types and therefore topic detection algorithms are directly applicable to secondary structure prediction at the residue level. The application of the context-sensitive vocabulary provided results that are comparable to the current state-of-the-art methods using "black-box" classification approaches, in particular neural networks, with Q_3 accuracy of about 70%. The advantage of the use of the context-sensitive vocabulary over these "black-box" methods is that it allows analysis of the word-association matrix with singular value decomposition to identify co-occurring word pairs, corresponding to regular expressions with a specific "meaning" for secondary structure. For example, one of the most highly associated word pair corresponded to the pattern "CPxxAI". The pattern describes the loop region at the C-terminal end of a beta-sheet. Thus, the context-sensitive vocabulary encodes some of the complex dependencies between amino acids that determine formation of secondary structure.

3   Identification of Functional Building Blocks in Proteins as a Signal Processing Task

The lack of knowledge on what are the break points separating words from each other is not new to the language arena. In fact, it is found in many speech applications. In a spoken sentence, words are not separated from each other by spaces as in written text. Thus, automatic speech analysis and synthesis methods also have to deal with identification of meaningful units. The task therefore shifts from statistical analysis of word frequencies to a stronger focus on signal identification and differentiation from noise in speech recognition applications. Similarly, the task of mapping protein sequences to their structure, dynamics and function can also be seen more generally as a signal processing task. Just as the speech signal is a waveform whose acoustical features vary with time, a protein is a linear chain of chemico-physical features that vary with position in the sequence. However, while a speech sample can take unlimited continuous values, or digitized values within a given digital resolution, for proteins the value can be only one of the possible twenty, corresponding to the twenty types of amino acids (see above). Hence assigning a symbol or value to each of the twenty amino acids is one alternative for digital representation. This is however, not a meaningful representation for signal processing. We will review below the approaches by which signal processing techniques become applicable to the identification of meaningful building blocks in protein sequences. We will demonstrate in detail using this example how scientific and technological advances in the specialized area of automatic speech recognition become relevant for the specialized area within computational biology of protein secondary structure prediction. Both areas separately have been extensively researched for several decades; the complete solution has not been accomplished; in both cases the underlying principles are understood, yet are difficult to model for decoding by a computer practically, "as the physics of simplicity and complexity meet" [26]. For a deeper understanding of protein structure and protein biochemistry, see [27] and [28]. Readers interested further in speech recognition may refer to [29, 30].

3.1 Digital Representation

Speech waveform is a superposition of signals of various different frequencies. By way of Nyquist criterion, the information in the signal can be completely captured by sampling the signal at a rate that is at least twice that of the largest frequency in the signal. Since most information in human speech is band-limited to about 8 kHz, sampling it at a rate of 16 kHz is sufficient. A typical digitized speech signal is a series of discrete-time samples of its amplitude. The amplitude of each sample is further coded into discrete levels to allow digital representation. To apply signal processing techniques to protein sequences, the protein must be represented by some numerical representation of its property at each position. To derive a meaningful representation of the protein signal, we must understand the chemical structures of the amino acids and their resulting physico-chemical properties (see above). The scales relating the 20 amino acids to each other based on these properties can be used to replace the amino acid symbols with numeric representations more similar to speech waveforms. In principle, any one of the property scales can be used, depending on the type of protein sequence analysis required. Consider the example speech utterance, "how to recognize speech with this new display", whose waveform is shown in Fig. 6A. The signal has been sampled at 16 kHz. Typically, the signal also contains background noise and therefore the pauses in between words are not entirely flat. The waveform shows how the amplitude of the sound varies as time progresses from the beginning of the utterance to the end. In contrast consider a protein. Figures 6B and 6C show how a protein may be represented as numerical signals. Figure 6B shows the protein in terms of charge and Fig. 6C shows the protein represented in terms of hydrophobicity of the amino acids. While speech is represented with respect to time, protein is represented in physical dimension from one end to the other end of the amino acid chain.

The goal of speech recognition is to identify the words that are spoken. There are several hundred thousand words in a typical language. These words are formed by a combination of smaller units of sound called phones. Recognizing

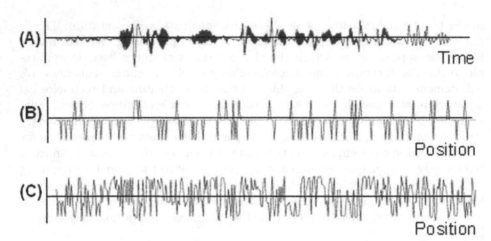

Fig. 6. Digital Representation. (A) Digital waveform of a speech signal of the utterance "how to recognize speech with this new display". The x-axis shows the time, while the y-axis shows the amplitude (loudness) of the signal. (B) Protein signal, where the sequence is represented by a binary scale of charge of the residues. (C) Protein signal in terms of hydrophobicity of the residues. X-axis in (B) and (C) shows the residue number along the length of the protein, and y-axis is the value of the property of the residues (here charge or hydrophobicity).

a word in speech amounts to recognizing these phones. There are typically 50 phones in speech. Thus, identification of "word" equivalents in protein sequences using the signal processing approach is equivalent to "phone" identification.

3.2   Information Required to Decode the Signal

The content of a speech signal is not only dependent on the signal itself; its interpretation relies on an external entity, the listener. For example, consider the phrases:

How to recognize speech with this new display
How to wreck a nice beach with this nudist play

The two phrases are composed of almost identical phone sequences, but result in two different sentences. Spectrograms showing the frequency decomposition of the sound signals are shown in Fig. 7B and 7C, for these two sentences spoken by the same speaker.

Given the speech signal or a spectrogram, which utterance was meant by the speaker can be found by the context in which it was spoken. Thus the complete information for interpretation is not contained in the speech signal itself, but is inferred from the context. On the other hand, the linear strings of amino acids that make up a protein contain in principle all the information needed to fold it into a 3-D shape capable of fulfilling its designated function.

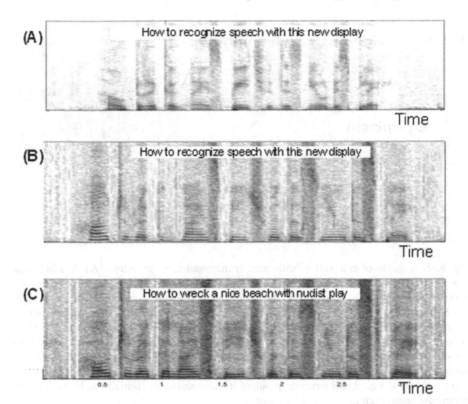

Fig. 7. Spectrograms of same utterances between different speakers and different utterances by same speaker: X-axis shows progression of time and y-axis shows different frequency bands. The energy of the signal in different bands is shown as intensity in grayscale values with progression of time. (A) and (B) show spectrograms of the same sentence "How to recognize speech with this new display" spoken by two different speakers, male and female. Although the frequency characterization is similar, the formant frequencies are much more clearly defined in the speech of female speaker. (C) shows the spectrogram of the utterance "How to wreck a nice beach with this nudist play" spoken by same speaker as in (B). (A) and (B) are not identical even though they are composed of the same words. (B) and (C) are similar to each other even though they are not the same sentences. See text for discussion.

3.3 Speaker Variability

Consider the signal characteristics of a word spoken by two different persons, especially if one is female and the other is male. Although the fundamental nature of the sounds remains the same, the overall absolute values of signal composition would be different. For example, a vowel sound would still have the same periodic nature in both utterances, but the frequency would be different. See for example, the frequency compositions of the same sentence spoken by a male and female speaker shown in Fig. 7A and 7B.

The analogy of speaker variability in the protein world can be found in the following broad categorization of proteins: the majority of a cell's proteins are

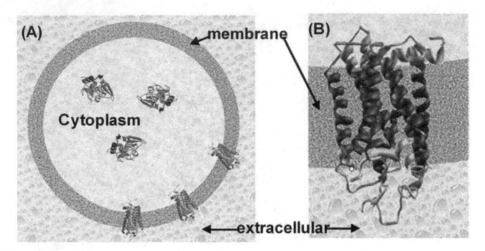

Fig. 8. Schematic of cell and soluble and transmembrane proteins. (A) A schematic of a cell: The cell is enveloped by a cell-membrane (brown) and is surrounded by water medium (blue bubbles). The medium inside the cell is made of water as well. Soluble proteins are found completely inside the cell. Membrane proteins are partly embedded in the cell-membrane. (B) Transmembrane protein Rhodopsin: It starts in the cytoplasmic region (top), traverses through the cell membrane (brown) to go into the extracellular region (bottom) and then transverses the membrane again to enter the cytoplasm. This protein has 8 helices in all, 7 of which are located mostly in the transmembrane region and extending out of it, and one helix (horizontal in picture) in the cytoplasmic region.

found inside the cells (soluble proteins), whereas, some proteins traverse through the cell membrane (membrane proteins). In contrast to soluble proteins, which are always in an aqueous environment, membrane proteins have parts that are like soluble proteins located either inside or outside of the cells, while a significant portion is located in a chemically different environment, the membrane lipid bilayer, as shown in Fig. 8. Since the environment around parts of these transmembrane proteins is different, the characteristics displayed by these parts are also different. Transmembrane helix prediction is closely related to protein secondary structure prediction given the primary sequence. Secondary structural elements described before, namely helix, strand, turn and loop are still the basic components of the three dimensional structure of membrane proteins also; however their characteristics are different from those of the soluble proteins when they are located in the membrane embedded parts. This difference may be seen as the speaker variability in speech. The intracellular, transmembrane and extracellular segments can be thought of as speech that is spoken by three different speakers.

Consider a domain specific speech recognition task where the number of speakers and the size of the vocabulary are very small. A method that is often adopted for this task is to recognize the words by speaker-specific word models. The approach adopted in transmembrane protein structure prediction is similar-the structural elements are modeled specifically for each environment separately. Consider another domain specific task where the goal is to perform only speaker recognition out of three speakers (cytoplasmic, transmembrane and extracellular). The protein shown in Fig. 8B is an example of a transmembrane protein called rhodopsin. It consists of 8 helical segments and a beta sheet. Seven of the helices are transmembrane, one helix is soluble. A speaker-segmentation like task on this protein, would label these seven segments as transmembrane, and the rest of the protein as cytoplasmic and extracellular segments.

3.4 Signal Analysis of Transmembrane Proteins

The duration of the transmembrane segment is usually about 20-25 amino acid residues which corresponds to the 30 + thickness of the cell membrane. (A residue is the equivalent of a sample in speech signal, whose value can be any one of the twenty amino acids). The cross-section of the cell-membrane is highly hydrophobic, thus imposing the requirement on amino acids within its environment to be predominantly hydrophobic. The properties most meaningful in this context to allow application of signal processing techniques are therefore related to hydrophobicity and polarity.

The most important mathematical tool in signal processing is the Fourier transform [31]. For a comprehensive review of signal processing methods in pro-

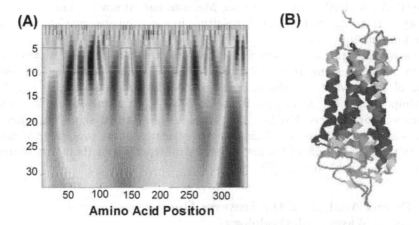

Fig. 9. Wavelet features of rhodopsin (swiss-prot id: OPSD_BOVIN) using a binary polar non-polar vocabulary: (A) Scalogram of the wavelet features: The primary sequence is mapped to polar nonpolar (1, 0 respectively) numerical scale and wavelet transform is computed at scales from 1 to 32 with the Mexican-hat analyzing function. The resulting 2D array is shown in image format after scaling the result to range between 0 and 1, with a rainbow color map VIBGYOR going from 0 to 1. The x-axis corresponds to the residue number and the y-axis corresponds to the scale at which the wavelet is computed, with the smallest scale at the top. (B) Wavelet features mapped onto the 3D structure of rhodopsin (pdb id: 1F88): The wavelet transform at a scale of 9 is normalized to a range of 0-150 and mapped onto the 3D structure of the protein, using 'temperature' field in the pdb format.

tein structure analysis, see [32]. A protein sequence is very short in length, being on an average 300 residues long. There are proteins as short as 50 residues and those that are larger than 1000 residues, but most of the proteins are a few hundred residues long. The duration of secondary structure elements are even shorter. Hence it is not suitable to use Fourier transform in the analysis of protein signal. Also, while Fourier transform can capture periodicities at any scale in the overall signal, it cannot identify the location of occurrence of periodicity. To capture local periodicities, Wavelet transform appears to be a more suitable mathematical tool [33] and has been applied earlier to speech recognition [34, 35]. Previously, the application of Wavelet transform in the context of transmembrane helix prediction has primarily been to de-noise the hydropathy signal by removing high frequency variations [36–39]. In the work presented here, wavelet transform is used to derive features from amino acid sequences.

In order to facilitate the use of signal analysis for the transmembrane helix prediction problem, polar/non-polar characteristics are mapped polar = 1, non-polar = 0. Other mappings such as by electronic properties, viz., mapping from strong electron donor to strong electron acceptors to numerical values +2 to -2, have also been studied. However, the best results were observed empirically by the choice of polar/non-polar representation. Application of wavelet transform to the polar/non-polar representation of one particular membrane protein, bovine rhodopsin (Swissprot ID: OPSD_BOVIN), is shown in Fig. 9. The numerical mapping of the sequence with polar/non-polar property is the same as shown in Fig. 6. A standard analysis function, Mexican-hat, at scales from 1 to 32 has been applied to this protein signal, resulting in a continuous wavelet transform of the protein sequence.

The wavelet transform gives rise to patterns that are distinct between the transmembrane regions from non transmembrane regions. An image representation of the wavelet transform, called the scalogram is shown in Fig. 9A. Superimposed on the scalogram is the location of transmembrane and non-transmembrane regions. Further, the wavelet transformed signal at different scales is also mapped onto the 3-dimensional structure of the protein, to visually analyze the distribution of feature values in different segments of the protein, here for scale 9 in rhodopsin (Fig. 9B).

3.5   Formal Analysis of the Features Derived Using Wavelet Methodology

Comparing the scalogram of a transmembrane protein in Fig. 9A to the spectrograms of speech in Fig. 7, it can be seen that the durational characteristic of transmembrane segments is very similar to that of phones in speech. The observations are very similar from one sample (or frame) to the next; there is an onset period and offset period from the transmembrane segment. In the absence of such durational feature, a classifier would have been suitable to classify the protein residues as transmembrane or non-transmembrane. However, to capture the time (or position) specific characteristics of the wavelets with respect to transmembrane domains, hidden Markov modeling (HMM) like architecture is

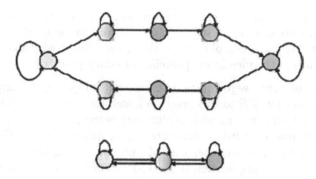

Fig. 10. HMM topology used for transmembrane prediction. The fully green state corresponds to the cytoplasmic loop, blue state to the extracellular loop, and the fully orange state to the core of the transmembrane region. The shaded states of green/orange and blue/orange colors correspond to transmembrane regions nearer to the lipid bilayer on cytoplasmic and extracellular sides. Although positive-inside rule [40] applies to the loop region thus characterizing cytoplasmic loops differently from extracellular loops, no distinction has been made in this work between cytoplasmic and extracellular loops. Hence, the topology shown on top reduces to that on the bottom, with just three states.

best suited. Here, we considered an HMM with a simple architecture as shown in Fig. 10. Each state is modeled with a mixture of 8 Gaussians. The vector of wavelet coefficients computed for scales 4 to 16 at each residue position in the protein, is considered the feature vector corresponding to that residue. In Fig 9A, the feature vectors correspond to columns in the 2D image of wavelet coefficients, considering only rows 4 to 16. The data set used is the set of 160 proteins [41]. The data set is available as 10 disjoint sets so that separate data may be used for training and testing. We used the first set (numbered 0) for testing, and the remaining sets for training. The accuracy of classification of each residue as transmembrane or non-transmembrane is found to be 80.0% (Q_2). Q_2 refers to the percentage of residues that have been classified correctly into the two states transmembrane and non-transmembrane. Although hidden Markov models have been used earlier towards transmembrane prediction, what is unique here is the demonstration of the use of wavelet coefficients as feature vectors. Within the speech recognition framework, wavelets have traditionally been used for speech enhancement (similar to hydrophobicity smoothing in case of transmembrane prediction), but a recent paper has demonstrated the use of wavelet coefficients as features for phoneme classification [35].

3.6   Membrane Helix Boundary Prediction Using N-Gram Features

The above work on transmembrane helix boundary prediction using signal processing techniques borrowed from language technologies strongly complements other applications of language technologies to the same task. As with phoneme identification, other language technologies applications use segmentation ap-

proaches, for example in document classification and topic detection. Traditionally, these methods have relied on n-gram features and statistical associations
between them. We have complemented the above study with two n-gram approaches to address the membrane protein boundary prediction problem.

(1) Similar to topic segmentation in natural language, we applied Yule's
measure of association [42] to this problem based on its use in natural language
processing [43]. Given a text with n different words, an n x n table of Yule
values for every pair of words is computed. The distribution of Yule values in
the table differs for different categories of text, indicating the positions of the
boundaries. In a model application to the G-Protein Coupled Receptor (GPCR)
family of membrane proteins, we found that Yule values can differentiate between
transmembrane helices and loops connecting the helices [18].

(2) Using the same n-gram features but a different association measure, Mutual Information, it was also shown that language technologies can discover
known functional building blocks, the transmembrane helices, without prior assumption on the length, type or properties of these building blocks. While the
above Yule statistics required prior knowledge in the form of a training set for examples of transmembrane versus non-transmembrane applications, using mutual
information, no such knowledge was required. Computing Mutual Information
statistics on the entire dataset of a membrane protein family, the GPCR family, without prior knowledge on the positions of extracellular-transmembrane
and cytoplasmic-transmembrane boundaries, can rediscover these boundaries,
as shown in Fig. 11 [19]. In topic segmentation, topic boundaries are indicated by minima in Mutual Information. Similarly, in membrane proteins sequences, both membrane-cytoplasmic and membrane-extracellular boundaries
are detected with high accuracy [19].

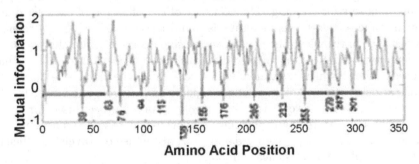

Fig. 11. Mutual information values along the rhodopsin sequence using different
datasets GPCR to generate mutual information values [19]. Horizontal lines use the
same color code as in Figure 1 indicating the positions of the segments belonging to
each of extracellular, cytoplasmic and helices domains based on expert knowledge. The
positions of breakpoints indicated by mutual information minima are shown as blue
labels. The figure is JKS's version of the work. It is posted here by permission of ACM
for your personal use. Not for redistribution. The definitive version was published in
[19] http://doi.acm.org/10.1145/967900.967933.

(3) Finally, an n-gram language modeling approach has also been adopted. The method builds a language model for each 'topic' representing transmembrane helices and loops and compares their performance in predicting the current amino acid, to determine whether a boundary occurs at the current position. The language models make use of only n-grams probabilities, but surprisingly still produced promising results [14, 18, 19].

4   Other Applications of Language Technologies in Computational Biology of Proteins

4.1   Genome Comparison

The secondary structure and transmembrane helix prediction tasks are only two examples of many tasks in computational biology where language technologies are relevant. For example, the features most often used in language technologies are word n-grams and there are many other tasks where n-grams do form meaningful building blocks. Probably the most widely known application of n-grams in computational biology is their use in the BLAST algorithm, where they enhance computational efficiency in sequence searching in the initial step [44]. However, n-grams have also proven useful in a number of other bioinformatics areas. The distributions of n-grams in biological sequences have been shown to follow Zipf's

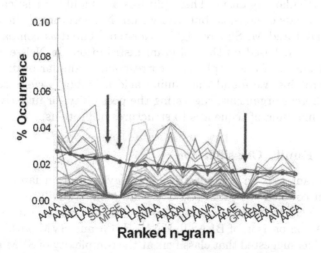

Fig. 12. Distribution of amino acid n-grams with n=4 in Neisseria meningitidis in comparison to the distribution of the corresponding amino acids in 44 other organisms [61]. N-grams of Neisseria are plotted in descending order of their frequency in the genome (in bold red). Numbers on x- indicate the ranks of the specific n-grams in Neisseria. Frequencies of corresponding n-grams from genomes of various other organisms are also shown (thin lines). The second thin line closely following the bold red line corresponds to a different strain of Neisseria meningtidis. Arrows indicate the positions of 4-grams that are over-represented in Neisseria, but are rare in other genomes. The figure is reproduced from [61] with permission from the publisher.

law [45–51]. Zipf's law states that the frequency of a word is related to its rank by a power law [52, 53]. While there is some debate as to the meaning of this observation for biological sequences [45–51], the Zipf plot of n-gram frequencies has found application in identification of genome signatures [16].

The Zipf-like analysis of protein sequences allows addressing the question of whether the sequences in proteins of different organisms are statistically similar or if organisms may be viewed as representations of different languages. We compared the n-gram frequencies of 44 different organisms using the n-gram comparison functions provided by the Biological Language Modeling Toolkit. (1) A simple Markovian uni-gram (context independent amino acid model from the proteins of Aeropyrum pernix was trained. When training and test sets were from the same organism, a perplexity (a variation of cross-entropy) of 16.6 was observed, whereas data from other organisms varied from 16.8 to 21.9. Thus, even the simplest model can automatically detect the differences in amino acid usage of different organisms. (2) We developed a modification of Zipf-like analysis that can reveal specific differences in n-grams in different organisms. First, the amino acid n-grams of a given length were sorted in descending order by frequency for the organism of choice. An example is shown in Fig. 12 for Neisseria meningitidis for n=4. Remarkably, there are three n-grams (shown by red arrows in the figure) that are among the top 20 most frequently occurring 4-grams in Neisseria, but that are rare or absent in any of the other genomes.

These highly idiosyncratic n-grams suggest "phrases" that are preferably used in the particular organism. These phrases are highly statistically significant, not only across organisms, but also within Neisseria itself. In particular, the 4-grams SDGI and MPSE are highly over-represented as compared to the frequencies expected based on the uni-gram distributions in Neisseria [16]. (3) While it is not known if these "phrases" correspond to similar or different substructures of proteins, we found that amino acid neighbor preferences are also different for different organisms, suggesting the possibility for underlying subtle changes in the mapping of sequences to structures of proteins.

4.2   Protein Family Classification

Another important task in computational biology is protein family classification. G-protein coupled receptors (GPCRs) are a superfamily of proteins and particularly difficult to classify into families due to the extreme diversity among its members. A comparison of BLAST, k-NN, HMM and SVM with alignment-based features has suggested that classifiers at the complexity of SVM are needed to attain high accuracy [54]. However, we were able to show that the simple Decision Tree and Naïve Bayes classifiers in conjunction with chi-square feature selection on counts of n-grams perform extremely well, and the Naïve Bayes classifier even outperforms the SVM significantly [55]. We also generalized the utility of n-grams for high-accuracy classification of other protein families using the Naïve Bayes approach [55, 56]. In line with these observations, Wu and co-workers have observed that neural networks perform well with n-gram features in the protein family classification task [57].

4.3   Prediction of Protein Folding Initiation Sites

The demonstrated success of language technologies for a number of typical computational biology tasks suggests that these methods may also prove useful in studies of tasks that have been studied less extensively. Prediction of folding initiation sites in proteins is a formidable task that requires novel approaches. We investigated if inverse frequencies may correlate with experimentally determined folding initiation sites in the protein folding model system, lysozyme. Our hypothesis was based on the observation that in natural languages, rare words carry the most relevant meaning of a text. Shown in Fig. 13 are inverse tri-gram frequencies plotted along the lysozyme sequence. Indeed, we observed a correlation between the locations of rare trigrams and the location of residual structure in the unfolded protein as evidenced by maxima in relaxation rates measured in NMR spectroscopic experiments. The statistical significance of this observation remains to be established by extension to other proteins, but lysozyme is the only protein for which the locations of folding initiation sites are known. However, the steady growth in the size of the protein databank will allow a systematic comparison between the sequences of n-grams and the number of structures that each n-gram can occur in. Such statistics are already beginning to be reported in the I-sites database [59] and in the analysis of sequences encoding certain types of structures [60]. Thus, it is expected that n-gram analysis may significantly contribute to the protein tertiary structure prediction problem in the future.

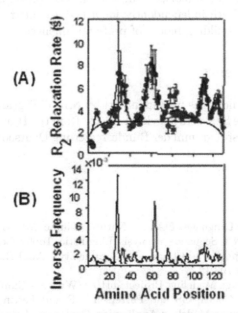

Fig. 13. Location of folding initiation sites in model protein Lysozyme (see Fig. 1) A. Transverse relaxation rates [58]. Large values above the black line indicate the presence of residual structure. B. Inverse trigram frequency in human lysozyme. The figure is reproduced from [61] with permission from the publisher.

5   Biological Language Modeling Toolkit and Website

A large number of linguistic methods for protein sequence analysis are provided at http://flan.blm.cs.cmu.edu/.

6   Conclusions

Here, we have shown that the use of an intuitive analogy allows direct application of methods developed in one specialized area of research to that of another. In particular, we demonstrated the use of language and speech technologies for a variety of computational biology problems. We described the major hurdle in the use of this analogy, the identification of functional equivalents of "words" in protein sequences with the long-term goal of preparing a dictionary for "protein sequence language". Although we are far from building such a dictionary, we demonstrate that a number of different vocabularies can provide meaningful building blocks in protein sequences. The utility of these vocabularies depends on the specific type of application in computational biology, and we provided examples from secondary structure prediction of soluble and of membrane proteins, of motif identification in genomes, protein family classification and protein folding and tertiary structure. Vocabularies range from individual chemical groups, to single amino acids, to combinations of amino acids (n-grams) with and without context information to chemical property representation. Automatic identification of functional building blocks using speech recognition and topic boundary detection methods both independently identified secondary structure elements as major functional building blocks of protein sequences.

Acknowledgements

Research presented here was funded in part by NSF ITR grants EIA0225656 and EIA0225636 and the Sofya Kovalevkaya Award from the Humboldt Foundation / Zukunftsinvestitionsprogramm der Bundesregierung Deutschland and NIH grant NLM108730.

References

1. Searls, DB: "The Language of Genes" Nature. volume 420. issue 6912. (2002) 211-7
2. Bolshoy, A: "DNA Sequence Analysis Linguistic Tools: Contrast Vocabularies, Compositional Spectra and Linguistic Complexity." Appl Bioinformatics. volume 2. issue 2. (2003) 103-12
3. Biological Language Modeling Project: http://Www.Cs.Cmu.Edu/ Blmt/
4. Huang, CC and Couch, GS and Pettersen, EF and Ferrin, TE: "Chimera: An Extensible Molecular Modeling Application Constructed Using Standard Components" http://Www.Cgl.Ucsf.Edu/Chimera. PSB1996: Pacific Symposium on Biocomputing. (1996) 50-61
5. Baldi, P: Bioinformatics. MIT Press. (1998)

6. Durbin, R and Eddy, S and Krogh, A and Mitchison, G: Biological Sequence Analysis: Probabilistic Models of Proteins and Nucleic Acids. (1998)
7. Bolshoy, A and Shapiro, K and Trifonov, E and Ioshikhes, I: "Enhancement of the Nucleosomal Pattern in Sequences of Lower Complexity." Nucl. Acids. Res. volume 25. issue 16. (1997) 3248-3254
8. Burge, C and Karlin, S: Prediction of Complete Gene Structures in Human Genomic DNA. 1997
9. Baxevanis, AD and Ouellette, BFF: Bioinformatics. A Practical Guide to the Analysis of Genes and Proteins. Wiley-Interscience. (1998)
10. Bussemaker, HJ and Li, H and Siggia, ED: "Building a Dictionary for Genomes: Identification of Presumptive Regulatory Sites by Statistical Analysis." Proc Natl Acad Sci U S A. volume 97. issue 18. (2000) 10096-100
11. Gibas, C and Jambeck, P: Developing Bioinformatics Computer Skills. O'Reilly & Associates. (2001)
12. Troyanskaya, OG and Arbell, O, Koren and Y, Landau, GM and Bolshoy, A: Sequence Complexity Profiles of Prokaryotic Genomic Sequences: A Fast Algorithm for Calculating Linguistic Complexity. (2002)
13. Coin, L and Bateman, A and Durbin, R: Enhanced Protein Domain Discovery by Using Language Modeling Techniques from Speech Recognition.(2003)
14. Cheng, BYM and Carbonell, J and Klein-Seetharaman, J: Application of Topic Segmentation Techniques to Protein Sequences: Identification of Transmembrane Helix Boundaries in Gpcrs. (2004)
15. Ganapathiraju, M and Klein-Seetharaman, J and Rosenfeld, R and Carbonell, J and Reddy, R: "Rare and Frequent Amino Acid N-Grams in Whole-Genome Protein Sequences." RECOMB'02: The Sixth Annual International Conference on Research in Computational Molecular Biology. Washington, USA. (2002)
16. Ganapathiraju, M and Weisser, D and Rosenfeld, R and Carbonell, J and Reddy, R and Klein-Seetharaman, J: "Comparative N-Gram Analysis of Whole-Genome Sequences" HLT2002: Human Language Technologies Conference. California, USA. (2002)
17. Ganapathiraju, M and Klein-Seetharaman, J and Balakrishnan, N and Reddy, R: "Characterization of Protein Secondary Structure Using Latent Semantic Analysis." IEEE Signal Processing magazine, May 2004 issue 15 (2004) 78-87
18. Ganapathiraju, M and Weisser, D and Klein-Seetharaman, J: "Yule Value Tables from Protein Datasets" SCI2004: World Conference on Systemics Cybernetics and Informatics. Florida, USA. (2004)
19. Weisser, D and Klein-Seetharaman, J: Identification of Fundamental Building Blocks in Protein Sequences Using Statistical Association Measures (2004)
20. PDBase: http://Www.Scsb.Utmb.Edu/Comp_Biol.Html/Venkat/Prop.Html In Silico Biol, volume 4, issue 2. (2004) 0012
21. ProtScale: http://www.Expasy.Ch/CgiBin/Protscale.Pl In Silico Biol, volume 4, issue 2. (1992) 0012
22. Landauer, T and Foltx, P and Laham, D: "Introduction to Latent Semantic Analysis." Discourse Processes, volume 25, issue 5212. (1998) 259-284
23. Berry, MW and Browne, M: Understanding Search Engines: Mathematical Modeling and Text Retrieval. Soc for Industrial & Applied Math. (1999)
24. Rost, B: "Review: Protein Secondary Structure Prediction Continues to Rise" J Struct Biol, volume 134, issue 2-3. (2001) 204-18
25. Liu, Y and Carbonell, J and Klein-Seetharaman, J and Gopalakrishnan, V: "Comparison of Probabilistic Combination Methods for Protein Secondary Structure Prediction." Bioinformatics, volume 16, issue 4. (2004) 376-82

26. Frauenfelder, H and Wolynes, PG: "Proteins: Where the Physics of Simplicity and Complexity Meet." Physics Today, volume 47, issue 15. (1994) 58-64
27. Carl-Ivar Branden, JT: Introduction to Protein Structure. Garland Publishing. (1999)
28. Voet, D and Voet, JG: Biochemistry. J. Wiley & Sons. (1995)
29. Rabiner, L and Juang, B-H: Fundamentals of Speech Recognition. Pearson Education POD. (1993)
30. Deller, JR and Hansen, JHL and Proakis, JG: Discrete-Time Processing of Speech Signals. Wiley-IEEE press. (1999)
31. Proakis, JG and Manolakis, D: Digital Signal Processing: Principles, Algorithms and Applications. Macmillan USA. (1992)
32. Giuliani, A and Benigni, R and Zbilut, JP and Webber, CL Jr and Sirabella, P and Colosimo, A: "Nonlinear Signal Analysis Methods in the Elucidation of Protein Sequence-Structure Relationships." Chem Rev, volume 102, issue 5. (2002) 1471-92
33. Graps, A: "An Introduction to Wavelets." Computational Science and Engineering, IEEE [see also Computing in Science & Engineering], volume 2, issue 2. (1995) 50-61
34. Tan, BT and Fu, M and Spray, A and Dermody, P: "The Use of Wavelet Transforms in Phoneme Recognition." ICSLP96: Fourth International Conference on Spoken Language Processing. (1996) 148-55
35. Gupta, M and Gilbert, A: "Robust Speech Recognition Using Wavelet Coefficient Features." ASRU01: IEEE Workshop on Automatic Speech Recognition and Understanding. (2001) 50-61
36. Lio, P and Vannucci, M: "Wavelet Change-Point Prediction of Transmembrane Proteins." Bioinformatics, volume 16, issue 4, (2000) 376-82
37. Fischer, P and Baudoux, G and Wouters, J: "Wavpred: A Wavelet-Based Algorithm for the Prediction of Transmembrane Proteins." Comm. math. sci, volume 1, issue 1, (2003) 44 - 56
38. Pashou, EE and Litou, ZI and Liakopoulos, TD and Hamodrakas, SJ: "Wavetm: Wavelet-Based Transmembrane Segment Prediction" In Silico Biol, volume 4, issue 2. (2004) 0012
39. Qiu, J and Liang, R and Zou, X and Mo, J: "Prediction of Transmembrane Proteins Based on the Continuous Wavelet Transform." J Chem Inf Comput Sci, volume 44, issue 2. (2004) 741-7
40. von Heijne, G: "Membrane Protein Structure Prediction. Hydrophobicity Analysis and the Positive-inside Rule" J Mol Biol, volume 225, issue = 2. (1992) 487-94
41. Sonnhammer, EL and von Heijne, G and Krogh, A: "A Hidden Markov Model for Predicting Transmembrane Helices in Protein Sequences." Proc Int Conf Intell Syst Mol Biol, volume 6, issue 6912. (1998) 175-82
42. Bishop, YMM and Fienberg, SE and Holland, PW: Discrete Multivariate Analysis. (1975)
43. Cai, C and Rosenfeld, R and Wasserman, L: "Exponential Language Models, Logistic Regression, and Semantic Coherence." Proc. NIST/DARPA Speech Transcription Workshop. (2000) 10096-100
44. Altschul, SF and Gish, W and Miller, W and Myers, EW and Lipman, DJ: Basic Local Alignment Search Tool. (1990)
45. Mantegna, RN and Buldyrev, SV and Goldberger, AL and Havlin, S, Peng and CK, Simons, M and Stanley, HE: "Linguistic Features of Noncoding DNA Sequences." Phys Rev Lett, volume 73, issue 23. (1994) 3169-72
46. Konopka, AK and Martindale, C: "Noncoding DNA, Zipf's Law, and Language" Science, volume 268, issue 5212. (1995) 789

47. Chatzidimitriou-Dreismann, CA and Streffer, RM and Larhammar, D: "Lack of Biological Significance in the 'Linguistic Features' of Noncoding DNA – a Quantitative Analysis." Nucleic Acids Res, volume 24, issue 9. (1996) 1676-81

48. Israeloff, NE and Kagalenko, M and Chan, K: "Can Zipf Distinguish Language from Noise in Noncoding DNA?" Physical Review Letters, volume 76, issue 11. (1996) 1976

49. Strait, BJ and Dewey, TG: "The Shannon Information Entropy of Protein Sequences." Biophys J, volume 71, issue 1. (1996) 148-55

50. Tsonis, AA and Elsner, JB and Tsonis, PA: "Is DNA a Language?" J Theor Biol, volume 184, issue 1. (1997) 25-9

51. Li, W: "Statistical Properties of Open Reading Frames in Complete Genome Sequences." Comput Chem, volume 23, issue 3-4. (1999) 283-301

52. Zipf, GK: "Selective Studies and the Principle of Relative Frequency in Language." ICSLP96: Fourth International Conference on Spoken Language Processing. (1932) 3544-57

53. Miller, GA and Newman, EB: "Tests of a Statistical Explanation of the Rank-Frequency Relation for Words in Written English." American Journal of Psychology, volume 71, issue 23. (1958) 209-218

54. Karchin, R and Karplus, K and Haussler, D: Classifying G-Protein Coupled Receptors with Support Vector Machines. (2002)

55. Cheng, BYM and Carbonell, J and Klein-Seetharaman, J: Document Classification Approach Leads to a More Accurate G-Protein Coupled Receptor Classifier. (2004)

56. Vries, J and Munshi, R and Tobi, D and Klein-Seetharaman, J and Benos, PV and Bahar, I: A Sequence Alignment-Independent Method for Protein Classification. (2004)

57. Wu, C and Whitson, G and McLarty, J and Ermongkonchai, A and Chang, TC: Protein Classification Artificial Neural System. (1992)

58. Klein-Seetharaman, J and Oikawa, M and Grimshaw, SB and Wirmer, J and Duchardt, E and Ueda, T and Imoto, T and Smith, LJ and Dobson, CM and Schwalbe, H: "Long-Range Interactions within a Nonnative Protein." Science, volume 295, issue 5560. (2002) 1719-22

59. Simons, KT and Bonneau, R and Ruczinski, I and Baker, D: Ab Initio Protein Structure Prediction of Casp Iii Targets Using Rosetta. (1999)

60. Kuznetsov, IB and Rackovsky, S: On the Properties and Sequence Context of Structurally Ambivalent Fragments in Proteins. (2003)

61. Ganapathiraju, M and Manoharan, V and Klein-Seetharaman, J: "BLMT: Statistical Sequence Analysis using N-Grams." J. Applied Bioinformatics, volume 3, issue 2. (2004)

Interactive Comprehensible Data Mining

Andy Pryke and Russell Beale

University of Birmingham, United Kingdom
{A.N.Pryke,R.Beale}@cs.bham.ac.uk

1 Problem

1.1 What Is Interesting?

In data mining, or knowledge discovery, we are essentially faced with a mass of data that we are trying to make sense of. We are looking for something "interesting". Quite what "interesting" means is hard to define, however – one day it is the general trend that most of the data follows that we are intrigued by – the next it is why there are a few outliers to that trend. In order for a data mining to be generically useful to us, it must therefore have some way in which we can indicate what is interesting and what is not, and for that to be dynamic and changeable.

Once we can ask the question appropriately, we then need to be able to understand the answers that the system gives us. It is therefore important that the responses of the system are represented in ways that we can understand. Whilst complex statistical measures of the data set may be accurate, if they are not comprehensible to the users they do not offer insight, only description.

One concept that we consider to be vital is to recognize the relative strengths of users and computers. The human visual system is exceptionally good at clustering, at recognizing patterns and trends, even in the presence of noise and distortion. Computer systems are exceptionally good at crunching numbers, producing exact parameterizations and exploring large numbers of alternatives. If we can combine the best of human and computer processing, we should be able to develop systems that are superior to one or other approach alone.

An ideal data mining system should, we would argue, offer the above characteristics; the ability to define what is interesting, using the abilities of the user and the computer in tasks to which they are best suited, and providing explanations of the data that are understandable and provide deep insights.

This leads us towards a system that will be interactive, in order to be flexible and work towards a solution. It should use visualization techniques to offer the user the opportunity to do both perceptual clustering and trend analysis, and to offer a mechanism for feeding back the results of machine-based data mining. It should have a data mining engine that is powerful, effective, and which can produce humanly comprehensible results as well.

The Haiku system was developed with these principles in mind, and offers a sym-biotic system that couples interactive 3-d dynamic visualization technology with a novel genetic algorithm.

Y. Cai (Ed.): Ambient Intelligence for Scientific Discovery, LNAI 3345, pp. 48–65, 2005.

1.2 Key Concepts

The key concepts in the Haiku system are

- Interaction via visual representation of data – visualization used to present data which can be manipulated and explored by the user
- Presentation of results in visual form – integration of the results of machine-based data mining back into the visualization to show things like coverage, accuracy, and the interrelationships between rules
- Bridging the human-computer communications gap – producing textual rules that are simple to understand and showing the effects of those visually, and allowing the data mining process to iterate
- Exploratory approach – allowing the user to pose questions about different parts of the data and follow lines of enquiry, focussing on whatever is interesting
- Comprehensible rules – tunable to give overviews or detail as required

1.3 Innovation

The innovative parts of the system are the data visualization approach, the discovery visualization, and the ability to produce rules that can be overviews (less accurate but painting a broad-brush picture) or specific (precise, and often more complex) or anywhere in between. However, the key point is that these approaches are combined into one system whose holistic effect is greater than the sum of the individual advances.

1.4 Relationship to Ambient Intelligence

One of the characteristics of ambient systems is that they utilize a much larger proportion of the information and context inherent in data in order to produce results. The Haiku system works in sympathy with these goals. Since the approach is iterative, as facts and knowledge about the data are discovered, these could be feed back into the system to guide further discoveries and results, allowing the system to build upon the knowledge it has created. In addition, the visualization allows information to be presented to the user, or to a group of users, allowing them to liaise and collectively explore the space.

Since the system can work in real time, new data could be constantly added into the system – users are not constrained to working with a fixed data set. The plasticity of both the visualization approach and the GA-based knowledge discovery system ensures that if new parameters or features of the current data set are discovered these can be added in as well. Haiku could therefore utilize new contextual and environmental information in real time, tapping in to both machine and human capabilities for adaptively processing changing data.

2   Approach

2.1   Visualization

The visualization engine used in the Haiku system provides an abstract 3-d perspective of multi-dimensional data based on the Hyper system[7–9] for force based visualization. The visualization consists of nodes and links (similar to a ball-and-stick model, only dynamic), whose properties are given by the parameters of the data. Data elements affect parameters such as node size, mass, link strength and elasticity, and so on. Multiple elements can affect one parameter, or a subset of parameters can be chosen.

Many forms of data can be visualized in Haiku. Typical data for data mining consists of a number of individual "items" (representing, for example, customers) each with the same number of numerical and/or nominal attributes. This is similar to standard dimension reduction methods used for solely numerical data such as Projection Pursuit [5] and Multi Dimensional Scaling [6], but applicable to data with a mix of nominal and numeric fields. What is required for Haiku visualization is that a similarity can be calculated between any two items. The similarity metric should match an intuitive view of the similarity of two items. In most cases, a simple and standard distance measure performs well.

To create the visualization, nodes are initially scattered randomly into the 3d space, with their associated links. Movement in this space is determined by a set of rules similar to the laws of physics. Links want to assume a particular length, determined by their elasticity and the nodes they are connected to – and the parameters of these are affected by the data. They pull inwards until they reach that length, or push outwards if they are compressed, just as a spring does in the real world. The more similar an item, the stronger the link connecting them. Nodes repel each other, based on their mass. This whole approach can be seen as a force directed graph visualization. This initial state is then allowed to evolve, and the links and nodes shuffle themselves around until they reach a low energy, steady state. Since the strongest forces are between the items that are the most similar, they tend to cluster in the same area of space – items unrelated to each other are not connected and hence occupy different areas of space. The repulsive force between nodes is used to spread them out.

The physics of the space are adjustable, but are chosen so that a steady state solution can be reached that is static – this is unlike the real world, in which a steady state exists that involves motion, such as we see in planetary orbits. Having a static steady state is easier to explore, since the visual system is especially sensitive to motion and hence orbiting systems tend to become the focus of attention.

The system effectively reduces the data dimensionality to 3D. However, unlike traditional dimension reduction methods, there is no predefined mapping between the higher and lower dimensional spaces.

Computationally, the process scales exponentially with the number of links, which is usually proportional to the number of data points. For small data sets (up to 1000 nodes) the process can be allowed to run in real time. For larger data

Fig. 1. A collapsed graph (of Soybean data shaded by class).

sets there needs to be a number of optimizations: only considering the strongest links, introducing locality of influence and so on.

2.2   Perception-Oriented Visualization

The interface provides full 3D control of the structure, from zooming in and out, moving smoothly through the system (flyby), rotating it in 3D, and jumping to specific points, all controlled with the mouse.

Some typical structures emerge, recognizable across many data sets. These include clusters of similar items, outlying items not in any particular cluster, and internal structures within perceived clusters. For example, the data may be seen as divided into two main groups, both of which contain a number of subgroups. Examples of data visualization are shown in the case studies (Sections 4.1 and 4.2).

2.3   Interaction with the Data Visualization

When features of interest are seen in the visual representation of the data they can be selected using the mouse. This opens up a number of possibilities:

- Data identification
- Re-visualization
- Explanation

The simplest of these (data identification) is to view the identity or details of items in the feature, or export this information to a file for later use.

Another option is to re-visualize the data set without the selected data or to focus in and only visualize the selected data. This can be used to exclude distorting outliers, or to concentrate on the interactions within an area of interest. Of course, we can data mine the whole data set without doing this, the approach taken by many other systems. One of the features of the Haiku system is the interactive indication of the things that we are currently interested in, and the subsequent focusing of the knowledge discovery process on categorizing or distinguishing that data.

A key feature of the system is that the user selection process takes full advantage of the abilities of our visual system: humans are exceptionally good at picking up gross features of visual representations. Our abilities have evolved to work well in the presence of noise, of missing or obscured data, and we are able to pick out both simple lines and curves as well as more complex features such as spirals and undulating waves or planes. By allowing user input into the knowledge discovery process, we can effectively use a highly efficient system very quickly as well as reducing the work that the computational system has to do.

The third option asks the machine to process the selected data. This is the most striking feature of the system: its ability to "explain" why features of interest exist. Typical questions when looking at a visual representation of data are: "Why are these items out on their own?", "What are the characteristics of this cluster?", "How do these two groups of items differ?". Applying a machine learning component generates answers to these types of question.

The interaction works as follows: first, a group or number of groups is selected. Then the option to explain the groups is selected. The user answers a small number of questions about their preferences for the explanation (short/long; highly accurate/general characteristics etc.) The system then returns a set of rules describing the features selected, and ensures that the rules conform to the level of detail that the user requires.

As an alternative, the classic machine learning system C4.5 [4] may be used to generate classification rules. Other data mining systems may also be applied by saving the selected feature information to an external file.

2.4   Knowledge Visualization and Feedback

The results from the GA can be fed back into the visualization to give extra insight into their relationships with the data. Identified clusters can be colored, for example, or rules added and linked to the data that they classify, as in Fig. 2.

In this figure, classification rules are the large spheres, with the data being the smaller spheres. Both are colored by class. Rules form part of an ordered rule set. If the first matching rule in the rule set correctly classifies an item of data, they are linked with a white line. If the rule set classification is incorrect, the rule and data are linked with a red (dark grey) line. Cyan (or light grey) links are between the rules and the data that are covered by rules further down the rule set. The visualization reorganizes itself to show these relationships clearly.

A number of things are immediately more apparent from this visualization than from a textual description. On the left of the figure is a group of five green (mid grey) rules, floating between them is the data they classify correctly. The rule at the top of the group can be seen to also classify some blue (dark grey) data incorrectly. Most interesting in the group is the right most rule, which not only "wins" the competition to classify the data correctly, it also misclassifies a number of other data points (red/dark grey links to right and below). This rule is obviously too general. From the visualization we can see that removing this rule would reduce the number of incorrect classifications, without affecting the number of items correctly classified.

It is interesting to note that as this visualization depends solely on the relationship between knowledge (e.g. classification rule) and data, it can be applied to a very wide range of discoveries, including those made by non-symbolic systems such as neural networks.

The system is fully interactive. The user can identify different characteristics and instruct the GA to describe them, and so the process continues. This synergy of abilities between the rapid, parallel exploration of the structure space by the computer and the user's innate pattern recognition abilities and interest in different aspects of the data produces a very powerful and flexible system.

2.5   Genetic Algorithms for Data Mining

We use a genetic algorithm (GA) approach for a number of reasons. First, a GA is able to effectively explore a large search space, and modern computing power means we can take advantage of this within a reasonable time frame. Secondly, one of the key design features is to produce a system that has humanly

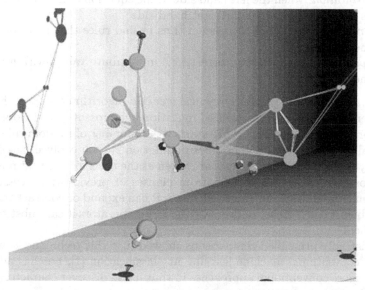

Fig. 2. Rule Coverage and Accuracy. Dark links indicate incorrect classification.

comprehensible results. Rules are inherently much more understandable than decision trees or probabilistic or statistical descriptions.

Thirdly, the genetic algorithm aims to discover rules and rule sets which optimize an objective function ("fitness"), and manipulation of this allows us to explore different areas of the search space. For example, we can strongly penalize rules that give false positive in order to obtain rules that can be used to determine the class of new data examples. Alternatively, we can bias the system towards rules that indicate the typical characteristics of items in a group, whether these characteristics are shared with another group or not. Short rules with few terms are going to be easier to comprehend than longer ones, but longer rules reveal more information. We can allow the user to choose which they would prefer by controlling the fitness function. Initially we might prefer short rules, in order to get an overview. Note that since the Haiku system is interactive and iterative, when we have a higher level of comprehension, we can repeat the process but allow the rules to become longer and hence more detailed, moving our understanding from a broad overview to comprehending the details.

We use a special type of GA that evolves rules; these produce terms to describe the underlying data of the form:

IF *term* OP value|range (& ...) THEN *term* OP value|range (& ...)

where *term* is a class from the data set, OP is one of the standard comparison operators $(<, >, =, \pounds, ^\wedge)$, value is a numeric or symbolic value, and range is a numeric range. A typical rule would therefore be:

IF *colour*=red & *texture*=soft & *size* < 3.2 THEN *fruit*=strawberry

There are three situations that are of particular interest to us:

- *Classification:* when the left hand side of the equation tries to predict a single class (usually known) on the right hand side
- *Characterization:* when the system tries to find rules that describe portions of the data set
- *Association:* which detects correlations in attribute values within a portion of the data set

The algorithm follows fairly typical genetic algorithmic approaches in its implementation, but with specialized mutation and crossover operators, in order to explore the space effectively. We start with a number of random rules created using values from the data. The rules population is then evolved based on how well they perform. The fittest rules are taken as the basis for the next population, with crossover creating new rules from clauses of previously successful rules. Mutation is specialized: for ranges of values it can expand or contract that range; for numbers it can increase or decrease them; for operators it can substitute them with others.

Statistically principled comparisons showed that this technique is at least as good as conventional machine learning at classification [1], but has advantages over the more conventional approaches in that it can discover characteristics and associations too.

3 Case Studies

3.1 Case Study 1: Interactive Data Mining of Housing Data

The Boston Housing Data [3] is a classic, well-known dataset available from the UCI Machine Learning repository [2]. Haiku was used to visualize the data. The complex clustering shown in Fig. 3 was revealed.

Two fairly distinct groups of data are visible, which show smaller internal features such as sub-groups. The two main groups were selected using the mouse, and short, accurate, classification rules were requested from the data mining system. These rules are shown:

```
Bounds_river = true ⇒ GROUP_1
Accuracy: 100% Coverage:43%

PropLargeDevelop = 0.0 AND 9.9 ≤ older_properties_percent
≤ 100.0 AND Pupil_teacher_ratio = 20.2 ⇒ GROUP_1
Accuracy: 94% Coverage: 83%

Bounds_river = false AND 4 ≤ Highway_access ≤ 8 ⇒ GROUP_2
Accuracy: 100% Coverage: 77%

Bounds_river = false AND 264 ≤ Tax_rate ≤ 403 ⇒ GROUP_2
Accuracy: 100% Coverage:69%

2.02 < Industry_proportion ≤ 3.41 ⇒ GROUP_2
Accuracy:98% Coverage: 13%
```

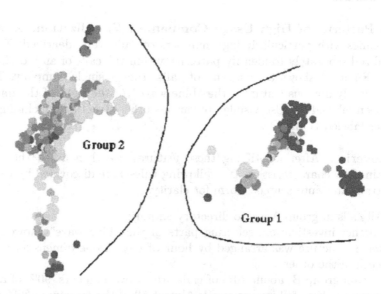

Fig. 3. Clustering of Boston Housing Data.

```
5.68 ≤ Lower_status_percent ≤ 6.56 ⇒ GROUP_2
Accuracy: 96% Coverage: 75%

Bounds_river = false ⇒ GROUP_2
Accuracy: 73% Coverage: 100%
```

This case study illustrates the following characteristics:

- The interactive visual discovery approach has revealed new structure in the data by visual clustering.
- We have used human visual perception to determine features of interest, and application of the data mining algorithm has generated concrete information about these "soft" discoveries.
- Together, interactive data mining has delivered increased knowledge about a well known dataset.

3.2 Case Study 2: Applying HAIKU to Telecoms Data

Justification. Massive amounts of data are generated from monitoring telecommunications switching. Even a small company may make many thousands of phone calls during a year. Telecommunications companies have a mountain of data originally collected for billing purposes. Telecoms data reflects business behavior, so is likely to contain complex patterns. For this reason, Haiku was applied to mine this data mountain.

The data considered detailed the calling number, recipient number and duration of phone calls to and from businesses in a medium sized town. Other information available included business sector and sales channels. All identity data was anonymized.

Call Patterns of High Usage Companies: Visualization. A number of companies with particularly high numbers of calls were identified. These were visualized separately to identify patterns within the calls of an individual company. Figure 4 shows a clustering of calls from a single company. The most immediately obvious feature is the "blue wave" to the right of the image. This has been labeled A. Also visible are various other structures, including the two cluster labeled B and C.

Discoveries. After identifying these features, we then asked the system to explain their characteristics. The following rules were discovered by the system, and translated into sentence form for clarity.

- All calls in group A are to directory enquiries.
- Further investigation, selecting parts of the "blue wave" showed that the wave structure was arranged by hour of day in one dimension and day of week in the other.
- Within group B, about 70% of calls are to two numbers. 90% of all calls to these numbers fall into group B. Almost all of the remaining 30% of calls in

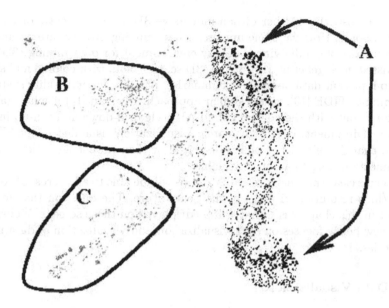

Fig. 4. Visualization of Telephone Calls from one Site – User Selected Groups are Marked.

    group B are to another two numbers. Most long distance ISDN calls are in group B. All but one call in the group has these properties. Most calls in the group are also charged at the same rate.
- About 80% of Group C calls are ISDN calls, and about 10% are from Payphones. About one third occur between 21:00 and 22:59, and about one half start at 15 minutes past the hour. Most are long distance calls. About 50% of the calls are very long, lasting between 8 and 15.5 hours.

    For this data set, Haiku discovers some very interesting facts about the calling patterns of a company. Notice that we can produce short, comprehensible rules that cover a significant portion of the data set, which are intrinsically much more usable than detailed descriptions of 100% of the data. These insights can then be used by the company to optimize their phone usage, or, as for this study, to feed back to the telecoms company some concepts for marketing and billing strategies.

4   Survey of Relevant Studies

4.1   Ambient and Virtual Reality Approaches to Data Mining

Ambient visualization systems are getting closer to becoming commonplace. Real and immersive 3D visualization system are becoming cheaper (e.g. GeoWall [10]) and so are high-resolution multi screen or "tiled" displays such as those used in the TeraScope system [11]. These hardware developments are reflected in a growth in data mining and data visualization systems using virtual reality.

Due to cost, the number of non-immersive 3D systems greatly outnumbers immersive ones. However some immersive data mining projects are up and running. For example, a 3D virtual reality environment for data mining (3DVDM) is discussed in Nagel et al. [12]. It uses 3D scatter plots with colored and shaped icons to represent data points and summaries. Another virtual reality system for data mining, TIDE [13], take a similar approach. Dive-On [14] displays take the same form, but with the addition of OLAP style drill-down and roll-up in a immersive environment. In [15] "Dynamic Visualization" is added to the 3DVDM system, changing either the points displayed or their properties (color, size etc) over time according to a fourth variable.

It seems clear that many research groups will be able to afford real 3D or large screen/high-resolution displays in the near future. The question that interests us most in this chapter is "what will be displayed on those screens?" Therefore, the review below focuses on data visualization and visualization of data mining discoveries.

4.2   Data Visualization

Approaches to Multivariate Data Visualization. The visualization of multi-dimensional data is hard for two major reasons. First, the human visual system is designed to perceive objects in three spatial dimensions (and one temporal dimension). Secondly, most computer displays are normally only capable of displaying information in two spatial dimensions (and one temporal dimension). So, to display objects with greater than 2 or 3 dimensions on a normal screen, we need to do more than simply place an object at a particular position in a 2-dimensional space. There are several approaches to the visualization of multi-dimensional data that lacks natural spatial axes including: traditional simple methods; object mapping; pixel based methods; dimension reduction; and network visualization. These are summarized below with references to key or examplary work. A comprehensive overview of database visualization techniques for exploratory analysis can be found in Daniel Keim and Mihael Ankerst's tutorial [22].

Simple Methods. Simple, traditional, non-computer based methods of graphically presenting data include scatter plots, histograms and line graphs. The computerization of these methods has had two major effects: firstly, these visualizations are now quicker and easier to generate and secondly, they have been extended into 3 dimensions. 3D effects may be obtained on paper by use of perspective, but a more effective method is to combine this with animated rotation.

Scatter plots represent the occurrence of data points with 2 numeric variables, by plotting symbols on a 2D plane. A third (normally nominal) variable is often used to determine which symbol is plotted. Computers have made it possible to extend scatter plots to 3 dimensions. Rotating the plot, and using motion parallax clues may obtain a 3D effect. In addition, more than 3 dimensions may be displayed by collapsing several dimensions into one using techniques such as projection pursuit or by using time as a fourth dimension.

Object Mapping. Object mapping embeds information about some or all of the dimensions in the appearance of an object representing an item of data. Most of this work takes an iconic approach, for example, Chernoff faces [17] map different dimensions to the appearance of eyes, ears, mouth etc. on a computer-generated face. Another technique, parallel co-ordinates [18–21,38], uses the crossing points of a line on parallel axes to represent an object in dimensional space. These lines can be thought of as dynamically generated icons.

Pixel Based Methods. Pixel based methods achieve a high information density by using individual pixels to represent fields in data items, or even items as a whole [44, 22]. One major problem to be addressed is how to choose a unique pixel for each item. Keim [44, 22] solves this problem in two parts. First, he imposes an order on the tuples. Secondly, he makes use of space-filling curves to transform one-dimensional ordering into two dimensions.

Spenke and Beilken [23] detail the use of the interactive visualization based data mining tool InfoZoom to the large financial data set used for the PKDD'99 Discovery Challenge. InfoZoom uses a spreadsheet-like approach to interaction. When too many values are present to be shown numerically, each value is replaced by a single pixel, giving a scatter plot like view of the data. The visible data can be constrained to subsets with particular properties, or sorted by an attribute to reveal correlations. When a subset is selected, animation is used to show a gradual change between the values for the whole data set and the values for the subset. Formulas can also be added to the "spreadsheet", for example to calculate averages. InfoZoom can be used either in an exploratory or hypothesis driven manner and seems simple enough to be used by domain experts after training. The system appears best suited to smaller data sets, the example in [23] uses around 700 items.

Dimension Reduction. Dimension reduction methods are normally applied to purely numeric data. They map the original dimensions (fields) of data into a smaller number of numeric dimensions, while attempting to retain or illustrate relevant properties of the original space, such as distances between items or patterns in item distribution.

Projection maps positions in N dimensions into 2 (or 3 or N) dimensions in a similar way to a 3D object casting a shadow on a 2D surface. As the 3D object is rotated, its shadow changes, and different features of the object become visible.

The grand tour [26, 27] is an automatically generated sequence of projections from N-dimensions that show the data from almost every possible angle. However, this can be time consuming and many of the views will not be of interest.

Projection pursuit [5] automates the identification of interesting views. A heuristic measure, the "projection index", is optimized to find an "interesting" view, typically by simulated annealing. Different projection indices may, for example, maximize the clustering of points or spread points over the 2D space. A number of variants on the original projection pursuit algorithm are discussed in [25]. XGobi [28, 30] and GGobi [31, 30] are the most commonly available implementations of the grand tour and projection pursuit.

Fastmap [32] can be used to reduce N-dimensional data sets to two or three dimensions for visualization. As the algorithm attempts to preserve distances in the reduced space, visual identification of clusters can be made. FastMap's advantage over other methods of transforming multidimensional data into a 3D space is its speed – O(Nk) for N objects projected into a k dimensional space. One disadvantage is that, compared with Multi Dimensional Scaling (MDS), it fares less well in preserving the distance between objects when they are projected into a lower dimensional space. Another disadvantage is that FastMap uses a line between two of the further apart objects ("pivot objects") to provide an axis for the first reduced dimension. Other axes are then placed perpendicular to this. If the pivot objects chosen are atypical (outliers), then this initial axis could be unsuitable.

Despite these possible problems, FastMap gives good visualizations on both synthetic and real world data, with clusters and patterns in the data clearly visible. Its scalability means that it is suitable for interactive use with large amounts of data.

Network Visualization. Netmap [33] is a successful commercial data mining visualization package. Typical applications include fraud identification, criminal investigation, and social network analysis.

Nodes representing entities in the database are placed around the perimeter of a circle. Links representing relationships between entities are drawn across the circle. Nodes can be grouped, and then appear next to each other. Nodes and links can be labeled and pruned according to their attributes. Nodes with few links can be removed reducing clutter.

4.3   Discovery Visualization

Discovery visualization is important; as data mining systems grow more powerful, we risk entering the era of "discovery overload" while trying to solve our "data overload" problems. There has been comparatively little work on the visualization of discoveries, and much work tends to be limited to specialized forms of rules, or unable to cope with modest numbers of discoveries. Below we briefly outline some of the approaches that have been tried, and identify some of their strengths and weaknesses. Another useful review of visualization for clustering and association discoveries can be found in Celar et al. [41].

Two Antecedent Association Rules. Fukuda et al. [34] present a system for visualization of individual rules. However, it is limited to rules with 2 numeric conditions, and a single boolean conclusion. For example:

`18 < Age < 25 and 10,000 ≤ Income < 25000 Implies Bad_risk=true`

Rules are visualized on a plane, with one axis representing each numerical attribute. The plane is divided into a number of pixels by partitioning the values into fixed size buckets. Pixel color represents rule confidence with redder pixels representing more confident rules. Pixel brightness approximates support. A good rule appears as a bright red region of the plane. Regions meeting a threshold of support and confidence can be selected interactively. The main advantages of this method are that it is visually simple, and the rules it discovers are not limited to rectangular regions.

Purple Insight's MineSet product (originally marketed by SGI), contains a number of discovery visualization methods. The most relevant is a graphical table illustrating the co-occurrences of "true" values for pairs of binary attributes. Again this is limited to discoveries with two antecedents. MineSet also provides decision tree and class probability visualizations [36, 37].

Han et al.[40] present a framework for interactive knowledge discovery, and a number of examples of the AVis system. AVis uses scatter plots and similar visualizations for data preparation and cleaning, a choice of discretization boundaries for numerical data, and visualization of associations between pairs of attributes.

Graph Based Approaches. Klemettinen's system [35] visualizes interactions between attributes in sets of rules using an attribute graph. Nodes represent attributes, and links their co-occurrence. The number of rules visualizable is greatly limited by the use of arc thickness to convey statistical information, and also by clutter and crossing of arcs.

Hao et al.[39] describe the "Directed Association Visualization" (DAV) system for 3D force based graph visualization of two item association rules. The term "association rule" is a common one, however, when only two items are involved, "association" might also be used. The visualization aims to identify pairs of products that are bought together, one of their examples being that 85% of purchasers of computer printers also buy paper.

The system visualizes graphs in which nodes represent items and directed links represent associations. Colors of links represent confidence, and support is reflected in the distance between items. In addition, clusters of items can be detected and wrapped in a surface. This reduces visual complexity and is a form of discovery in itself, indicating that items in the cluster a similar.

An example in [39] shows a graph with approximately 180 nodes and 1400 links, summarizing 250,000 transactions. This can be visualized in real time.

Attribute Utility. Bruzzese and Davino [38] present a method for the visualization of multiple antecedent association rules, for pruning of rule sets and identification of relevant attributes. Multiple rules can be plotted on parallel co-ordinates using "Item Utility" for each of their attributes, based on the contribution of the attribute to rule accuracy.

Hofmann et al [42] present a method for visualizing the support and confidence of association rules with multiple conditions using mosaic plots and double decker plots. These show bar chart like representations with an area proportional to support, partially colored to reflect confidence.

Clustering. Discoveries Bruzzese and Davino [38] use Multiple Correspondence Analysis to project rule antecedents and consequents into a 2D space, where clustering is observed. Tsumoto and Hirano [43] calculate rule similarity measures based on both shared attributes (syntactic similarity) and shared coverage of data (semantic similarity). Multi Dimensional Scaling is applied to these to visualize the rules in 2D, and clustering of similar rules becomes clearly visible.

5   Conclusion

The Haiku system for information visualization and explanation provides a useful interface for interactive data mining. By interacting with a virtual data space created dynamically from the data properties, greater insight can be gained than by using standard machine learning based data mining. It allows users to explore features visually, to direct the computer to generate explanations and to evaluate the results of their exploration, again in the visual domain. This combination of intuitive and knowledge driven exploration with the mechanical power of the learning algorithms provides a much richer environment and can lead to a deeper understanding of the domain.

Acknowledgements

This work was partially supported by grants from British Telecom, Integral Solutions Ltd and British Maritime Technology. Thanks to Nick Drew and Bob Hendley for their work on the visualization parts of the system, and to colleagues for their comments and help.

References

1. Pryke, Andy: Data Mining using Genetic Algorithms and Interactive Visualization (Ph.D Thesis), The University of Birmingham. (1998)
2. Blake, C.L. and Merz, C.J.: UCI Repository of machine learning databases, http://www.ics.uci.edu/~mlearn/MLRepository.html. Irvine, CA: University of California, Department of Information and Computer Science. (1998)
3. Quinlan,R.: Combining Instance-Based and Model-Based Learning. In Proceedings on the Tenth International Conference of Machine Learning, 236-243, University of Massachusetts, Amherst. Morgan Kaufmann. (1993)
4. Quinlan, R.: C4.5: Programs for Machine Learning, Morgan Kaufmann. (1992)
5. Friedman, J. H. and Tukey, J. W., A projection pursuit algorithm for exploratory data analysis, IEEE Trans. Computers, c-23(9) (1974) 881
6. T. F. Cox and M. A. A. Cox: Multidimensional Scaling., Chapman and Hall, London. (1994)
7. Hendley, RJ, Drew, N, Beale, R, Wood, AM.: Narcissus: visualizing information. Readings in information visualization. eds Stuart Card, Jock Mackinlay, Ben Shneiderman. January. (1999) 503-511
8. Beale, R, McNab, RJ, Witten, IH.: "Visualizing sequences of queries: a new tool for information retrieval." 1997 Proc IEEE Conf on Information Visualization, London, England, August. (1997) 57-62
9. Wood, A.M., Drew, N.S., Beale, R., and Hendley, R.J.: "HyperSpace: Web Browsing with Visualization." Third International World-Wide Web Conference Poster Proceeding, Darmstadt Germany. April. (1995) 21-25

10. Daniel Steinwand, Brian Davis, Nathan Weeks: "GeoWall: Investigations into Low-cost Stereo Display Systems", U.S. Geological Survey Open File Report 03-198. (2002)
11. Charles Zhang, Jason Leigh, Thomas A. DeFanti, Marco Mazzucco, Robert Grossman: "TeraScope: Distributed Visual Data Mining of Terascale Data Sets Over Photonic Networks," Journal of Future Generation Computer Systems (FGCS), Elsevier Science Press, Volume 19, Issue 6, August. (2003) 935-944.
12. Nagel, H.R., Granum, E., and Musaeus, P.: Methods for visual mining of data in virtual reality. In PKDD 2001 International Workshop on Visual Data Mining. (2001)
13. Sawant, N., Scharver, C., Leigh, J., Johnson, A., Reinhart, G., Creel, E., Batchu, S., Bailey, S., and Grossman, R.: The tele-immersive data explorer: A distributed architecture for collaborative interactive visualization of large data-sets. Pro- ceedings of 4th International Immersive Projection Technology Workshop, Ames, Iowa, June. (2000)
14. Ammoura, A.: Dive-on: From databases to virtual reality. ACM Crossroads Database Special Edition, 7(3). (2001)
15. Nagel, Henrik. R., Vittrup, Michael, Granum, Erik, Bovbjerg, Søren: Exploring Non-Linear Data Relationships in VR using the 3D Visual Data Mining System, Proceedings of the International Workshop on Visual Data Mining, in conjunction with The Third IEEE International Conference on Data Mining, Melbourne, Florida, USA, November. (2003)
16. Keim, D.A. and Ankerst,M.: Visual Data Mining and Exploration of Large Databases, Tutorial T08, at European Conference on Machine Learning (ECML) and the 8th European Conference on Principles and Practice of Knowledge Discovery in Databases (PKDD). (2001)
17. Chernoff, H.: Using Faces to Represent Points in K-Dimensional space graphically, Journal of the American Statistical Association, 1973, volume 68, pp 361-368
18. Wegman, E. J.: Hyperdimensional Data Analysis Using Parallel Coordinates, Journal of the American Statistical Association, September 1990, 85(411). (1990) 664-675
19. Lee, H.Y. and Ong, H.L.: Visualization support for data mining, IEE Expert-Intelligent Systems and Their Applications. (1996) 11:69-75
20. Zhao K., Liu, B., Tirpak, T. and Schalle, A., Detecting patterns of change using enhanced parallel coordinate visualization, ICDM 2003. (2003)
21. Zhao K., Liu, B., Tirpak, T. and Schalle, A., V-Miner: Using Enhanced Parallel Coordinates to Mine Product Design and TestData, KDD. (2004)
22. Keim, D., Hao, M.C., Ladisch, J., Hsu, M., Dayal, U., Pixel Bar Charts: A New Technique for Visualizing Large Multi-Attribute Data Sets without Aggregation, IEEE Symposium on Information Visualization 2001 (INFOVIS'01) October 22-23. San Diego. (2001) 113
23. Spenke, M., Beilken, C.: Visual, Interactive Data Mining with InfoZoom – the Financial Data Set, PKDD'99 Discovery Challenge, http://lisp.vse.cz/pkdd99/, 3rd European Conference on Principles and Practice of Knowledge Discovery in Databases, September 15-18. Prague, Czech Republic. (1999)
24. Friedman, J.H. and Tukey, J.W.: A Projection Pursuit Algorithm for Exploratory Data Analysis, IEEE Transactions on Computers, September, c-23(9). (1974) 881-889
25. Jones, M.C. and Sibson, R: What is Projection Pursuit?, Journal of the Royal Statistical Association A, 150(1). (1987) 1-36

26. Asimov, Daniel: The grand tour: a tool for viewing multidimensional data, SIAM Journal on Scientific and Statistical Computing, v.6 n.1, Jan. (1985) 128-143
27. Asimov, D. and Buja, A.: Grand Tour and Projection Pursuit. Journal of Computational and Graphical Statistics, 4(3). (1995) 155-172
28. Swayne, D. F., Cook, D., Buja, A.: XGobi: Interactive Dynamic Graphics in the X Window System with a Link to S. In: 1991 Proceedings of the Section on Statistical Graphics. American Statistical Association, Alexandria, VA, (1991) 1-8.
29. Swayne, D. F., Cook, D., Buja, A.: XGobi: Interactive Dynamic Graphics in the X Window System. Journal of Computational and Graphical Statistics 7 (1). (1998) 113-130.
30. Symanzik, J., Swayne, D. F., Temple Lang, D., Cook, D.: Software Integration for Multivariate Exploratory Spatial Data Analysis, New Tools for Spatial Data Analysis: Proceedings of the Specialist Meeting, Santa Barbara, California, May 10-11, 2002, Center for Spatially Integrated Social Science. (2002)
31. GGobi: Swayne, D. G. and Buja, A. and Temple-Lang, D.: Exploratory Visual Analysis of Graphs in GGobi(draft), Proceedings of the 3rd International Workshop on Distributed Statistical Computing (DSC 2003), March 20-22, 2003, Technische Universität Wien, Vienna, Austria, Editors: Kurt Hornik, Friedrich Leisch and Achim Zeileis, ISSN 1609-395X. (2003)
32. Faloutsos, C., Lin, K-I.: "FastMap: A Fast Algorithm for Indexing, Data-Mining and Visualization of Traditional and Multimedia Datasets", SIGMOD Record, June, 24(2). (1995) 163-174
33. Netmap Analytics Website, July. http://www.netmapanalytics.com (2004)
34. Fukuda, Takeshi, Morimoto, Yasuhiko, Morishita, Shinichi, and Tokuyama, Takeshi: Data mining using two-dimensional optimized association rules: Scheme, algorithms, and visualization. In H. V. Jagadish and Inderpal Singh Mumick, editors, Proceedings of the 1996 ACM SIGMOD International Conference on Management of Data, Montreal, Quebec, Canada, 4-6 June. (1996) 13-23
35. Klemettinen, Mika, Mannila, Heikki, Ronkainen, Pirjo, Toivonen, Hannu, and Verkamo, A. Inkeri: Finding interesting rules from large sets of discovered association rules. In Nabil R. Adam, Bharat K. Bhargava, and Yelena Yesha, editors, Third International Conference on Information and Knowledge Management (CIKM'94). ACM Press, November. (1994) 401-407
36. Brunk, C., Kelly, J., and Kohavi, R.: MineSet: an integrated system for data mining. In Heckerman, D., Mannila, H., Pregibon, D., and Uthurusamy, R., editors, Proceedings of the third international conference on Knowledge Discovery and Data Mining. AAAI Press. (1997) 135-138
37. MineSet http://www.purpleinsight.com/products/mineset/detail.html
38. Bruzzese, Dario and Davino, Cristina: Visual Post-Analysis of Association Rules, proceeding of Second International Workshop on Visual Data Mining held in conjunction with the 13th European Conference on Machine Learning (ECML'02) and The 6th European Conference on Principles and Practice of Knowledge Discovery in Databases (PKDD-02), Helsinki, Finland, 19-23 August. (2002)
39. Hao, M.C., Dayal, U., Hsu, M., Sprenger,T., and Gross, M.H.: Visualization of Directed Associations in E-Commerce In Ebert, D.S., Favre, J.M., Peikert,R, editors, Transaction Data In Data Visualization 2001 (proceedings of the EG+IEEE VisSym in Ascona, 22-30 May, 2001) ISBN 3-211-83674-8. (2001)
40. Han, J., Hu, X., and Cercone, N.: A visualization model of interactive knowledge discovery systems and its implementations, Information Visualization, vol. 2, no. 2, June. (2003) 105-125

41. Ceglar, A., Roddick, J. F. and Calder, P.: Guiding Knowledge Discovery through Interactive Data Mining. Technical Report KDM-01-002. KDM Laboratory, Flinders University, Adelaide, South Australia. (2001

42. Hofmann, H.,Siebes, A.P.J.M. and Wilhelm, A.F.X.: Visualizing association rules with interactive mosaic plots in Proceedings of the sixth ACM SIGKDD international conference on Knowledge discovery and data mining, ISBN:1-58113-233-6. (2002)

43. Tsumoto, S., Hirano, S.: Visualization of rule's similarity using multidimensional scaling, in Proceedings of Third IEEE International Conference on Data Mining (ICDM) 2003 Third International Workshop on Visual Data Mining, ICDM2003. (2003)

44. Keim, D. A.: Pixel-oriented database visualizations. SIGMOD Record (ACM Special Interest Group on Management of Data), December. (1996) 25(4):35–39

Scientific Discovery Within Data Streams

Andrew J. Cowell, Sue Havre, Richard May, and Antonio Sanfilippo

Pacific Northwest National Laboratory, USA
{andrew.cowell,sue.havre,richard.may,antonio.sanfilippo}@pnl.gov

1   Introduction

The term 'data-stream' is an increasingly overloaded expression. It often means different things to different people, depending on domain, usage or operation. Harold (2003) draws the following analogy:

> "A [stream] analogy might be a queue of people waiting to get on a ride at an amusement park. As people are processed at the front (i.e. get on the roller coaster) more are added at the back of the line. If it's a slow day the roller coaster may catch up with the end of the line and have to wait for people to board. Other days there may always be people in line until the park closes...There's always a definite number of people in line though this number may change from moment to moment as people enter at the back of the line and exit from the front of the line. Although all the people are discrete, you'll sometimes have a family that must be put together in the same car. Thus although the individuals are discrete, they aren't necessarily unrelated."

For our purposes we define a data-stream as a series of data (e.g. credit card transactions arriving at a clearing office, cellular phone traffic or environmental data from satellites) arriving in real time, that have an initiation, a continuous ingest of data, but with no expectations on the amount, length, or end of the data flow. The data stream does not have a database or repository as an intrinsic part of its definition–it is a 'one-look' opportunity from the perspective of data stream analytics. We call each data element in the stream a token and the complexity of these tokens ranges from simple (e.g. characters in a sentence: "T H I S I S A S T R E A M...") to extremely complex (e.g. a detailed transaction record). The volume of data-streams is usually massive, and while each individual token may be rather uninformative, taken as a whole they describe the nature of the changing phenomena over time.

The properties of data streams differ from conventional stored relations in many ways. They have no width or flow boundaries, meaning that there is no control over the total amount of data flowing, or differences in flow volume arriving at any particular moment. They are also time varying and unpredictable; flow can start or stop at any point and the number of tokens per unit time that are delivered to a receiver vary. In addition, we have no control over the order in which data items arrive; some data-streams provide tokens in order, while

Y. Cai (Ed.): Ambient Intelligence for Scientific Discovery, LNAI 3345, pp. 66–80, 2005.

others do not. Due to the volume of data, after tokens are processed they are typically discarded and cannot (usually) be retrieved for further analysis (i.e. they are non-persistent). Finally, data streams usually carry data of a known structure. Transmitters of stream data may insert data that does not subscribe to the agreed format, and the stream mechanism may carry these 'false' tokens but without a receiver to process them, they simply become noise. While our work on streaming data is aimed at covering multiple media types (VAST: video, audio, still image and text), our initial focus is on textual information, abridged from structured or unstructured documents.

Many examples of streaming data can be found on the internet:

- Real-time raw traffic loop sensor data: At http://128.95.29.3:8411, self-describing data from the Seattle metropolitan area highway system may be viewed in a browser. This information is processed to display the area's traffic flow map available at http://www.wsdot.wa.gov/PugetSoundTraffic/.
- Real-time stock quotes: At http://www.pcquote.com, clicking on the 'stock ticker' button brings up a streaming ticker of stock prices and averages at the top of your browser.
- Audio news feeds: At http://www.npr.org/audiohelp/progstream.html, clicking on the NPR audio online button, delivers a streaming news broadcast, available via RealAudio and other audio players.
- Video news feeds: At http://www.cnn.com/video/, several video clips are available to review the daily news. Although these are not continuous streams of video, they are representative of the type of video information becoming available in streaming format.

Browsers and other applications are able to process and present this information in formats that are often very convenient to the casual user. Yet, data streams represent a significant challenge to information analysts wishing to use information in more complex ways. To look at potential future issues with respect to streaming data, Lyman and Varian [1] examined the data flows associated with two common information broadcast media: television and radio. They used the CIA World Factbook to find that there are 33,071 television stations in the world. Assuming these stations broadcast about 16 hours per day, this would equal about 193 million hours total programming. They estimated that 25% of the programs were original, leading to a figure of 48 million hours each year. Using the low end of their storage estimates that one-hour of video requires 1.3 GB of storage, then worldwide, program storage would be about 63,000 TB. For radio, they estimated that FM radio stations broadcast 20 hours per day, AM stations 16 hours per day, and shortwave stations 12 hours per day. Therefore, they estimated that there is approximately 290 million hours (188 million FM, 98 million AM, and 6 million shortwave) of radio programming per year. Applying a 50 MB/hour rule of thumb, we come to an estimate of the annual storage requirement of about 14,500 TB if one were to record everything broadcast on radio. At the time of writing, a typical desktop workstation comes equipped with an 80 GB hard disk. Assuming all disk space is available for storage (an incorrect, but simplifying assumption, as some space needs to be used to hold the system software), this allows a mere 53 hours of local video storage or 1600 hours of radio. This example of potential information overload provides some support for the argument that one-look stream processing is a desirable capability for the desktop system. Being selective and only choosing elements of interest drastically reduces the burden.

Data-streams are essential parts of the scientific discipline, intrinsic to a growing number of research areas. 'Knowledge workers' who find themselves working in these areas are in dire need of tools that help them deal with the substantial volume and high complexity that modern streamed data possesses. Our goal in this paper is to put forth a concept for a future generation analytical environment for scientific discovery within data-streams. We take a component approach, utilizing prototypical elements designed under different auspices for diverse purposes and describe an approach to bring them together to provide an ambient environment for collaborative study and a platform for data-stream research.

First, we discuss our stream-processing component, designed as a first step in marshalling complex data streams into something actionable.

2   Stream Processing Component

The concept of our stream-processing engine (shown in Fig. 1) is to provide the ability to drastically reduce incoming data-streams to more manageable levels by allowing the knowledge worker to implicitly define filters that restrict content to only those tokens of intellectual value. We utilize a Content-based Messaging System (CBMS) [2], an optimized J2EE Java Messaging Service (JMS) that provides highly efficient message formatting and filtering. In our prototype, this reduced stream is then routed through a set of algorithms that produce signatures (a compressed representation of the original token). A signature expresses the semantic content of the data sub-stream it encodes with reference to topics that are discovered through an unsupervised classification model. Such a classification model is augmented with a process of ontological annotation that identifies relevant entities and relations among them in terms of reference generic and domain specific ontologies. The topics, entities and relations discovered are then utilized to provide users with an information rich visualization of the data stream.

As signatures are generated, they are consumed into a descriptive profile (a representation of the status quo of the reduced stream). On a token-by-token basis, the profile may grow or remain the same depending on what that particular signature adds to the current knowledge of this stream. After a user-defined training period, new signatures from arriving tokens in the stream are compared against the profile and evaluated for novel content that the knowledge worker may be interested in.

One of the advantages of this approach is that, depending on the requirements of the user, different sets of algorithms may be used to perform different actions. For example, if the user wants to monitor a data stream for new, novel content (as described above), a change detection mode of operation is selected.

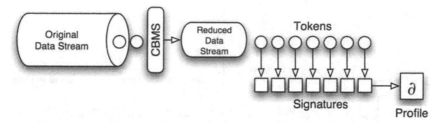

Fig. 1. Data Stream Processing Engine Concept.

If, on the other hand, a classification mode of operation is required, a different set of algorithms could be substituted to perform clustering of documents into specific folders dependant on content. This 'plug and play' nature of our streams processing concept can be seen in Fig. 2.

Viewing this process from the user's standpoint, prior to any stream processing the user of the system creates a 'stream tap': a description of what particular stream they are interested in, and what operations they wish to perform. This tap also defines report settings such as how they wish to be notified (e.g. email, SMS text messaging, etc). Figure 3 shows a schematic of the user interface elements that produce the steam tap. First of all, the set of streams available to the user are presented. This usually includes all the streams that have been processed for inclusion in our prototype (i.e. had XML stream format descriptors created) although security mechanisms could be incorporated so to present only streams that a particular user is cleared to use. After selecting a stream, the prototype verifies that the stream is available and running (i.e. currently being received). It would be inefficient to have our system receive streams that are not currently being tapped, so a stream is only received when there is interest in it. The next step is to allow the user to reduce the stream, if applicable. For operations like change detection, users are often interested in specific parts of a

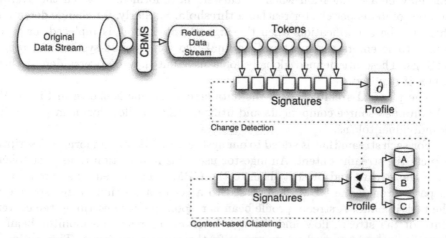

Fig. 2. Component Nature of the Data Stream Processing Engine.

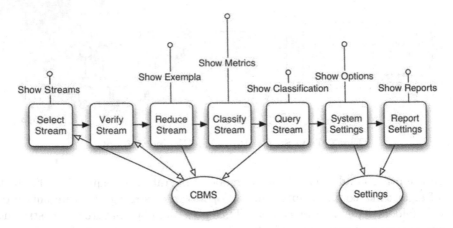

Fig. 3. A schematic of the Stream Tap User Interface.

data stream. For example, if a user wanted to tap a data stream of news stories, and only wanted to know of new events in the Middle East, they may restrict the data stream to news stories that contain specific keywords in the title. To help with this step, an exempla from the data stream is presented, and the user may utilize the filtering capabilities of the CBMS to restrict the stream to a more manageable level. In some cases, for example when classifying stream content into concept bins, no reduction is performed. The next step is to classify the tokens flowing in the data stream. This step allows the system to present the early results of data reduction and gives the user the opportunity to revise their reduction criteria. Again, elements of the user interface are specific to the task in hand. From a clustering perspective this stage would include a breakdown of what clusters have formed. From a change detection standpoint, the top 'n' topics could be presented. The next step allows the user to define what elements of the process they wish to be notified about. For example, for the clustering task, this may be a notification when 'n' clusters have formed, or when the average number of items per cluster reaches a threshold. Similarly, for change detection, this may be a notification when the highest rated topic is replaced, or when a new topic enters the top ten. The final two steps define system and report settings. These are defined globally for a user but may be overridden at these stages if required.

The physical architecture of the data stream engine is shown in Fig. 4. We rely on open-source components and utilize J2EE to allow for bean processing of individual tokens.

For each stream that is added to our system, a XML stream format descriptor depicts the stream content. An ingestor uses this information to extract tokens from the stream and present them to the CBMS. The tokens that are allowed to pass through the CBMS are passed to a set of algorithm beans, specific to the task in hand. A stream profile bean is responsible for describing the current state of the stream flow and through interactions with the monitor bean, a decision is made as and when to notify the user of an event. This action is

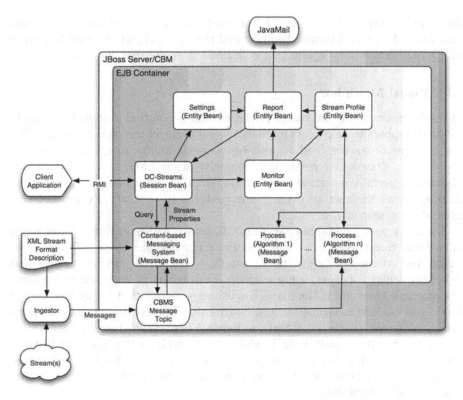

Fig. 4. Physical Architecture of the Data Stream Processing Engine.

performed by the report bean, using input from the monitor bean (and based on a method of notification and notification address supplied by the setting bean) via JavaMail. The system currently supports email and SMS text message notifications, however, as is true for the entire system, new methods may be plugged into the architecture.

For the purposes of our overarching concept here, we rely on this architecture to reduce the initial data-stream to a manageable and interesting set, providing a dynamic corpus of documents for the visualization component.

3 Visualization Component

One goal in exploratory information visualization is to present information so that users can easily discern patterns. These may reveal trends, relationships, anomalies, and structure in the data, and could potentially help confirm knowledge or hypotheses. Patterns may also raise unexpected questions leading users to new insights. The challenge is to create visualizations that enable users to find patterns quickly and easily. Researchers at the Pacific Northwest National Laboratory have developed a suite of visualization tools that help the knowledge worker in these tasks [3]. Here, we present ThemeRiver[TM1] [4]. We shall discuss

---

[1] ThemeRiver is a registered trademark of the Pacific Northwest National Laboratory.

the visual metaphor that ThemeRiver used, the human perceptual processes that ThemeRiver used to its advantage and the layers of context used to provide additional information beyond that contained in the source material.

3.1 Visual Metaphor

ThemeRiver draws on the power of the human perceptual system by using familiar metaphors to help users more easily comprehend the data presented. The graphic layout was designed to leverage a user's ability to quickly assimilate information, drawing on research in cognitive science and psychophysics. The addition of useful contextual information, such as time lines and event annotations, allows the user to connect the patterns in content to events or time intervals (e.g. seasons).

Ideally, a visual metaphor facilitates discovery by presenting data in an intuitive way that is consistent with the user's perceptual and cognitive abilities. Lakoff and Johnson [5] argue that metaphors are wired into our understanding of particular concepts, using evidence from common linguistic expressions. One example they cite is the many English expressions that imply that Anglo-Americans understand time in terms of motion relative to themselves. Some figures of speech characterize time as moving (e.g., "the time will come" and "don't let the opportunity pass"), while others imply that people are the ones moving through time (e.g., "as we go through the years"). We believe the river metaphor of theme currents changing over time derives part of its strength from this cultural understanding.

We use a river metaphor to convey several key notions. The document collection's time evolution, selected thematic content, and thematic strength are indicated by the river's directed flow, composition, and changing width, respectively. The directed flow from left to right is interpreted as movement through time. In Fig. 5, the river flows from November 1959 to June 1961. The horizontal distance between two points on the river defines a time interval. For example, the time interval represented by the distance between the two vertical dotted lines is almost two months. Like a histogram, ThemeRiver uses variations in width to represent variations in strength or degree of representation. At any point in time, the total vertical distance, or width, of the river indicates the collective strength of the selected themes. The collective theme strength of the river is quite strong in March 1961 (near the right side of the figure) where the river is wide; the collective theme strength is much weaker in June 1961 (the far right of the figure) where the river is narrow.

Colored 'currents' flowing within the river represent individual themes. A current's vertical width narrows or broadens to indicate decreases or increases in the strength of the individual theme at any point in time. In Fig. 5 the cyan current represents 'weapons'; the weapons theme is relatively weak in November 1959 and relatively strong in December 1959. A current maintains its integrity as a single entity over time. If a theme ceases to occur in the documents for a period of time and then recurs, the current likewise disappears and then reappears in the same color and position relative to the other themes. The weapons theme

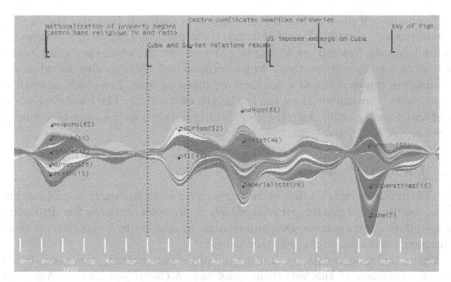

Fig. 5. The ThemeRiver Visual Metaphor.

disappears in the months of January and February 1960 but reappears in March 1960. The entire river may 'dry up' for a period of time if the composite currents all disappear. This is possible because a river can effectively represent only a subset of themes from a document collection, typically a few dozen selected themes. In context of the concept presented in this paper, these may represent the major clusters from a stream or the most significant events that are being queried for change.

3.2 Perceptual Considerations

During the perception process humans do not organize individual, low-level, sensed elements but sense more complete 'packages' that represent objects or patterns. In a recent book, Hoffman [5] presents a compelling discussion of how our perceptual processes identify curves and silhouettes, recognize parts, and group them together into objects. Numerous aspects of the image influence our ability to perceive these parts and objects, including similarity, continuity, symmetry, proximity, and closure. For example, it is easier to perceive objects that are bounded by continuous curves than objects that contain abrupt changes [6].

Smooth, continuous curves bound a theme current in the ThemeRiver visualization. A theme current is assigned a single color for the entire length of the river. The smooth bounds and distinct color help the user track and compare a current's behavior along the river. At a glance the user can see the pattern of the current as an object - where it bulges, where it shrinks, and where it remains unchanged. We naturally associate the size (area) of the object with strength; a larger area indicates more strength, while a smaller area indicates less strength. The absence of the object indicates no use or strength at that time.

Proximity afforded by stacking the currents makes it easy to compare the current shapes (smoothly bounded within the same time interval or across neighboring intervals. We can see when two patterns match, when they complement each other, or when they appear to be uncorrelated. We can also see when the patterns are concurrent and when they are offset in time. The stacking order of the currents is consistent along the full length of the river. The consistent use of color and stacking order helps the user identify currents as the locus of attention moves across the visualization.

3.3   Layers of Context

The ThemeRiver visualization includes the river of theme currents, a time line below the river, and markers for related historical events along the top. Providing such context allows users to evaluate content in relation to issues beyond those contained within the documents themselves.

Figure 5 shows an interesting example of a related theme and event in the sudden expansion of the 'oil' theme just before Castro confiscated American oil refineries in 1960. On occasion we find patterns than cannot be explained until further investigation uncovers events not included in our event stream. For example, in a later period (not shown) ThemeRiver reveals the use of themes 'kennedy' and 'missiles' in March 1992. These themes seem outdated for 1992. On further investigation of events in 1992, we discovered that Castro spoke in March at a conference marking the 30th Anniversary of the Cuban Missile Crisis (October 1962). In such cases we can easily add a marker to the event stream. A user could also add analysis annotations in the same way.

Some additional elements of the ThemeRiver user interface help the user in their analytical task. A histogram (Fig. 6, right) can show whether stream content is light on a particular topic for a reason, or simply due to seasonal causes (for example, the fact that less news is reported at the weekend).

In addition, showing multiple streams head-to-head can allow the user to compare them (Fig. 6, left). Finally, tracking related themes is simplified by assigning them to the same color family. This ensures that related themes appear together and are identifiable as a group.

By associating a mechanism for collecting and simplifying data-streams with a themed visualization tool, we shall be taking a step towards providing knowledge workers with the types of tools they require for successful stream processing. While this is certainly a step in the right direction, we are intrigued by the notion of being subsumed by the data, being perceptually linked to its flow. For these reasons we consider a third component, a means to engulf the user in the data.

4   Ambient Component

The key to developing the next generation human to information interface is to move beyond the limitations of small computer monitors as our only view into the electronic information space and keyboards and mice as the only interaction devices.

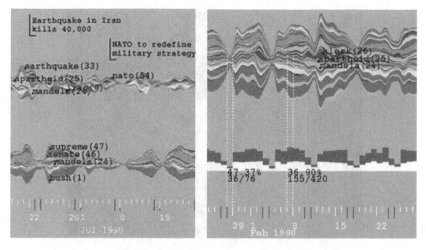

Fig. 6. Additional ThemeRiver user interface elements.

```
germany(36)
unification(37)
gdr(38)
kohl(39)
ceausescu(40)
hungary(41)
iliescu(42)
bucharest(43)
```

Fig. 7. ThemeRiver uses color family to relate themes.

Our physical information space, which includes walls, tables, and other surfaces, should now be our view into the electronic information space. People perform physical interactions with information every day by picking up a book, building a model, or writing notes on a page. Similar interactions need to be developed for electronic information. Providing these types of interactions in the electronic world would allow us to interact more quickly, naturally, and hopefully more effectively in the broader context of information exploration. For these reasons, Battelle, in association with the HITLab, have created the Human Information Space (HI-Space) [7] (Fig. 8). This system utilizes knowledge from many areas of research, including Psychology, Human-Computer Interaction, Virtual Reality, Kinesiology, and Computer Science, to create a physical workspace that blurs the boundaries between physical and electronic information. The most desirable aspects of both the physical and electronic information spaces are used to enhance the ability to interact with information, promote group dialog, and to facilitate group interaction with information to solve complex tasks.

Fig. 8. Demonstration of the HI-Space system.

In a HI-Space system, the sensors (camera, radio frequency tagging antenna and microphone array) are placed over the table to capture user interactions with a table display. The display itself is a rear-view screen being fed by a standard LCD projector. The HI-Space creates an interaction space between the sensor array and the 2D display surface, as depicted in Fig. 9. This creates a 3D interaction volume that allows the user a much greater degree of freedom than in conventional systems. The system has the potential to interpret gestures or actions anywhere in the interaction volume and respond accordingly, giving the HI-Space much greater potential for advanced interactions than technologies that only mimic touch screen type functionality. The emphasis of our research has been the development of new interaction techniques and technologies as well as creating the information workspace. Towards this objective, we are taking advantage of technologies that are already in the mainstream pipeline, including new projector technology, large-screen displays, and high-resolution cameras. Battelle has a working proof-of-concept HI-Space system at its facilities [8] and has a second system at the University of Washington's Human Interface Technology Laboratory (HITL) [9]. Other HI-Space systems are in use at other sites around the USA (e.g. the GeoVISTA Center at Penn State [10]).

The core software of the HI-Space system is the underlying computer vision library that takes incoming video images and recognizes two new classes of input devices: pointers and objects. Pointers are anything that is reaching into the interaction volume, for example, a hand or handheld stylus. An object is something that has been placed on the display surface and left there. The use of objects in video tracked systems has been discussed extensively under the topic of tangible interfaces [11] and hand tracking has occurred in a variety of systems [12–14]. HI-Space uniquely brings these and other functionality into a group environment where neither the user nor objects are instrumented or tethered in any way. All tracking and recognition is from physical characteristics derived only from the video camera. The system will track as many pointers and objects

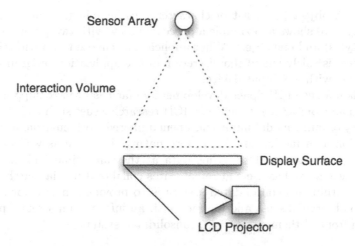

Fig. 9. The HI-Space System.

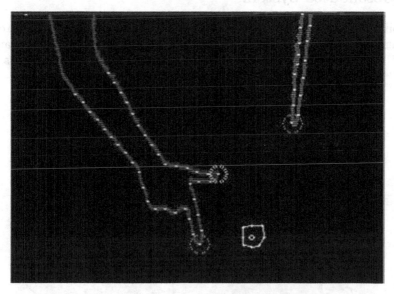

Fig. 10. Pointers and objects within the HI-Space System.

as are placed inside the interaction volume, however, there is a practical limit due to problems of recognizing when pointers overlap one another.

When a pointer or object is recognized by the HI-Space library routines, it passes to the application a set of characteristics about each and every pointer or object being tracked. These characteristics are updated with each new video frame. For pointers, the application is sent the location it entered the interaction volume, where the tip of the pointer is located, length of the pointer, how many fingers (in the case of a hand) are on the pointer, and if the pointer is in a recognized pose state. The pose is used for hands and is part of a gesture recognitions system. Each object has a list of characteristics including, location, size, and shape. Figure 10 shows an example a processed view with two points (one hand and one stylus) and one object. What applications choose to do with these new input devices is solely left to the discretion of the application programmer, just as is the case with any input device.

The main focus of HI-Space development so far has been to support a number of Human Computer Interaction (HCI) research issues such as investigating redundancy of multi-modal input and unencumbered work environments, direct manipulation as a mechanism for a more natural interface as well as collaborative group interaction of the same data at the same time and in the same physical space, as well as users at remote sites collaborating via matched tables. Our focus within this consolidated system is to provide a means for a number of users to observe, discuss and interact with an information stream, presented visually in front of them as part of a consolidated system.

5   Consolidated System

The consolidated environment takes each of these elements together to produce a rich environment for collaborative investigation. Knowledge workers standing around the HI-SPACE could observe the themes of the selected streams flow,

Fig. 11. Next generation environment for scientific discovery in data-streams (Concept).

changing dimensions as new token influence the status quo. Monitors covering the walls could hold representations of individual data items or other miscellaneous statistics. They could also provide expressions of other researchers, connected in from a remote location. We envision the HI-SPACE itself holding the ThemeRiver visualization, but enhanced to allow users to use hand gestures to indicate topics of interest. They may use phicons [15], physical objects registered with the HI-SPACE as placemarkers. These could be placed as stopblocks on themes that are not considered essential to the current study, or in some alternative manner so to affect the themes presented. Usability studies will be required to ascertain the usefulness of an ambient approach to such scientific discovery, but we believe that by becoming more intrinsically involved with the data, scientists may be able to uncover unique findings, previously undiscovered. An artist's rendition of our concept can be seen in Fig. 11.

6 Summary

We have presented our vision for a next generation analytical environment for scientific discovery within data-streams. By utilizing components from our research portfolio in Information Analytics, Rich Interaction Environments and Knowledge Engineering, we envision a system that can handle massive data streams of differing data types, present the most important elements of these streams visually and allow for advanced interactions within a group context.

Acknowledgements

The authors would like to thank their colleagues across numerous departments at PNNL that made these individual components possible.

References

1. Lyman, P. and Varian, H.: How Much Information? A project report of the Regents of the University of California, available at http://www.sims.berkeley.edu/how-much-info. (2000)
2. Gorton, I., Almquist, Justin, Cramer, Nick, Haack, Jereme, Hoza, Mark: "An Efficient, Scalable Content-Based Messaging System", in Proc. 7th IEEE International Enterprise Distributed Object Computing Conference (EDOC 2003), pg. 278-285, Brisbane, Australia. (September 2003)
3. Pacific Northwest National Laboratory's IT Showcase http://showcase.pnl.gov/show?it/triver-prod webpage
4. Havre SL, Hetzler BG, Whitney PD and Nowell LT.: "ThemeRiver: Visualizing Thematic Changes in Document Collections". IEEE Transactions on Visualization and Computer Graphics. (2002) 8(1):9-20
5. Hoffman, D.D.: "Visual Intelligence: How We Create What We See." W.W. Norton and Company, Inc., New York. (1998)
6. Ware, C.: "Information Visualization: Perception for Design." San Diego: Academic Press. (2000)

7. May, R.: "Hi-Space: A Next Generation Workspace Environment." Masters Thesis in Electrical Engineering Computer Science. Pullman, Washington, Washington State University.
8. http://showcase.pnl.gov/show?it/hispace-prod
9. http://www.hitl.washington.edu/hispace.html
10. MacEachren M.A., et al: "Visually-Enabled Geocollaboration to Support Data Exploration and Decision-Making." Proceedings of the 21st International Cartographic Conference, Durban, South Africa. (August 2003) 10-16
11. Ullmer, B. and H. Ishii: "The metaDESK: Models and Prototypes for Tangible User Interfaces." UIST. (1997)
12. Matsushita, N. and Rekimoto, J.: "HoloWall: Designing a Finger, Hand, Body, and Object Sensitive Wall." UIST. (1997)
13. Krueger, M. W.: "Artificial Reality II", Addison-Wesley Publishing Company. (1991)
14. Wellner, P.: "Interactions with Paper on the DigitalDesk." Communications of the ACM. (1993) 36(7): 87-96.
15. Ohshima, T., K. Sato, et al.: "AR2 Hockey; A Case Study of Collaborative Augmented Reality." VRAIS. (1998)

Shape as Memory Storage

Michael Leyton

DIMACS & Rutgers University, USA
mleyton@dimacs.rutgers.edu

1 New Foundations to Geometry

In a sequence of books, I have developed *new foundations to geometry* that are directly opposed to the foundations to geometry that have existed from Euclid to modern physics, including Einstein. The central proposal of the new foundations is this:

SHAPE ≡ **MEMORY STORAGE**

Let us see how this contrasts with the standard foundations for geometry that have existed for almost three thousand years. In the standard foundations, a geometric object consists of those properties of a figure that do not change under a set of actions. These properties are called the *invariants* of the actions. Geometry began with the study of invariance, in the form of Euclid's concern with *congruence*, which is really a concern with invariance (properties that do not change). And modern physics is based on invariance. For example, Einstein's principle of relativity states that physics is the study of those properties that are invariant (unchanged) under transformations between observers. Quantum mechanics studies the invariants of measurement operators.

My argument is that the problem with invariants is that they are *memoryless*. That is, if a property is invariant (unchanged) under an action, then one cannot infer from the property that the action has taken place. Thus I argue: *Invariants cannot act as memory stores.* In consequence, I conclude that geometry, from Euclid to Einstein has been concerned with *memorylessness*. In fact, since standard geometry tries to maximize the discovery of invariants, it is essentially trying to maximize memorylessness. My argument is that these foundations to geometry are inappropriate to the *computational* age; e.g., people want computers that have greater memory storage, not less.

As a consequence, I embarked on a 30-year project to build up an entirely new system for geometry – a system that was recently completed. Rather than basing geometry on the *maximization of memorylessness* (the aim from Euclid to Einstein), I base geometry on the *maximization of memory storage*. The result is a system that is profoundly different, both on a conceptual level and on a detailed mathematical level. The conceptual structure is elaborated in my book *Symmetry, Causality, Mind* (MIT Press, 630 pages); and the mathematical structure is elaborated in my book *A Generative Theory of Shape* (Springer-Verlag, 550 pages).

Y. Cai (Ed.): Ambient Intelligence for Scientific Discovery, LNAI 3345, pp. 81–103, 2005.

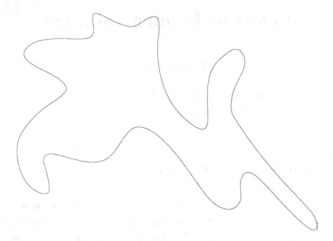

Fig. 1. Shape as history.

2   The Process-Grammar

The purpose of the present chapter is to give an example of the theory without going deeply into the extensive technicalities. The example we shall choose is the extraction of memory stored in *curvature extrema*. I show that curvature extrema contain an extremely high amount of memory storage, and furthermore that this storage is organized in a hierarchy I called a *Process-Grammar*. After I published this grammar in the 1980's it was applied by scientists in over 20 disciplines: radiology, meteorology, computer vision, chemical engineering, geology, computer-aided design, anatomy, botany, forensic science, robotics, software engineering, architecture, linguistics, mechanical engineering, computer graphics, art, semiotics, archaeology, anthropology, etc.

Let us begin by understanding the purpose for which the grammar was developed: inferring history from shape; e.g., from the shapes of tumors, embryos, clouds, etc. For example, the shape shown in Fig 1 can be understood as the result of various processes such as protrusion, indentation, squashing, resistance. My book *Symmetry, Causality, Mind* (MIT Press), was essentially a 630-page rule-system for deducing the past history that formed any shape. The Process-Grammar is part of that rule-system – the part related to the use of curvature extrema.

3   The PISA Symmetry Analysis

It is first necessary to understand how symmetry can be defined in complex shape. Clearly, in a simple shape, such as an equilateral triangle, a symmetry axis is easy to define. One simply places a straight mirror across the shape such that one half is reflected onto the other. The straight line of the mirror is then defined to be a symmetry axis of the shape. However, in a complex shape, it is often impossible to place a mirror that will reflect one half of the figure onto the other. Fig 1, is an example of such a shape. However, in such cases, one might still wish to regard the figure, or part of it, as symmetrical about some *curved* axis. Such a generalized axis can be constructed in the following way.

Consider Fig 2. It shows two curves c_1 and c_2, which can be understood as two sides of an object. Notice that no mirror could reflect one of these curves onto the other. The goal is to construct a symmetry axis between the two curves. One proceeds as follows: As shown in Fig 3, introduce a circle that is tangential simultaneously to the two curves. Here the two tangent points are marked as A and B.

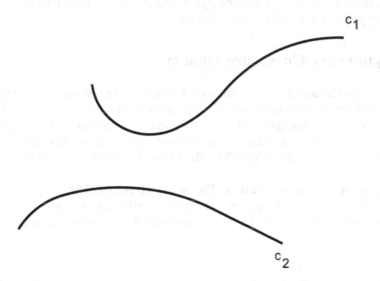

Fig. 2. How can one construct a symmetry axis between these to curves?

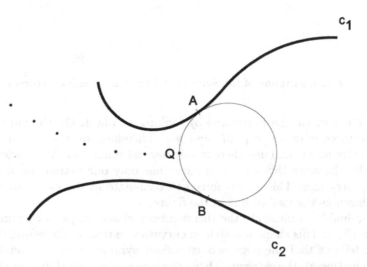

Fig. 3. The points Q define the symmetry axis.

Next, move the circle continuously along the two curves, c_1 and c_2, while always ensuring that it maintains the property of been tangential to the two curves simultaneously. To maintain this double-touching property, it might be necessary to expand or contract the circle. This procedure was invented by Blum in the 1960s, and he defined the symmetry axis to be the center of the circle as it moved. However, in my book, *Symmetry, Causality, Mind*, I showed that there are serious topological problems with this definition, and I defined the axis to be the trajectory of the point Q shown in Fig 3. This is the point on the circle, half-way between the two tangent points. As the circle moves along the curves, it traces out a trajectory as indicated by the sequence of dots shown in the figure. I called this axis, *Process-Inferring Symmetry Axis*, or simply PISA. It does not have the problems associated with the Blum axis.

4   Symmetry-Curvature Duality

The Process-Grammar to be elaborated relies on two structural factors in a shape: symmetry and curvature. Mathematically, symmetry and curvature are two very different descriptors of shape. However, a theorem that I proposed and proved in [4] shows that there is an intimate relationship between these two descriptors. This relationship will be the basis of the entire chapter.

Symmetry-Curvature Duality Theorem (Leyton, 1987): *Any section of curve, that has one and only one curvature extremum, has one and only one symmetry axis. This axis is forced to terminate at the extremum itself.*

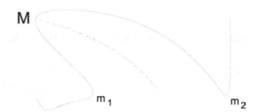

Fig. 4. Illustration of the Symmetry-Curvature Duality Theorem.

The theorem can be illustrated by looking at Fig 4. On the curve shown, there are three extrema: m_1, M, and m_2. Therefore, on the section of curve *between* extrema m_1 and m_2, there is only one extremum, M. What the theorem says is this: Because this section of curve has only one extremum, it has only one symmetry axis. This axis is forced to terminate at the extremum M. The axis is shown as the dashed line in the figure.

It is valuable to illustrate the theorem on a closed shape, for example, that shown in Fig 5. This shape has sixteen curvature extrema. Therefore, the above theorem tells us that there are sixteen unique symmetry axes associated with, and terminating at, the extrema. They are given as the dashed lines in the figure.

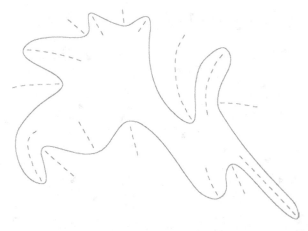

Fig. 5. Sixteen extrema imply sixteen symmetry axes.

5   The Interaction Principle

The reason for involving symmetry axes is that it will be argued that they are closely related to process-histories. This proposed relationship is given by the following principle:

Interaction Principle (Leyton, 1984): *Symmetry axes are the directions along which processes are hypothesized as most likely to have acted.*

The principle was extensively corroborated in Leyton [7], in several areas of perception including motion perception as well as shape perception. The argument used in Leyton [7] to justify the principle, involves the following two steps: (1) A process that acts along a symmetry axis tends to preserve the symmetry; i.e. to be structure-preserving. (2) Structure-preserving processes are perceived as the most likely processes to occur or to have occurred.

6   The Inference of Processes

We now have the tools required to understand how processes can be recovered from the curvature extrema of shape; i.e., how curvature extrema can be converted into memory stores. In fact, the system to be proposed consists of two inference rules that are applied successively to a shape. The rules can be illustrated by considering Fig 6.

The first rule is the Symmetry-Curvature Duality Theorem (section 4) which states that, to each curvature extremum, there is a unique symmetry axis terminating at that extremum. The second rule is the Interaction Principle (section 5), which states that each of the axes is a direction along which a process has acted. The implication is that the boundary was deformed along the axes; e.g. each protrusion was the result of pushing out along its axis, and each indentation was the result of pushing in along its axis. In fact, each axis is the trace or record of boundary-movement!

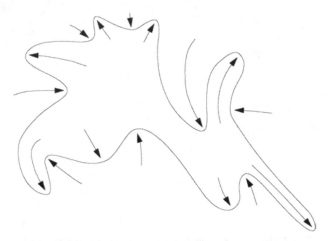

Fig. 6. The processes inferred by the rules.

Under this analysis, processes are understood as creating the curvature extrema; e.g. the processes introduce protrusions and indentations etc., into the shape boundary. This means that, if one were to go backwards in time, undoing all the inferred processes, one would eventually remove all the extrema. Observe that there is only one closed curve without extrema: the circle. Thus the implication is that the ultimate starting shape must have been a circle, and this was deformed under various processes each of which produced an extremum.

7   Corroborating Examples

To obtain extensive corroboration for the above rules, let us now apply them to all shapes with up to eight curvature extrema. These are shown as the outlines in Figs 7–9. When our inference rules are applied to these outlines, they produce the arrows shown as the inferred histories. One can see that the results accord remarkably well with intuition.

Further considerations should be made: Any individual outline, together with the inferred arrows, will be called a *process diagram*. The reader should observe that on each process diagram in Figs 7–9, a letter-label has been placed at each extremum (the end of each arrow). There are four alternative labels, M^+, m^-, m^+, and M^-, and these correspond to the four alternative types of curvature extrema. The four types are shown in Fig 10 and are explained as follows:

The first two have exactly the same shape: They are the sharpest kinds of curvature extrema. The difference between them is that, in the first, the solid (shaded) is on the inside, and, in the second, the solid (shaded) is on the outside. That is, they are figure/ground reversals of each other. The remaining two extrema are also figure/ground reversals of each other. Here the extrema are the flattest points on the respective curves.

Now notice the following important phenomenon: The above characterizations of the four extrema types are purely structural. However, in surveying the

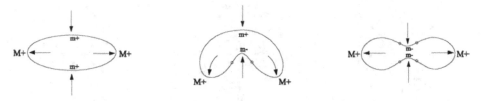

Fig. 7. The inferred histories on the shapes with 4 extrema.

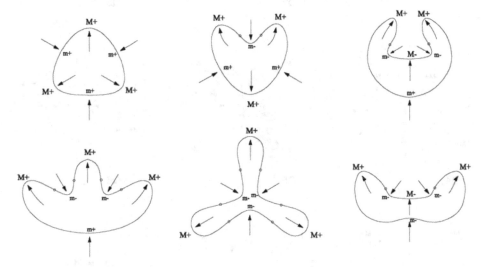

Fig. 8. The inferred histories on the shapes with 6 extrema.

shapes in Figs 7–9, it becomes clear the four extrema types correspond to four English terms that people use to describe *processes*. Table 1 gives the correspondence:

Table 1. Correspondence between extremum type and process type.

EXTREMUM TYPE ⟷ PROCESS TYPE

M^+	⟷	protrusion
m^-	⟷	indentation
m^+	⟷	squashing
M^-	⟷	resistance

What we have done so far is to lay the ground-work of the Process Grammar. What the grammar will do is show the way each of these shapes deforms into each other. It turns out that there are only six things that can happen as one shape transforms into another: i.e., *six phase-transitions*. These will be the six rules of the grammar. Let us now show what they are.

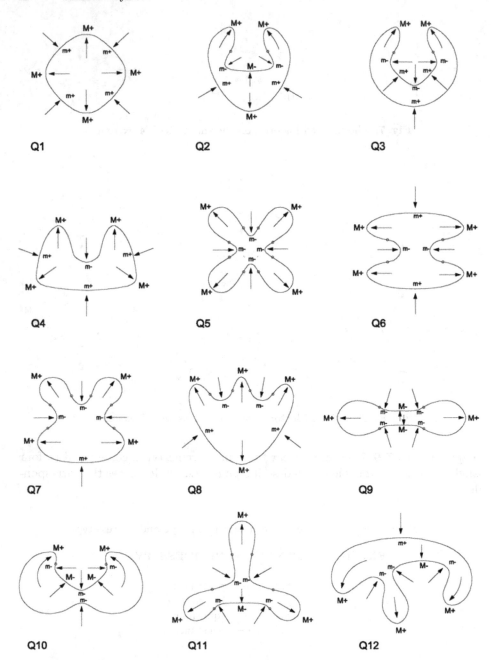

Fig. 9. The inferred histories on the shapes with 8 extrema.

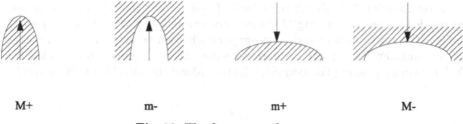

$M+$ $m-$ $m+$ $M-$

Fig. 10. The four types of extrema.

8 The Method to Be Used

The purpose of the Process Grammar is to yield additional information concerning the past history of the shape.

Our procedure for finding this information will be as follows: Let us imagine that we have two stages in the history of the shape. For example, imagine being a doctor looking at two X-rays of a tumor taken a month apart. Observe that any doctor examines two such X-rays (e.g., on a screen), in order to assess what has happened in the intervening month. If one considers the way the doctor's thinking proceeds, one realizes that there is a basic inference rule that is being used: The doctor will try, as much as possible, to explain a process seen in the later shape as an *extrapolation* of a process seen in the earlier shape. That is, the doctor tries to maximize the description of *history as extrapolations*. We will show how to discover these extrapolations.

Recall that the processes we have been examining are those that move along symmetry axes, creating extrema. As a simple first cut, we can say that extrapolations have one of two forms:

(1) Continuation: The process simply continues along the symmetry axis, maintaining that single axis.

(2) Bifurcation: The process branches into two axes, i.e., creating two processes out of one.

Now recall, from Fig 10 that there are four types of extrema M^+, m^-, m^+, and M^-. These were discussed at the end of section 7. It is necessary therefore to look at what happens when one continues the process at each of the four types, and at what happens when one branches (bifurcates) the process at each of the four types. This means that there are *eight* alternative events that can occur: four continuations and four bifurcations.

9 Continuation at M^+ and m^-

Let us start by considering continuations, and then move on to bifurcations. It turns out that, when one continues a process at either of the first two extrema, M^+ or m^-, nothing significant happens, as follows:

First consider M^+. Recall from Table 1 (p87), that the M^+ extremum corresponds to a protrusion. Fig 11 shows three examples of M^+, the three protrusions. We want to understand what happens when any one of the M^+ processes is continued. For example, what happens when the protruding process at the top M^+ continues pushing the boundary further along the direction of its arrow?

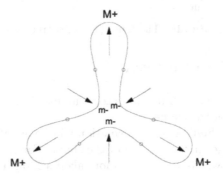

Fig. 11. Continuation at M^+ and m^- do not change extremum-type.

The answer is simple: The boundary would remain a M^+ extremum, despite being extended further upwards. Intuitively, this is obvious: A protrusion remains a protrusion if it continues. Therefore, from now on, we will ignore continuation at M^+ as structurally trivial.

Now observe that exactly the same considerations apply with respect to any m^- extremum. For example, notice that the same shape, Fig 11, has three m^- extrema. Notice also that, in accord with Table 1 (p87), each of these corresponds to an *indentation*. It is clear that, if the process continues at a m^-, the boundary would remain m^-. Again, this is intuitively obvious: An indentation remains an indentation if it continues. As a consequence, we will also ignore continuation at m^- as structurally trivial.

In summary, the two cases considered in this section, continuation at M^+ and at m^-, are structurally trivial. It will now be seen that continuations at the remaining two extrema, m^+ and M^-, induce much more interesting effects on a shape.

10   Continuation at m^+

According to Table 1 (p87), a m^+ extremum is always associated with a *squashing* process. An example is shown in the top of the left shape in Fig 12. Notice therefore that the process explains the flattening at this extremum, relative to the greater bend at either end of the top.

Our goal is to understand what happens when the process at this m^+ extremum is continued forward in time; i.e., the downward arrow pushes further downward. Clearly, a continuation of the process can result in the indentation shown at the top of the right shape in Fig 12.

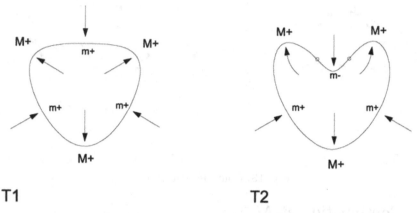

T1   T2

Fig. 12. Continuation at m^+.

The structural change, in going from the left to the right shape, should be understood as follows: First, the m^+ at the top of the left shape changes to the m^- at the top of the right shape. Notice that the m^- extremum corresponds to an indentation, as predicted by Table 1 (p87).

An extra feature should be observed: On either side of the m^- extremum, at the top of the right shape, a small circular dot has been placed. Such a dot marks a position where the curvature is zero; i.e., the curve is, locally, completely straight. If one were driving around this curve, the dot would mark the place where the steering wheel would point straight ahead.

With these facts, one can now describe exactly what occurred in the transition from the left shape to the right shape: The m^+ extremum at the top of the left shape has changed into a m^- extremum at the top of the right shape, and two points of zero curvature, 0, have been introduced on either side of the m^-. One can therefore say that the transition from the left shape to the right shape is the replacement of m^+ (left shape) by the triple, $0m^-0$ (right shape). The transition is therefore:

$$m^+ \longrightarrow 0m^-0.$$

This transition will be labelled Cm^+ meaning *Continuation at m^+*. Thus the transition is given fully as:

$$Cm^+ : m^+ \longrightarrow 0m^-0.$$

This mathematical expression is easy to translate into English. Reading the symbols, from left to right, the expression says:

Continuation at m^+ takes m^+ and replaces it by the triple $0m^-0$.

It is worth having a simple phrase defining the transition in Fig 12. Notice that, since the extremum m^+ in the left shape is a squashing, and the extremum m^- in the right shape is an indentation, the transition can be described as:

A squashing continues till it indents.

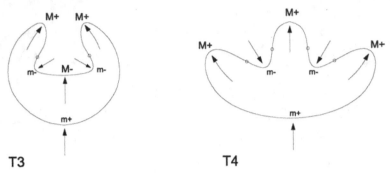

T3   T4

Fig. 13. Continuation at M^-.

11   Continuation at M^-

We will now investigate what happens when the process at the fourth and final extremum M^- is continued forward in time. As an example, consider the M^- in the center of the bay in the left shape in Fig 13. In accord with Table 1 (p87), the process at this extremum is an *internal resistance*. In order to understand this process, let us suppose that the left shape represents an island. Initially, this island was circular. Then, there was an inflow of water at the top (creating a dip inwards). This flow increased inward, but met a ridge of mountains along the center of the island. The mountain ridge acted as a resistance to the inflow of water, and thus the bay was formed. In the center of the bay, the point labelled M^- is a curvature extremum, because it is the point on the bay with the *least* amount of bend (i.e., extreme in the sense of "least").

Now return to the main issue of this section: What happens when the upward resistive arrow (terminating at the M^- extremum) is continued along the direction of the arrow. This could happen for example, if there is a volcano in the mountains, that erupts, sending lava down into the sea. The result would therefore be the shape shown on the right in Fig 13. In other words, a protrusion would be formed into the sea.

The structural change, in going from the left to the right shape, should be understood as follows: First, the M^- in the center of the bay (left shape) changes into the M^+ at the top of the right shape, the protrusion.

An extra feature should be observed: On either side of the M^+ extremum, at the top of the right shape, a small circular dot has been placed. Such a dot again marks a position where the curvature is zero; i.e., the curve is, locally, completely straight.

Thus we can describe what has happened in the transition from the left shape to the right shape: The M^- extremum in the bay of the left shape has changed into a M^+ extremum at the top of the right shape, and two points of zero curvature, 0, have been introduced on either side of the M^+. In other words, the M^- in the left shape has been replaced by the triple, $0M^+0$ in the right shape. The transition is therefore:

$$M^- \longrightarrow 0M^+0.$$

This transition will be labelled CM^- meaning *Continuation at* M^-. Thus the transition is given fully as:

$$CM^-\ :\ M^- \longrightarrow 0M^+0.$$

This mathematical expression is easy to translate into English. Reading the symbols, from left to right, the expression says:

Continuation at M^- *takes* M^- *and replaces it by the triple* $0M^+0$.

It is worth having a simple phrase defining the transition in Fig 13. Notice that, since the extremum M^- in the left shape is a resistance, and the extremum M^+ in the right shape is a protrusion, the transition can be described as:

A resistance continues till it protrudes.

Comment: We have now gone through each of the four extrema, and defined what happens when the process at the extremum is allowed to continue. The first and second extrema involved no structural change, but the third and fourth extrema did.

12   Bifurcation at M^+

We now turn from continuations to bifurcations (branchings) at extrema. Again, each of the four extrema will be investigated in turn.

First we examine what happens when the process at a M^+ extremum branches forward in time. As an example, consider the M^+ at the top of the left shape in Fig 14. In accord with Table 1 (p87), the process at this extremum is a *protrusion*. The effect of bifurcating is shown in the right shape. One branch goes to the left, and the other goes to the right.

The structural change, in going from the left to the right shape, should be understood as follows: First observe that the single M^+ at the top of the left

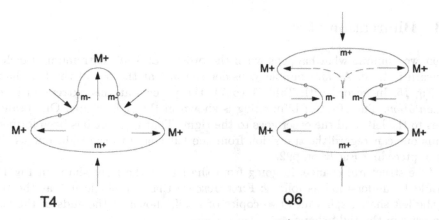

Fig. 14. Bifurcation at M^+.

shape, splits into two copies of itself, shown at the ends of the two branches in the right shape.

There is also another feature. In the center of the top of the right shape, a new extremum has been introduced, m^+. Note that the process at this extremum is a *squashing*, as predicted in Table 1 on p87. This process explains the flattening in the middle of the top, relative to the sharpening towards either end of the top. The m^+ extremum is a minimum, and is required mathematically, because the two branching extrema are maxima M, and two maxima cannot exist without a minimum in between.

With these facts, one can now describe exactly what occurred in the transition from the left shape to the right shape: The M^+ extremum at the top of the left shape has split into two copies of itself in the right shape, and a new extremum m^+ has been introduced. That is, the transition from the left shape to the right shape is the replacement of M^+ (left shape) by the triple, $M^+m^+M^+$ (right shape). The transition is therefore:

$$M^+ \longrightarrow M^+m^+M^+.$$

This transition will be labelled BM^+, meaning *Bifurcation at* M^+. Thus the transition is given fully as:

$$BM^+ \ : \ M^+ \longrightarrow M^+m^+M^+.$$

This mathematical expression is easy to translate into English. Reading the symbols, from left to right, the expression says:

Bifurcation at M^+ takes M^+ and replaces it by the triple $M^+m^+M^+$.

It will also be worth having a simple phrase to summarize the effect of the transition in Fig 14. The structure formed on the right shape has the shape of a *shield*, and therefore, the transition will be referred to thus:

Shield-formation.

13   Bifurcation at m^-

Next we examine what happens when the process at a m^- extremum branches forward in time. As an example, consider the m^- at the top of the left shape in Fig 15. In accord with Table 1 (p87), the process at this extremum is an *indentation*. The effect of bifurcating is shown in the right shape. One branch goes to the left, and the other goes to the right. That is, a *bay* has been formed! Thus one can regard the transition from the left shape to the right one as the stage preceding Fig 13 on p92.

The structural change, in going from the left to the right shape in Fig 15, should be understood as follows: First observe that the single m^- at the top of the left shape, splits into two copies of itself, shown at the ends of the two branches in the right shape.

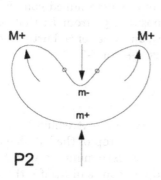

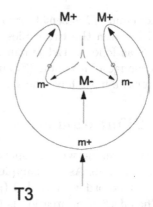

Fig. 15. Bifurcation at m^-.

There is also another feature. In the center of the top of the right shape, a new extremum has been introduced, M^-. Note that the process at this extremum is a *resistance*, as predicted in Table 1 on p87. This process explains the flattening in the middle of the bay, relative to the sharpening towards either end of the bay.

With these facts, one can now describe exactly what occurred in the transition from the left shape to the right shape: The m^- extremum at the top of the left shape has been replaced by the triple, $m^- M^- m^-$ in the right shape. The transition is therefore:

$$m^- \longrightarrow m^- M^- m^-.$$

This transition will be labelled Bm^- meaning *Bifurcation at* m^-. Thus the transition is given fully as:

$$Bm^- : m^- \longrightarrow m^- M^- m^-.$$

This mathematical expression is easy to translate into English. Reading the symbols, from left to right, the expression says:

Bifurcation at m^- *takes* m^- *and replaces it by the triple* $m^- M^- m^-$.

It will also be worth having a simple phrase to summarize the effect of the transition in Fig 15. The obvious phrase is this:

Bay-formation.

14   The Bifurcation Format

The previous two sections established the first two bifurcations: those at M^+ and m^-. The next two sections will describe the remaining two bifurcations. However, before giving these, it is worth observing that the first two bifurcations allow us to see that bifurcations have the same format as each other, which is shown as follows:

$$E \longrightarrow EeE.$$

An extremum E is sent to two copies of itself, and a new extremum e is introduced between the two copies. The new extremum e is determined completely from E as follows: Extremum e must be the opposite type from E; that is, it much change a Maximum (M) into a minimum (m), and vice versa. Furthermore, extremum e must have the same sign as E, that is, "+" or "-".

15   Bifurcation at m^+

Next we examine what happens when the process at a m^+ extremum branches forward in time. As an example, consider the m^+ at the top of the left shape in Fig 16. In accord with Table 1 (p87), the process at this extremum is a *squashing*.

The effect of bifurcation is that m^+ splits into two copies of itself – the two copies shown on either side of the right shape. One should imagine the two copies as *sliding* over the surface till they reached their current positions.

The other crucial event is the introduction of a new extremum M^+ in the top of the right shape. This is in accord with the bifurcation format described in the previous section. Notice that the upward process here conforms to Table 1 on p87, which says that a M^+ extremum always corresponds to a protrusion.

Thus the transition from the left shape to the right shape is the replacement of the m^+ extremum at the top of the left shape by the triple $m^+M^+m^+$ in the right shape. The transition is therefore:

$$m^+ \longrightarrow m^+M^+m^+.$$

This transition will be labelled Bm^+ meaning *Bifurcation at m^+*. Thus the transition is given fully as:

$$Bm^+ \; : \; m^+ \longrightarrow m^+M^+m^+.$$

This mathematical expression is easy to translate into English. Reading the symbols, from left to right, the expression says:

Bifurcation at m^+ takes m^+ and replaces it by the triple $m^+M^+m^+$.

It will also be worth having a simple phrase to summarize the effect of the transition, as follows: Notice that the main effect in Fig 16 is that the initial

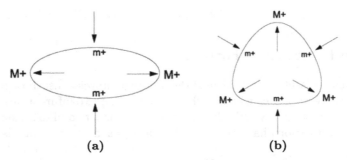

(a)   (b)

Fig. 16. Bifurcation at m^+.

squashing process is pushed to either side by the breaking-through of an upward protrusion. Thus the transition can be summarized by the following phrase:

Breaking-through of a protrusion.

16   Bifurcation at M^-

Now we establish the final bifurcation. We examine what happens when the process at a M^- extremum branches forward in time. As an example, consider the M^- in the center of the bay, the left shape, in Fig 17. In accord with Table 1 (p87), the process at this extremum is an *internal resistance*.

The effect of bifurcation is that M^- splits into two copies of itself – the two copies shown at the two sides of the *deepened bay* in the right shape. One should imagine the two copies as *sliding* over the surface till they reached their current positions.

The other crucial event is the introduction of a new extremum m^- in the bottom of the right shape. This is in accord with the bifurcation format described in section 14. Notice that the downward process here conforms to Table 1 on p87, which says that a m^- extremum always corresponds to a resistance.

Thus the transition from the left shape to the right shape is the replacement of the M^- extremum in the middle of the left shape by the triple $M^-m^-M^-$ in the right shape. The transition is therefore:

$$M^- \longrightarrow M^-m^-M^-.$$

This transition will be labelled BM^- meaning *Bifurcation at M^-*. Thus the transition is given fully as:

$$BM^- \; : \; M^- \longrightarrow M^-m^-M^-.$$

This mathematical expression is easy to translate into English. Reading the symbols, from left to right, the expression says:

Bifurcation at M^- takes M^- and replaces it by the triple $M^-m^-M^-$.

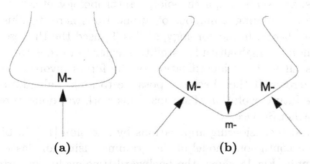

(a)   (b)

Fig. 17. Bifurcation at M^-.

It is also worth having a simple phrase to summarize the effect of the transition, as follows: Notice that the main effect in Fig 17 is that the initial resistance process is pushed to either side by the breaking-through of an downward indentation. Thus the transition can be summarized by the following phrase:

Breaking-through of an indentation.

17   The Process-Grammar

Having completed the bifurcations, let us now put together the entire system that has been developed in sections 8 to 17. Our concern has been to describe the shape evolution by what happens at the most significant points on the shape: the curvature extrema. We have seen that the evolution of any smooth shape can be decomposed into into *six types of phase-transition* defined at the extrema involved. These phase-transitions are given as follows:

Process Grammar

$$
\begin{aligned}
Cm^+ : & \quad m^+ \longrightarrow 0m^-0 & \text{(squashing continues till it indents)} \\
CM^- : & \quad M^- \longrightarrow 0M^+0 & \text{(resistance continues till it protrudes)} \\
BM^+ : & \quad M^+ \longrightarrow M^+m^+M^+ & \text{(sheild-formation)} \\
Bm^- : & \quad m^- \longrightarrow m^-M^-m^- & \text{(bay-formation)} \\
Bm^+ : & \quad m^+ \longrightarrow m^+M^+m^+ & \text{(breaking-through of a protrusion)} \\
BM^- : & \quad M^- \longrightarrow M^-m^-M^- & \text{(breaking-through of an indentation)}
\end{aligned}
$$

Note that the first two transitions are the two continuations, as indicated by the letter C at the beginning of the first two lines; and the last four transitions are the bifurcations, as indicated by the letter B at the beginning of the remaining lines.

18   Scientific Applications of the Process-Grammar

As soon as I published the Process-Grammar in 1988, scientists began to apply it in several disciplines; e.g., radiology, meteorology, computer vision, chemical engineering, geology, computer-aided design, anatomy, botany, forensic science, software engineering, urban planning, linguistics, mechanical engineering, computer graphics, art, semiotics, archaeology, anthropology, etc.

It is worth considering a number of applications here, to illustrate various concepts of the theory. In meteorology, Milios [9] used the Process-Grammar to analyze and monitor high-altitude satellite imagery in order to detect weather patterns. This allowed the identification of the forces involved; i.e., the forces go along the arrows. It then becomes possible to make substantial predictions concerning the future evolution of storms. This work was done in relation to the Canadian Weather Service.

It is worth also considering applications by Shemlon [11], in biology. Shemlon developed a continuous model of the grammar using an elastic string equation. For example, Fig 18 shows the backward time-evolution, provided by the equation. It follows the laws of the Process-Grammar. Notice how the shape goes back to a circle, as predicted in section 6. Fig 19 shows the corresponding tracks of the curvature extrema in that evolution. In this figure, one can see that the rules of the Process-Grammar mark the evolution stages. Shemlon applied this technique to analyze neuronal growth models, dental radiographs, electron micrographs and magnetic resonance imagery.

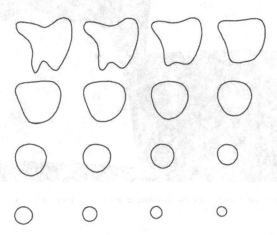

Fig. 18. Continuous realization of the Process-Grammar for biological applications, by Shemlon [11], using an elastic string equation.

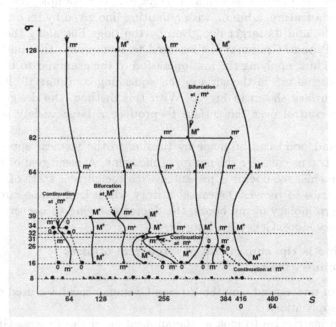

Fig. 19. Shemlon's use of the Process-Grammar to label the transitions in the above biological example.

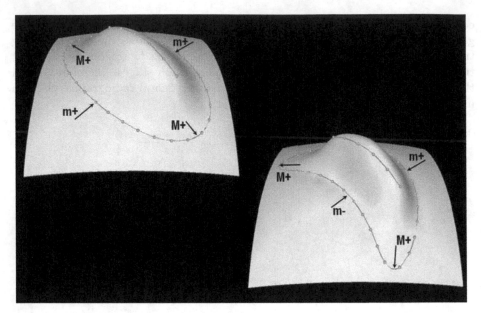

Fig. 20. Application of the Process-Grammar to computer-aided design by Pernot et al [10].

Let us now turn to an application by Pernot et al. [10] to the manipulation of free-form features in computer-aided design. Pernot's method begins by defining a limiting line for a feature as well as a target line. For example, the first surface in Fig 20 has a feature, a bump, with a limiting line given by its oval boundary on the surface, and its target line given by the ridge line along the top of the bump. The Process-Grammar is then used to manipulate the limiting line of the feature. Thus, applying the first operation of the grammar to the left-hand squashing process m^+ in the surface, this squashing continues till it indents in the second surface shown in Fig 20. With this method, the designer is given considerable control over the surface to produce a large variety of free-form features.

A profound point can be made by turning to the medical applications for illustration. Let us consider the nature of medicine. A basic goal of medicine is *diagnosis*. In this, the doctor is presented with the current state of, let's say, a tumor, and tries to *recover* the causal history which lead to the current state. Using the terminology of my books, the doctor is trying to *convert* the tumor into a memory store. Generally, I argue:

Medicine is the conversion of biological objects into memory stores.

Thus one can understand why the Process-Grammar has been used extensively in medical applications.

It is also instructive to look at the application of the Process-Grammar to chemical engineering by Lee [2]. Here the grammar was used to model molecular

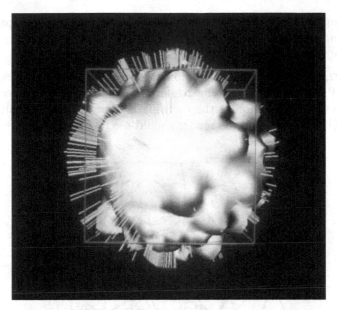

Fig. 21. Application of the Process-Grammar in molecular dynamics, by Lee [2].

dynamics – in particular, the dynamical interactions within mixtures of solvent and solute particles. Fig 21 represents the data shape, in *velocity space*, of a single solute molecule as it interacts with other molecules.

The initial data shape is given by a sphere (in velocity space). This is deformed by the successively incoming data in such a way that, at any time, one can use my curvature inference rules on the current shape, in order to infer the *history of the data*. In other words, one does not have to keep the preceding data – one can use the rules to *infer* it. Incidently, the lines in Fig 21 correspond to the axes associated with curvature extrema as predicted by the rules.

Lee stated that the advantage of basing the system on my rules was that inference can be made as to how the shape-altering "data-forces" have acted upon the data shape over the time course, thus giving insight into the nature of the computational force itself. In this, Lee shows a particularly deep understanding of my work. As I have said in my books, because the inference rules give a method of converting objects into memory stores, they give a method of *extending the computational system to include those objects as memory stores*.

19   Artistic Applications of the Process-Grammar

In section 18, we saw that the Process-Grammar has been applied by scientists in many disciplines. However, the grammar has also received applications in the arts. Here I will briefly discuss its application to the analysis of paintings: One of the chapters of my book *Symmetry, Causality, Mind* gives lengthy analyses of paintings showing the power of the grammar to reveal their compositional structures. In fact, one of the main arguments in my books is this:

**Paintings are structured by the rules of memory storage.
That is, the rules of artistic composition
are the rules of memory storage.**

In Fig 22, the rules for the extraction of history from curvature extrema, are applied to Picasso's *Still Life*. The reader can see that this gives considerable insight into the composition of the painting. For an extensive analysis of this painting and several others, the reader should see my books.

Fig. 22. Curvature extrema and their inferred processes in Picasso's *Still Life*.

20   Final Comment

This paper has shown only a small part of the extensive rule-system, developed in my books, for the inference of history from shape. The books elaborate several hundred rules, of which the Process-Grammar, given here, consists of only six. The rules are divided into systems which each take different properties of a shape as different sources of information of actions that determined the shape; i.e., in the same way that the Process-Grammar takes the curvature extrema as the information source.

As stated earlier, the rules give new foundations for geometry, which oppose the conventional foundations based on invariants. Invariants are those properties that do not store the effects of actions applied to them. The invariants program was defined in Euclid's concept of congruence, and generalized by Klein in the nineteenth century, to become the basis of modern mathematics and physics. In contrast, the new foundations elaborated in my books, take the opposite program, that of making geometry not the study of invariants, the memoryless properties, but making geometry the study of those properties from which past applied actions can be inferred, i.e., the memory stores.

References

1. Blum, H.: Biological shape and visual science. *Journal of Theoretical Biology*, **38**(1973) 205-287
2. Lee, J.P.:*Scientific Visualization with Glyphs and Shape Grammars*. Master's Thesis, School for Visual Arts, New York. (1991)
3. Leyton, M.: Symmetry-curvature duality. *Computer Vision, Graphics, and Image Processing, 38*, . (1987b) 327-341
4. Leyton, M.: A Limitation Theorem for the Differential Prototypification of Shape. *Journal of Mathematical Psychology, 31*. (1987d) 307-320
5. Leyton, M.: A Process-Grammar for Shape. *Artificial Intelligence, 34*. (1988) 213-247.
6. Leyton, M.: Inferring Causal-History from Shape. *Cognitive Science, 13*. (1989) 357-387
7. Leyton, M.:*Symmetry, Causality, Mind*. Cambridge, Mass: MIT Press. (1992)
8. Leyton, M.: *A Generative Theory of Shape*. Berlin: Springer-Verlag. (2001)
9. Milios, E.E.: Shape matching using curvature processes. *Computer Vision, Graphics, and Image Processing, 47*. (1989) 203-226.
10. Pernot, J-P., Guillet, S., Leon, J-C., Falcidieno, B., & Giannini, F.: Interactive Operators for free form features manipulation. In SIAM conference on CADG, Seattle, 2003. (2003)
11. Shemlon, S.: *The Elastic String Model of Non-Rigid Evolving Contours and its Applications in Computer Vision*. PhD Thesis, Rutgers University. (1994)

Spatial Cues in 3D Visualization

Geoffrey S. Hubona[1] and Gregory W. Shirah[2]

[1] Georgia State University, USA
ghubona@savannah.cis.gsu.edu
[2] NASA Goddard Space Flight Center, USA
greg.shirah@nasa.gov

1 Introduction

The ever-increasing power and complexity of available hardware and software has enabled the development of a wide variety of visualization techniques that allow the ever more concise presentation of data. Associated with this trend is the challenge to condense and convey ever-increasing amounts of useful information into smaller and smaller spaces. Depicting computer-generated visualizations in three dimensions (3D), similar to how we perceive the real world, is one approach to condense these visual presentations of information. However, there is an inherent dilemma in this approach; the visual medium on which the vast majority of 3D imagery is displayed is inherently two dimensional (2D): a flat computer monitor. Although there are some immersive or 'true 3D devices' on the market, such as the fishbow rotating display, the LCD layered 3D monitor, and 3D displays marketed by companies such as SeeReal Technologies, most of these devices are either too small or too expensive for the average user.

Humans visually discover and interact with their environment by: (1) perceiving visual information; (2) recognizing the "external source" of the information; and (3) interpreting its meaning and significance. The process of human perception and the interpretation of visual information is extremely complex, involving many levels of anatomical, neurochemical and psychophysical processing in vision and cognition. The human eye does not operate like a camera, but rather serves as an 'optical interface' between the external environment and the internal neural components of human vision and cognition which convey the basic visual attributes of form, field, color, motion, and depth. It is the design of computer visualizations to promote the accurate understanding of the relative depths (e.g. in the 'z' dimension) of objects that is particularly challenging.

The visual cues that enable us to perceive depth have been extensively documented. However, the use of these cues, and the combination of these cues, to effectively convey depth information in computer-generated imagery is still an ongoing topic of contemporary research. Depth cues are often placed into two categories: (1) primary depth cues, with a physiological basis, that include binocular disparity (which enables stereopsis), convergence and accommodation; and (2) secondary (or pictorial) cues, including texture and texture gradients, shading and shadow, relative motion, occlusion, reference frames, linear and aerial perspective, height in plane (or elevation), apparent size, and others (please see [1] and [2] for a complete discussion of primary and secondary depth cues).

Y. Cai (Ed.): Ambient Intelligence for Scientific Discovery, LNAI 3345, pp. 104–128, 2005.

Examining basic perceptual techniques that promote the design of realistic 3D computer-generated imagery is directly relevant to the topic of ambient intelligence for scientific discovery. This visualization topic addresses questions and issues such as: (1) How do we significantly reduce information while maintaining meaning? (2) How do we enhance the perception of patterns from massive and growing data resources? and (3) How do we design common information spaces for collaboration enabled by 2D and 3D interfaces?

In this chapter, we survey recent human computer interaction (HCI) and perceptual research that examines the relative efficacies of different depth cues in promoting an understanding of the spatial relationships of objects visually presented in 2D and 3D visual environments. Some of the spatial relationships include the relative sizes, shapes and positions of abstract objects presented in visualized scenes. The depth cues that we closely examine include motion, stereopsis, shadowing techniques, and scene background characteristics. We also review the impact of gender as it affects the perceptual understanding of these basic spatial relationships of objects presented in 2D and 3D visualizations. Finally, we conclude the chapter with a summary discussion of conclusions and recommendations for future visualization research in this area.

2   Problem and Issues

System-level interaction design for scientific discovery has gained recent attention as a result of potential payoffs in applications ranging from biomedical discovery, earth science, nano-materials and telecommunications. With the availability of growing volumes of visual data, there is the opportunity to develop novel ambient interfaces and interaction methods that maximize the user's discovery and understanding of the visual information. One challenge in this regard is to leverage what is known about human perception so as to design these interfaces in a way that the typical viewer can intuitively extract the greatest amount of accurate, relevant information.

For example, the National Aeronautics and Space Administration (NASA) has routinely stored terabytes of visual information about the Earth's surface, atmospheric and oceanic conditions that has been downloaded from satellites orbiting our planet. But the challenge is: How can we best present this visual information to the general public in such a way that it can be used most effectively for educational and other purposes? As another example, immersive technologies often utilize the characteristics of objects that 'pop up' in the users' field of view to represent information about that virtual world. In these cases, an important issue is: How do we visually present these objects such that most users can readily perceive and understand the information presented? To address and inform these issues, basic research regarding the human perception of visual information and objects presented in artificial 2D and 3D worlds is warranted.

2.1   Background

To create computer visualizations that effectively promote the perception, discovery and understanding of spatial arrangements of displayed objects (that can represent data or other information), it is useful to draw from established theory that explains how we naturally and effectively perceive objects in the real world. How does our perceptual and cognitive systems ascertain the relative depths and understand the spatial relationships of objects that are viewed in our natural environment? This issue becomes more complicated when there are multiple sources of information that may incrementally support (or conflict with) our cognitive assessments of the relative sizes, positions, and orientations of objects viewed in space.

Cue Theory. [1–5] maintains that the human visual system infers the distance of environmental objects based on information relating to the posture of the eyes and to visual patterns projected onto our retinas. The operative visual depth cues that serve these purposes are many and varied, and are often placed into the two categories of primary and secondary cues discussed in the Introduction to this chapter. The general tenets of cue theory, that these primary and secondary cues impact our perception and understanding of the relative spatial attributes of objects viewed in space, are widely accepted. However, the particular processes used by the visual system in selecting and/or combining multiple depth cues to arrive at a singular, stable perception of the depth of objects in space are widely debated. What happens when there are multiple cues that complement (or conflict with) each other in providing information about the depth of objects seen within our visual fields? In these circumstances, there are at least two countervailing views [3–5], that the perceptual system: (1) selects certain cues that dominate over other cues; or (2) integrates the multiple available cues, fostering a perception of depth that is incrementally affected by each individual cue. Additionally, there are variants of both the selection and integration approaches.

Two variants of the selection approach include vetoing and fusion models. In [3], they suggested a vetoing mechanism that is operative when conflicting information is provided by multiple cues. In these situations, the more dominant depth cue simply overrides the effect of the weaker cue(s) and the perception of depth is provided by the stronger cue alone. Furthermore, [3] and [4] discuss weak and strong fusion mechanisms that combine characteristics of both the selection and integration approaches. In the weak fusion model, depth information is cognitively processed separately from each cue, and subsequently combined in a weighted linear manner to produce an overall depth effect. In strong fusion, there is a non-linear interaction among multiple depth cues. As an example, one cue may work to disambiguate information, allowing depth information to be extracted from another cue.

Two variants of the integration approach include additive and multiplicative models. In [5], they provide an comprehensive summary of the additive and multiplicative depth cue integration approaches. However, the crux of the additive model is that depth information provided by multiple individual cues is aggregated such that additional cues always provide more information about depth. In contrast, the multiplicative model maintains that there is a synergy among multiple depth cues which creates either a "greater than" or a "lesser than" overall effect. Thus, instead of multiple cues incrementally adding more information about depth, the multiple cues interact, and may, in the aggregate, provide more, or less, perceptual information about the depth of objects seen within our visual fields.

2.2 Key Depth Cue Concepts

Motion. The typical human perceptual experience occurs within a context of nested motions. The movement of the eyes, as well as the movement of objects, provide important perceptual cues about the environmental and spatial properties of objects perceived in space.

Motion, or motion parallax, has previously been demonstrated to be a powerful depth cue [6–11]. However, there is conflicting evidence whether user-controlled object motion provides more depth information than uncontrolled motion. In [12], they reported no differences in performance due to controlled and uncontrolled motion, whereas [8] reported improved performances with user-controlled motion. Furthermore, there is evidence that it does not matter whether the object or the observer is moving [13]. Research has indicated that the motion cue can be introduced simply through the observer's own head movement [14, 15]. For example, [16] and [17] reported that introducing the motion cue through the use of head-tracking displays had performance effects as powerful as stereo viewing.

Stereopsis. Stereopsis, or the perception of stereoscopic images, is enabled by the physiological condition of binocular disparity. Because human eyes are positioned approximately six centimeters apart, an environmental object that is viewed with both eyes within a distance of about thirty meters projects two separate and displaced images onto the retinas of the left and right eyes. The brain fuses these two images, and in the process, the viewer is provided with significant depth cues regarding the relative size, shape, orientation and distance of the viewed object. However, we nevertheless perceive depth, and can make reasonable estimates about the relative sizes and locations of even the most distant objects viewed in our environment. Thus, stereoscopic viewing is not the only effective visual mechanism for perceiving depth.

Human performance in a variety of task domains using stereoscopic user interfaces has been previously investigated. Relevant domains and tasks have included the viewing, manipulation, and/or recognition of object images [7, 8, 12, 18–22]; relative depth perception [23]; medicine [9]; and cockpit situational awareness [24–26]. Stereo viewing has been demonstrated to be a powerful visual cue for understanding depth information [27, 28], and is sometimes used as a baseline condition for assessing the relative efficacies of other 2D and 3D visualization techniques [8, 16, 19, 20].

Studies have demonstrated task performance advantages from stereo viewing, particularly in perceiving, recognizing, grasping, moving, positioning and resizing objects viewed in depth, as well as in recognizing and understanding object shapes [8, 9, 12, 18–22, 29]. Nevertheless, it is not universally accepted that stereoscopic viewing is a predominant depth cue [7]. Some researchers have suggested that the benefits of stereo viewing are task-specific [21, 30]. However, there is largely a consensus that stereo viewing is a powerful, and perhaps dominant, depth cue for engaging in a variety of tasks involving the spatial manipulation of objects perceived in depth.

Shadows. The application of lighting techniques to promote realism and to improve the perception and understanding of computer visualizations has many approaches, including luminance, ambient and diffuse lighting, specular high-lights, object surface shading, and attached and cast shadows, to name just a few. Because contemporary hardware has just recently become powerful enough to easily compute and render realtime, moving objects casting shadows cre-ated by different (unseen) light sources on various background surfaces, this issue has not been fully explored in contemporary human factors visualiza-tion research. (For a thorough online summary of research in this area, see http://artis.imag.fr/Recherche/RealTimeShadows/index.html).

In [31], he distinguished between two types of object shadows: the primary or attached shadow created when the shadow of an object is visible on that same object (sometimes called 'self-shadowing'); and the derived or cast shadow, cre-ated when the shadow of one object is visible on a different object or background surface. Attached shadows are created by the surface anomalies of an object that self-shade other surface areas of that same object relative to some light source. In contrast, cast shadows are created by a light-occluding object positioned be-tween the light source and another detached, but otherwise illuminated, object surface. Yonas [31] was one of the first to demonstrate that both attached and cast shadows can affect the perceived relative size, shape, elevation, and depth of a object viewed within a scene. However, because shadows cast by moving objects 'cascade' over objects and surfaces that are displaced at various distances and orientations from the light-occluding object, cast shadows are potentially more useful than attached shadows for extracting depth information about objects viewed in the scene.

Scene Background Complexity. It has been demonstrated that complex scene backgrounds impede spatial task performances, especially in the presence of objects casting shadows [19]. However, in that experiment, background scene complexity was manipulated by varying the entire *configuration* of the back-ground (i.e. flat floor with no walls, 'stair-step' floor with no walls, or room with walls). In a subsequent experiment [20], they manipulated the (simple or com-plex) characteristics of room walls (as textured and/or 'zig-zag') that contained the visual worlds. They again reported that more complex background scenery can impair understanding the spatial characteristics and relationships of objects depicted in 2D and 3D space. Studies [32, 33] have discussed forces that can help or hinder task performances that require the integration of depth cues that are in close proximity. Specifically, they state that increased perceptual *information access cost* (IAC) can disrupt performance. They state [33]: "when noise or vi-sual clutter is close to relevant indicators, it will disrupt the movement of visual attention to the indicator, often imposing greater uncertainty as to where the target is located."

Gender. Researchers have long acknowledged the relevance of gender as impacting human computer interaction. Gender has been regarded as an important factor affecting: computer skills and computer design issues [34]; the design of user interfaces [35]; and the achievement of the 'universal usability' of internet-based and other computer services [36]. It has been demonstrated that men and women report different perceptions and preferences with respect to the use and satisfaction of electronic commerce web site features [38].

Furthermore, gender differences in both innate (e.g. cognitive test scores) and applied (e.g. external task-oriented) cognitive abilities have been actively studied for decades. Although cognitive task performances of men and women have been shown to overlap considerably [38], and although some studies report that women outperform men in many aspects of verbal ability [39, 40], many studies report that men outperform women in certain spatial tasks [40–44].

Differences between the genders performing spatial tasks are generally attributed to innate gender differences in cognitive spatial abilities. Prominent meta-analytic studies [45, 46] have indicated higher male scores on certain cognitive spatial tests, but individual studies report inconsistent results in this regard. Assessing differences between the genders in spatial abilities is also complicated by the fact that the different studies often use different test instruments to measure so-called 'spatial ability.' To clarify this issue, Linn and Petersen [45] categorized the cognitive test instruments used in the literature into three distinct groups, including those that measure: (1) *spatial perception*; (2) *mental rotation*; and (3) *spatial visualization*. 'Spatial perception' is described as "the ability to determine spatial relations despite distracting information." 'Mental rotation' is the ability to quickly and accurately imagine the rotation of two- and three-dimensional figures. 'Spatial visualization' refers to "the ability to manipulate complex spatial information when several stages are needed to produce the correct solution." Using these categories, meta-analyses [45, 46] have concluded that men score higher than women on *spatial perception* and *mental rotation* tests, but that there are no aggregate gender differences on *spatial visualization* cognitive test scores.

One theory that offers an evolutionary perspective on contemporary gender differences in innate spatial abilities is the hunter-gatherer theory of the origin of gender-specific spatial attributes [47]. This theory suggests that ancient differentiated sex roles from prehistoric times are responsible for modern-day men and women having different cognitive skill predispositions. According to this theory, prehistoric women, or 'gatherers,' who were effective at foraging for food, and who were successful at keeping track of relationships, activities, objects, locations, and landmarks near their habitats, were also successful at acquiring resources for bearing and raising offspring. Moreover, prehistoric males, or 'hunters,' who were better at traveling through unfamiliar territory, estimating distance, and generally at navigating with a 'bird's eye view' orientation were, as a consequence, more successful at hunting, competing with other males, finding mates, and, consequently, at fathering children.

Through evolutionary selection, the 'hunter-gatherer' theory maintains that these male-female predispositions in cognitive abilities persist today. In support of this theory, there is evidence that contemporary females exhibit superior performance to males on spatial tasks mimicking foraging-related activities, such as remembering the location of landmarks in their environment [48]. In addition, it has been shown that women are better than men at keeping track of objects, and at finding objects that are lost [47, 49]. Moreover, studies report that women remember the locations of previously viewed items better than men [50], and that women are better than men at remembering the locations of specific objects [51]. In contrast, men generally outperform women at spatial tasks involving the manipulation of objects in space [45, 52–57]. Furthermore, studies have shown that men are better than women at 'mental rotation' spatial abilities [48, 58], reportedly as an evolutionary artifact of the ability to track an animal through unfamiliar terrain and then expeditiously navigate their way home.

3   Approach

We report three experiments in which subjects perform visual, spatial tasks using 2D and 3D 'virtual worlds.' The first experiment is an object matching experiment and the second and third experiments require subjects to reposition and to resize objects viewed in space against some predefined standard. The three experiments were designed to manipulate similar conditions under different task circumstances such that comprehensive conclusions could be drawn regarding the efficacy of particular depth cues in promoting spatial task performances.

3.1   Experiment #1: Object Matching

Method. The object matching experiment [8] utilized a variant of the mental rotation paradigm [59]. Subjects were presented with pairs of object images at different angles and orientations and the task was to determine whether the two objects were identical or different. Figures 1 through 4 show examples of the four types of solid and wire frame, cubical and spherical object images. Figure 1 also depicts the experimental user interface with "start," "same" and "different" buttons embedded. One half of the presented image pairs were identical and the other half were different. The left object of each pair was always stationary and the right object was always in motion. In one half of the trials, subjects controlled the motion of the right object by rotating it around the center point in any direction. In the remaining trials, the right object rotated automatically in a fixed direction and speed.

Design. The experiment used a within-subjects design, manipulating the independent variables: viewing mode (stereo, mono); type of motion (controlled, uncontrolled); object surface characteristic (wire frame, solid); and object shape characteristic (cube, sphere). Stereo viewing was achieved using CrystalEyes stereoscopic glasses. The measured dependent variables included error rate, the

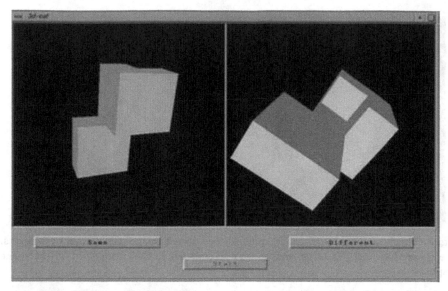

Fig. 1. Subjects were presented with pairs of object images. The above is a solid cube-based image pair with "start," "same" and "different" user interface buttons embedded. One half of the presented image pairs were identical and the other half were different. The left image was always stationary and the right image was always capable of motion.

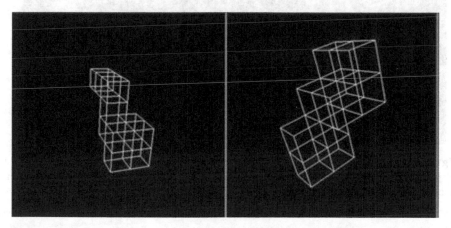

Fig. 2. This is an example of wire-frame cube-based object image pair viewed by subjects. There is no opaque surface on the wire-frame images, permitting subjects to "see through" the objects.

percentage of incorrect responses, and response time, measured in milliseconds. The test software, developed in the C++ programming language and SGI's Open Inventor graphics toolkit, automatically recorded repeated measures of the dependent variables. Fourteen female and sixteen male professional employees of the Goddard Space Flight Center (GSFC) volunteered as subjects. Although this subject population may not be a representative sample of the general popula-

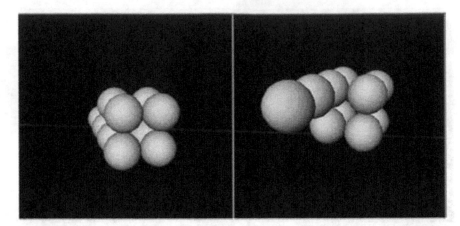

Fig. 3. This is an example of a solid sphere-based object image pair viewed by subjects. The sphere-based object image shapes were in contrast to the cube-based object image shapes.

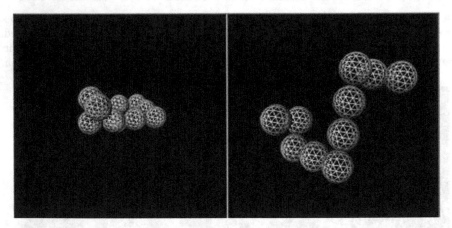

Fig. 4. This is an example of a wire frame sphere-based object image pair viewed by subjects. As in Fig. 2, wire-frame object surfaces enabled subjects to "see through" each object.

tion, they comprised a 'visualization-savvy' subject pool, and, as such, represent the 'strong case' for generalizing the results. Each subject engaged in four sets of fifty two trials each, for a total of 208 observations per subject. Each subject was presented with the same 208 image pairs, and each image pair was unique, although the presentation order varied.

Results. The data were fitted to a repeated measures multivariate analysis of variance model (MANOVA). The MANOVA model tested each of the four main effects (viewing mode, type of motion, surface characteristic and object shape) on the error rate and response time dependent variable measures. There were significant differences (at the 95% confidence level) in the mean values of the error rate and response time measures as a function of three main effects: viewing mode; type of motion; and surface characteristic. The main effect of the (cube or sphere) object shape was not significant with respect to error rate nor response time.

The mean error rate across all experimental trials was 11.04%. The mean overall response time per image pair was 13.01 seconds. Subjects viewing image pairs in stereo made fewer errors, and responded more quickly, than did subjects viewing the image pairs in mono. Moreover, subjects controlling the object motion of the right-hand object image were more accurate, although they took longer to make their object comparison decisions, than did the subjects who did not control this motion. Furthermore, subjects viewing wire frame images took longer to complete trials than did subjects viewing solid objects, although they were no more nor less accurate in their object matching judgments. Complete quantitative results will be provided by requesting same from the lead author of this chapter.

3.2   Experiment #2:
Object Positioning and Resizing in Virtual Worlds

Method. The second experiment involved object positioning and resizing tasks in 2D and 3D 'virtual worlds' [19]. In the positioning task, subjects were presented with object images arranged to outline the vertices of larger, symmetrical figures, either cubes or octahedrons. The task was to reposition the misplaced vertex object in the x, y and z dimensions, as quickly and accurately as possible, so as to complete the symmetrical arrangement (see Figs. 5 and 6). In the resizing task, the vertex objects were correctly positioned, but one of the objects was either larger or smaller than the remaining objects (see Fig.. 7). The task was to resize this object, as quickly and accurately as possible, to make it correspond with the uniform size of the other objects. In both the positioning and resizing tasks, subjects used a spaceball input device to manipulate (i.e. move or resize) the target objects. A 'spaceball' is a six-degrees-of-freedom input device that has a large round, graspable ball mounted on a flat base. In the positioning task, the spaceball was programmed such that 'pushing' or 'pulling' the ball forward, backward, up or down, or in any direction caused the selected object on the screen to move in that corresponding direction. In the resizing task, the spaceball was programmed such that 'pushing' forward, or 'pulling' backward, caused the selected object to increase, or decrease in size, respectively.

Design. The positioning and resizing virtual world experiment also used a within-subjects, repeated measures design, manipulating the independent variables: shadows (on, off); number of shadow-casting light sources (one, two); viewing mode (stereo, mono); and scene background (flat plane, room, 'stair-step' plane). The number of shadow casting light sources was a condition nested within the shadows on condition. The dependent variables included error magnitude and response time. Error magnitude for the positioning task was defined as

Fig. 5. This is an example of an initial virtual world positioning task trial in a "room with walls" scene background with each object casting one shadow. The task was to reposition the misplaced sphere so as to outline a larger, isometric cube figure. The spheres in this example outline the vertices, or corners, of the larger, isometric cube figure.

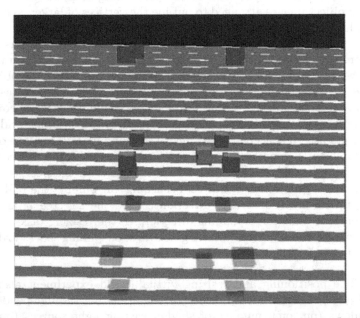

Fig. 6. This is an example of an initial virtual world positioning task trial over a "stair-step" scene background with each object casting one shadow. The task was to reposition the misplaced cube so as to outline a larger, isometric cube figure. Once correctly placed, the cubes in this example outline the vertices, or corners, of a larger, isometric cube figure.

Fig. 7. This is an example of an initial virtual world resizing task trial over a "stair-step" scene background with objects casting no shadows. The task was to resize the larger sphere so as to match the size of the remaining spheres, some of which were displaced in depth. The spheres in this example outline the vertices of an octahedron.

the Euclidean summation of the three directional errors in the x, y, and z dimensions (i.e. error magnitude $= (e_x^2 + e_y^2 + e_z^2)^{1/2}$). This metric constitutes the exact distance of the repositioned object from its correct position in three dimensional space. Error magnitude for the resizing task was defined as the absolute value of the error in length of either the radius (in task trials using spheres as vertex objects) or the diagonal (in task trials using cubes or tetrahedrons as vertex objects) of the resized object. Trial completion time was the period of time, measured in milliseconds, from when the scene first appeared until the subject pushed a button on the spaceball, causing the next scene to appear. Written in the C programming language and OpenGL, repeated measures of the dependent variables were automatically recorded by the task trial software. There were a total of 288 trials per subject, 144 trials for each task. All subjects viewed the same 288 scenes, although the presentation order varied. The volunteer subject population consisted of 14 male and 16 female professional employees of GSFC.

One half of all trials randomly presented shadows on, and the remaining trials presented shadows off. In the shadows on condition, one half of the trials randomly used one light source to produce the shadows, and the remaining trials used two light sources. One half of all trials were viewed in stereo, and the remaining trials were viewed in mono. One third of the background conditions randomly used a flat plane for the scene background; one third used the room; and the remaining third used the 'stair-step' plane.

In all positioning and resizing task trials, the location of the misplaced or incorrectly sized vertex was randomly located with respect to the other vertices. In addition, light sources were consistently positioned 'from above' and at various angles from the zenith. Moreover, in trials with two light sources, their angle of separation varied from trial to trial. Thus, the relative locations and separation of the light sources changed from trial to trial.

Results. The data was again analyzed by fitting a repeated measures MANOVA model to the experimental observations. The MANOVA model tested each of the four main effects (shadows on/off, viewing mode, number of shadow-casting lights, and background) on the error magnitude and response time dependent variables. The data from the positioning and resizing tasks were segregated and analyzed separately. In both the positioning and resizing tasks performance data, there were significant differences (at the 95% confidence level) in the mean values of the dependent variables (error magnitude and response time) as a function of all four main effects: use of shadows; viewing mode; number of shadowing lights; and scene background. Complete quantitative results for both the positioning and resizing tasks will be provided by requesting same from the lead author.

In the positioning task with shadows on, subjects were more accurate, although they took *longer* to position the misplaced vertex object than when there was no shadow present. Moreover, subjects viewing the vertex objects in stereo were more accurate and faster performing the positioning task than they were when viewing the virtual worlds in mono. Also, subjects viewing the vertex objects shadowed by two lights sources were *less* accurate and took *more* time than they were when viewing the vertex objects shadowed by one light source. Subjects viewing the vertex objects in a room, or over a flat plane background were more accurate than were subjects viewing the vertex objects over the stair-step background. The error magnitude difference between the room and plane background conditions was not significant. Furthermore, subjects viewing the objects over a stair-step background took more time performing the positioning task than did subjects viewing the objects in a room or over a flat plane background. The difference in the response times between the room and flat plane scene background conditions was not significant.

In the resizing task with shadows on, there was no difference in resizing accuracy, but subjects *took longer* resizing the vertex objects using shadows than they did without the shadows. Furthermore, subjects viewing the scenes in stereo were more accurate and faster than they were viewing the scenes in mono. There was no difference in accuracy with shadows created by two lights compared to one light source, although subjects viewing the objects shadowed by two light sources took more time performing the resizing task than they did when viewing the objects shadowed by one light source. Finally, the scene background also significantly impacted subjects' resizing task performances, but only with respect to resizing accuracy, not response time. Subjects viewing the vertex objects in a room were more accurate than they were when viewing the objects over either a flat plane or stair-step background condition. The differences in the response times among the three scene background conditions were not significant.

3.3   Experiment #3:
Object Positioning and Resizing in Virtual Rooms

Method. The third experiment involved object positioning and resizing tasks in 2D and 3D 'virtual rooms' [20]. These virtual rooms were bounded by four surfaces: a floor, and left, right and rear walls. The objects to be manipulated

Fig. 8. This is an example of an initial positioning task trial with no shadow in a room with a flat background surface of solid texture. The task was to reposition the misplaced sphere so as to create a straight line vector segment with one sphere located exactly at the midpoint of the straight line segment.

Fig. 9. This is an example of an initial resizing task trial with one shadow in a room with a flat background surface of solid texture. The task was to resize the smaller sphere so as to match the size of the other larger sphere displaced in depth.

were resident within this 'virtual room.' It was similar to the second experiment, but differed in several respects: (1) it utilized different positioning and resizing tasks; (2) subjects could rotate (i.e. move) their view of each virtual room 45

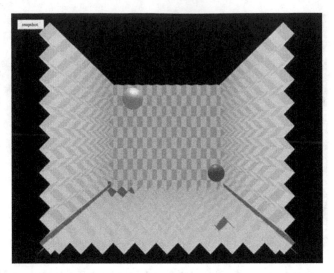

Fig. 10. This is an example of an initial resizing task trial with one shadow in a room with a 'zig-zag' background surface of checkerboard texture. The task was to resize the smaller sphere so as to match the size of the other slightly larger sphere displaced in depth.

degrees in either the left or right directions; (3) the target and referent objects were always displaced at different distances, or depths (i.e. the z dimension), from the viewer; (4) the experimental trial software created 2D and 3D 'virtual rooms' instead of 'virtual worlds;' and (5) the shadow condition always used exactly one (unseen) light source, fixed and stationary at the azimuth position. In the positioning task, subjects viewed 'virtual rooms' containing three equally-sized, spherical objects suspended in space (see Fig. 8). Subjects were asked to reposition one of the spheres, the target object, in 3D space (i.e. in the x, y and z dimensions) as quickly and accurately as possible so as to symmetrically complete a straight line segment (or vector/vector segment) characterized as three spheres located equidistant from each other. In each positioning trial solution, the correctly placed spheres always subtended an oblique angle from the viewer's perspective, so that each of the three spheres were displaced at different depths from the viewer.

In the resizing task, subjects viewed 'virtual rooms' containing two differently-sized spheres suspended in 3D space (see Figs. 9 and 10). Unlike the positioning task, in the resizing task, the objects were fixed in position. Subjects were asked to adjust the size of the target object, as quickly and accurately as possible, to make it correspond with the perceived size of the referent object. The target and referent spheres were always positioned at different depths from the viewer, and were always presented in different, and random, sizes and locations, relative to each other. In one half of the trials, the target sphere was initially larger than the referent, and in the other half of the trials, initially smaller. Consequently, from trial to trial, subjects were randomly increasing, or decreasing, the size of the target sphere. In both the positioning and resizing tasks, subjects manipulated the target objects using a spaceball input device.

Design. The positioning and resizing virtual room experiment again used a within-subjects design, manipulating the independent variables: *viewing mode* (stereo, mono); *number of shadows cast by objects* (none, one); *background scene surface shape* (flat, zig-zag); and *background scene surface texture* (solid, checkerboard). The dependent variable performance measures included: accuracy, measured as *error magnitude*; completion time, measured as *response time*; and scene *rotational distance*, measured as the total number of degrees that a subject rotated the scene in either a left or right direction. Distance error magnitude for the positioning task was again defined as the Euclidean summation of the three directional errors in the x, y, and z dimensions (i.e. distance error magnitude $= (e_x^2 + e_y^2 + e_z^2)^{1/2}$). Radius error magnitude for the resizing task was defined as the absolute value of the difference between the radius length of the resized target sphere compared to the radius length of the correctly-sized referent sphere. Trial completion time was the period of time, measured in milliseconds, from when the scene first appeared until the subject pushed a button on the spaceball, causing the next scene to appear. The positioning and resizing task trials consisted of 144 unique virtual room scenes presented in random order to the subjects.

The volunteer subject population consisted of 16 male and 14 female professional employees of GSFC. For each subject, one half of all trials were viewed in stereo, with the remaining trials viewed in mono. One half of the trials randomly presented scenes with no shadow, and the remaining trials had one shadow cast by each object. In all scenes utilizing cast shadows, the shadow-casting lighting position was fixed and stationary, directly overhead at the azimuth position. One half of all trials randomly presented a 'flat' background scene surface, characterized as a three-walled 'room' with a flat floor and walls (see Figs. 8 or 9). Similarly, one half of the trials randomly presented a 'zig-zag' background scene surface, characterized as a room with a 'corrugated' floor and walls (see Fig. 10). Also, one half of the scenes were presented with a solid background surface texture (see Figs. 8 or 9), whereas the remaining scenes appeared with a checkerboard texture (see Fig. 10).

Results. The data was again analyzed by fitting a repeated measures MANOVA model to the performance measures. The MANOVA model tested each of the four main effects (viewing mode, presence of cast shadows, background scene surface shape, and background scene surface texture) on the error magnitude, response time and rotational distance dependent variable performance measures. In the positioning task performance data, there were significant differences (at the 95% confidence level) in the mean values of the dependent variables (distance error magnitude, response time and rotational distance) as a function of all four main effects. In the resizing task performance data, there were significant differences (at the 95% confidence level) in the mean values of the dependent variables (distance error magnitude, response time and rotational distance) as a function of three of the four main effects. However, objects casting shadows did not significantly influence subjects' resizing performance measures. Complete quantitative results for both the positioning and resizing tasks will be provided by requesting same from the lead author.

In the positioning task, subjects viewing the objects in stereo were more accurate, faster, and used less rotational distance than when positioning objects viewed in mono. With objects casting a shadow, subjects were more accurate, took more time, and used less rotational distance than when positioning objects viewed with no cast shadows. While positioning objects against a (more complex) zig-zag background surface shape, subjects were equally accurate, but took more time and used less rotational distance than when positioning objects against a (more simple) flat background surface shape. Finally, while positioning objects against a (more complex) checker-board background texture, subjects were equally accurate, but again took more time and used less rotational distance than when positioning objects against a (more simple) solid background texture.

In the resizing task, subjects viewing the objects in stereo were more accurate, faster, and used less rotational distance than when resizing objects viewed in mono. Objects casting shadows had no significant effect on the resizing performance measures. While resizing objects against a (more complex) zig-zag background surface shape, subjects were less accurate, took more time, and used less rotational distance than when resizing objects against a (more simple) flat background surface shape. Finally, while resizing objects against a (more complex) checkerboard background texture, subjects were equally accurate, but again took more time and used less rotational distance than when resizing objects against a (more simple) solid background texture.

4   Results Summary

Instead of summarizing the results across the three experiments together, we summarize the results for each of the depth cues of interest separately in the sections that follow. In general, stereo viewing was the most effective cue for enhancing performance in each task. However, motion was 'a close second' in this regard. Finally, we discuss a limited number of salient implications for the design of effective 2D and 3D user interfaces and for depth cue theory in Section 5: Conclusions and Discussion.

4.1   Motion

Motion is a powerful depth cue that rivals stereo viewing in providing information about the relative distances of viewed objects. Consequently, motion, in general, can enhance spatial task performances and can provide useful information about the spatial properties (such as size, orientation, distance) of objects viewed in space. However, the utility of motion in promoting spatial task performances is also a function of the task type, and is tied to individual characteristics, as well (for example, see the discussion of gender that follows).

The incorporation of motion cues in visual activities can take many forms, from moving or rotating a viewed object, to moving or changing the perspective of the viewer, to moving or rotating the entire field of view. In general, motion enables parallax, which is instrumental in stereo viewing. In our three experiments, we incorporated several types of motion: (1) controlled versus uncontrolled motion (in the object matching experiment); (2) moving the viewed objects themselves (in the positioning tasks of both the 'virtual world' and 'virtual room' experiments); and (3) moving, or rotating, the viewed scenes (in both the positioning and resizing 'virtual room' experimental tasks). To summarize our observations about the effects of motion on these spatial task performances:

1. Controlling the motion of the rotating object in the mental rotation experiment enabled more accurate object recognition and object matching performances. However, subjects took longer judging whether the objects were the same or different when they controlled this motion. However, we can conclude that motion improved the quality of their object recognition and matching judgments.
2. Moving the objects (especially in the presence of a cast shadow) in both positioning tasks of the 'virtual world' and 'virtual room' experiments was instrumental in providing distance (i.e. depth) information about the target object, especially in relation to the other (stationary) objects in each scene.
3. The ability to left- and right-rotate the 'virtual room' scenes was used to a much greater degree to extract depth information when other available depth cues were diminished.

Stating this last point differently, 'virtual room' scenes, in both the positioning and resizing tasks, were always rotated more when there was less depth information available from the other cues present. That is, the scenes were rotated more when viewed: (1) in mono compared to stereo; (2) with no shadow, compared to one shadow, present; and (3) when the rooms were viewed against the more simple flat surface shape or solid texture characteristics, compared to the more complex 'zig-zag' surface shape or checkerboard textures. We observe that the rotational distance depth cue was used to supplement, or directly substitute, depth information as it became less available from other existing cues.

4.2   Stereo Viewing

Stereo viewing was a dominant and powerful depth cue for promoting task performances in all three experiments. While viewing scenes in stereo, in comparison to mono viewing, subjects were consistently more accurate and faster: (1) recognizing and matching objects shapes in the first experiment; and (2) positioning and resizing objects in both the second and third experiments. Furthermore, in the third experiment, subjects relied less on the rotational distance depth cue in the presence of stereo viewing. In short, stereo viewing consistently supported every aspect of the spatial task performance measures in these three controlled experiments.

We conclude that stereo viewing is a dominant depth cue for spatial task performances of these kinds. Consequently, it may be more useful to test stereo viewing conditions as a baseline against which to measure the relative efficacy of other perceptual cues, rather than testing the effects of stereo viewing per se.

4.3   Shadows

Objects casting shadows can provide more depth information about the relative positions of objects viewed in space. When moving and positioning objects that are casting shadows, the viewer recovers information about the location of the object through the geometry that is implied by the position of the object's shadow on the background surface.

However, the utility of shadows to improve spatial task performances in 2D and 3D visual scenes is focused and limited. In our experiments, shadows were most useful for enhancing object positioning (and not resizing) performances when the scenes were viewed monoscopically, in 2D. The contributions of shadows to the enhancement of object positioning performances when the scenes were viewed in 'true 3D' stereo were negligible. Furthermore, when the object shadows were cast on increasingly complex background surfaces and textures, positioning task performances suffered. Also, shadows were useful only when there was one light source. In scenes (in the 'virtual world' experiment) in which there were two light sources, positioning performances were diminished to the same level at which no shadows were present. Thus, there are caveats and limitations to the efficacy of cast shadows in promoting spatial task performances in general.

4.4   Scene Background Complexity

The findings of the 'virtual world' and 'virtual room' experiments both suggest that the introduction of more complex background scenery in visual 3D scenes can impair the perception and understanding of the spatial attributes of other objects contained within the scene. In general, having less complex detail in the scenery background promotes a better understanding of the relative positions and sizes of foreground objects. More complex background scenery introduces "perceptual clutter" that seemingly disrupts the visual attention afforded to foreground objects.

4.5   Gender

We deliberately balanced each of the three experiments by gender so that we could analyze the effects of gender on these particular spatial tasks performances. We expand the results originally presented in [60].

Table 1 summarizes relative task performances by gender. Males were more accurate and faster than females recognizing and matching object shapes. Consistent with the spatial abilities literature indicating a male advantage on mental rotation tasks, it is not surprising that the male subjects outperformed the

Table 1. Summary of gender-based differences in the experimental performance measures. We observed definite gender biases for performing particular spatial tasks that are largely consistent with existing literature. In our experiments, males excelled at tasks involving mental rotation (i.e. object matching) and object movement (i.e. object positioning), whereas females were more accurate resizing objects that were fixed in location.

Object Task:	Accuracy/Gender:	RT/Gender:	Rot. Dist./Gender:
Matching	Males more accurate	Males faster	Not Applicable
Positioning	Males more accurate	No M/F difference	Males use more
Resizing	Females more accurate	No M/F difference	Males use more

females in accurately and quickly matching objects. Moreover, controlling the motion of the right hand 'comparison object' significantly reduced male object matching error rates, but had no effect on female error rates. Furthermore, males were more accurate positioning objects, whereas females were more accurate resizing objects (although there were no significant differences in male-female response times for either of the positioning and resizing tasks). Also, males made more use of the rotational distance feature in both the positioning and resizing tasks, evidently finding the ability to rotate the objects more useful than did the females in attempting to position and resize the objects.

How do these findings suggest approaches to develop 'gender neutral' visual interfaces? One suggestion is to add meaningful landmarks and to diminish the viewer's reliance on 'spatial presence' and, particularly, on mental rotation ability. Visual interfaces that enable the stationary viewer to 'look right' or 'look left' (or up, down, backward, etc.) for familiar landmarks may be an effective, gender-neutral alternative to the use of typical motion cues, such as 'flying around' virtual spaces, to extract information from a scene. The reliance on motion cues, in particular, to extract information from the visual features of objects presented in a scene is especially problematic.

5   Conclusions and Discussion

What do these cumulative findings tell us about the relative efficacy of visual cues in extracting spatial information from visual objects and features presented in computer-generated scenery? Which depth cues are most important in this regard? How can we make use of these findings so as to better enable the perceptual discovery of information embedded and represented in 2D and 3D visual scenery and user interfaces?

With respect to extracting spatial information, especially regarding the relative depths and placements of objects, stereoscopic viewing was the most powerful and useful depth cue among those examined in these particular tasks. Motion cues are also useful in this regard, although there is evidence that motion is more useful for male, as compared to female, viewers. Moreover, it is clear that the relative efficacy of the individual depth cues tested are tied to the nature of the task. For example, the cast shadows were very useful for positioning objects, but not for resizing objects. So it is problematic to state that any one particular cue will be universally useful in all visual tasks. The nature of the task itself must also be considered.

Additional implications for the design of 3D user interfaces, particularly with respect to applications that involve positioning and resizing objects, include: (1) stereoscopic viewing is a powerful depth cue, superior to monoscopic viewing, and, overall, to the use of objects casting shadows, for enhancing positioning and resizing task performances; (2) shadows cast by objects can improve the accuracy of spatial task performances, particularly when those tasks entail the user-controlled motion of those objects; (3) introducing a cast shadow to a scene viewed in mono enhances positioning accuracy to a level equivalent to that of viewing the scene in stereo with no shadow present; and (4) increasingly complex background scenery tends to impede the performance of spatial tasks conducted against those backgrounds.

Additionally, there are implications for the design of 'virtual worlds.' One implication is that such virtual worlds should be simple and natural to the viewer. Users can more easily relate to what they are viewing when there is a minimum of complexity, particularly with respect to background surface characteristics. Another implication is that thorough and detailed task analyses should precede any design activity. User performance is maximized by first analyzing and detailing the immediate task requirements, and by then matching the characteristics of the available 2D and 3D interface features and cues to these requirements. A third implication is that navigational issues are a major concern. Certain bounded 3D environments, such as rooms, can greatly assist navigation. Additionally, the user-controlled motion of visible objects can be useful, not only to provide depth information, but also to assist the user in 'feeling around' the environment, and therefore supporting navigational needs. A final implication is that users' performances are better supported when objects in the scene are related by position to: background surfaces; other objects in the scene; and to the viewer's point of reference. Reference cues such as cast shadows (or objects otherwise 'touching' background surfaces and other objects), help in this regard.

Finally, how do these findings inform on the issue of whether the perceptual system *selects* or *integrates* depth cues to provide a stable and holistic sense of the spatial properties of objects presented visually in 2D and 3D scenes? Our findings do not suggest that one source of depth information simply takes precedence over others, a defining characteristic of the *selection* approach. Rather, our cumulative findings support an integrative framework: that different cues have different effects, depending on the task involved. Moreover, the statistically significant interactions among some of the viewing (depth cue) conditions suggests a *multiplicative* (as opposed to an *additive*) integrative approach to cue theory. Different cues have interactive 'greater than' or 'lesser than' effects on performance, largely related to characteristics of the task and of the individual viewer.

5.1   Recommendations for Future Research

More research is needed to assess the performance effects of additional 2D (pictorial) depth cues while interacting with visual computer applications. It would also be useful to assess the relative utilities of 2D cues as effective alternatives to primary, physiological 3D depth cues, such as stereopsis. As computer hardware and software continue to evolve in power and capabilities, a wider variety of alternative 2D cues become available for practical use. With the demonstrated power of stereo viewing as a dominant cue, there is a need for testing the efficacies of additional pictorial cues against this baseline 3D cue. The use of real time, moving object shadows to convey depth information is but one example of a 2D cue that was impractical to use just a few years ago.

Finally, we need more research investigating how depth cues are integrated in assisting visual, spatial task performances, particularly in tasks extracting information embedded in novel visualizations. To this end, it would be useful to work toward a taxonomy of prototypical visual tasks that are performed with computers, particularly those in which information is extracted from visual interfaces, and to develop conceptual and/or mathematical models explicating how particular cues, or sets of cues, are integrated so as to improve task performances.

References

1. Kelsey, C.A.: Detection of Visual Information. In: Hendee, W.R., Wells, P. (eds.): The Perception of Visual Information. Springer, New York (1993) 30-51
2. Gibson, J.J.: Perception of the Visual World. Houghton Mifflin, Boston (1950)
3. Johnston, E.B., Cumming, B.G., Parker, A.J.: Integration of Depth Modules: Stereopsis and Texture. Vision Research. 33 (1993) 813-826
4. Clark, J.J., Yuille, A.L.: Data Fusion for Sensory Information Processing Systems. Kluwer Academic Publishers, London (1990)
5. Cutting, J.E., Bruno, N., Brady, N.P., Moore, C.: Selectivity, Scope, and Simplicity of Models: A Lesson from Fitting Judgments of Perceived Depth. Journal of Experimental Psychology: General. 121 (1992) 364-381
6. Braunstein, M.L.: Depth Perception Through Motion. Academic Press, New York (1976)
7. Gallimore, J.J., Brown, M.E.: Visualization of 3-D Computer-Aided Design Objects. International Journal of Human-Computer Interaction. 5 (1993) 361-382
8. Hubona, G.S., Shirah, G.W., Fout, D.G.: The Effects of Motion and Stereopsis on Three-Dimensional Visualization. Int. J. Human-Computer Studies. 47 (1997) 609-627
9. Sollenberger, R.L., Milgram, P.: Effects of Stereoscopic and Rotational Displays in Three-Dimensional Path-Tracing Tasks. Human Factors. 35 (1993) 483-499
10. Todd, J.T.: Perception of Structure from Motion: Is Projective Correspondence of Moving Elements a Necessary Condition? Journal of Experimental Psychology: Human Perception and Performance. 11 (1985) 689-710
11. Wallach, H., O'Connell, D.H.: The Kinetic Depth Effect. Journal of Experimental Psychology. 45 (1953) 205-217
12. Ware, C., Franck, G.: Evaluating Stereo and Motion Cues for Visualizing Information Nets in Three Dimensions. ACM Transactions of Graphics. 15 (1996) 121-140

13. Van Damme, W.J.M., Van De Grind, W.A.: Active Vision and the Identification of Three-Dimensional Shape. Vision Research. 11 (1993) 1581-1587
14. Overbeeke, C.J., Stratmann, M.H.: Space Through Movement. Ph.D. Dissertation. Delft University of Technology, Delft, The Netherlands (1988)
15. Smets, G.J.F.: Designing for Telepresence: The Interdependence of Movement and Visual Perception Implemented. Proceedings of the 5th IFAC/IFIP/IFORS/IEA Symposium on Analysis, Design, and Evaluation of Man-Machine Systems. Permagon Press, Inc., Elmsford, New York (1993)
16. Arthur, K.W., Booth, K.S., Ware, C.: Evaluating 3D Task Performance for Fish Tank Virtual Worlds. ACM Transactions on Information Systems. 11 (1993) 239-265
17. Ware, C., Arthur, K., Booth, K.S.: Fish Tank Virtual Reality. Proceedings of the ACM Conference on Human Factors in Computing, April 24-29, 1993, ACM Press, NY, 37-42
18. Brown, M.E., Gallimore, J.J.: Visualization of Three-Dimensional Structure During Computer-Aided Design. International Journal of Human-Computer Interaction. 7 (1995) 37-56
19. Hubona, G.S., Wheeler, P.N., Shirah, G.W., Brandt, M.: The Relative Contributions of Stereo, Lighting, and Background Scenes in Promoting 3D Depth Visualization. ACM Transactions on Computer-Human Interaction. 6 (1999) 214-242
20. Hubona, G.S., Shirah, G.W., Jennings, D.K.: The Effects of Cast Shadows and Stereopsis on Performing Computer-Generated Spatial Tasks. IEEE Transactions on Systems, Man, and Cybernetics - Part A: Systems and Humans. 34 (2004) 483-493
21. Wickens, C.D., Merwin, D.H., Lin, E.L.: Implications of Graphics Enhancements for the Visualization of Scientific Data: Dimensional Integrality, Stereopsis, Motion, and Mesh. Human Factors. 36 (1994) 44-61
22. Zhai, S., Buxton, W., Milgram, P.: The Partial-Occlusion Effect: Utilizing Semitransparency in 3D Human-Computer Interaction. ACM Transactions on Computer-Human Interaction. 3 (1996) 254-284
23. Reinhart, W.F.: Effects of Depth Cues in Depth Judgments Using a Field-Sequential Stereoscopic CRT Display. Unpublished Ph.D. Dissertation, Virginia Polytechnic Institute and State University, Blacksburg, Virginia (1990)
24. Bridges, A.L., Reising, J.M.: Three-Dimensional Stereographic Pictorial Visual Interfaces and Display Systems in Flight Simulation. SPIE Proceedings. 761 (1987) 102-109
25. Reising, J.M., Mazur, K.M.: 3-D Displays for Cockpit: Where They Payoff. SPIE Proceedings. 1256 (1990) 35-43
26. Yeh, Y., Silverstein, L.D.: Visual Performance with Monoscopic and Stereoscopic Presentations of Identical Three-Dimensional Visual Tasks. SID International Symposium Digest of Technical Papers. 21 (1990) 359-362
27. McAllister, D.F.: Stereo Computer Graphics and Other True 3D Technologies. Princeton University Press, Princeton, N.J. (1993)
28. Wickens, C.D., Todd, S., Seidler, K.: Three-Dimensional Displays: Perception, Implementations and Applications. CSERIAC Tech. Report 89-001, Wright Patterson Air Force Base, Ohio (1989)
29. WcWhorter, S.W., Hodges, L.F., Rodriguez, W.E.: Comparison of 3D Display Formats for CAD Applications. Tech. Report GIT-GVU-91-04. Georgia Institute of Technology, Graphics, Visualization and Usability Center (1991)
30. Liu, Y., Wickens, C.D.: Use of Computer Graphics and Cluster Analysis in Aiding Relational Judgment. Human Factors. 34 (1992) 165-178

31. Yonas, A.: Attached and Cast Shadows. In Perception and Pictorial Representation. Nodine, C.F.: Ed. Praeger, New York (1979) 100-109

32. Wickens, C.D.: The Proximity Compatibility Principle: Its Psychological Foundation and Relevance to Display Design. Technical Report ARL-92-5/NASA-92-3. University of Illinois Institute of Aviation, Aviation Research Lab, Savoy, IL (1992)

33. Wickens, C.D., Carlswell, C.M.: The Proximity Compatibility Principle: Its Psychological Foundation and Relevance to Display Design. Human Factors. 37 (1995) 473-494

34. Balka, E.: Gender and Skill in Human-Computer Interaction. Proceedings of CHI '96. (Vancouver, British Columbia, Canada) ACM Press, New York (1994) 325

35. Leventhal, L., Teasley, B., Stone, B.: Designing for Diverse Users: Will Just A Better Interface Do? Proceedings of CHI '94. (Boston, MA) ACM Press, New York (1994) 191-192

36. Shneiderman, B.: Universal Usability. Communications of the ACM. 43 (2000) 85-91

37. Simon, S.J.: The Impact of Culture and Gender on Web Sites. The DATA BASE for Advances in Information Systems. 32 (2001) 18-37

38. McKeever, V.F.: Hormone and Hemisphericity Hypothesis Regarding Cognitive Sex Differences: Possible Future Explanatory Power, But Current Empirical Chaos. Learning and Individual Differences. 7 (1995) 323-340

39. McGlone, J.: Sex Differences in Functional Brain Asymmetry: A Critical Survey. Behavioral and Brain Science. 3 (1980) 216-263

40. Halpern, D.F.: Sex Differences in Cognitive Abilities. Lawrence Erlbaum Associates, Hillsdale, NJ (1986)

41. Hyde, J.S.: How Large Are Cognitive Gender Differences? American Psychologist. 36 (1981) 892-901

42. McGee, M.G.: Human Spatial Abilities: Psychometric Studies and Environmental, Genetic, Hormonal, and Neurological Influences. Psychological Bulletin. 86 (1979) 889-918

43. Voyer, D.: On the Magnitude of Laterality Effects and Sex Differences in Functional Literalities. Laterality. 1 (1996) 51-83

44. Waber, D.P.: Maturation: Thoughts on Renewing an Old Acquaintanceship. In Biological Studies of Mental Processes. Caplan, D.: Ed. MIT Press, Cambridge, MA (1982) 8-26

45. Linn, M.C., Petersen, A.C.: Emergence and Characterization of Sex Differences in Spatial Ability: A Meta-Analysis. Child Development. 56 (1985) 1479-1498

46. Voyer, D., Voyer, S., Bryden, M.P.: Magnitude of Sex Differences in Spatial Abilities: A Meta-analysis and Consideration of Critical Variables. Psychological Bulletin. 117 (1995) 250-270

47. Silverman, I., Eals, M.: Sex Differences in Spatial Abilities: Evolutionary Theory and Data. In The Adapted Mind: Evolutionary Psychology and the Generation of Culture. Barkow, J.H., Cosmides, L., Tooby, J.: Eds. Oxford Press, New York (1992) 531-549

48. Dabbs, J.M., Chang, E.-L., Strong, R.A., Milun, R.: Spatial Ability, Navigation Strategy, and Geographic Knowledge Among Men and Women. Evolution and Human Behavior. 19 (1998) 89-98

49. Eals, M., Silverman, I.: The Hunter-Gatherer Theory of Spatial Sex Differences: Proximate Factors Mediating the Female Advantage in Recall of Object Arrays. Ethological Sociobiology. 15 (1994) 95-105

50. McBurney, D.H., Gaulin, S.J.C., Devineni, T., Adams, C.: Superior Spatial Memory of Women: Stronger Evidence for the Gathering Hypothesis. Evolution and Human Behavior. 18 (1997) 165-174

51. James, T.W., Kimura, D.: Sex Differences in Remembering the Locations of Objects in an Array: Location-Shift Versus Location-Exchanges. Evolution and Human Behavior. 18 (1997) 155-163

52. Collins, D.W., Kimura, D.: A Large Sex Difference on a Two-Dimensional Mental Rotation Task. Behavioral Neuroscience. 111 (1997) 845-849

53. Goldstein, D., Haldane, D., Mitchell, C.: Sex Differences in Visual-Spatial Ability: The Role of Performance Factors. Memory & Cognition. 18 (1990) 546-550

54. Kimura, D.: Sex Differences in Cerebral Organization for Speech and Praxis Functions. Canadian Journal of Psychology. 37 (1983) 19-35

55. Kolb, B., Whishaw, I.: Human Neuropsychology. Freeman, New York (1990)

56. Lohman, D.F.: The Effect of Speed-Accuracy Tradeoff on Sex Differences in Mental Rotation. Perception and Psychophysics. 39 (1986) 427-436

57. Maccoby, E.E., Jacklin, C.N.: The Psychology of Sex Differences. Stanford University Press, Stanford, CA (1974)

58. Silverman, I., Choi, J., Mackewn, A., Fisher, M., Moro, J., Olshansky, E.: Evolved Mechanisms Underlying Wayfinding: Further Studies on the Hunter-Gatherer Theory of Spatial Sex Differences. Evolution and Human Behavior. 21(2000) 201-213

59. Shepard, R.N., Metzler, J.: Mental Rotation of Three-Dimensional Objects. Science. 171 (1971) 701-703

60. Hubona, G.S., Shirah, G.W.: The Gender Factor Performing Visualization Tasks on Computer Media. Proceedings of the 37th International Conference on System Sciences (CD/ROM), January 5-8, 2004, Computer Society Press, Nine pages.

Cognitive Artifacts in Complex Work

Peter H. Jones[1] and Christopher P. Nemeth[2]

[1] Redesign Research, USA
peter@redesignresearch.com
[2] The University of Chicago, USA
cnemeth@uchicago.edu

1 Introduction

The Indian folk tale recorded in the well-known John Saxe poem tells of six blind men, each grabbing a different part of an elephant, and describing their impression of the whole beast from a single part's perspective. So the elephant appears to each blind man to be like a snake, a fan, a tree, a rope, a wall, a spear. As the poem concludes:

> "And so these men of Indostan, Disputed loud and long, Each in his own opinion, exceeding stiff and strong. Though each was partly right, All were in the wrong."

Although this tale suggests a general metaphor for poor collaboration and social coordination, the insinuation of *blindness* indicates an inability to share the common information that is normally available through visual perception. When fundamental cognitive resources such as shared information or visual cues are missing, collaborative work practices may suffer from the "anti-cognition" suggested by the elephant metaphor. When individuals believe they are contributing to the whole, but are unable to verify the models that are held by other participants, continued progress might founder. We may find such "blind men" situations when organizations value and prefer independent individual cognition at the expense of supporting whole system coordination. Blindness to shared effects is practically ensured when those who work together are not able to share information.

Our research shows the importance of artifacts that are created and used by multiple participants in collaborative practices. Artifacts analysis, in the context of ethnographic field research, admits access and insight into the cognitive work underlying observed practices. For example, the blind men might have benefited from the use of a common artifact to integrate the attributes of the partially-observed animal. Those who work in science and medicine perform research and work on phenomena with only a partial grasp of function and mechanisms. People use what are termed cognitive artifacts, usually physical, tangible written objects such as the operating room schedule or the laboratory notebook, to note status, maintain current knowledge through cryptic but well-understood markers, distribute memory among participants, and manage emergent conditions. We contend that digital artifact design (including ambient intelligent systems as

Y. Cai (Ed.): Ambient Intelligence for Scientific Discovery, LNAI 3345, pp. 152–183, 2005.

well as conventional computing) must successfully support the cognitive functions physical artifacts already assist.

Cognitive artifacts embody what is relevant in distributed work settings because those who perform work create and use them as an essential part of their work environment. The life scientists and acute health care clinicians we studied routinely create and use physical cognitive artifacts as a way to manage uncertainty and complexity. In these technical environments, artifacts reveal processes that are supported more effectively by paper than computer. In acute health care, physical artifacts including a hard copy printout and white marker board serve team members more effectively than electronic displays. In life sciences research, computer-based and traditional information artifacts do not support the distributed cognitive processes described in scientific discovery. These two studies of cohesive work groups and their manual cognitive artifacts therefore reveal gaps between current practices and technology use.

We present the two cases as models for researching distributed artifact use, and to show how cognitive artifacts embody implicit requirements for effective computer-supported information systems. Current computer-supported information systems can be inadequate to support distributed cognitive work because the system developers do not grasp the work that is being performed. We argue such artifacts must be analyzed in a distributed context, to avoid designing information technology for discrete tasks at the expense of cooperative work. The acute care study shows how artifacts can be used as a means to efficiently get at the underlying cognitive work that clinicians perform. As scientific discovery is also a joint cognitive process, we use this second case to argue for redesign of information artifacts for distributed cognition in the life sciences laboratory.

Scientific discovery is a cognitive work process conducted in a highly uncertain environment. In much of life sciences, while research projects are generally planned, experiments follow the lead of findings, not plans. New experiments are formulated on a daily basis to tease out and learn from phenomena. In experimental research, we find discovery described as a process; accounts of the "eureka" event are in reality few, if not nonexistent in modern science. Cognitive studies of discovery in practice are few, and have only recently emerged in the literature [7, 8, 32, 19], suggesting much remains unexplored. Cognitive studies of social reasoning and information use in scientific discovery have focused on behaviors that facilitate the emergence and recognition of "meaningful novelty" in research findings and patterns of scientific reasoning. Simon [32], shows the general importance of discovery as a cognitive process due to its engagement with ill-structured problems that explore the entire range of human cognitive resources, with the capability to access deep insights into complex and creative human thinking.

In terms of distributed cognition, Dunbar's research is noteworthy for its insights into the social process of discovery in natural sciences, and the unexpected use of distributed information in experimental reasoning. Dunbar [8] describes the importance ascribed to unexpected findings in lab meetings. Measuring the contribution of reasoning statements, Dunbar finds that reasoning is widely distributed among participants toward a goal of making sense of findings. The empirical data show scientists using analogies to exchange metaphorical ideas in arguing for interim approaches and toward obtaining consensus toward discovery.

In designing information systems for discovery, we must identify information objects that assist scientists in the process. But where do we look for information and cognitive structures that support analogy, and scientific reasoning? We must also understand how scientists use search and retrieval to acquire knowledge to confirm, disconfirm, or build upon incomplete but potentially important unexpected findings. We suggest that current information resources, as powerful and complete as they are, are insufficient to support the cognitive processes of discovery.

2   Research into Distributed Cognition

Distributed cognition is commonly shared knowledge that benefits a group but cannot be known by any single individual [12]. It is the collective cognitive activity in which individuals participate in order to accomplish shared goals. This team mind [18] draws on the experience of all team members to create new, unexpected ideas that are beyond individual ability. Because it is human behavior, distributed cognition exists separate and apart from computer systems. As the activity that computing systems intend to assist, it is essential to understand distributed cognition according to its particular applications.

The two research studies reported in this chapter used two known research approaches to investigate distributed cognition in complex tasks. The acute health care study's author (CN) followed an ethnographic research approach, using methods such as direct observation, informal interview, and artifacts analysis to gather field data. Analysis then revealed the process and strategies that anesthesia coordinators use to develop assignment schedules. Case studies were developed to synthesize field notes, showing how team members translated the schedule into the reality of daily work. The life sciences research study's author (PJ) employed cognitive ethnography, using contextual interview and task diaries to gather data, analyzing practice using an activity theory approach [16].

The approaches are different but their goals are similar. Both studies seek to understand complex technical work domains. Both seek to understand distributed cognitive processes and to describe requirements for information technology to support it. There is no single approach to the study of cognitive work. Each work domain evokes different questions, based on its unique demands.

2.1   Using Ethnography to Understand Work

As it is practiced by design-oriented researchers, ethnography has been described as "ethnographically-informed ethnomethodology" [2]. This is a hybrid approach to studying people in workgroups and their engagement with technological artifacts. Ethnography derives from cultural anthropology, in which researchers of human culture literally record their observations of human social behavior with minimal interpretation and representation. Ethnographic field research differs from the case study in its investigation of culture [20], and engages multiple data collection methods to study behavior within the group context. Within occupational cultures such as acute care or life sciences, we find certain shared uses and meanings for artifacts, revealing why these artifacts are employed in joint work, and suggesting limits to adoption of information technology.

Cognitive ethnography [10, 1], has been specifically developed to understand cognitive work using an ethnographic research approach. Cognitive ethnography integrates observation, interview, and interaction study toward rich descriptions and ecologically valid representations of cognitive phenomena in the work setting. Although researchers employ a collection of techniques in this approach, the research setting, questions, domain, and participant activities determine the selection of techniques to study distributed nature of cognition and activity. While individual behavior is studied, the approach focuses "on the material and social means of the construction of action and meaning." [10]. Multiple research methods were employed to gather field data and analyze findings.

The likelihood of obtaining ecologically valid data was improved by triangulation (using multiple methods to account for subject behavior). Drawing from ethnography, observations followed the participant's natural course of work practice. Cognitive artifacts were analyzed to identify how information was used and exchanged. Other methods were used in both studies to examine issues of specific interest. The acute care study used laboratory style observation of schedule writing to understand how coordinators plan staff assignments. The life sciences study used information task diaries with faculty and graduate students, to gather detailed information behaviors on a daily basis for up to 10 response days over a 3-week period. Semi-structured interviews and information task walkthroughs were used to gather additional contextual data. We describe the integration and interpretation of these data with the case study.

2.2 Cognitive Artifacts as a Tool for Work and Research

Cognitive artifacts are physical objects such as a calendar, a shopping list, or a computer that humans make to aid, enhance, or improve cognition [13]. Norman [26] expands cognitive artifacts beyond physical objects to include any artificial device that displays information, including computer systems, heuristic rules of thumb, and mnemonics. Kaptelinin [17] makes the distinction that cognitive artifacts rightly extend to collective use and that they serve not only to improve whole system performance. They are instruments that improve and change cognition.

We further distinguish between two types of artifacts. What we might call *endogenous* cognitive artifacts are made by users to make their own work better or easier. *Exogenous* artifacts are developed outside of the workplace and installed for use there. We describe endogenous artifacts, which are created and implemented by their users, and show how they can be used to articulate the nature and boundaries of (exogenous) information systems. Users maintain these objects in spite of "leading edge" technology being available. This is not due to legacy work routines, but because they support distributed cognitive work better.

Individuals develop and use cognitive artifacts so that it is possible to perform otherwise impossible tasks, such as the process of care coordination for acute care patients. As the patient length of stay and the number of procedures increase, the need for more powerful cognitive artifacts also grows in order to support increased demands for patient care coordination.

Artifacts can be used to distribute cognition in a variety of ways. They can be used by an individual to hold information related to plan and status, which are distributed across time. For example, an anesthesia coordinator who develops a plan for the day's activities embeds intentions, speculations and anticipations in it to mold what is to come. Later in the day, the same coordinator can use the artifact that has been annotated and adjusted throughout the day to perform trade-off decisions and re-plan to balance staff resources against changing care demands. Artifacts can also distribute cognition socially by holding both the patient care procedure plans and status to be distributed among staff members. Earlier in the day, team members can use the artifact to anticipate their role in the events that are expected. The artifact serves as a means to develop consensus about, and embody, future needs. Later in the day, staff members use the artifact as a platform to track progress and reconcile conflicts as they evaluate demands for care that remain.

Computer systems make it possible to develop digital versions of cognitive artifacts. In many instances, computer-based artifacts have been designed as mimics of physical artifacts. In such cases, the traits of simple physical items that made the artifacts so useful have been replaced by electronic analogs that may not be as easy to use in complex work. Digital artifacts that are developed with insufficient research into people's work practice can make work more difficult instead of easier. Problems include creating lags in information updates, truncating information by forcing it to fit into limited display real estate, and requiring users to drill down through levels of hierarchical menus. The result increases, rather than decreases, the amount of work an individual performs. Operators who are confronted with such circumstances can reject such digital artifacts and return to physical artifacts. This is because physical artifacts embed well-understood but tacit cognitive tasks and have already been proven to successfully support the shared practices of individuals.

2.3   New Information System Development

New approaches to computing systems are often couched in terms of the promise of technology. Human participants are cast as the beneficiaries of advantages that will accrue from new systems. Rather than considering abstractions of what might be possible, it is more productive to portray real applications that new systems could benefit. Scientific research and acute healthcare have genuine needs for improved information system performance that make this more practical discussion possible. Both domains require constant access to time-sensitive information for all participants. Both differ in the way information is used through time. As an operational system, acute care requires current information on patient and system status, as well as the ability to review, update, and anticipate that information. As an exploratory process, life sciences share little need for monitoring and scheduling critical events. Instead, experimental work requires review of information and event over long durations and dynamic updates of emergent data that inform ongoing processes.

While both domains use the latest *operational* equipment, they lag in support for information technology systems. Life sciences quickly adopted experimental systems, biological databases and visualization. Their use of information resources is surprisingly traditional, with a continuing reliance on the traditional printed article. Acute care relies on information to provide patient care and coordinate the resources that are required to provide it. As important as information is in healthcare, computer support has been largely devoted to the blunt (management) side of the organization for purposes such as billing. The acute care case is presented first to illustrate the use of cognitive artifacts in a complex communicative process.

3   Cognitive Work in Acute Care: Scheduling

Health care organizations include tightly constrained teams of service providers who perform complex procedures that routinely have significant consequences. At the sharp end of health care, these practitioners apply expertise through actions in order to produce results [6]. The circumstances for adverse outcomes are embedded in the conditions and constraints in the workplace. Those conditions can result from many influences including management (blunt end) policy and practice [29].

The site where this research was conducted handles roughly 50 to 80 procedures every day in 24 operating rooms (OR). Some of these are brief and take 30 minutes while others last most of the day. Some are routine and their duration can be predicted reliably, while others are complex and less predictable. Some procedures will go on as scheduled, while others will be delayed and canceled. There is always the possibility of an emergent need for an OR and staff to perform a procedure. The coordinator's responsibility is to manage staff activities to accommodate these demands efficiently [23].

The work of health care practitioners includes diagnostic and therapeutic interventions that enable a practitioner to influence the patient's future course. This work is supported by a large body of knowledge, a tradition of training, and many artifacts. Practitioner work is not simply about clinical details. It also includes what has been termed technical work [5]. Each individual procedure depends on the timely synchronization of people, equipment, tools and facilities. The collective management of that process throughout an entire day for the entire suite of operating rooms also requires coordination.

Technical work coordination involves many practical but essential activities that are needed to carry out clinical care: resource availability assessment, resource allocation, anticipation, prediction, trade-off decisions, speculation, and negotiation among others [5]. Many practitioners consider this type of activity to be the "background noise" of the workplace. When asked about such issues,

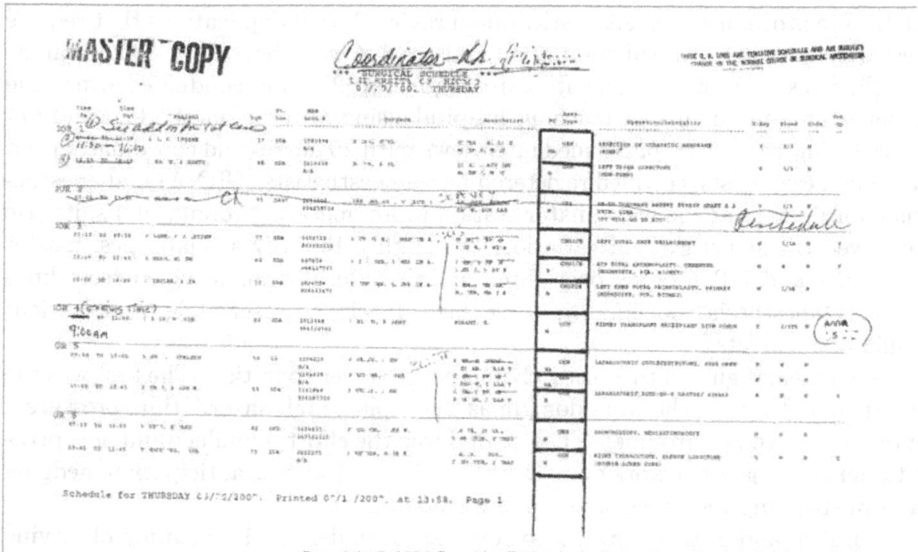

Fig. 1. Hard Copy of the Master Schedule.

clinicians identify technical work issues as merely "the way we do things around here." Yet the details of technical work are not trivial. Technical work is intimately related to clinical care and it exerts real influences on decisions that are made [25]. Practitioners have created cognitive artifacts in order to assist the technical work of scheduling and managing anesthesia resources. The master schedule (Fig. 1) is the primary artifact that a coordinator creates the day before procedures and embodies all of the assignment information that matters in this work setting. It is one of many artifacts that are created in order to reduce uncertainty to a minimum, which is essential to effectively manage resource allocation in this variable, ever-changing, contingent, high risk setting.

Berg [3] and Heath and Luff [9] describe the failure of computer-supported information systems that were intended to support sharp end cognitive work. Those failures were due in large part to the system developers' poor grasp of the actual nature of work at the sharp end. Those who would develop ambient information systems for health care need to understand what they intend to support. The following section describes a research approach to accomplish that.

3.1   Research Method

Research into cognitive activity in surgical and critical care is difficult for a number of reasons. Care settings, patient populations and system constraints vary widely. Practitioners often suffer from poor insight into how their work is organized. Information and interaction at the sharp end is dense and complex. In addition, technical work is poorly recognized as an aspect of medical care. Recent initiatives to protect care provider and patient privacy have resulted in elaborate procedures such as institutional review board applications that require researchers to perform substantial administrative work beyond actual research.

This research study in acute care cognition [23] was conducted over nine months at a major urban teaching hospital using an ethnomethodological approach. The researcher performed interviews with 25 nurses and coordinators and 40 anesthesiologists/certified registered nurse anesthetists (CRNA) and anesthesia coordinators at the coordinator station in an operating room (OR) suite. He reviewed the structure and variations of roughly 15 daily availabilities, master schedules and OR Graphs over three months. He also made video recordings of three anesthesia coordinators while each developed a schedule of outpatient clinic assignments.

Two themes guided this research into practitioner cognition. The first was the effort to understand the work domain as a complex, high hazard, time-pressured, interrupt-driven environment. The second was the effort to understand how practitioners manage their work domain using strategies such as anticipation, hedging and husbanding resources, and making trade-offs.

Surgical and critical care is too complex to understand by simply observing what happens. So much information is embedded in this environment that the investigator needs some additional means to understand it. Cognitive artifacts are that means. Artifacts embody the nature of the technical work that is necessary to plan and manage anesthesia assignments. Artifacts represent the structure and boundaries of the work domain. This research used four observation and cognitive systems engineering methods [33] to understand how acute care team members learn, remember, and make decisions about anesthesia resource allocation.

Artifact Analysis. Xiao et al [34] describes how practitioners develop artifacts such as white marker boards on their own. Observing the way that such artifacts are organized and used enables the researcher to identify critical features of the domain and work situation. This is because cognitive artifacts typically are used to support important, difficult activities. The work that the artifact is designed to support can also be improved by making a better artifact. Better information design or improved use of information technology can make technical work more enjoyable, more efficient, and more reliable.

Direct Observation. The researcher watched how clinicians acted, interacted, and used cognitive artifacts to coordinate work. Understanding emerged from the researcher's own observations and interviews in the real world. Neither laboratory study, simulation, nor reading, could discover the richness of team activity in the context that observation captures.

Interviews. Discussions with practitioners can be in-depth, structured sessions, or informal, spur-of-the-moment queries. Questions can be designed to elicit critical information. Follow-up queries were used to seek further information beyond the initial answers that subjects gave. Information from interviews helped to understand the reasons behind observed behaviors and to discover more about the context for opinions and actions than the other methods revealed.

Laboratory Study. One senior anesthesia staff member per day plans the daily schedule in the OR unit and outpatient clinic, then manages those assignments the following day. Anesthesiologists with coordinator experience were invited to each write a schedule while being recorded on videotape. Four coordinators out of eight were available and three agreed to participate. Summaries of the sessions removed all identifying information and included three elements: verbal transcript, annotated artifacts, and comments on coordinator cognitive work. Categorization, classification and analysis were used to produce a formalized performance description for a number of anesthesia coordinators who wrote daily schedules. Recording and analysis of master schedule writing sessions showed how the anesthesia coordinator formulates a feasible future for the following day. Observation and interviews with acute care team members revealed the cognitive work that is involved in translating the schedule's intentions into the daily reality of acute care.

3.2   Implications of Replacing Physical Artifacts with Digital Versions

The installation of an electronic scheduling system at the same site (Fig. 2) made it possible to observe how a digital version fared as a replacement for a simple paper artifact. In this new display (Fig. 3) cases were listed in the same manner as the paper artifact shown in Fig. 1.

As a mimic of the paper master schedule, it did not improve the information that it conveyed or the way that the information was displayed. In fact, the electronic display imposed difficulties that had not been a problem when the paper version was in use. For example, limitations to the information display such as field size restrictions resulted in problems with display use that had not been anticipated.

Fig. 2. Electronic scheduling system at coordinator station.

iOR	OR Time	End Time	Cls/R'	Patient Name	Age	Primary Surgeon	Anesthes	Anes	Procedures	Progress St	Event
iOR1	07:30	11:30	SDA	Smith, Christine	17yrs	Barnes	Connor Watts	GEN	Resection of Subaortic Membr	In OR	
iOR1 iOR2	12:15	16:15	SDA	Delano, Ashley	4mos	Barnes	Connor Watts	GEN	Left Upper Lobectomy	R-404	
iOR3	07:30	09:30	SDA	Malone, Anna	77yrs	Potter	Ellenson Morey	GEN	Left Total Knee Replacement	In OR	
iOR3	10:15	11:45	SDA	Perry, Helen	62yrs	Potter	Ellenson Morey	GEN	Hip Total Arthroplasty, Cement	R-325	

Fig. 3. Electronic master schedule format (all names are fictitious).

The research also revealed traits that are essential to artifacts that are intended to support that work. At a minimum, any cognitive artifact in this environment, whether paper or computer-supported, must be accurate, efficient, reliable, informative, clear, and malleable [25]. Each has implications for the development of digital cognitive artifacts.

Accurate. *Current and valid in its representation of the system state.* Each coordinator updated the paper artifact with simple pen notations upon learning new information. Under the computer-based system, case status information is frequently posted late by a half hour or more. This forces team members to do extra cognitive work as they make in-person trips and phone calls to verify case status.

Efficient. *Impose the least burden on users to create and obtain information.* Practitioners could look down the paper master schedule on display at the coordinator station and find cases scheduled throughout the day. The roster on the electronic display shifts each time a case is deleted, causing the reader to search for cases. In addition, the computer interface requires practitioners to drill down as far as four menu levels to find information that was previously available in one glance using the paper version of the master schedule.

Reliable. *Available for use when needed.* The paper artifact was displayed daily at the coordinator station. Computer-supported displays that go "down" prevent team members from seeing or entering information. This causes great difficulty in making the kind of moment-by-moment decisions that are necessary for resource allocation.

Informative. *Contain information that pertains to circumstances of interest to the team.* Coordinators evaluate the day of procedures according to what has already happened and how the remainder of the day can be planned. The paper master schedule allowed for the collection of information that was related to cases through the day. The computer-based version removes a case from the display after the patient has been sent to post-anesthesia recovery. Displays that offer only a restricted "keyhole" view of the day prevent practitioners from making connections that are a necessary part of their cognitive work.

Clear. *Unambiguous and free from confusion.* Procedures must be completely and precisely described in order to specify what is to be done. Minor differences in wording result in major differences in the kind of supplies and equipment that will be required for a procedure. The paper artifact contained complete descriptions of each procedure to be performed. The computer-based display only allows truncated descriptions, which create misleading procedure descriptions that have caused departments to plan for the wrong procedure.

Malleable. *Able to be manipulated by those who use them.* Practitioners interact with many artifacts frequently as they obtain and provide information among the team. They also use artifacts in a variety of subtle ways, depending on their confidence in the information they have. Nursing and anesthesia coordinators were able to write notes on the paper artifact to track pertinent information. The structure of artifacts can also be changed. For example, the team can modify the OR board layout to better support cognitive work as it evolves. The computer-based display does not allow for this kind of interaction.

4   Cognitive Work in the Laboratory: Life Sciences Research

In 2002-2003 a phased field study [15] investigated information behaviors in life sciences research at two North American universities, at a molecular biology research center and a large pharmacology department. Information behaviors are the everyday repeatable search, review, exchange, and other uses of scientific information drawn from print and electronic resources. The study focused on understanding the actual information behavior of life scientists in their daily work practice in research projects, which have discovery and publication as goals.

   A cognitive ethnography examined information practices and cognitive artifacts within collaborative research projects. An activity theory framework was adopted to model and understand distributed cognitive work as revealed in information practices. The study investigated cognitive drivers within experimental research that trigger selection and use of information resources. A major purpose of this exploratory study was to identify opportunities for improving information services design, as well as to understand information behavior.

   Two observations of information activity in research motivate analysis of cognitive artifacts in discovery. One, after nearly a decade of having electronic research articles available online, scientists constantly print important articles and generally ignore electronic (PDF and HTML) versions. The electronic file is convenient for scanning and review, but serious reading is done from the printed article. Even with the very limited bench space available for information work, scientists print and stack (or bind) selected articles. Two, nearly all these researchers used only one search engine for retrieval of research articles, either

PubMed or MEDLINE exclusively. These two observations indicate highly stable patterns of information use over time.

Information artifacts are not merely analogous to the cognitive work of research, they are the result, target, and product of cognitive work. Scientists are immersed in information artifacts. They often scan or read over a dozen articles a week, run numerous searches related to experimental work, and may simultaneously work on research papers and grant proposals while running experiments or managing lab work. While not obvious from the view of the lab bench, a life sciences lab is a dynamic, highly productive information environment. But from a production perspective, much of the information work is churn, extensive and repeated reading to draw specific information objects from the context of research articles. This difference between artifact and information object is central to information use in discovery.

4.1   Research Method

Information tasks and artifacts provide a "trail" of cognitive work, matching task and cognitive artifacts (e.g. search results, articles, abstracts) with participants' representations of goals, intentions, and observed practice. Cognitive distribution of information tasks was studied using several methods unique to information behavior research. The unit of analysis was the research project activity, with data collected and coded by individual tasks and joint information practices by project. Information tasks were examined over the time period of identified research projects. Collaborative processes were described in semi-structured interviews and specified in response to questions in task diaries. Multiple accounts were obtained and compared

The studies were conducted as cognitive ethnographies, observing information behaviors as empirical actions in the work setting and identifying cognitive artifacts used in information-driven practices. Field data collected included video and audio recorded observations and interviews, information task walkthroughs, and diaries recording detailed information tasks. From a total of 32 life scientists (molecular biologists and pharmacologists), 20 graduate students and faculty scientists kept electronic diaries for 10 days each, recording their information tasks as they occurred. Across the diary sampling periods of 3 weeks, over 90% of the recorded information tasks originated from the demands of experimental research projects.

Multiple research methods were employed to gather field data and analyze findings. Drawing from cognitive ethnography, observations followed the participant's natural course of work practice. The likelihood of obtaining ecologically valid data was enhanced by triangulating other methods to acquire specific records of information use (within participants and between sample groups).

Task diaries were used with 5 faculty and 15 graduate students, gathering detailed information behaviors on a daily basis for up to 10 response days over 2-3 weeks. The purpose of the diary was to sample actual information tasks as they occurred during everyday practice. By distributing the diary activity across a range of participants, different information tasks were described for self-defined periods of research work. The diary was a standard Word file designed to collect detailed responses on a daily basis, with each response associated with an information episode, using 6-10 open-ended prompt questions per response day. Questions were varied each day, to elicit a wide range of information tasks over the task diary period.

The field research sessions consisted of one-week of full-day visits to the scientists' laboratories and work locations. Two researchers conducted observations and interviews, recording sessions with digital video and/or audio. During the field period, 2 one-hour semi-structured interviews were held with principal investigators (PIs) and selected researchers. The interview protocols for PIs collected information use data on research projects, grant and manuscript practices, and program development. Researcher protocols gathered data on experiments, computer and information service use, use of journals and articles, and specific information tasks. Cognitive walkthroughs of specific information services used by these researchers were conducted to capture and evaluate actions, decisions, and resources used.

Research practices and associated information activities were reconstructed using a research information life-cycle diagram. This analytical instrument was designed to capture a temporal model of information activities within the project unit of analysis. Participants further described research project events, decisions and processes, experiments, and other associated research tasks. After describing a complete project history (supported by searches, papers, posters, and other documentation) we recorded information tasks associated with each event. While based on a retrospective method, we attempted to maintain construct validity relative to actual and current information tasks by specifying current or recent research projects. We related the diagram's data to diary and interview data to compare task descriptions and information services used. In some cases, participants gathered supporting documentation such as printouts of searches, reference lists, abstracts, and other materials in advance of the field visit. This method enabled participants to describe project and experimental activities, related information tasks, and collaborative tasks along a defined time line representing the process of a current experimental research project.

4.2   Discovery as an Information Practice

Studying the work of scientists from task diaries, interviews and observations shows multiple projects, competing demands, and the unplanned events of research practice. Faculty and graduate students conducted experiments, organized projects, and sought information through searches, artifacts, and requests to colleagues. We identify seven continuous practices; tasks that refer to cognitive artifacts are shown in italics.

- Managing research: Organizing *schedules*, activities and commitments for research
- Conducting research: Preparing equipment and materials for experiments, running experiments, *documenting experiments* and procedures, *sharing findings*

- Generating inquiries (*searches*, questions) prompted by experimental findings
- Seeking validation of specific experimental findings: Seeking clarifications, *alternative findings*, *prior literature*, other valid approaches
- Finding relevant published *articles*, and scanning and reading for specific questions (very little broad reading)
- Preparing article *manuscripts* – writing *sections of articles*, sharing findings and making sense of data, reviewing current literature, internal review of *drafts*
- Research conversation – Phone calls and *emails* with other scientists, current and potential collaborators, maintaining social networks

The goal of the research project, and the end goal of these practices, can be considered original scientific discovery, with an *outcome* of publication of findings. But cognitive research shows discovery a highly distributed, social cognitive process with no clear milestones of activity. Scientific discovery is a process that depends on both individual and shared knowledge practices. It builds on tacit knowledge, experience with research practice and literature, and the ability to frame findings from experiments within a research context. Dunbar [8] describes discovery as a *communicative* process, with no specific associated cognitive artifacts. Information artifacts (manuscripts, lab notebooks, research articles) contribute to this process, but are not central. We examine cognitive artifacts to better understand this relationship.

The triggering event for research discovery is the initial discovery of unexpected experimental findings. Dunbar [8] shows that over 70% of scientists' inductions, 50% of their deductions, and 70% of their causal reasoning statements were devoted to unexpected findings. Life scientists revealed the importance of "new findings in the lab" as a triggering event for specific information tasks.

"I have weekly meetings with my supervisor to brainstorm or to discuss my progress and what my research findings could mean."

"Weekly meetings ... to discuss findings from articles that may back up my research."

Dunbar [8] also shows the importance of distributed cognition. In molecular biology lab meetings, more than 50% of the reasoning process was distributed, shared and generated among a number of scientists. This suggests that distributed reasoning (in collaborations of small research teams) significantly contributes to the process of discovery. However, no studies are found that examine information use and information artifacts in this process.

Analogies were frequently generated in lab discussions, to formulate hypotheses, design experiments, or to explain results to other scientists. However, an interesting cognitive operation was found that scientists tended to forget their analogies and other "cognitive scaffolding" used in reasoning, and they recalled and subsequently relied on the results of their reasoning. While analogies are important in leading scientists to discovery, they were undervalued and even invisible. Further, the identification and appropriation of analogies in the process of "discovery dialogue" requires access to deep sources of both related and divergent literatures. The structure or depth of such analogies may differ widely by discipline, but the access to related concepts presents itself as a design opportunity in the processes of discovery.

4.3   Artifacts and Resources in the Information Ecology

An institution's information ecology [22] provides infrastructure and resources for scientific information practices, as well as constraints which guide and permit certain actions and not others. In this infrastructure, scientists develop regular patterns of use, as described in this model. Even as the institution adds resources and services (through growth, acquisition of new content holdings, and new services on the Web), the post-Internet information ecology now provides a stable set of resources. With this stability, little demand is exhibited for new services or features beyond those currently available. Instead of the dozens, if not potentially hundreds of possible information resources available in the natural sciences, we find two resources (PubMed and Google) consistently used, in the specified context of research projects.

Another indication of resource stability in this ecology shows in the regularity of information tasks performed by scientists on an everyday basis. Table 1 describes six information tasks found across all participants. These tasks are regular, repeatable discrete information seeking actions. Each task represents a different common objective, with scientists locating specific information artifacts associated with the task. These tasks are driven by seeking information artifacts, following current theories in information seeking that identify a putative information need. But the task's cognitive drivers are not located in this context. The cognitive work required by the research project demands specific information objects, irrespective of artifact.

Habituated Stable Behaviors. An important finding disclosed by this model shows these six information tasks are habituated; people resist switching to alternative resources or information seeking methods after cognitive accommodation to sufficient tools. Habituated information tasks are *cognitively economical*, requiring minimal conscious attention to perform successfully. These tasks tend to become internalized as routine operations, demanding from the user only minimal, if any, reflection on their interaction. Because they are stable, continually performed, transparent tasks, we predict such tasks may translate as complete functions in an information ecology enhanced by ambient systems, since the resources and resulting artifacts will be recognized by all participants. This finding has significant implications for design. First, these six "canonical" stable tasks might be incorporated into information ecologies that distribute the artifacts used in research discovery. Second, because these information tasks do not directly support research discovery, we identify a substantial gap between the current ecology of information resources and the potential for supporting the cognitive demands of distributed discovery. This gap delineates the boundary of cognitive artifacts used in discovery, and the limits of technology.

Table 1. Information tasks and artifacts.

Information task	Information artifact
1. Locating materials and methods, by searching, locating, and selecting information from the Internet, primarily using Google.	"Answer" – In many cases a specific material or method
2. Seeking journal articles by searching, locating, and selecting from titles and resources listed in the university library website. This task links to primary resources such as PubMed or MEDLINE, and specialized services such as Web of Science.	Article – PDF format to print and read later
3. Direct searching and selecting of abstracts from primary search resources (PubMed), linking to PDF versions of desired articles through library-provided article linking.	Set of abstracts or citations to topic – Print and scan or read at later time
4. Occasional access of disciplinary websites and tracking topics through email newsletters.	General research topic or news item
5. Regular scanning of 10-20 journals of specific research interest, typically online.	Journal, to access articles
6. Continual use of local resources prepared and collected by the researcher for reading, reference, and immediate use in research work. Artifacts include printed and annotated articles, reference lists, abstracts, and electronic versions of these.	Range of artifacts – Locality serves rapid access to self-assigned topical information

Highly Constrained Resource Use. Even though the information resources in this ecology undergo continual and incremental revision, scientists used only a very limited set. Across observations, a narrow range of habitual information tasks were found for all roles studied in the field sample. These six categories accounted for 91% of cited information tasks, and for nearly all the online tasks and common resources recorded. Although this finding, while correct, may seem an apparently impoverished profile of information activity, this task model is compared with a time-based model of research information practices (Table 2). A weakness of the task model is its insistence on a single-user, resource-use model of information use. The "task" model fails to advance understanding of how information is used in discovery.

4.4   Information Practices in Research

Information research practices are defined as goal-oriented information behaviors that mediate research activity. Everyday, non-directed interactions are information tasks, as shown in Table 1. The difference hinges on the validity, which we question, of studying user interaction with information resources as a unit of analysis. Such information tasks are not independent activities, but are contingent on a research purpose. This study established "research project" as the analysis unit, focused on information use as required by experimental research. This analysis revealed seven major research information tasks over the life-cycle of experimental projects. These research tasks are mediated by certain information practices as shown in Table 2.

Cognitive Tasks Vary in the Research Life-Cycle. A research project may require a duration of a year or much longer, depending on how the project is defined. Discovery occurs as a distributed cognitive process, building upon unexpected findings and learning gained from multiple events during the course of the project. Information practices were analyzed for the entire life-cycle of 10 case projects, examining the information practices of experimental life sciences projects.

Information Practices in Research Life-Cycle. Table 2 specifies seven *information practices* that define the information use life-cycle within a research project, based on analysis of 10 cases, all long-term research projects in the life sciences field studies. As information tasks, they are all complex (multiple steps over time), and are defined here by the intent and goal of the researcher, not by artifact type. These practices are performed to fulfill requirements of a research project, and as cognitive tasks are independent of resource or system. They can be performed manually, verbally, or online, using resources in the information ecology to acquire artifacts and objects.

It is beyond the scope of this chapter to describe the research projects contributing to this model. The significance of this description is to show how research tasks are performed as distributed information processes toward discovery. Scientists conduct independent and discrete information actions, but over the year-plus time periods of research projects, these individual information tasks inform both individual and the research project members as a distributed cognitive system.

All seven research tasks are often conducted to satisfy collaborative objectives. The tasks are described relative to research needs: PIs delegating literature reviews, scientists discussing the design or validity of procedures, exchanging data to support findings or assessments, or relating findings to other known literature.

The practices are complex, typically requiring multiple tasks and hours or even days to complete. Each is directed toward a defined *object* of action. In-

Table 2. Research tasks and associated information practices.

Research task	Information practices
Exhaustive review	Finding all studies (broad search) in a topic area.
Resolve issues in experiments	Immediate inquiries regarding issues emerging from research data.
Evaluate findings	Assessing or validating experimental findings through comparison with other research.
Assess procedures	Locating information unavailable locally on an as-needed basis – especially methods, materials, and procedures.
Establish context for findings	Locating background and supporting information for establishing context and fitting findings into precedent literature.
Assess current state of knowledge	Updating known studies in a topic area with new articles.
Building a case	Analyzing references, and finding competing and complementary authors supporting or arguing against findings.

formation objects represent the information objective, its use. An information object may be defined as the "required or desired objective of use from an information artifact." The information objects consist of components drawn from artifacts such as articles and abstracts, and meet the unique requirements of a research project. Bishop [4] refers to these components as "document surrogates," but here we find the objects inherently containing the objective of information seeking. For the information object, the document is often the "surrogate." These surrogate objects are "building blocks" of research, but are not complete artifacts or sources of knowledge. Objects are often drawn from the defined components of an artifact (e.g., part of a method from the Methods section of an article), but they are not the text of the component.

Individuals are also sought within this distributed system as information and memory resources for specific knowledge. Lab members often first ask a colleague for an answer, if known as a resource for that topic. This is supported by behaviors such as the public act of distributing *printed* research articles to other lab members; this displays personal interest in a particular line of research and one's capacity to discuss or address issues represented by those papers.

4.5   Information Behavior and Search Patterns

While scientists in the study had a wide variety of information resources from which to draw, they limited their research to only two services (PubMed and Google) and were found to use few other resources available to them for published research. The data show (across both field locations) over 90% used the *PubMed* search engine for published scientific research. Most used Google for publicly available information such as other scientists' web sites and chemical suppliers, with 4-5 alternative search engines used on only an individual basis. While they may spend hours locating and scanning papers online, and hours finding referenced papers unavailable online, they spend very limited amounts of time and cognitive resources in the task of *searching*.

Scientists preferred using the simplified search interfaces of the PubMed service and Google search engine over the more sophisticated or specialized search tools and interfaces available in their information ecology. They paid little attention to user interface features and showed no trend toward skill development by using advanced search forms or features such as saved searches (e.g., PubMed's *Cubby*). Over time, search tasks become routinized operations.

Few scientists in the study sought new resources to supplement those in regular use. Instead we observed that, once a set of resources and pattern of use was established, it tended to remain in use over time, even as the available resources in the ecology changed. We found scientists predominantly using the research tools they had learned in graduate school. The PIs preferred MEDLINE to PubMed, having learned its interface as graduate students before PubMed was available. The current graduate students used PubMed almost exclusively.

We make a distinction between (cognitive) information artifact and information object. The artifact is the physical printed document or digital file. An information object is the component "objective" extracted from an artifact. It is defined by the user's need, and not by content. These objects are transformed in research and discovery processes from latent components in the artifact to referenced observations, support for findings, arguments. Scientists conduct many small steps of gathering information, following the direction of an experiment or finding, and build upon the contributed information and reasoning of collaborators and other authors. Within these small steps of information behavior information is transformed from artifact to object to embedded knowledge.

4.6   Printed Article as Cognitive Artifact

During an information task, such as locating articles referenced in a research report, a researcher pursues two types of objects. First an information *artifact* (e.g., published abstract) is sought, followed by locating an *information object* (e.g., the object of searching, the answer of interest). The researcher's cognitive task attends to locating the information object, and the artifact embodying the object. For the most part, the mediating tool (search engine) is used as a transparent appliance and, while necessary to retrieve artifacts of interest, is much less significant as a cognitive artifact.

Information artifacts such as articles, abstracts, and lists of references and components (objects) such as experimental methods are printed and distributed throughout the individual researcher's workspace, computer, notebooks, and memory. By volume and frequency of use, the printed article is the most common information artifact. The printed format was preferred by all participating scientists to electronic formats, primarily for its readability and portability. As a cognitive artifact, the printed copy supports ad hoc perusal and internalization to personal memory, as it may be scanned and read at different times at the scientist's convenience. Because printed articles occupy valuable space on the lab bench's desk, only research papers considered important or relevant to current research are printed and kept available, with the most important and timely articles commonly copied to other scientists. Several participants in different labs indicated how they located currently useful papers in a stack in or on the desk, personally ordered by time of interest of reference. Topics of the most current interest, or being monitored, were represented by full papers toward the top of the stack, with weeks or months of prior topics below the most current issues further down the stack. This natural ordering by currency suggests a monitoring approach for electronic services.

The printed article is in fact an external artifact, drawn from a public source for a specific use in research work. But a distributed cognitive view shows it functions as an endogenous shared computational resource. By its selection and use, it functions as if created by the lab, being read by research project members and discussed in lab and journal meetings. As a researcher inscribes notes and highlights the pages, an article becomes personalized and internalized for memory. Compare adoption of an important article to other cognitive artifacts. Numerous citations, references to authors, and other notes become committed to memory over time, but less critical artifacts serve their purpose and are discarded. Key references to methods and data may be integrated into the more persistent form of a manuscript draft or lab notebook. But unimportant articles are often screened and not even printed or read. The selection and distribution of specific printed articles mediates group awareness of current research issues, publishing trends, competition, quality standards, and of course, emerging findings and applicable facts. Such purposes and uses of paper documents in collaborative knowledge work have been recently validated [31].

The article is maintained as a printed artifact, and as a persistent personal artifact. But these artifacts were explicitly distributed among other lab members. Scientists indicated they commonly shared newsworthy articles or those relevant to research projects by photocopying and distributing them to the desks of intended readers. While we might expect frequent distribution of PDF articles as email attachments, graduate students in two different cases explained it was "just as easy" to copy the article, and this practice was observed during the field visit.

It appears another reason for personally distributing a hard copy article was the meaning attributed to the act of this distribution. One graduate student admitted they preferred to photocopy the printed article because it was "more likely to be read" than if sent via email. The recipients were aware of the specific individual responsible for the distribution. There follows the expectation of reading the article and its contribution to distributed memory, now available for future research (discovery-oriented) discussions in referring to these articles. But the printed article as artifact also carries meanings in its very format, and may be considered a more direct expression of the intent of the research. People annotate the articles and note key paragraphs. When copying articles to senior investigators, graduate students often highlighted or annotated within the article, managing the memory load of intended recipients. These annotations refer to components we consider information objects, which signal an intention or literally, an "objective."

4.7   Laboratory Notebook as Cognitive Artifact

In all lab locations in both field study locations, life sciences researchers maintained traditional bound laboratory notebooks to record experiments. The printed lab notebook is required as both a personal record of experiments for a project, and a legal document representing findings to establish original discovery or to file for patents. These are compelling reasons to maintain the paper notebook artifact, but interest in electronic notebooks has grown. Although electronic lab notebooks have been identified as an emerging technology at the lab bench, they have yet to reach significant adoption. Field evaluations of early prototypes have only started to gain some interest among chemists and other scientists [30], but many issues of form factor, user interface, and data management remain to be established.

Scientists keep the lab notebook as a document of record for every experiment conducted. Notebooks are portable, and often reviewed by the supervisors and other research project members in discussions of findings and procedure. In some molecular biology labs, scientists set up and run one experiment a day, following methodical steps and recording every step by hand in the notebook. In other labs, the notebook may be updated on a regular basis, but is kept current at least weekly.

The notebook is used as a personal, yet distributed cognitive artifact in every step of an experimental cycle, and then as a document supporting findings for discovery, lab discussions, and documenting experiments in a manuscript. As a personal document, it represents the actual work of setting up experiments, with a record of materials, measures, and equipment, sufficient to enable duplication by any other researcher. As a distributed artifact, the notebook is property of the research lab and is shared (at times) with and by other members of a research project. It is archived as a bound volume for safekeeping and future review. According to Mackay, et al [21], biologists "are heavy computer users, but most appreciated the simplicity and flexibility of their paper notebooks. They particularly liked the ability to highlight or annotate images or data and create free-form drawing to illustrate a point." These properties illustrate some of the existing boundary conditions that must be exceeded or accommodated by an electronic notebook artifact.

Discoveries that emerge from experimental findings are noted in the lab notebook, and the "unexpected findings" hoped for by research projects are shared in discussion from this artifact. However, we have little insight into the extent to which using the notebook may contribute to the cognitive processes of discovery. Given prior research recognizing how the distributed contributions of scientists help interpret discovery, distributed access and display of lab notebook data might assist this process.

Recent projects have identified some factors associated with adoption of electronic notebook. Mackay [21] examined three approaches to electronic lab notebooks, and found it most effective to augment the paper notebook with electronic capability using a graphics tablet, a PDA, and cross-interaction software that translates writing and commands on the notebook itself to an electronic record. It supplements the paper notebook by transferring written details as text to a database, supporting data operations such as tagging and documenting mice or samples, and linking to online source data or articles on the web. By transferring document data to electronic format, scientists can store shareable records of experiments to the database, and generate tables of contents across the notebook entries.

Other recent studies [30] have suggested scientists are not yet ready to switch to electronic notebooks, even in highly computerized labs. Schraefel's [30] team compared current electronic lab book approaches, and identified problems preventing adoption. They co-designed a Tablet PC-based notebook with chemists, making a prototype that addressed perceived adoption issues with electronic notebooks. Initial results of the prototype were promising, but these studies also show how far removed such systems remain from wholesale adoption in research labs.

There are certainly multiple factors establishing the cognitive boundary conditions for endogenous artifacts in research practices. A technology-based view of boundaries may assert that current information technology has not met the conditions sufficient to adoption. However, a cognitive view suggests the interaction of many factors, both individual and collective, may constrain electronic artifacts in established practices.

5   Using Cognitive Artifacts for System Design

Intelligent ambient environments show promise for many situations where individuals interact with complex technological devices, such as medical treatment facilities, smart homes and public spaces, and learning spaces such as museums and schools. Ambient systems that can be designed to sense individual presence, collect and organize appropriate data, and respond situationally [27], might also serve distributed cognition in research laboratory and acute health care applications.

Ambient intelligence concepts vary across a wide range, partly because the field remains in the early stages of technological development. The findings from both of the studies that are described in this chapter demonstrate how to link research with system design and development. This section relates the findings from the analysis of distributed cognition to the development of advanced computing systems that are intended to support that cognition.

5.1   Acute Care Anesthesia Scheduling

Research into acute care cognition has provided a number of insights into methods, cognitive artifacts, and practitioner individual and group behavior in the health care setting. The study of physical cognitive artifacts showed how members of the organization seek to reduce uncertainty to the smallest possible amount to make it manageable on the day of procedures. Artifacts show how practitioners apply their expertise to the creation and management of a plan in order to perform a complex set of procedures. Artifacts also reveal organizational change. For example, the master schedule evolves from a plan of procedures that may be performed at day's start into a log of procedures that have been performed by day's end. Artifacts can make research efficient by enabling the researcher to get in at the right level (where help is useful), and to deal with the most meaningful aspects of a complex technical work setting.

Practitioner cognition is distributed in order to strike and manage the balance of constrained resources with the continually changing demand for services. Their cognition is also temporal, shifting attention forward and backward as the day evolves. Team members view past, present and expected events through the day as it progresses. All participants rely on other departments through a daily set of expectations and anticipated action in order to execute the procedures.

The research methods that have been described here get at the nature of practitioner behavior, including the goals and strategies that practitioners use to achieve them. Methods make it possible to evaluate new cognitive artifacts by determining the fit between an artifact and the work domain for which it is intended. Those who seek a way to understand the cognitive work in a domain will need to use such an approach in order to develop information technology that is authentically suited to practitioner needs.

Cognitive artifacts that are computer-supported can add value to resource planning through prompting, and support for speculation, consequence assessment, and value-based decisions.

Prompting. Coordinator interviews indicated that schedule development expertise relies on deep domain knowledge that can only be cultivated through time. Computer-supported artifacts might survey information in the distributed cognition for gaps and inconsistencies that go unnoticed. Nominating such item(s) for the schedule writer to consider would enrich and improve the cognition.

Speculation. Coordinators and team members were routinely observed to speculate about different courses of action in anticipation of known and possible demands for care. Computer-supported artifacts can make it possible for coordinators to speculate about possible courses of action and then choose among them. Making it possible for coordinators to evaluate multiple options would make their consideration more thorough.

Consequences. During schedule writing sessions, coordinators routinely mentioned the implications of the decisions they made while assigning resources. However, coordinators varied in their attention to implications. In one instance, a coordinator writing the same sample schedule as a previous coordinator noticed an opportunity for Medicare reimbursement that the other coordinator had not mentioned. Applying evaluation criteria to potential courses of action could make it possible to display the consequences of choices. For example, a system might show how billing could be increased or how costs could be minimized by opening one room or closing another.

Value-Based Decisions. Schedule writing sessions showed how coordinators vary in their approach to scheduling decisions, based on different preferences that include making the day easy for the coordinator to manage, giving residents the optimal learning opportunity, and making the best match among practitioners and procedures. Digital artifacts can be used to develop templates of schedule planning strategies. Coordinators can review and employ a template that best matches their values and preferences. Templates can capture scheduling expertise and make it available for use by others, expanding schedule writing best practices beyond a single individual. Study of template use through time might open the way to insights about coordinator training and the development of schedule models to ease coordinator work loads.

Developing a Conceptual Solution Based on Findings. Any distributed cognition includes cognitive artifacts that participants develop and use to support cognitive work. Naturalistic decision making environments such as health care are time pressured and resource constrained. For this reason, artifacts that participants create embody information that matters in that work setting. Artifacts are maintained as a part of everyday work because they are valued.

Acute care cognitive research such as the work that has been described here reveals information about the work setting that can be used to create displays that are well-suited to staff work. Findings can also show how to create other types of displays that might add value to practitioner and coordinator daily activities. Displays of information that are related to staff assignments for patient procedures are typically organized according to the location where they are to be performed. As Figs. 1 and 3 show, the cases that are slated to be performed in the OR suite are listed according to each OR room. However, most of the cognitive work that coordinators perform in making and managing staff assignments is temporal – organized according to time.

Any tools that are created to assist these complex and highly sensitive interactions need to reflect the underlying complexity of the work that is to be performed. An effective computer-supported version of the master schedule could improve team performance by supporting work in ways the research had revealed.

How would an ambient intelligent environment assist clinician needs to schedule and manage anesthesia resource assignments? Because time is the key aspect here, designing a display according to time would allow the staff to easily track changes, to anticipate future events, and to respond to emerging situations. What has happened, what has been set in motion, what can be expected, and when each occurs is best depicted in time series representations. Figure 4 illustrates

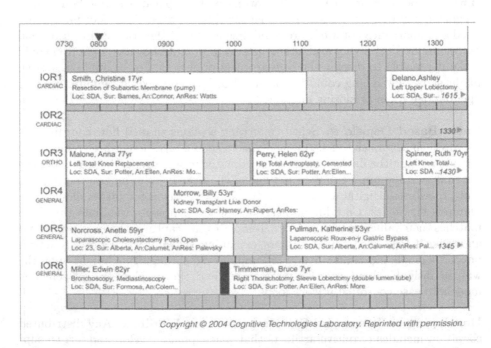

Fig. 4. Conceptual approach for temporal master schedule (all names are fictitious).

the conceptual design of a display that would complement cognitive work needs for resource scheduling and management. It also promises to improve on the previous paper copy of the master schedule by providing information that is structured, consolidated, retained, and explicit.

Structured. The visual organization of the temporal display remains the same as it evolves. By using a graphic representation of time, the team can understand and evaluate relationships among events through time.

Consolidated. Relevant variables such as age are shown within each case window, which saves the need to locate and assemble information that is related but is displayed separately.

Retained. Cases that were performed remain on the display in sequence. Comments and related information can be added. Retaining information makes it possible to review the entire day's activities while they are still underway.

Explicit. Aspects of schedule management that were previously hidden are made evident. These include requirements that are the objects of coordinator cognitive work such as showing conflicts and gaps in timing, and constraints on schedule management such as operating room clean-up and restocking.

Taking a longer-term view, AmI displays could also support prompting, speculation, consequence assessment and value-based decisions in ways that physical artifacts cannot [24]. Further features that such displays might provide include prompting, speculation, evaluation of consequences, and support for value-based decisions.

Prompting. Digital artifacts might survey information in the distributed cognition for gaps and inconsistencies that go unnoticed and unaccounted for. Nominating the item(s) for consideration would enrich and improve the cognition.

Speculation. Digital artifacts can enable coordinators to simulate, speculate, and choose among possible courses of action. For example, speculation about plans for the afternoon staff is currently limited to the coordinator's white marker board cognitive artifact (OR Board). Developing potential courses of action would make it possible to evaluate how desirable they might be.

Consequences. Applying evaluation criteria to potential courses of action could make it possible to display the consequences of choices. One example is to show how billing could be increased, or costs minimized, by opening one operating room or closing another.

Value-Based Decisions. Digital artifacts can be used to develop templates of schedule planning strategies. Coordinators could review and use the template that best matches their values and preferences. Such templates can capture scheduling expertise and make it available beyond a single individual. Study of template use through time might open the way to insights about coordinator training and the development of further schedule models that might ease coordinator workloads.

The cognitive artifact's design must represent constraints and opportunities that are relevant in this domain. Because time is the key consideration, organizing display design according to time allows users to easily track changes, to anticipate future events, and to respond to emerging situations.

5.2   Experimental Life Sciences Laboratory

The case findings enable specification of information services to support information use *toward discovery* in the research laboratory. As with the acute care case, we must build upon an understanding of the use of significant artifacts. Artifacts analysis can reveal numerous needs of collaborating scientists in the discovery process.

As with acute care, an "endogenous" issue remains to first understand the cognitive work practices in research and design interfaces and information services that meet the requirements of the work. The major purpose of reporting detailed findings from life sciences information use is to share real world situations of research practice and discovery with system designers, and reveal some key constraints to adoption of any new service. Again, these constraints come down to the cognitive artifacts, the printed article and lab notebook. These artifacts are so closely coupled to research work that design initiatives must focus on enhancing their properties for cognitive work.

In this discussion we maintain focus on cognitive artifacts and related information objects in the context of scientific discovery. The article and the lab notebook offer a bottom-up perspective based on actual artifact use. The translation to design derives from both the stable, *physical* qualities appreciated in the artifacts, and the *cognitive use* of artifacts and information objects.

We suggest a design challenge of augmenting the laboratory as a designed information space, and to enhance inherently effective physical artifacts to afford interaction with this information space. The field research into scientific information use surfaces three opportunities:

- Redesign searchable information resources and artifacts to access information objects, and not just retrievable artifacts.
- Activate cognitive artifacts, specifically the printed article and lab notebook, to enable communication between these artifacts and distributed information systems.
- Reengineer the contemporary life sciences laboratory as an intelligent environment with pervasive access to information objects at the point of need.

Activating Cognitive Artifacts. Two primary cognitive artifacts involved in discovery were analyzed, the research article and the lab notebook. Both of these artifacts are significantly used and preferred in physical, printed format. These are tangible artifacts with well-defined use characteristics, and people will continue to work with them as tangible artifacts for the foreseeable future, regardless of technology. As relatively stable genres, they provide natural platforms for augmentation starting with minimalist interactivity.

We are encouraged by the innovation of ambient systems that start with tangible objects that translate physical actions on workspaces, desks, and walls to computational actions [14]. AmI designers should consider enhancing the interaction of lab artifacts with various resources through specific information assignments to open interaction from the physical artifact to information services and databases.

The augmented A-Book [21] demonstrates such an example of combining the paper artifact and electronic tools for the lab notebook. Biologists cooperatively designed the A-Book prototype as a portable system to record genetic data from lab mice used in experiments. The paper notebook was used as a base writing template, using an A4 size graphics tablet, a PDA, and a 4D mouse. The PDA was used as an "interaction lens" to transparently display formats and writing from the notebook. Gestures and interactions with this PDA filter electronically record data from tagged objects. The recorded data can be transmitted and viewed as high fidelity images and data. The biologists both record data in the notebook with a pen, and interact with these recordings by interaction with the PDA interaction lens using a non-inking pointer. While the data recording requires somewhat belabored interaction with both notebook and a graphics tablet/PDA interface, this prototype was very well received for its intended purpose of portability. This approach portends the ability to record, transmit, and redisplay data in real time from multiple experiments, providing experimental data to collaborating labs, meetings, and shared information displays.

"Ambient articles" could be printed like any other scientific paper, providing the lightweight, readable, portable format best supplied by paper. Tagging the article with an electronic DOI (document object identifier) or citation link would enable sensors in the lab environment to locate the sensed article online, providing transparent access to online features missing from the print copy. While electronic ID tags could be used to locate print articles in a physical stack, most researchers have indicated that to find an article lost among the stacks is to run an online search and save a PDF copy.

Ambient Information in the Laboratory. Essentially we are aiming to facilitate discovery by integrating information to support its known cognitive conditions (unexpected findings, analogous thinking, and distributed reasoning). A scenario for "ambient collaboration" considers the status and needs of each researcher's experimental work and their current and persistent information needs. Without ranging into exotic and potentially disruptive input systems (voice, gesture, tagged chemicals and experimental systems) we focus primarily on the output dimension (data display, feedback, visualization).

Before adapting new information technology regimes and genres to the scientific workplace, we should analyze social and institutional factors to understand the opportunity or space for design. In research practice, we find scientists working in ways proscribed to a great extent by the traditions and demands of their discipline, and the requirements of the institution. These factors may motivate acceptance or constrain the effectiveness of ambient interfaces in the discovery process. We propose evaluating collaborative research projects as a space for augmenting reasoning with ambient information. The cognitive conditions for discovery (unexpected findings, analogous thinking, distributed reasoning) and the drivers for collaboration (extending research network, parallel experimental regimes, wider distribution of reasoning and feedback) provide a significant opportunity for supporting scientific discovery.

The field study reveals a high-intensity everyday work practice that admits little time for ad hoc peripheral interactions or discussions. The regularly scheduled lab meeting will continue for some time as the basis for research-related exchange and brainstorming to develop interpretations. While the social practices of meetings on the surface may suggest using the one-to-one or one-to-many interfaces of online "collaboratories," the reality of limited attention and participation with information tools suggests a less obvious approach. Rather than attempting a groupware-based system to facilitate discovery in multi-location lab meetings, an ambient approach should adapt to the human perceptual system through peripheral information space.

Users are free to engage or dismiss the information streamed to multiple participants sourced from both peers and information servers. New information genres should be designed; information objects are not targets of searches, but are "pushed" or "syndicated" based on associations and collaborative or scripted filters constructed by participant interaction. As an initial application, this might be as simple as a shared computer and display monitor in each participating workspace, displaying organized threads of data, findings, and article suggestions posted by other collaborators. A running electronic inventory of significant papers retrieved by lab members over time would assist in providing views of literature in constant reference or use, or to display visualizations of research topics and areas explored within and across projects in a particular lab or the research center.

By using electronic lab notebooks and automated data logging, streams of experimental data and lab notes forward to all participants linking to a thread. As ongoing findings are logged and discussed, and participants select key ideas, an analogy agent searches online resources and presents analogous information objects (excerpts or keywords in context) to the shared space. While few of these "suggested analogies" may be perfect, the object is to facilitate the interpretation process, and not an accurate analogy. The goal, using peripheral (unattended) information display and visualization, might be to augment the social process of discovery for collaborators on a continuous basis. A running stream of discovery-oriented analogies, tuned to match research topics, may be attended to at any time as a peripheral task.

Over time these information collaborations will integrate vast amounts of data, translated to specific research objects that might be transferred and reused. Individual interaction and feedback with the system tunes collaborative filter algorithms and increases information specificity, serving to reduce data and noise to minimize attentional overload for individuals and other collaborators. The "intelligence" in such information collaboration develops as a network effect, as each participant and lab's inputs, research data, and information resources are stored, developed, and selected.

6 Conclusions

The chapter shows the nature of distributed cognition that can be found through artifacts that participants develop and use to manage cognitive work. Two case studies presented approaches to distributed cognition. Both studies described highly-uncertain work domains with strong common collaborative objectives. We show how cognitive artifacts reveal distributed cognition processes that support production and performance. The preference that workers show for physical artifacts may be a factor in many distributed systems. Such artifacts reveal significant *boundaries* in the ecology of practice that have yet to be reached or surpassed by sufficiently designed information technologies. Designers should carefully approach known boundaries "marked" by artifacts to avoid disrupting essential cognitive work, or to avoid outright failure of systems or their adoption in complex work domains.

Advanced technologies such as ambient systems may eventually fulfill the promise of a rich information ecology in research and medical practice. In order to create such systems, we urge designers to involve the tangible in distributed computing systems. The use of printed artifacts in distributing memory and knowledge should be considered a "way in" to understand information tasks, and not merely as printed output from searching electronic databases. The augmented A-Book [21] demonstrates such an example of combining the paper artifact and electronic tools for the lab notebook.

The life sciences study shows how information practice in research has become routine and habituated. We describe an information ecology with highly stable tasks, and a preference trend among life scientists converging on only two search tools, PubMed for scientific publications and Google for everything outside of the literature. After nearly 10 years of online scientific publishing, the printed research article remains the end product of successful searching, and very little online reading or use of electronic article formats was found across multiple labs. And the process of collecting the complete set of research articles continues to demand extensive time, even in the online information ecology, given the uneven distribution of available online articles. The substantive finding is that scientists prefer using the printed artifact, and most important articles are printed and maintained as hard copy. Several conclusions about cognitive artifacts in discovery follow from these findings.

Information and Memory Are Maintained by Cognitive Artifacts. In complex, collaborative work domains as described in the case studies, cognitive artifacts provide a means of distributing information and maintaining collaborative memory.

Physical Cognitive Artifacts Reveal the Boundaries of Information Technology. In complex, high risk or high uncertainty settings, workers create or appropriate endogenous artifacts to guide knowledge practices such as planning and discovery, and to supplement collaboration. These cognitive artifacts represent boundary conditions that may not be readily replaced by information technology. Their success lies in how well they reflect cognitive work in their particular setting.

Tangible Artifacts Are Key Markers for Design. Physical artifacts that are used in cognitive work in high-uncertainty domains offer a way to support the underlying cognitive requirements of the cognitive work. In life sciences, the highly-stable use of simple online search resources and preference for printed articles reveals the continuing primacy of the printed article format. The printed article has maintained its role as a primary cognitive artifact because of its affordance for reading and portability, and the shared practices that have evolved with its use over many years. Electronic versions of the same article exhibit few of the physical affordances. To support effective distributed use of information artifacts, a new electronic model of the information object should be designed that provides specific information at the level of detail required for use, and provides another channel for accessing the full artifact.

People Work Through Information Artifacts, but Attend to Objects. Information artifacts (e.g., research articles) are carriers of information objects, and participants locate and share these objects when using information. Discovery processes should identify and represent information objects from the multiple sources of artifacts in the information ecology. Systems designed to aid distributed discovery practices must account for the situated relevance of information objects as they are actually used in practice.

Research Guides Development. Computing systems that are developed without an understanding of the cognition that is to be supported will impede, not improve, work. Methods that have been described in this chapter will lead the researcher toward that understanding. Artifacts embody what matters in a work setting. Artifact analysis leads us to understand work settings by pointing to what matters in that domain. This makes research efficient, allowing the researcher to dismiss the inconsequential for the consequential and to avoid wasting valuable resources, time, and effort.

Systems Design for Distributed Cognition. Computing systems have regularly been developed to exploit a technology opportunity. This technology-driven approach has often been pursued at the expense of understanding the nature of human involvement. Developers of AmI systems have the opportunity to break with the traditional optimism that accompanies new technology and, instead, ground it in the reality of actual cognitive requirements.

Acknowledgements

Dr. Nemeth's work was supported by a grant (RO3LM07947) from the National Library of Medicine, NIH. Dr. Jones' research was supported by Elsevier, as part of a field research program investigating information behavior in experimental life sciences.

References

1. Ball, L.J and Ormerod, T.C.: Putting ethnography to work: the case for a cognitive ethnography of design. International Journal of Human-Computer Studies, 53 (1). (2000) 147-168
2. Bentley, R., Hughes, J.A., Randall, D., Rodden, T., Sawyer, P., Shapiro, D. and Sommerville, I.: Ethnographically-informed systems design for air traffic control. In Proceedings of Computer-Supported Cooperative Work, CSCW 92, Toronto. (1992) 123- 129
3. Berg, M. Rationalizing Medical Work. Cambridge, MA: The MIT Press. (1997)
4. Bishop, A.P.: Document structure and digital libraries: how researchers mobilize information in journal articles. Information Processing and Management, 35. (1999) 255-279
5. Cook, R., Woods, D. and Miller, C.: A tale of two stories: Contrasting views of patient safety. Chicago: National Health Care Safety Council of the National Patient Safety Foundation, American Medical Association. The National Patient Safety Foundation: http://www.npsf.org (1998)
6. Cook, R.: A brief look at the New Look in complex system failure, error, safety, and resilience. Cognitive Technologies Laboratory http://www.ctlab.org (2004)
7. Dunbar, K.: How scientists really reason: Scientific reasoning in real-world laboratories. In R.J. Sternberg, and J. Davidson (Eds.), Mechanisms of Insight. Cambridge MA.: MIT Press (1995)
8. Dunbar, K.: How scientists think in the real world: Implications for science education. Journal of Applied Developmental Psychology, 21 (1). (2000) 49-58
9. Heath, C. and Luff, P.: Technology in Action. New York: Cambridge University Press. (2000)
10. Hollan, J., Hutchins, E., and Kirsh, D.: Distributed cognition: Toward a new foundation for Human Computer Interaction research. ACM Transactions on Computer-Human Interaction, 7 (2). (2000) 174-196
11. Hutchins, E.: The social organization of distributed cognition. In L. B. Resnick, J. M. Levine, & S. D. Teasley (Eds.), Perspectives on Socially Shared Cognition (pp. 283-307). Washington, DC: American Psychological Association Press (1991)
12. Hutchins, E.: Cognition in the Wild. Cambridge, MA: The MIT Press (1995)
13. Hutchins, E.: Cognitive Artifacts. In R.A. Wilson and F.C. Keil (Eds.), The MIT Encyclopedia of the Cognitive Sciences, http://cognet.mit.edu/MITECS/Entry/hutchins (2002)
14. Ishii, H. and Ullmer, B.: Tangible bits: Towards seamless interfaces between people, bits and atoms. In Proceedings of ACM SIG CHI Conference on Human Factors in Computing Systems, CHI 97, Atlanta, GA. (1997) 234-241
15. Jones, P.H.: Distributed information seeking in research collaboration: An extended economy of resources, memory, and cognition. CSAPC'03, 9th European Conference on Cognitive Science Approaches to Process Control, Amsterdam, September. (2003)

16. Kaptelinin, V.: Activity theory: Implications for human-computer interaction. In B.A. Nardi (ed.), Context and Consciousness: Activity theory and human-computer interaction. Cambridge, MA: The MIT Press. (1996)
17. Kaptelinin, V.: Learning with artefacts: integrating technologies into activities. Interacting with Computers, 15 (2003) 831-836
18. Klein, G.: Sources of Power. Cambridge, MA: The MIT Press. (2000)
19. Kulkarni, D., and Simon, H.A.: The processes of scientific discovery: The strategy of experimentation. Cognitive Science, 12. (1988) 139-175
20. LeCompte, M.D. and Schensul, J.J.: Designing and Conducting Ethnographic Research, Vol., 1, Ethnographer's Toolkit. Walnut Creek, CA: AltaMira Press. (1999)
21. Mackay, W.E., Pothier, G., Letondal, C., Boegh, K., and Sorenson, H.E.: The missing link: Augmenting biology laboratory notebooks. CHI Letters, 4(2), ACM Press, Paris, France, October. (2002) 41-50
22. Nardi, B.A. and O'Day, V.L: Information Ecologies: Using Technology with Heart. Cambridge, MA: The MIT Press. (1999)
23. Nemeth, C.P.: The Master Schedule: How Cognitive Artifacts Affect Distributed Cognition in Acute Care. Dissertation Abstracts International 64/08, 3990, (UMI No. AAT 3101124). (2003)
24. Nemeth, C. and Cook, R. Discovering and Supporting Temporal Cognition in Complex Environments. Proceedings of the National Conference of the Cognitive Science Society. Chicago, August. (2004)
25. Nemeth, C., Cook, R., O'Connor, M., and Klock, P.A.: Using cognitive artifacts to understand distributed cognition. In Nemeth, C., Cook, R., and Woods, D. (Eds). Special Issue on Studies in Healthcare Technical Work. IEEE Transactions on Systems, Man and Cybernetics-Part A. Institute of Electrical and Electronic Engineers. (in press)
26. Norman, D.A.: Cognitive artifacts. In J. Carroll (Ed.), Designing Interaction: Psychology at the Human-Computer Interaction Interface. New York: Cambridge University Press. (1991)
27. O'Hare, G. M. P. and O'Grady, M. J.: Gulliver's Genie: A multi-agent system for ubiquitous and intelligent content delivery, Computer Communications, 26 (11). (2003) 1177-1187
28. Patterson, E., Cook, R. and Render, M.: Improving patient safety by identifying side effects from introducing bar coding in medication administration. Journal of the American Medical Information Association 9. (2002) 540-553
29. Reason, J.: Managing the Risk of Organizational Accidents. Aldershot: Ashgate. (1997)
30. Schraefel, M.C., Hughes, G.V., Mills, H.R., Smith, G., Payne, T.R., and Frey, J.: Breaking the book: Translating the chemistry lab book into a pervasive computing environment. In Proceedings of ACM CHI 2004, Vienna. (2004) 25-32
31. Sellen, A.J. and Harper, R.H.R.: The Myth of the Paperless Office. Cambridge, MA: The MIT Press. (2002)
32. Simon, H.A. and Okada, T.: Collaborative discovery in a scientific domain. Cognitive Science, 21 (2). (1997) 109-146
33. Woods D, and Roth E.: Cognitive Systems Engineering. In M. Helander (Ed.), Handbook of Human-Computer Interaction, 3-43. Amsterdam: North-Holland. (1988)
34. Xiao, Y., Lasome, C., Moss, J., Mackenzie, C.F., and Farsi, S.: Cognitive Properties of a Whiteboard. In Prinz, W., Jarke, M., Rogers, Y., Schmidt, K., and Wulf, V. (Eds.), Proceedings of the Seventh European Conference on Computer-Supported Cooperative Work, September, 16-20. Bonn: Kluwer Academic Publishers. (2001)

Multi-modal Interaction in Biomedicine

Elena V. Zudilova and Peter M.A. Sloot

University of Amsterdam, The Netherlands
{elenaz,sloot}@science.uva.nl

1 Introduction

Everybody agrees that user tasks and preferences should play a central role in the design and development of applications oriented to non-computer experts. Nevertheless, even biomedical applications are sometimes developed in a relative vacuum from the real needs of end-users and environments where they are supposed to be used.

To provide a clinician with an intuitive environment to solve a target class of problems, a biomedical application has to be built in such a way that a user can exploit modern technologies without specialized knowledge of underlying hardware and software [18]. Unfortunately, in reality the situation is different. Many developers do not take into account the fact that their potential users are people, who are mostly inexperienced computer users, and as a result they need intuitive interaction capabilities and a relevant feedback adapted to their knowledge and skills.

User comfort is very important for the success of any software application [13]. But very often we forget that usability problems may arise not only from an 'uncomfortable' graphical user interface (GUI), but also from a projection modality chosen incorrectly for deploying an interactive environment [16].

Existing projection modalities have not been sufficiently investigated yet in respect to usability factors. Meanwhile, the selection of an appropriate projection modality in accordance with the user's tasks, preferences and personal features might help in building a motivated environment for biomedical purposes. In this chapter we summarize our recent findings related to this research and introduce a new concept of multi-modal interaction based on the combination of virtual reality (VR) and desktop projection modalities within the same system. For the case study of the research we used a biomedical application simulating vascular reconstruction [2, 22].

The rest of the chapter is organized as follows. Section 2 introduces concepts of a multi-modal interaction and projection modalities. Section 3 describes the biomedical application for vascular reconstruction deployed for two different projection modalities. Section 4 is devoted to the experiments on user profiling. Both the methodology, on which the user profiling was based, and the results are presented here. In section 5 the possibilities of how VR and desktop projection modalities can be combined are discussed. Finally, conclusions and plans for future research are presented in section 6.

Y. Cai (Ed.): Ambient Intelligence for Scientific Discovery, LNAI 3345, pp. 184–201, 2005.
© Springer-Verlag Berlin Heidelberg 2005

2 Multi-modal Interaction and Projection Modalities

Section 2 introduces concepts of multi-modal interaction and projection modalities.

Traditionally, multi-modal interaction is considered as interacting with a computer system using more than one input or output modality at a time, usually suggesting drastically different modalities to be used simultaneously [16]. The simplest example of multi-modal interaction is the simultaneous use of a mouse and a keyboard. More advanced multi-modal interfaces may combine voice input with a mouse and/or tactile feedback.

Today's advanced computer technologies provide different forms of input/output modalities. The possibility to combine them while using the same application leads to the development of a multi-modal interaction style. We may use command dialogue, speech recognition, data entry, graphics, web and pen-based interfaces, direct manipulation, haptics, gestures and even interacting via GPRS enabled cell phones. For example, one can draw simple images by walking round the streets of a city and entering data points along the way via a cell phone [25]. Virtual and augmented reality can be also considered as input/output modalities used for providing the interaction-visualization support [16]. These two relatively new interaction paradigms are alternatives to a desktop solution applied on a common PC (or a PDA). They are usually referred to as projection modalities [6].

Virtual reality (VR) is a projection modality, invented in 1965 by Ivan Sutherland [20] and intended to make the interaction process with a computer more intuitive and appealing. The main difference of an immersive[1] [5] application in comparison to a desktop one is that it can provide the user with a sense of presence. In VR an artificial world is created around the user, which gives the impression of being in that world and able to navigate through and manipulate objects in the world [5]. Ideally, VR has to provide an environment, where users can interact freely in a 3D space. However, in practice the utilization depends on hardware and software solutions chosen for deploying this projection modality.

When VR is combined with the real world, this projection modality is called augmented reality (AR). AR is a combination of a real scene viewed by a user and virtual objects generated by a computer that augment the scene with additional information. So if in VR the artificial world is generated completely, in AR the real world is combined with elements from the artificial one [11]. Actually AR is a projection modality, which is the closest to the real world because a user mainly perceives the real world with just a bit of computer-generated data (Fig. 1). As for a desktop, we here refer to a conventional PC. A conventional PC is highly refined to support office work, which is characterized by a user sitting in a chair, at a desktop preferably with a lot of space for a keyboard and a mouse [15]. The user is typically situated at the same desktop the entire day and primarily

---

[1] Immersive VR offers the user a stereoscopic, head tracked, as much as possible surrounding visual experience using either head-mounted displays or (multiple) projection screens, such as in the CAVE environment. Such systems are deemed 'semi-immersive', when an all around picture is not offered [5].

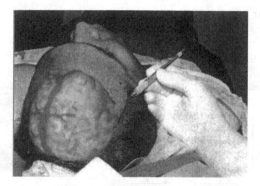

Fig. 1. AR in medicine.

works alone. In the case of a desktop projection modality, a 3D environment is projected on a computer screen (Fig. 2) and users' manipulation and navigation capabilities become limited within a 2D projected world.

We focus our research on investigation of differences arising from the interaction in VR and desktops.

3 The Virtual Radiology Explorer in VR and Desktop

The Virtual Radiology Explorer (VRE) is a biomedical simulation system for vascular reconstruction, which has been deployed both for VR and desktop projection modalities. Unhealthy life style and dangerous habits may affect our arteries and veins. The purpose of a vascular reconstruction is to redirect and increase blood flow in the case of stenosis[2] or repair an artery if it is affected by

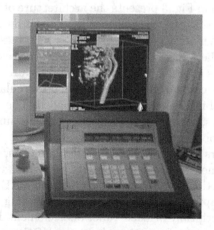

Fig. 2. An example of a medical virtual environment on a desktop: the Philips Medical Systems' "Easy Vision".

---

[2] Stenosis is a narrowing or blockage of the artery [21].

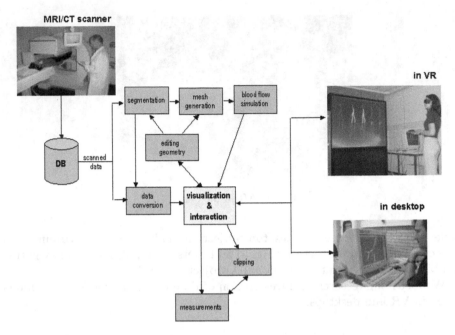

Fig. 3. An interactive simulated vascular reconstruction system.

aneurysm[3]. To find the best solution for the treatment of a particular vascular disorder is not always an easy task and depends to a great extent on the current stage of a disease and the exact location of the affected zone of an artery [21]. The aim of the VRE is to provide a clinician with an interactive virtual simulated environment to visualize and explore the patient's vascular condition to help in finding solutions for further treatment.

The scheme shown in Fig. 3 presents the architecture of the VRE system. The input data for conducting an experiment is a patient's data, which comes either directly from a scanner in a hospital or from a remote storage or a database (DB). By means of the VRE system the end-user may assess medical scans in 2 or 3D, simulate the vascular reconstruction procedure and validate possible ways of treatment by comparing a patient's blood circulation before and after the simulated surgical intervention has been applied. The VRE solver simulates blood flow parameters, which are visualized to give a surgeon a possibility to check whether the blood flow in the affected area will be normalized or not.

The potential users of the VRE are vascular surgeons, radiologists and technologists, as well as medical novice specialists, students, and trainers. [8]

A detailed description of the functionality of the VRE system is far beyond the scope of this chapter. To add to the understanding of the VRE Table 1 provides a brief description of each functional element from Fig. 3. Readers interested in getting more information about the VRE may refer to earlier work [2, 18, 22].

---

[3] An aneurysmal disease is a balloon like swelling in the artery [21].

Table 1. An overview of the VRE functionalities.

Segmentation	The segmentation is applied to extract the arterial structure of interest from a raw data set
Data conversion	At this stage a scanned data in DICOM [17] format is converted into VTK [26] format so that it can be visualized and processed further.
Mesh generation	The segmented and converted data set is then modified into a 3D mesh for the VRE solver.
Blood flow simulation	The VRE solver simulates the parameters of the blood flow: velocity, pressure and shear stress. The solver is based on the lattice-Boltzmann method, which is a mesoscopic approach for simulating fluid flow based on the kinetic Boltzmann equation [2, 18].
Grid (geometry) editing	A user may edit interactively the geometry of an artery: add a bypass, remove insignificant elements or restore the fragments lost during the segmentation.
Measurements (probing)	The interactive measurement component of the VRE provides the possibility to measure quantitatively a distance, angle, diameter and some other parameters characterizing an artery.
Clipping	Using clipping planes a user may cut off the display of a scene such that anything in front of the near-plane, or behind the far-plane, is not visible. If needed measurements and clipping can be combined. [14]
Visualization and interaction	Several visualization techniques are used within the VRE to represent the patient's data and the parameters of a blood flow [18]. Surface and volume rendering are used for the visualization of arteries and of the patient's body. We use currently glyphs, streamlines and streaklines to visualize the results of the blood flow simulation. As for the interaction capabilities, the VRE supports two interaction styles: – the Virual Operating Theatre for VR (section 3.1); – a Personal Desktop Assistant for desktop (section 3.2).

Many of the VRE components are non-interactive due mostly to their complexity (e.g., simulation, segmentation, data conversion). A user may only run, pause or stop the execution of a routine. As for the interaction capabilities, they are supported currently only by several components of the VRE: grid (geometry) editing, data exploration (e.g., clipping engine) and measurements.

The system is available both on the Distributed Realtime Interactive Virtual Environment (DRIVE) system [1, 22] and on a PC-based workstation. Two independent versions of the VRE have been developed to give a possibility to exploit the system in two projection modalities: in VR and desktop.

3.1   The Virtual Operating Theatre

We called the interaction style of the VRE system deployed for the VR projection modality 'the Virtual Operating Theatre', because a user 'plays a role' of a physician applying the treatment of a vascular disease on a simulated patient [2].

To support better the user's interaction within an operating theater, a multi-modal interface [18] to the VRE system has been built. It combines context sensitive interaction by voice and manipulation of 3D virtual objects using a wand[4] and hand gestures. Although, the main VRE functionality can be accessed both via a direct selection or manipulation and via a voice command, for time consuming procedures related to grid editing, interactive measurements and data exploration the direct manipulation technique remains the most reliable.

For the end-user of the VRE system, grid editing is the most important functionality, since it permits to simulate the surgical procedure of the placement of a bypass[5] on an artery. In VR users are capable to manipulate 3D objects directly. They deal with 3D representations of an artery and a bypass. For representing a bypass we use spline primitives. So the procedure of adding a bypass comes down to re-scaling of a spline and positioning it correctly on an artery. These manipulations are conducted using a wand. The same procedure can be applied to the placement of a stent within an artery in the case of aneurism.

Measurements are crucial both for diagnosis and for planning the treatment. Clinical decision making relies on evaluation of the vessels in terms of a degree of narrowing for stenosis and dilatation[6] for aneurysms. The shape, length, diameter, and even material of a bypass or a stent depend to a great extent on the size and geometry of an affected vessel.

Interactive measurements in VR are organized as follows. For conducting a measurement, a user has to position an appropriate number of active markers on an object. Markers are building blocks of the distance, angle and line-strip measurements. The number of necessary active markers depends on a measurement to be done. For measuring a distance, a user has to add two markers and if it is an angle, three. For conducting line-strip or tracing measurements – at least two [22]. In VR a user can add a marker via direct manipulation using the position and orientation of a wand.

A free clipping engine [12], which has been developed recently as a part of the VRE system, is an interactive component aimed to help in the exploration of big data sets. By restricting a view via a clipping plane the user may look inside the patient's body or specific part of an artery. In VR a user may change the orientation of a clipping plane by changing the direction of a wand and as a result see the original data, obtained from a scanner, slice by slice (Fig. 4).

---

[4] A wand is a hand driven controller combined with tracking sensors to allow the VR system to receive user commands and to track the position of the hand with respect to virtual objects; provides 6 degrees of freedom (position and orientation) [22].

[5] A bypass is a graft rerouting a blood flow around blockages. Usually it is a piece of vein taken from elsewhere in the body or an implant made from an organic material [21].

[6] Dilatation is an increase over the normal arterial diameter [21].

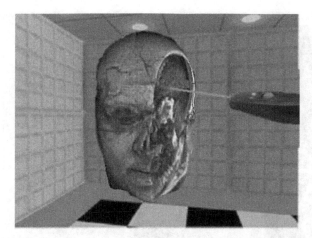

Fig. 4. Free clipping in VR (The original data set was provided by Dr. A. Koning, SARA, the Netherlands).

Using a wand the user may navigate through a virtual world, explore the patient's body and even walk through an artery. However, to navigate and manipulate successfully in a 3D virtual world a user should possess special motor skills, which is not an easy task for all people [6].

3.2   A Personal Desktop Assistant

It is known that the desktop projection modality suits the individual work the best [6]. That is why we called the interaction style provided by the desktop VRE 'a Personal Desktop Assistant'. In principle a user does not need additional motor skills to interact with the desktop VRE. The biggest problem arises from the fact that within a desktop application we cannot manipulate 3D objects directly, we always deal with 2D projected representations of these objects [7]. Even though the 3D representation of data is provided by many desktop applications, it does not play an important role with respect to the manipulation or navigation capabilities. It is used mostly as a passive viewer, which helps a user to orient better.

Thus, to add a bypass or a stent within the desktop VRE a user has to deal with several projected representations of an artery and auxiliary dialogue menus. The same concerns interactive measurements in a desktop. The procedure of adding a marker is similar to the procedure of grid editing. If in VR a user can add a marker via a direct manipulation using the position and orientation of a wand, switching to the desktop projection modality leads to the necessity to deploy extra menus and sliders to help the user to orient him or herself in a projected 3D world.

The GUI of the clipping engine of the VRE deployed for the desktop projection modality is shown in Fig. 5. In comparison to VR versions, additional interface capabilities have been applied. Thus, a user may select a slice of interest

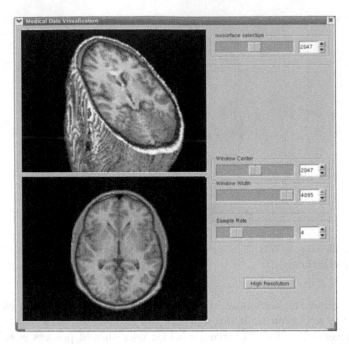

Fig. 5. Clipping in the desktop VRE (The original data set was provided by Dr. C. Taylor, Stanford University, USA).

by means of a menu or a slider. A unique identification number helps to identify a concrete slice. The GUI contains two viewers: one presents the 3D object and another one shows a high-resolution slice of interest, which has been generated as a result of the intersection of a 3D object with a clipping plane built by a user. The combination of these two views provides several advantages. First of all, a user can have a 3D view of an object, which is important for planning a further intervention; and at the same time he or she can get a more detailed view of a slice of interest by varying scale or contrast parameters. It is also important that the technique used is quite similar to the standard approach for the visualization of CT/MRI scans familiar to the end-users of the VRE [12]. Even though, like it was mentioned above, for the manipulation and navigation in a desktop environment a user does not need to possess extra motor skills, the necessity to deal with the increasing number of GUI's elements may lead at a certain moment to the deterioration of the users' orientation capabilities.

4   User Profiling

The existing prototypes of the VRE provide a sufficient set of functionalities, enabling us to take a much closer look at the usability problems. To make sure that the system is developed in accordance with real life demands, the choice was made to conduct a small exploratory study as a first step to investigate the daily working context of two focus user groups of the VRE: radiologists and vascular surgeons. Seven interventional radiologists and seven vascular surgeons from nine Dutch hospitals participated in the experiment on user profiling.

4.1 Methodology

The most effective way to find usability problems of the VRE is the extensive involvement of users in prototyping and development of the system. However, clinicians are not unlimitedly available for extensive design sessions and repeated laboratory testing. The advantage of contextual analysis [3] applied is in studying users' tasks and preferences in a real life environment without having to rely on self-reporting methods.

The combination of exploratory interviews and observation sessions leads to a better understanding of tasks and processes surrounding the diagnosis and treatment planning for vascular disorders. It also permits us to get a better view to the possible place of the VRE system in a real life medical environment.

Observations have been carried out to gain detailed understanding of tasks and the context in which each task is performed. The whole trajectory of tasks related to diagnosis and treatment planning has been observed in a manner resembling contextual inquiry by an individual researcher [10]. Forms containing data recorded and reported by clinicians in certain assessment tasks have been gathered. Notes and photographs have been taken when possible and permitted.

The interviews served as a preparation for observation sessions. During series of 'one-to-one' interviews the subjects have been asked about their daily activities related to diagnosis, treatment planning and surgical interventions. Working processes and information used in these processes have been identified. Current bottlenecks and high-risk elements of each task have been assessed to gain understanding when the system's support might be useful. The usage of 3D data by subjects has been evaluated. Expectations concerning the improvement of existing medical tools have been gathered. The subjects' attitudes towards different projection modalities have been analyzed.

To summarise, the user profiling permits us to:

- Identify the processes related to the tasks of diagnosis and planning interventions for vascular disorders and specify the place of the VRE in respect to these processes;
- Classify potential users of the VRE and analyze their attitudes towards VR and desktop projection modalities.

The next subsections present these findings.

4.2 Task Analysis

Diagnosis starts when a patient comes to the First Health Care, where a therapist confirms that a patient is suffering from a vascular disorder. At this early stage information processed by a therapist may vary from a story told by a patient to a complete scan data set made earlier.

The next step is consultancy, which is usually conducted by a vascular surgeon. The consultation includes diagnosis and identification of contraindications with the corresponding explanations for minimization of risk factors in future (e.g., stop smoking or low cholesterol level) [8]. Physical examination can also be conducted: it includes measurements of blood pressure and pulse rhythm, as well as special tests, e.g., the 'walk test' [9]. If a vascular surgeon is an experienced practitioner, this examination will be sufficient to make a diagnosis and to plan the further treatment for a typical case, even including a surgical intervention if necessary.

As for non-typical cases, further testing is required, which implies collaborative work of radiologists and surgeons to make correct diagnosis and plan a proper treatment. Several imaging techniques can be used to determine the location of the obstruction or narrowing of the artery. One of them is echo-doppler (duplex) examination. It permits to picture the vein to determine the location of a vascular disorder. The echo-doppler examination utilizes an ultrasound probe to visualize the vein structure either through the chest wall or by placing a probe through the mouth into the esophagus [17].

If the echo-doppler examination does not help in better understanding of the patient's conditions, computed tomography (CT), magnetic resonance imaging (MRI) or magnetic resonance angiography (MRA) can be used for the further examination [17]. 3D data acquired by CT or MRI is always converted into a set of 2D slices that can be displayed and evaluated from various perspectives and levels. MRA is a technique for imaging blood vessels that contain flowing blood. It is very popular among cardiovascular specialists because of its ability to non-invasively visualize a vascular disease. The choice of the imaging technique is determined by the structure or anomaly that needs to be observed, given that some techniques are better suited for certain cases than others [21].

Although, the data acquired by imaging techniques is always presented in 2D, radiologists and surgeons can easily process it. However, for complicated non-typical cases 3D reconstruction of scans is also performed to get an extra insight in the geometry. In this respect the VRE system might be very helpful, for the prediction of the behavior of a bypass or even a stent in the future. In any case, the VRE will always remain only an assistant in making a decision. Nevertheless to the available functionality of the VRE in future, the final decision will be made always by clinicians. Thus, currently the final decision about the diagnosis and further intervention is usually made during a 'vascular meeting' where both radiologists and surgeons are present.

A simplified use-case diagram for the VRE system is shown in Fig. 6. This diagram corresponds only to assisting in decision-making. As for another possibility of using the VRE as a training environment for medical students and novice clinicians, currently it is only possible if the training process is guided and controlled by a teacher, who is a confident user of the VRE.

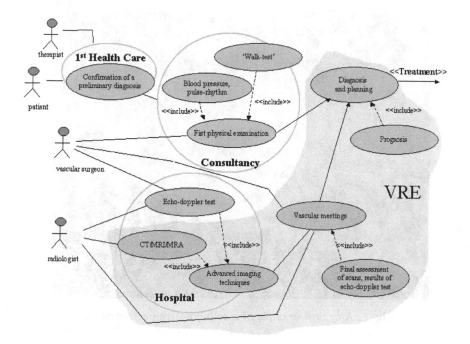

Fig. 6. Simplified use-case diagram for the VRE system.

4.3   User Groups and Types

End-users of the VRE are people who use the system as a tool for conducting experiments. It is expected that the VRE will be used for the interactive decision support by vascular surgeons, radiologists (both diagnostic and interventional) and technologists[7].

An unexpected finding of the experiment conducted was the identification of an extra potential user group – technicians [8]. They form one of the most perspective user groups of the VRE, since they currently use diagnosis and planning systems to prepare scan images for radiologists and surgeons, so that they could assess these images as quick as possible. In some cases, technicians and radiologists perform the first assessment of these images together. Depending on the scope of the VRE in future the needs and requirements for this user group may need to be taken into consideration as well.

Like it was mentioned earlier, two user groups participated in the experiment on user profiling: vascular surgeons and interventional radiologists. We tried to categorize people that we interviewed and observed and as a result came up with the following classification of the potential users of the VRE system.

---

[7] Vascular technologists are people from scientific or radiography background. They conduct patients' testing using special equipment, including MRA/MRI/CT scanners, for diagnosis of arterial and venous diseases.

Fig. 7. A typical example of a collaborative environment.

1. *Highly Cooperative Clinicians.* The work of these people is highly cooperative (Fig. 7) and may require fast intervention. They are very dependent on each other, nurses and anesthetists. It is very important for these clinicians to have access to different types of technology 'on-fly' (e.g., X-ray machines, the electronic patient data, ultrasonic equipment, etc.) The Virtual Operating Theatre is the best solution for this user type. However, it is important to take into account the fact that it is quite possible that they have to remain sterile, in which case a traditional wand and stereo glasses are not an option for them.

2. *Experts.* These people are usually very experienced clinicians. In making a decision they rely more on their own expertise, than on experience of other people and available technologies. However, it does not always mean that these clinicians are conservative. Many of them can be very enthusiastic about new advanced computer technologies, especially if the results are generated quickly and comply to their expectations. This user type prefers individual work, so a Personal Desktop Assistant might be a good solution for them.

3. *Mobile Clinicians.* These people move around treating the patients. It can be within a hospital but it could also be in the patients' home. These people are working in different environments with different needs for IT-support (e.g., the ward, the office, the outpatient department, the meeting room, the patient home). This user type is mostly interested in monitoring the patient's condition. Although, from time to time they can be interested in getting a quick access to the VRE system. The best solution for these clinicians is the VRE deployed for the desktop projection modality available on a PDA.

4.4   User Attitudes Towards VR and Desktop

Different people prefer different interaction styles. The Virtual Operating Theatre cannot always satisfy all potential users of the VRE, as well as a Personal Desktop Assistant. The choice of an interaction style is very closely related to users' tasks and preferences. We base this assumption on the results of user profiling. Both interviews and observations indicate that many surgeons and interventional radiologists would prefer to use desktop applications for accomplishing every-day tasks. As for the large immersive virtual environments, they would be more preferable for collaborative work and training.

Even though 3D visualization is now available in most hospitals, it has been found that existing systems are not always in use. Currently, no intervention is carried out based on the evaluation of 3D visualizations only. This is due, first of all, to the bad resolution of 3D stereoscopic images in comparison to 2D high-resolution scans.

The advantage of the VR projection modality is that it provides possibilities for collaborative work, which is crucial if we talk about clinicians. During observation sessions it has been found that medical people spend a significant part of their time in collaboration: for making a diagnosis and planning a treatment. However, the number of people involved in a work discussion usually does not exceed five. The exception is a weekly medical conference, in which all staff members of the medical department are present.

Table 2. An overview of the VRE functionalities.

VR	Desktop
Stereoscopic visualization and 'sense of immersion' add significantly to the task understanding or performance.	Stereoscopic visualization and immersion do not add to the task understanding or performance.
The 3D stereoscopic representation is vital.	Image resolution is crucial.
Insight view into a complex structure is more important than performance.	Performance is vital. No extra time can be spent for running the specialized equipment or conducting complicated manipulations.
Perception and field regard are important.	Perception and field regard do not add to the understanding of a task.
Collaborative work of a relatively big group of people (3 or more) is necessary to support.	Quick, informal collaboration needs to be provided for a relatively small group of people (2 maximum).
End-users are interested in new technologies and willing to spend time for training.	End-users are less inclined to learn using new equipment and technology.
There is enough space to place equipment.	Space limits.
Enough budget is available.	The available budget is limited.

A desktop application cannot be treated as an instant solution to usability problems experienced while working with a VR application [7], and vice versa. Success always depends on the usability of a desktop or VR version. However, the better understanding of the interaction capabilities provided by the desktop projection modality makes it a viable alternative to VR. Another factor is simulator sickness[8].

Simulator sickness occurs in conjunction with VR exposure. Users having simulator sickness cannot work in VR for a long time. According to [6] almost a quarter of computer users suffers from a form of simulator sickness. So approximately the same proportion of the VRE users are not capable of exploiting VR. For these users desktop solution remains the only possible option.

The heuristic evaluation of the VRE [13] coupled with the results of user profiling permit us to pick up criteria helping to choose between VR and desktop. Some of them are provided in Table 2. More information can be found in our other publications [6, 12]. These criteria can be applied not only to biomedical applications, but to other domains as well, especially if the interaction and visualization aspects are vital for the application under the development.

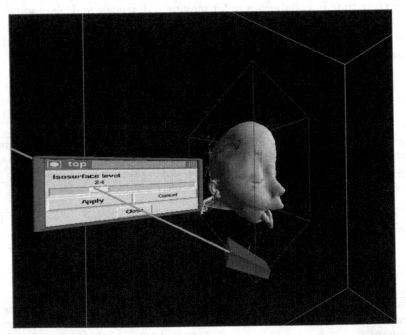

Fig. 8. Combination of VR and desktop within an immersive virtual environment [1] (The image is courtesy of Dr. R.G. Belleman, University of Amsterdam, the Netherlands).

---

[8] Simulator sickness is a kind of motion sickness except that it occurs in a simulated environment without actual physical motion [16].

5   VR and Desktop: An Integrated Solution

The results of the experiments on user profiling led us to the idea to combine VR and desktop projection modalities within the same interaction visualization system. In this case different types of users will be able to work within the same environment and switch between different projection modalities if necessary. We see at least three possibilities of how this idea can be deployed.

One of the possibilities of how VR and desktop applications can be combined is shown in Fig. 8. The main idea is to provide access to an already existing desktop application by "absorbing" its GUI into VR [1, 4]. A desktop application is represented in a separate window. For its activation and further manipulations a user must use a wand and/or a keyboard, which is not very intuitive and quite often leads to the significant meshing of the interaction process. Thus, if the position of a 'desktop window' in VR is not fixed, it is very easy to loose it while navigating in a 3D world.

Another possibility is to provide a user with an integrated workplace, where he or she can work in the virtual environment and at a desktop PC at the same time. Working alternating at a desktop PC and at a VR installation is the typical situation for a programmer and also for a CAD-Designer (e.g., the PIcasso system [19]). Because of repeatedly putting up and down input devices and glasses and also due to repeatedly standing up and sitting down when changing the workplace, this is very demanding and time consuming.

A Personal Space Station (PSS) is a relatively new concept for deploying the interaction-visualization support [15]. The main advantage of a PSS is that it initially combines the elements of VR and desktop projection modalities within the same system and it is possible to switch between them if necessary.

A PSS allows users to interact directly with a virtual world. A PSS consists of a semi-transparent mirror, in which a stereoscopic image is reflected. A user reaches under a mirror to interact with the virtual objects directly with his or her hands or by using task-specific input devices. Fig. 9 shows the experimental setup of a PSS that has been built at the University of Amsterdam. By definition a PSS is an individual environment, but there is a possibility to build a shared environment where users can manipulate the same virtual objects working on different PSSs [7]. More information about a PSS concept can be found in [24].

The idea to combine VR and desktop projection modalities on a PSS sounds very attractive. However, its deployment is not an easy task. Now both the VR and the desktop versions of the VRE system can run on a PSS. But to switch a user has to restart a system, which is very uncomfortable and does not allow using the functionality of both versions at the same time.

The interaction in VR and desktop projection modalities is different with respect to navigation, locomotion, manipulation and measurement capabilities [5]. To combine the Virtual Operating Theatre and a Personal Desktop Assistant, a PSS has to support input and output modalities provided by both VR and desktop simultaneously. This leads us to the development of a new concept of 'a multi-modal desktop-VR interaction'. This concept is based on the principle of exploiting interaction capabilities of VR and desktop simultaneously without changing devices and a workplace.

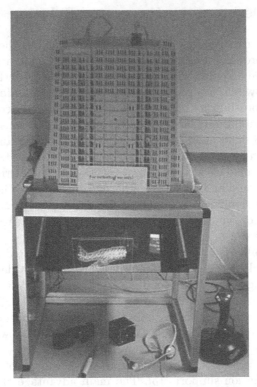

Fig. 9. A Personal Space Station – an experimental setup [24].

6   Conclusions and Discussion

In this chapter we introduced our findings related to the development of biomedical applications in different projection modalities. The case study for this research was a simulated environment for vascular reconstruction – the VRE system.

The heuristic usability evaluation that we conducted recently and the first results of user profiling indicate that the human-computer interaction depends to a great extent on a projection modality chosen for deploying interaction and visualization capabilities. It becomes especially crucial if we talk about biomedical applications. As clinicians are usually unfamiliar with modern computer technologies, it is very important to make the process of their interaction with an application as intuitive as possible.

In this chapter we introduce the concepts of a multi-modal interaction and projection modalities. We discuss two interaction styles of the VRE system based on VR and desktop – the Virtual Operating Theatre and a Personal Desktop Assistant. Although, both VR and desktop solutions are viable alternatives for the VRE users, the results of user profiling show that none of them can satisfy all potential users. That is why we decided to combine virtual and desktop interaction capabilities within the same environment. We are now working on deploying a Personal Space Station that will be capable to provide 'a multi-modal desktop-VR interaction'.

Our current research goal is to build a system, which will give users a possibility to switch between VR and desktop projection modalities without changing devices and a workplace. We focused on the development of a mechanism to support simultaneously input and output modalities of both VR and desktop. This will permit us to provide end-users of the VRE with a combined desktop-VR version of the system. We expect that it will help to satisfy the wider range of end-users and make their interaction with the VRE more intuitive. Our next research step related to HCI will be to compare navigation, locomotion, manipulation and measurement capabilities in VR and desktop projection modalities with respect to users' satisfaction, performance and mistake inflicting. We plan to use the VRE running on a PSS as a case study for this research.

The final research goal will be to develop a system able to dynamically change the interaction style, adapting itself to the situation, preferences and motor skills of each user. This system will be based on personalized interaction metaphors [22].

Acknowledgements

The authors would like to thank Dr. Robert Belleman, Denis Shamonin, Daniela Gavidia, Roman Shulakov and Hans Ragas for their contribution to the development of the VRE system. We also would like to acknowledge Dutch hospitals for their participation in user profiling, as well as Henriette Cramer and Dr. Vanessa Evers for their contribution to this research.

This work is partially sponsored by the EU CrossGrid Project IST-2001-32243 and the Token 2000 project "Distributed Interactive Medical Exploratory for 3D Medical Images."

References

1. Belleman, R.G.: Interactive Exploration in virtual environments, University of Amsterdam, PhD thesis (2003)
2. Belleman, R.G., Sloot, P.M.A.: Simulated Vascular Reconstruction in a Virtual Operating Theatre. Proceedings of CARS 2001 (2001) 18-27
3. Beyer, H., Holtzblatt, K.: Contextual Design: Defining Customer-Centered Systems, Morgan Kaufmann (1998)
4. Dykstra, P.: X11 in virtual environments: Combining computer interaction methodologies. In X Resource issue Nine. O'Reilly and Associates, 8th Annual X Technical Conference (1994)
5. Bowman, D.G., Hodges, L.F.: User Interface Constraints for Immersive Virtual Environment Applications. Graphics, Visualization and Usability Center Technical Report GIT-GVU-95-26 (1995)
6. Chen, C., Czerwinski, M., Macredie, R.: Individual differences in virtual environments-introduction and overview, Journal of the American Society for Information Science, v.51 n.6 (2000) 499-507

7. Crabtree, A., Rodden, T., Mariani, J.: Designing Virtual Environments to Support Cooperation in the Real World, Virtual Reality 6 (2002) 63-74
8. Cramer, H.S.M., Evers, V., Zudilova, E.V. and Sloot, P.M.A: Context Analysis to Inform Virtual Reality Application Development, Int. J. Virtual Reality (in press).
9. Enright, P.L., McBurnie, M.A., Bittner, V., Tracy, R.P., McNamara, R., Arnold, A., Newman, A.B.: The 6-min walk test: a quick measure of functional status in elderly adults, Cardiovascular Health Study. Chest. J., 123(2) (2003) 387-398
10. Forsythe, D.E.: It's just a matter of common sense: Ethnography as invisible work, Computer Supported Cooperative Work (8) (1999) 127-145
11. Jolesz, F.A. et al.: Image-Guided Procedures and the Operating Room of the Future, Radiology, 204 (1997) 601-612
12. Gavidia Simonetti, D.P., Zudilova, E.V., Sloot, P.M.A.: A Client-Server Engine for Parallel Computation of High-Resolution Planes, Proc. of International Conference on Computational Science – ICCS 2004, Krakow, Poland, June 2004, in series Lecture Notes in Computer Science 3038 (2004) 970-977
13. Nielsen, J.: Usability Engineering, Academic Press (2000)
14. Pierce, J., Forsberg, A., Conway, M.J., Hong, S.,Zeleznik, R.: Image Plane Interaction Techniques in 3D Immersive Environments, Proceedings of 1997 Symposium on Interactive 3D Graphics (1997) 39-43
15. Poston, T., Serra L.: Dextrous virtual work. Communications of the ACM, 39(5) (1996) 37-45
16. Raskin, J.: The Humane Interface: New Directions for Designing Interactive Systems, Addison-Wesley Pub Co (2000)
17. Robb, R.A.: Handbook of Medical Imaging: Processing and Analysis,Academic Press (2000)
18. Sloot, P.M.A., van Albada, G.D., Zudilova, E.V., Heinzlreiter, P., Kranzlmüller, D., Rosmanith, H., Volkert, J.: Grid-based Interactive Visualisation of Medical Images, Proceedings of the First European HealthGrid Conference (2003) 57- 66
19. Stefani, O., Hoffmann, H., Patel, H., Haselberger, F.: Extending the Desktop Workplace by a Portable Virtual Reality System, in CD Proceedings of the IPT2004 Immersive Projection Technology Workshop (2004)
20. Sutherland, I.E.: The Ultimate Display, Proceedings of IFIP Congress, New York (1965) 506-508
21. Yao, J.S.T., Pearce, W.H.: Current Techniques in Modern Vascular Surgery, 1st edition, McGraw-Hill Professional (2000)
22. Zudilova, E.V., Sloot, P.M.A., Belleman, R.G.: A Multi-modal Interface for an Interactive Simulated Vascular Reconstruction System, Proceedings of the IEEE International Conference on Multimodal Interfaces (2002) 313-319
23. Zudilova, E.V., Sloot, P.M.A.: A First Step to a User-Centered Approach to a Development of Adaptive Simulation-Visualization Complexes, Proceedings of the International Conference of the Systemics, Cybernetics and Informatics, Orlando, Florida, USA, July 2002, V.V (2002) 104-110
24. The Section Computational Science website: http://www.science.uva.nl/research/scs/
25. The GPS drawing project: http://www.gpsdrawing.com
26. The Visualisation Toolkit website: http://www.kitware.com

Continuous Body Monitoring

Jonathan Farringdon and Sarah Nashold

BodyMedia Inc., USA
jonny@bodymedia.com

1 SenseWear: A Body Worn Sensor System

When a person who usually wears a watch forgets to put it on one day, it is common for them to look at their wrist anyway expecting the watch to be there. Without looking or touching to check, they are not aware of the watch's presence or lack thereof. The watch becomes a part of their expected experience due to its comfort and continuous utility. It satisfies Thad Starner's definition of a wearable system as "always with you, always on, and always accessible"[22]. At another end of the ambient intelligence spectrum the design vision of Stefano Marzano is one where the " 'relationship' between us and the technology around us will be of utmost importance. This relationship will no longer be one of user towards machine but of person towards 'object-become-subject', thus towards something that is capable of reacting, of being educated and responding [18]." Amongst the myriads of applications envisioned in an "ambient culture" by Stefano's team are the person, their clothing, their home and furniture, and an amenable outside world [17].

The interdisciplinary team at Bodymedia, Inc. designed the SenseWear armband in the realms of both Starner's and Marzano's ideals. SenseWear is a multi-sensor system designed for wearing in contact with the body 24 hours a day, 7 days a week, with periodic removal for hygiene. Figure 1 shows the SenseWear armband being worn. SenseWear is designed to continuously provide, record, and share information about the state of the wearer through nearly all of their life activities. The SenseWear armband is an active data collection point and "hub" of physiological and context based ambient information systems. Like the watch, it is "always with you, always on, and always accessible". What SenseWear does for you, because it's accessible, may not be continuously apparent. Accessibility to information mediated by the device is completely dependent on particular associated applications. SenseWear is often used as a continuous silent and unobtrusive activity monitor. It's worn and in contact with the skin continuously because it's doing something for you continuously. We regularly observe that SenseWear users forget they are wearing the device during normal use. Indeed on the occasions when a SenseWear user has their armband off they occasionally reach or feel for it, just like they might with a watch. In the wearable computing field this takes SenseWear into the realms of Mann's eudaemonic wearable [15].

The SenseWear armband performs continuous monitoring of the person 24/7 in an unobtrusive way and can communicate its findings wirelessly to other devices around it. This has clear benefits for ambient environments and information

Y. Cai (Ed.): Ambient Intelligence for Scientific Discovery, LNAI 3345, pp. 202–223, 2005.

All graphics in this chapter are reprinted
with permission from BodyMedia Inc.

Fig. 1. The SenseWear PRO$_2$.

devices. The SenseWear Armband is commercially available from BodyMedia, Inc. based in Pittsburgh PA, as a research tool giving access to "raw" and derived data. Specifically configured SenseWear armbands, together with custom end-user software applications, are also commercially available from BodyMedia or their partners, for example the weight management system HealthWear available from Roche [21].

This chapter describes the armband's functionality and gives an overview of the technical capabilities of the armband and its construction. A breadth of applications are presented showing the feasibility and acceptance of a body worn continuous monitor. This illustrates the SenseWear armband's utility as an ambient intelligent device.

1.1 Why an Accessory and Not Apparel?

A study of suitable locations on the human body for both sensing physiology and locating hard components resulted in candidate locations and form factors for continuous body monitoring [7, 10] (See Fig. 2). The combination of sensors (discussed later) and the desired small unobtrusive form factor resulted in a decision to have multiple sensors and data collection inside a single unit worn on the triceps.

SenseWear occupies a body region that is new for skin-touching wearables – the upper arm. A custom stretch elastic was employed, the bottom of the unit and sensors conformed to maximize contact, and thousands of hours of testing performed to achieve a design that was comfortable and "completely forgettable" on vastly different arm sizes. A major achievement in this process was developing a design that was tight enough to keep the sensors in place against the arm without slipping, but loose enough not to constrict the user's arm and cause discomfort – a sensitive balance.

Flexible, symmetrical wings were developed to stabilize the device on the arm (ensuring good sensor contact) and molded to a circumference exactly between

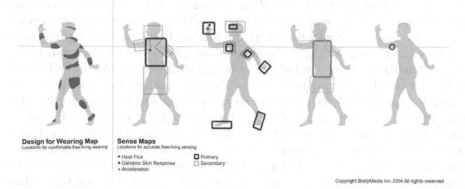

Fig. 2. Shapes and positions from the original "Design for Wearability" study [7], far left. To the right of this are four visualizations reflecting subsequent research in 1999. These highlight sensor locations for heat flux, galvanic skin response, and acceleration. The SenseWear armband location is identified far right.

the smallest and largest adult arm sizes. They fold inward to fit the smallest adult female arm (down to 203mm/8" circumference) and expand to accommodate the arms of large bodybuilders (up to 622mm/24.5" circumference) making the system usable by virtually all adults.

SenseWear is made from molded plastics and surgical grade stainless steel, materials approved in the USA for skin contact. The unit is easily cleaned. In home use the unit might be wiped clean when washing one's self. In a clinical setting the strap is changed and unit cleaned between subjects. The strap is made from nylon, polyester, and polyisoprene (no latex) in three sizes: small, one size fits most, and large. Specifically, the straps fit 140mm/5.5" − 241mm/9.5", 203mm/8.5" − 432mm/17" and 406mm/16" − 622mm/24.5" arm circumferences. By being readily cleanable, the sensor component is suitable for almost 24/7 wearing. When a user bathes they take it off with their clothes, replacing the clothes and the armband at the same time. The straps are detachable for washing. The suggested wearing duration is 23 hours in any 24 hour period.

The armband is minimally invasive. Furthermore, it is comfortable and invisible for most observers even if the user is wearing a short sleeved shirt. It is in skin contact, but only at the surface, and is thus less intimidating or uncomfortable than semi-invasive sensor devices such as some blood-glucose meters, or clinical heart rate monitors where electrodes are adhered to the skin. Completely invasive sensors such as implants have a certain positive unobtrusiveness and 24/7 monitoring capabilities. An example of such a device is an implanted loop recorder for cardiac care. However, by comparison, the process of implantation is extremely expensive, and carries a substantial psychological barrier for broad consumer use.

1.2   Real Time Versus Post Activity Analysis

The SenseWear armband is a ubiquitous computing device, however it is not always used as a real time device. Indeed for applications such as clinical study and clinical weight management SenseWear is usually used as a passive continuous data gatherer. The data is analyzed after the fact. In the weight management setting for example, a user may wear the armband all day, simply going about their business. Importantly, the armband does not restrict the user, but is simply constantly collecting data about them and their activity. At the end of each day, for example, the user retrieves the data to another system such as a PC where the data is analyzed and acted upon. In the clinical setting, experimenters can deploy subjects with SenseWear and have it collect data outside the lab for up to fourteen days. The subjects may keep diaries as well, but SenseWear is an objective observer, providing automatic journaling of the wearer's activities and body states. At the end of a study SenseWear provides a data set for the experimenter to manipulate in numerous ways not possible in real time. Many examples of SenseWear in real-life use are given later in this chapter.

Real-time data becomes more important for reactive ubiquitous devices and environments. In these cases, SenseWear is equipped with a short-range transceiver and can communicate with similarly equipped devices. SenseWear units are uniquely addressable. The transceiver is currently commercially available in additional sensory products such as weight-scales. In this case the user stands on the scale, and their weight is transmitted to the armband, where it is inserted into the data stream.

2   Architecture and System

SenseWear is a tool – a body worn, wearer focused, sensor and data hub that can perform an application on its own, or be part of a much more extensive system. Two generic frameworks are presented: stand-alone and supervised.

2.1   Supervised

Figure 3 illustrates SenseWear's place in a large-scale system. There is no specific application in this particular system view. All components are information systems, thus are customizable to specific applications. This particular system architecture illustration considers numerous SenseWear users wearing the armband and being constantly monitored. Elsewhere, connected by the internet, clinicians, care givers, fitness professionals or other concerned parties monitor the wearers after the raw sensor data has been analyzed. The Apex fitness system (described in Sec. 5) is an example of this architecture deployed commercially.

2.2   Stand Alone

A stand-alone system, with optional home PC support would have an architecture shown in Fig. 4. Third party devices can log their sensor readings or other pertinent information amongst the continuous armband data by using the transceiver kit. SenseWear research customers also can add the transceiver to their own devices.

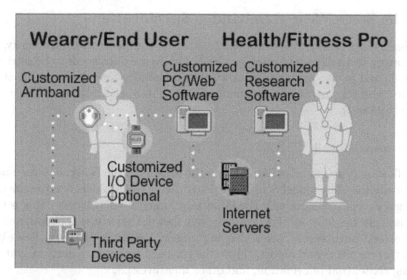

Fig. 3. Illustration of information communicated between SenseWear users and professional advisors.

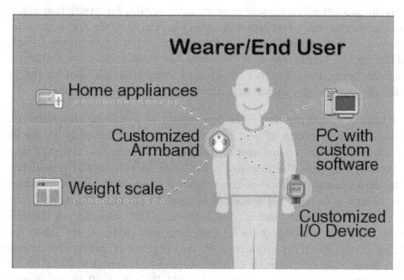

Fig. 4. A stand-alone home system architecture.

These architectures are realizable and in some circumstances already commercially deployed through the use of some modular components. On Microsoft Windows PC's there are both stand alone applications for accessing SenseWear data and internet transport mechanisms. A programmable transceiver kit allows for custom third party devices to communicate their data to the armband. Software systems exist for professionals to manage and view the data of their users remotely.

3   The SenseWear Armband – Specifications

The SenseWear armband is comfortable to wear, can be worn continuously, and will store up to 14 days of physiological data before the data needs to be retrieved. The armband is also equipped with wireless capability for retrieving the stored data and also for providing real-time feedback. The specifications in Table 1 are for SenseWear II.

3.1   Sensor Detail

The following provides more detail about the sensors in the Bodymedia armband. Specifically the 2004 model SenseWear Pro$_2$. After the physical sensors are characterized we will consider why the important thing is not what is being sensed, but what can be detected. For example, one can not purchase a pedometer sensor, a calorie-burn sensor, nor a sleeping sensor. Yet these are what SenseWear ultimately monitors and reports. From the physical sensors are derived synthetic sensors, contextual information, and other measures [2].

Accelerometer. The accelerometer is a 2-axis MEMS device that measures motion. The motion can be mapped to forces exerted on the body and the gravity information can provide valuable context information for predictive algorithms. The accelerometer has a resolution of approximately 0.005g and is presently calibrated to match a reference gravity of one g to within 0.05g on the longitudinal axis, 0.06g on the transverse axis. The axes are relative to an upright armband, longitudinal being from ground to sky and transverse parallel to the ground. Worn on the back of the upper arm, transverse is through the chest.

Heat Flux. The proprietary heat flux sensor is a robust and reliable device that measures the amount of heat being dissipated by the body at the location of the armband. The sensor uses materials with very low thermal resistance and extremely sensitive thermisters. It is placed in a thermally conductive path between the skin and the side of the armband exposed to the environment (see Fig. 5). A high gain internal amplifier is used to increase the resolution of the measurements to a resolution of < 0.3 W/m^2. The accuracy of the heat flux sensor is tested in a wide range of temperatures, with a low inter armband variability about room temperature. At two regions of particular interest, the heat flux sensor has a resolution of 0.267 W/m^2 in thermal equilibrium at 22°C (room temperature); and a resolution of 0.291 W/m^2 at 50 W/m^2 heat flux at 32°C (skin temperature). The high gain amplification results in a very sensitive instrument, highly suited to higher rate sampling.

Galvanic Skin Response. Galvanic skin response (GSR) represents electrical conductivity between two points on the wearer's arm. The GSR sensor in the armband includes two hypoallergenic stainless steel electrodes integrated into the underside of the armband connected to a circuit that measures the skin's conductivity between these two electrodes (see Fig. 5). Skin conductivity is affected by the sweat from physical activity and by emotional stimuli. GSR is used as an

Table 1. Detailed specifications for the SenseWear II armband.

Dimensions and weight
(l) 85.3mm x (w) 53.4mm x (h) 19.5mm. Weight 85g.
(l) 3.4" x (w) 2.1" x (h) 0.8". Weight 3.0 oz

Mechanical
Medical Device Grade ABS – monitor top and skin-touching bottom.
UV-stabilized Thermoplastic Urethane(TPU) – flexible wings, overmolded
to monitor top.
FDA-registered co-polyester – skin touching label covers screws providing
a smooth interface to skin.
Surgical grade stainless steel 304 – external sensors, progressive stamped
and insert molded to bottom.
Custom designed non-latex elastic – adjustable strap.

Hardware
Battery – 1 AAA, up to 14 days continuous use (24/7).
Memory – 512Kbytes of flash data storage, up to 14 days continuous use
(24/7) in standard configuration.
Processor – low power 16 bit w/integral program flash, scratch RAM,
A/D, and peripheral support.
USB – USB 2.0 interface with drivers for Windows 98, ME, 2000, and
XP.
Wireless – ISM band 916.5MHz radio transceiver for wireless communi-
cation.

Sensors
Accelerometer – 2-axis MEMs device
Heat Flux – patented configuration of injection molded heat pipe, sensor,
and differential amplification
Galvanic skin response – symmetrical stainless steel pads insert molded
into the ABS bottom
Skin temperature – thermistor-based sensor assemblies

indicator of evaporative heat loss by identifying the onset, peak and recovery of
maximal sweat rates. The GSR circuit records skin resistance to a high degree of
accuracy over a wide range of values, with a 2.5nSiemen maximum error up to
100nSiemens, and a 2.5% maximum error otherwise. Typically minute averages
in GSR show small changes from minute to minute. Subtle physiological effects
can be seen in GSR at higher sampling rates.

Skin Temperature. Skin temperature is measured using a highly accurate
thermistor-based sensor located on the backside of the armband near its edges
and in contact with the skin. Continuously measured skin temperature is approximately linearly reflective of the body's core temperature. The skin temperature sensor has a resolution < 0.05 degrees Celsius and is accurate to 0.5°C

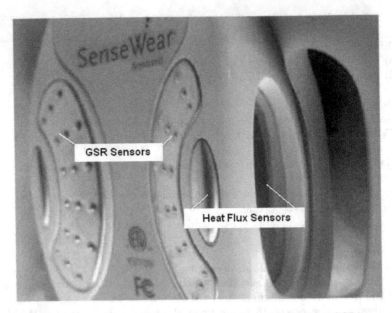

Fig. 5. Sensor positions on the back and side of SenseWear. The GSR sensors are a pair positioned on the underside of the unit, in contact with the skin. The heat flux sensor has a skin contact component on the underside and a cover component on the side of the unit.

between the 20 and 40 °C range (68°F-104°F). At room temperature the resolution is 0.02°C. Typically minute averages in temperature show small changes from minute to minute. Subtle physiological effects can be seen in temperature at higher sampling rates. The temperature sensor is recording the skin temperature, thus changes in the local thermal environment can also cause this reading to change indirectly by causing changes in skin temperature.

3.2   Derived Measures – Synthetic Sensors

The SenseWear armband samples all of the raw sensors at 32 Hz. From these signals, many other signals are calculated and derived. In many SenseWear systems a set of derived channels are then recorded at a much lower rate, such as once per minute. These synthetic sensors can include simple metrics such as averages and summations, but can also include complex computations such as activity classification and energy expenditure. In SenseWear systems these synthetic sensors appear as additional sensor data streams.

Energy Expenditure (EE). The medical standard for measuring caloric expenditure is the VO2 metabolic cart. But these machines tend to be large, lab-restricted devices that require a technician's supervision. The SenseWear armband was designed to provide results comparable to a metabolic cart but in a small wearable form factor, invisible to observers, usable in a free-living environment, easier to put on and as comfortable as a wristwatch (see Fig. 6).

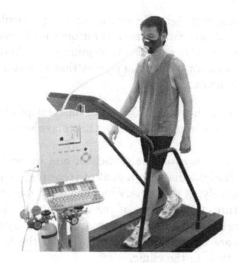

Fig. 6. VO2 metabolic cart in a lab setting.

The energy expenditure algorithm in the SenseWear system is multi-sensory. There are limitations to single-sensor products (e.g. pedometers, accelerometers) in deriving calorie expenditure. Such products are capable of seeing only one or two-dimensional activities and can not differentiate between the myriad activities performed throughout the day. The SenseWear system is a tested and proved first-of-its-kind multi-sensory design that can intelligently recognize contexts and apply the appropriate sensors to measure the activity being performed. This innovation not only improves accuracy, but in applications such as HealthWear allows the system to communicate the contexts (activities) that are most effective for achieving the wearer's weight loss goals.

BodyMedia has already developed software that integrates the signals from the sensors in the SenseWear armband and processes them using algorithms that provide estimates of energy expenditure during different types of physical activity. Energy Expenditure, often calculated in units of metabolic equivalents (METS) for exercise physiologists, is a size and weight independent measure of calories burned. Energy expenditure is predicted by first classifying the data into an activity class (e.g., ambulatory exercise, biking-like exercise, other exercise, or resting). An appropriate regression equation is then applied. The classifiers and equations were tuned on indirect calorimetry data collected from subjects performing the relevant activities (see Fig. 6).

Pedometer. An onboard algorithm in the armband calculates steps based upon the high rate two-axis acceleration data stream.

Wearer's Context. Many SenseWear systems can predict when the wearer is in a number of standard states, including lying down, sleeping, being restful, traveling in a moving vehicle, walking, running, biking, and other types of exercising. These categorizations can be important for other algorithms (e.g. energy expenditure) or in their own right, depending on the particular application. For example these classifications can be used to automatically record a person's activities during a day – in other words, auto-journaling. Another application is simply to record the amount of exercise or rest that a person undertakes in the course of wearing the armband.

Future Sensors. While not available as commercial products in 2004, there are additional applications and capabilities that make sense for the SenseWear platform.

Heart rate is a prime physiological indicator and an active area of research and development at BodyMedia with a goal of recording heart rate as comfortably and as unobtrusively as the SenseWear armband measures sleep, activity, and energy expenditure. Other areas of research and development include algorithm and software support for diabetes management, hydration monitoring, and sleep. All these are applicable for monitoring in the home and free-living environments rather than in the clinic.

3.3   System Embodiments

The SenseWear armband is currently commercially deployed in three different packages: research, weight management, and fitness.

The research and clinical system is a stand-alone system comprised of armbands and research software. The software allows for the initialization, sampling rate configuration, data retrieval, and viewing of collected data from the armbands. The research software gives the user a great deal of control over their armband and the collected data compared to the other applications. The raw data, and many of the derived measures such as sleep and energy expenditure are exportable as Microsoft Excel or comma separated value files for further analysis. HealthWear is the brand name of the clinical weight management package available from Roche. This combines the armband with a web site-based tracking system designed to be used in the context of a clinical setting, allowing individuals to monitor their progress from home PCs. The Apex Club Based Weight Manager is a managed fitness system available from the Apex Fitness Group that combines the armband with a personal training regimen and a web site-based meal and exercise planning and tracking system. Both these systems are now described in more detail.

4   Roche HealthWear

"The percent of persons who are overweight or obese (BMI of 25 or higher) increased from 56% in 1988 to 64% in 1999-2000 [23]."

"With obesity on the rise, we can expect a sharp increase in diabetes rates to continue. Unless these dangerous trends are halted, the impact on our nation's health and medical care costs will be overwhelming." Jeffrey P. Koplan, MD. Director, US Centers for Disease Control and Prevention 1998-2002 [12].

HealthWear[1] is an innovative and educational weight loss system consisting of a small wearable monitor (the HealthWear armband), a user friendly internet application (HealthWear Weight Center) and algorithms to provide wearers with the most accurate calorie balance system available. The HealthWear Armband uses a collection of sensors to gather personalized physiological data from the wearer. This information is downloaded to the Weight Center where algorithms

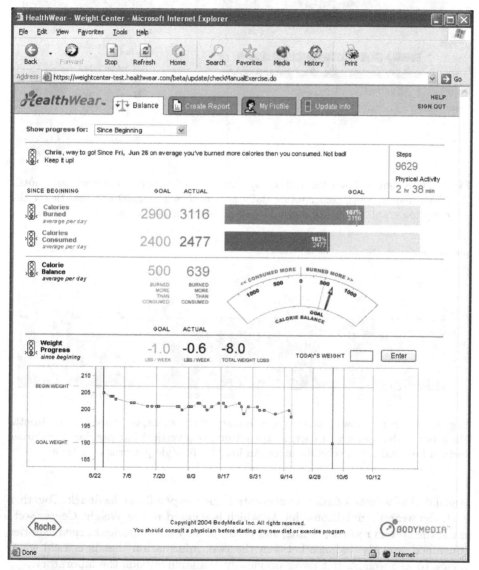

Fig. 7. This figure shows the overall view of HealthWear Weight Center, with charted weight and calorie balance.

---

[1] HealthWear is a trademark of a Member of the Roche Group. ©Roche Diagnostics.

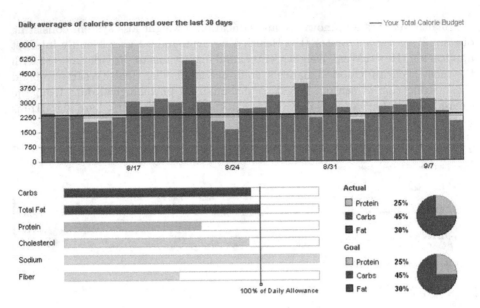

Fig. 8. This figure shows the thirty day summary of calories consumed and nutrition. The users' energy consumption daily goal is shown as 2260 calories. Below the consumption graph is a break down of their actual food intake against their goal.

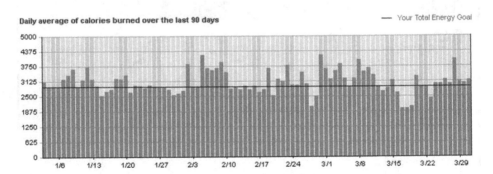

Fig. 9. This figure shows a ninety day summary of energy expenditure. The horizontal black bar is the user's goal energy expenditure, one vertical bar per day, the darker vertical lines indicate weekends. users can look for lifestyle patterns over time.

translate the wearer's data into accurate caloric expenditure feedback. Together with the wearer's nutritional intake which is entered in the Weight Center software, the system records, trends, and presents the user's calories burned, calories consumed, and the balance between the two; information that is critical when trying to lose weight, but never previously available outside the laboratory.

A calorie deficit is required if one is to lose weight. However, tracking calories consumed is difficult and accurately counting calories burned has been virtually impossible outside of a clinical environment (see Fig. 6).

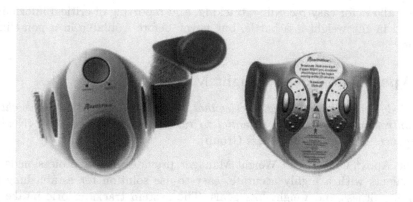

Fig. 10. The HealthWear armband. Back view, right, is without strap.

The HealthWear System automatically records and tracks calories burned. Tracking calories consumed is enhanced with an innovative online food diary. The system goes one step further to compare the data, report the results, and recommend to the user ways in which to reach their personal weight goals. Screenshots from the HealthWear application are shown in Figs. 7, 8 and 9.

From a technology perspective, HealthWear is both a medical device and wearable computer – two product categories often equated with technology-centric complexity. To reduce this perception, the team created a goal to take the best parts of these product categories: the accuracy implied in medical devices and leading-edge technology implied in wearable computers, and blend them into a new form and interaction experience that conveys empowerment and health. A highly ergonomic and body shaped form factor, integrated and seamless material transitions achieved through over and insert-molding, and soft, light colors help convey this perceptual message (see Fig. 10).

The HealthWear armband has only one button, which is used to view the memory and battery status. All other interactions are automated, increasing simplicity, reducing user error and reinforcing the advanced nature of the device.

The HealthWear armband turns on simply by sliding it on. Once the armband detects that it is being worn, the armband turns on. A short vibration and friendly sound sequence indicate that the armband is starting to monitor. When the wearer slides the armband off, it turns off.

Uploading the data stored on the armband to the HealthWear website is just as easy. While wearing the armband the user opens the Weight Center software and transmits their information through a small Wireless Communicator connected to the user's PC USB port. This device is a disk 65mm in diameter, domed to 20mm at the center and 4mm at the edge.

By reducing the size of the technology and enabling the system with online software, HealthWear liberates clinically accurate weight monitoring from the lab, allowing patients to proactively monitor their goals in a free-living fashion, see their progress in the context of everyday living, predict their weight loss or gain trend, and share results with their health care provider. The HealthWear

System allows for easy recording, tracking, and reporting of critical information required in the weight-loss battle, but never before available in a non-clinical setting.

5   Apex Club Based Weight Manager

"BodyMedia has developed a device that, properly integrated into a weight control program, has the potential to turn the tide on obesity." (Neal Spruce, CEO of Apex Fitness Group).

The Apex[2] Club Based Weight Manager provides fitness professionals and their clients with a highly accurate, easy-to-use solution for establishing and managing fitness and weight loss goals. The system tracks caloric intake and expenditure automatically, without the requirement of food logging. The system is supported by other features such as a state-of-the-art food menu generation engine and comprehensive reporting features for both fitness professionals and club members. Figure 11 shows the armband at use in the Apex program.

Apex Fitness specified this software system to take advantage of the continuous energy expenditure and context monitoring capabilities of SenseWear. The Apex web-based Weight Manager is deployed in clubs around the USA. For a club member this involves using a software system together with a fitness professional, and the option of wearing "the sleek wearable body monitor." The web-based nutrition and coaching software helps club members and their personal trainers establish and keep track of fitness and weight loss goals. The armband gives objective measures of energy expenditure during fitness sessions and during the rest of the day.

Apex programs are well established over the last twenty years, and are the most widely available fitness programs in the USA. 24-Hour Fitness is the leading health club chain in North America. This broad and timely experience is employed through a (human) supervised system architecture.

The inclusion of continuous energy expenditure monitoring enhances the weight control programs by informing the client about exactly how much food they can consume before they store it in all the wrong places. This is a calorie-counting program where users do not need to do anything other than wear the device and weigh themselves once a week. The fitness professional combines their experience, their knowledge of the client, and the recorded armband data to better advise the client.

One of the many functions of the BodyMedia armband is the ability to accurately measure a person's total calories burned in any timeframe, allowing the wearer to view the result and adjust their food intake accordingly. The ability to monitor total energy expenditure, together with the trainer's ability to accurately measure body mass changes, allows the system to report back to each user and their fitness professional what the user's total calorie intake has averaged without any manual recording. The system reports estimated food intake (calories in) and measured energy output (calories out).

---

[2] Apex is a trademark of the Apex Fitness Group.

Fig. 11. This figure shows armbands worn in the gym and a user with a fitness professional discussing the client's recorded results.

The Apex Club Based Weight Manager is personalized according to the user's eating and exercise preferences. The Apex program, using the guidelines of the American Dietetic Association, creates an individual program for each user according to their particular food likes and dislikes. As a result, Apex program participants are more likely to achieve a sustainable weight loss change.

6   SenseWear Everywhere

"My subjects like the Armband because they don't really notice they are wearing it. It's an exciting technology that combines physiological and activity monitoring information." Dr. Scott J. Strath, Ph.D. Research Fellow. Ann Arbor VA Hospital.

Researchers from a variety of fields have used the SenseWear Armband and InnerView Research Software (IRS versions 1.0-4.0) in various investigations.

In most cases researchers were willing to share their data and analysis, which has helped BodyMedia to continually improve both the SenseWear armband and the research software, to strengthen user and activity data pools, and to improve BodyMedia's ability to train, choose, and develop more sophisticated algorithms.

Often, research specialists provide the first instance of focused group data (e.g. obese, diabetic, cardiac and pulmonary subjects) affording unique opportunities to realize previously undiscovered physiological information that can lead to better understanding of typical and distinctive qualities in the data characteristics of a group or activity set. We expect this cyclical exchange to continue, improving the accuracy and scope of BodyMedia tools in both research and diagnostic settings.

The SenseWear Armband is particularly interesting as a data collection device for medical applications because it allows data collection in free-living environments without using cumbersome or invasive laboratory equipment (see for example Fig. 6). Similarly, SenseWear is a useful tool for studying psychosocial situations because of its noninvasive, constant, multisensor data logging capabilities. This can enhance qualitative field notes with physiological information overlays and, in some situations, reduce or eliminate note taking by hand. Furthermore, with data streaming technologies in place, SenseWear provides the potential for remote information collection, analysis, and synthesis.

6.1   Energy Expenditure and Exercise Physiology

Researchers have used BodyMedia Armbands in a variety of clinical studies often in relation to energy expenditure and fitness studies. University of Pittsburgh has collaborated with BodyMedia on a number of research initiatives including energy expenditure, sleep, and eating disorders. Dr. Kupfer, Chief of Behavioral Medicine at UPMC sees the armbands and associated software as an opportunity to "get information... we could previously get only in a lab" and sees great potential for using armbands for affordable public health studies.

Jakicic et al [9] and Fruin et al [6] tested the SenseWear PRO Armband against indirect calorimetry measurements for energy expenditure during rest and during use of multiple fitness machines such as treadmills and stationary bicycles. The Jakacic study [9] found "When exercise specific algorithms are used, the SenseWear Pro Armband provides an accurate estimate of energy expenditure when compared to indirect calorimetry during exercise periods examined in this study." The Fruin study [6] found "The SWA provided valid and reliable estimates of EE at rest and generated similar mean estimates of EE as IC on the ergometer; however, individual error was large. The SWA overestimated the EE of flat walking and underestimated inclined walking EE."

King et al [11] studied multiple activity monitors including CSA, TriTrac-R3D, RT3, BioTrainer-Pro accelerometers, and the SenseWear Armband. Their study concluded that "The CSA was the best estimate of total EE at walking and jogging speeds, the TriTrac-R3D was the best estimate of total EE at running speeds, and the SenseWear Armband was the best estimate of total EE at most speeds."

Chronic Obstructive Pulmonary Disease (COPD) physiopathologists at the University of Pittsburgh have found wearable body monitoring (WBM) devices useful for research, stating that for therapy study "exercise tests have gained popularity as outcome measures . . . [acting as] surrogates of 'free-living' activity, which. . . may represent the more meaningful outcome [20]." This group tested a portable telemetric breath-by-breath (EE-BXB) metabolic device against the BodyMedia SenseWear armband on COPD subjects concluding "A WBM is a reproducible and valid measure of physical activity in the laboratory setting and should, therefore, be a valid measure of 'free-living' activity and a highly meaningful outcome measure in COPD clinical trials [20]."

Other researchers are taking advantage of free-living information gathering capabilities for estimating energy expenditure, for example Cole et al[3].

Researchers at Virginia Tech are using BodyMedia armbands to monitor activity levels of human participants involved in diet and exercise studies concerning conjugated linoleic acid (CLA), a substance found to increase metabolic rates and decrease fats in lab rodents.

Health Management Consultants of Virginia are developing a children's game aimed at encouraging lifestyle changes based on activity levels – in this case footsteps recorded during a day. Children are given the choice to wear a SenseWear armband that automatically retrieves to the game or a pedometer with a parent controlled, daily log. Children's footsteps equal points necessary to continue game play, which gives an advantage to the armband option because of more frequent data updates. Preliminary feedback indicates decreased TV watching and increased footsteps in child subjects.

6.2   Telemedicine

One of the largest commercial markets in America is that of the "aging" baby boomer. There are projected shortages of health care professionals to tend to the future needs of this large socioeconomic group as well as a greater emphasis on quality of life issues. Remote medical monitoring is one answer to this growing need. It allows fewer health care professionals to diagnose and care for more patients at greater distances saving money, spreading the breadth of specialized expertise and allowing for patients to have more autonomy and a perceived higher quality of life by spending more time at home and less time in a hospital.

Along with remote medical monitoring capabilities for home health comes health monitoring capabilities for more dire situations.

Sandia National Laboratories, of Lockheed Martin Company, has included BodyMedia armbands in its survey of body monitoring systems with potential to support telemedicine for both military and social health initiatives.

Researchers at the Department of Computer Science, University of Central Florida find that a barrier to tele-health is the attenuation of information exchange between a health care provider and a remotely located patient. To improve communication, they are developing emotional maps derived in part from physiological data points collected by SenseWear armbands to help get "objective indicators of patients' emotional status in a useful form to enhance patient care [14]."

CERMUSA is an applied research and technology center located on the campus of Saint Francis University in Loretto, PA. They are working with Bodymedia in the field of monitoring technologies for patients in remote areas suffering from chronic diabetes and obesity. As part of this project, clinical researchers will use the SenseWear system together with wirelessly enabled glucose meters and weight scales to remotely monitor vital patient information such as blood-glucose levels, exercise habits, sleep quality, weight change, nutritional intake and overall compliance with programs administered by their caregiver.

6.3 Industry and the Work Place

Worker health, satisfaction, and productivity greatly effect manufacturing facilities fiscal gains. Better understanding worker stress, workload, and bottlenecks will provide the potential to improve training, working conditions, and work flow, increasing efficiency, safety, and yield.

PPG Industries, conducted a study to investigate whether differences in automation effected worker fatigue and effectiveness. Dr. Colombi, Corporate Medical Director for Environment, Health and Safety at PPG Industries, used BodyMedia armbands to measure workers' energy expenditure over shifts in two different facilities. He found "that the SenseWear armband accurately measured the levels of activity and amount of energy expended by the 40 plant workers who participated in the study" and further concluded "A wearable energy dosimeter is a viable alternative to oxygen consumption and heart frequency to evaluate workload assessment [4]."

ARUP, an architecture engineering and design firm, whose well known buildings include the Sydney Opera House, investigates the environmental conditions of its buildings for comfort. The company uses physiological data collected from BodyMedia armbands to better understand design performance in free-living situations [24].

NASA with the National Bio-Computation Center is investigating the potential for using SenseWear technology to monitor astronaut's health in space and during training.

6.4 Human Computer Interaction

Researchers from the Human Computer Interaction Department, Carnegie Mellon University used the armband to study comfort perceptions of wearable technology. Participants were given an armband or a hydration device and told the device served social, medical, or regulatory functions. Researchers noted that "significant differences in desirability and comfort ratings were found between functional conditions, indicating that functionality is a factor of comfort [1]."

6.5 Human Interaction

Not one person can be expert in all that is necessary, for instance, to bring a product to market; individuals are trained mostly in their field of expertise and not in collaborative work. To successfully work as a team it is helpful to be more aware of individual and team dynamics so participants can act progressively toward goals.

Sandia Collaborative Working [5], used BodyMedia armbands while it "explored the potential for real-time signal analysis to provide information that enables emergent and desirable group behavior and improved task performance" by mapping audio, video, physiological, and somatic data of test subjects playing a collaborative game. The group used an array of sensors, processors, and software to develop a tool that can identify individual and group trends, identify their states, and give warnings and help in decision-making [19]. This pointed to individual and group stress and efficiency trends useful for studying future group work situations.

Nasoz et al [16] looked at the ability to predict emotions from physiological information taken from SenseWear PRO_2 armbands while watching emotionally scored movie clips. "The affective intelligent user interfaces we plan to create will adapt to user affect dynamically in the current context, thus providing enhanced social presence." The team predicts that machines that identify and modify output based on users' emotions can optimize teaching, improve emotional communication between remote users, and suggest modifications to unsafe emotions in particular contexts.

A multi-university team used the BodyMedia armbands to detect whether a user is busy or not busy in order to determine interruptibility. "Our motivation is derived from the observation that context does not require a descriptive label to be used for adaptivity and contextually sensitive response. This makes an approach towards completely unsupervised learning feasible [13]." This investigation was a preliminary step towards making devices subservient to their users instead of the typical, opposite reality.

7   Application, Capability, and Acceptance

BodyMedia armbands and software are useful devices for comfortably collecting body measurements, which can lead to better understanding and detection of the user's physiological and emotional states, improved progress checking and training, and data collection in situations requiring high mobility. When coupled with environmental information or data from user groups, information can lead to better design of physical environments.

Contextual aware devices can calculate situation appropriate responses that may greatly change future context-specific human computer interaction and information feedback loops, leading to beneficial changes in education, health, work and leisure.

The SenseWear continuous body monitor is presently mainly deployed in health and fitness domains. Currently available are consumer products, professionally supervised products and scientific and social research products. The data from SenseWear remains a largely untapped diamond mine. At the 2004 International Conference on Machine Learning eight workshop papers discussed the process of discovering new information in a SenseWear data set of 64,000 multi-sensor samples. Topics included discovering if the wearer was watching television and identifying the gender of the wearer [8].

SenseWear is mostly worn as an everyday health and fitness diagnostic tool. However, SenseWear has also been used in out-of-the-ordinary situations and by extraordinary people. Armbands have been used while training guards in a mock prison riot and by airport fire fighters. SenseWear has gone up Mt. Everest, traveled to both the North and South Poles, and has been around the world on a yacht – all to better understand human physiology in extreme environments and situations. In the field of sports, the armband helps athletes better understand their bodies. Armbands have been worn by marathon runners, a super welter-weight boxing champion, a Wimbledon tennis champion, and a basketball Hall of Famer. SenseWear wearers include three gold medal Olympians.

SenseWear has been described as "a dashboard for your body." Wearing the armband has high value because it tells you objective information about yourself, at a very low personal cost. Measures such as hydration and fatigue can be indicated when they are difficult to impartially self observe. The fuel efficiency notion of miles-per-gallon can be transferred into human terms of caloric efficiency. With unobtrusive, noninvasive, continuous body monitoring, other ambient intelligent devices have the opportunity to know you better.

Sensing silently
Data doesn't know its worth
My ubiquity

Acknowledgements

Particular thanks for material and support from Chris Kasabach, Dave Andre, Scott Boehmke, Suresh Vishnubhatla, Chris Pacione, Ivo Stivoric, Astro Teller; and all the BodyMedia team past and present. Thanks also to John Beck at Gist Design. Good work chaps. Carry on.

References

1. Bodine, K. and Gemperle, F.: "Effects of Functionality on Perceived Comfort of Wearables." In Proceedings of the Seventh IEEE International Symposium on Wearable Computers, White Plains, NY. IEEE. (2003)
2. BodyMedia (2004)
   Armband specification. http://www.bodymedia.com/pdf/SW_Armband.pdf
   Sensors specification. http://www.bodymedia.com/pdf/Sensors.pdf
3. Cole, P.J., LeMura, L.M., Klinger, T.A., Strohecker, K., McConnel, T.R.: "Measure Energy Expenditure In Cardiac Patients Using The BodyMedia(tm) Armband Versus Indirect Calorimetry. A Validation Study." Journal of Sports Medicine and Physical Fitness. (September 2004)

4. Colombi, A.M., Vishnubhatla, S., Adams, K.J., Tollerud, D.J., Peele, P.B.: "SenseWear personal energy expenditure measurements for protracted, repetitive upper-extremity tasks with and without process automation." In Symposium Ergonomics In Action at 27th International Congress on Occupational Health. Brazil. (23-28 February 2003)

5. Doser, Adele B., Merkle, Peter B., Johnson, Curtis, Jones, Wendell, Warner, David, Murphy, Tim: "Enabling Technology for Human Collaboration" Sandia National Laboratories, Albuquerque, NM 87185 and Livermore, CA 94550. Document SAND 2003-4225. (2003)

6. Fruin, Margaret L, Rankin, Walberg, Janet: "Validity of a Multi-Sensor Armband in Estimating Rest and Exercise Energy Expenditure." Medicine and Science in Sports and Exercise. (June 2004) 36(6):1063-1069

7. Gemperle, F., Kasabach, K., Stivoric, J., Bauer, M., and Martin, R.: "Design for Wearability", in Proceedings of the 2nd IEEE International Symposium on Wearable Computers. IEEE. (1998) 116-123

8. ICML. International Conference on Machine Learning, Banff, 2004. "Physiological Data Modeling Contest." workshop papers
http://www.cs.utexas.edu/users/sherstov/pdmc/ (2004)

9. Jakicic,J. M., Marcus, M., Gallagher, K. I., Randall, C., Thomas, E., Goss, F. L., and Robertson, R. J.: "Evaluation of the SenseWear Pro Armband[TM] to Assess Energy Expenditure during Exercise." Medicine and Science in Sports and Exercise. Vol. 36, No. 5. (2004) 897-904

10. Kasabach, Chris, Pacione, Chris, Stivoric, John (Ivo), Teller, Astro, Andre, David: "Why The Upper Arm? Factors Contributing to the Design of an Accurate and Comfortable, Wearable Body Monitor."
http://www.bodymedia.com/pdf/Wearability_whitepaper.pdf (2003)

11. King, George A, Torres, Nancy, Potter, Charlie, Brooks, Toby J, Coleman, Karen J.: "Comparison of Activity Monitors to Estimate Energy Cost of Treadmill Exercise." Medicine and Science in Sports and Exercise. (July 2004) 36(7):1244-1251

12. Koplan, Jeffrey P. MD: Press release, "Diabetes Rates Rise Another 6 Percent in 1999." http://www.cdc.gov/diabetes/news/docs/010126.htm (2001)

13. Krause, Andreas, Siewiorek, Daniel P., Smailagic, Asim, Farringdon, Jonny: "Unsupervised, Dynamic Identification of Physiological and Activity Context in Wearable Computing." In proceedings of the Seventh IEEE International Symposium on Wearable Computers. White Plains, New York, USA. (2001) 21-23

14. Lisetti, C., Nasoz, F., LeRouge, C., Ozyer, O., and Alvarez, K.: "Developing Multimodal Intelligent Affective Interfaces for Tele-Home Health Care." To appear in International Journal of Human-Computer Studies (Special Issue on Applications of Affective Computing in Human-Computer Interaction). (2004)

15. Mann, Steve: "Eudaemonic computing (underwearables)." First international symposium on wearable computers. IEEE (13-14 October 1997) 177-8

16. Nasoz, Fatma, Alvarez, Kaye, Lisetti, Christine L., Finkelstein, Neal: "Emotion Recognition from Physiological Signals for Presence Technologies." International Journal of Cognition, Technology and Work. Special Issue on Presence, Vol 6(1). (2003)

17. Marzano, Stefano: "Smart Connections. From Ambient Intelligence to Ambient Culture." Philips Design. Exhibition first presented at the Milan Furniture Fair in 2001. http://www.design.philips.com/smartconnections/index.html (2001)

18. Marzano, Stefano: "The culture of Ambient intelligence." Philips Design.
http://www.design.philips.com/about_us/our_vision/
the_culture_of_ambient_intelligence.asp (2004)

19. Pancerella, C.M., Tucker, S., Doser, A.B., Kyker, R., Perano, K.J., Berry, N.M.: "Adaptive Awareness for Personal and Small Group Decision Making" Sandia National Laboratories, Albuquerque, NM 87185 and Livermore, CA 94550. Document SAND 2003-8701. (2003)

20. Patel, S. A. MD, MPH, Slivka, W. A., RPFT and Sciurba, F. C., MD: "Validation Of A Wearable Body Monitoring Device In COPD." American Journal of Respiratory and Critical Care Medicine. (September, 2004)

21. Roche. Roche Diagnostic. http://www.healthwear.com (2004)

22. Starner, Thad: "Interview of Thad Starner" by Peter Thomas. New Scientist. http://wearables.www.media.mit.edu/projects/wearables/newsci.html (1995)

23. United States Center for Disease Control (CDC) "Healthy weight, overweight, and obesity among U.S. adults", in National Health and Nutrition Examination Survey, July 2003. www.cdc.gov/nchs/data/nhanes/databriefs/adultweight.pdf

24. Wilson, D., Haglund, B.: "Workplace performance monitoring: analysing the combination of physiological and environmental sensory inputs." EuroWearables 2003. Arup, UK and University of Idaho, USA
http://conferences.iee.org/eurowearable 2003 (2003)

Ambient Diagnostics

Yang Cai[1], Gregory Li[1], Teri Mick[1], Sai Ho Chung[1], and Binh Pham[2]

[1] Carnegie Mellon University, USA
{ycai,gregli,teri}@cmu.edu, saic@andrew.cmu.edu
[2] Queensland University of Technology, Australia
b.pham@qut.edu.au

1 Introduction

People can usually sense troubles in a car from noises, vibrations, or smells. An experienced driver can even tell where the problem is. We call this kind of skill *'Ambient Diagnostics'*.

Ambient Diagnostics is an emerging field that is aimed at detecting abnormities from seemly disconnected ambient data that we take for granted. For example, the human body is a rich ambient data source: temperature, pulses, gestures, sound, forces, moisture, et al. Also, many electronic devices provide pervasive ambient data streams, such as mobile phones, surveillance cameras, satellite images, personal data assistants, wireless networks and so on.

The *peripheral vision* of the redundant information enables Ambient Diagnostics. For example, a mobile phone can also be a diagnostic tool. As the sounds generated by breathing in asthma patients are widely accepted as an indicator of disease activity [1, 2], researchers have investigated the use of a mobile phone and electronic signal transfer by e-mail and voice mail to study tracheal breath sounds in individuals with normal lung function and patients with asthma [3]. The results suggest that mobile phone recordings clearly discriminate tracheal breath sounds in asthma patients and could be a non-invasive method of monitoring airway diseases.

It is challenging to extract just one bit of diagnosis (positive or negative) from massive ambient data. First, we need pivotal heuristics or domain knowledge. In many cases, the heuristics just serve as an early warning rather than an accurate examination. For example, medical studies show that snoring may be related to hypertension, cardiac dysfunction, angina pectoris and cerebral infarction. The immediate rise in systemic blood pressure during snoring has been confirmed by polygraphic recordings [60]. A 'snoremeter' could be added into a mobile phone because it already has a microphone inside. It would provide valuable early warnings for related diseases.

Second, we need *physical heuristics* that effectively filter out the trivial data while only keeping the abnormities. Knowing the physical properties of the targeted system would greatly benefit a diagnosis. For example, if we know that the needle in a hay stack is metal, then we can work around the metal properties and make the hay disappear. Ideally, physical heuristics map the data to a feature space that only displays limited interesting features. Determining which

Y. Cai (Ed.): Ambient Intelligence for Scientific Discovery, LNAI 3345, pp. 224–247, 2005.

modality to use for mapping the feature space is sometimes called *'modality intelligence.'* For instance, classic Fourier Transformation algorithms map data from a time-domain to a frequency-domain. For many periodical data sets, this is a blessing because it is easier to see the patterns in the frequency domain. Wu and Siegel developed a sound recognition system that can identify types of vehicles by sound signatures [11]. The algorithm can also be used for analyzing the breathing patterns of asthma sufferers.

Third, we need effective feature descriptions. The human brain is mainly wired using languages, not for pixel computations. How to transform a verbal description into a digital representation is a non-trivial task. For example, how do we describe the texture on the human body? How do we sense group activities in a video from a nursing home?

Ambient Diagnostics can be traced back to ancient times. For over two thousand years, physical inspection has been a unique and important diagnostic method of Traditional Chinese Medicine (TCM). Observing abnormal changes in the tongue, blood volume pulse patterns, breath smells, gestures, etc., can aid in diagnosing diseases. TCM diagnosis is a black-box approach that involves only input and output data around the body. For many years, scientists have been trying to use modern technologies to unleash the ancient knowledge base. For example, a recent paper published on an IEEE conference presents a computer-based arterial blood-volume pulse analyzer. It is a 'rediscovery' of the diagnostic method originated from ancient TCM [65].

This chapter was inspired by the research of computerized TCM tongue inspection. Through this case study, the chapter discusses the components and potential of ambient diagnostics. We believe that it can be used in applications such as security intelligence, where the difference is deceiving.

2   Tongue Inspection

Visual inspection of the tongue has been a unique and important diagnostic method of Traditional Chinese Medicine (TCM) for thousands of years. Observing the abnormal changes in the tongue proper and in the tongue coating can aid in diagnosing diseases. The inspection of the tongue comprises the inspection of the tongue body and the coating. The tongue body refers to the tissue of the muscle and blood vessels, while the coating refers to something on the tongue like mosses, which are formed, according to the theory of TCM, by the rising of the 'qi' (energy) of the spleen and stomach. For decades, international TCM medical professionals have conducted an enormous number of scientific experiments on tongue inspection [26].

Clinical data has shown significant connections between various viscera cancers and abnormalities in the tongue and the tongue coating. Yao from China studied 4,000 clinical cases with gastroendoscopy images over a period of 20 years. He found significant connections between various viscera cancers and abnormalities in the tongue and the tongue coating. Yao found that viscera cancer patients showed less tongue coating at the tip or edge of the tongue and that the coating color had turned to purple. He published a book about his study, including in it 130 tongue inspection images, along with gastroendoscopy images and patient diagnoses [20].

Since the early 1980s, medical professionals in China have systematically studied the relationship between various cancers and tongue signatures. Their results have been published in national medical journals. For instance, China TCM Society, China Cancer Society and TCM Diagnosis Association conducted a national project that included cases of 12,448 cancerous patients, 1,628 non-cancerous patients and 5,578 normal patients. The results statistically showed that there are significant changes of color, coating, shape and dorsum shape of the tongues of cancerous patients versus those tongues of non-cancerous patients or normal subjects [23]. Fujin TCM Hospital in China conducted a survey of 168 stomach cancer patients and 200 healthy subjects in 1983. The results showed that the percentage of abnormal tongues were 4 to 10 times higher in cancerous patients than those of healthy subjects; for example, for cancer patients: 70.8% purple/bluish color, 76.5% abnormal proper coating, 20.8% with cracks, and 83.9% dorsum deformation, and for healthy subjects: only 12.5% purple/bluish color, 26.2% abnormal proper coating, 1.5% with cracks, and 10.5% with dorsum deformation [25]. PLA 211 Hospital in China conducted a series of surveys on liver cancer patients versus non-cancer patients who have liver diseases. Results showed that liver cancer patients' abnormal tongue percentage is about 2 to 3 times higher than those of non-cancerous patients [21]. The data shows the method has certain selectivity for cancer diagnosis. Another survey showed that the level of abnormal signatures on the tongue increased as the tumor size increased from less than 5mm, larger than 5mm, to wide spread. The data shows promise for cancer stage estimation and possible early diagnosis [63].

Visual inspection of the tongue offers many advantages: it is a non-invasive diagnosis method, is simple and inexpensive. However, the current practice in TCM is mainly experience based or subjective. The quality of the visual inspection varies between individuals. Although there are a few experts successfully diagnosing cancers based on inspection of the tongue, their skills are not easily transferable to other medical professionals. Their expertise is limited to qualitative descriptions, not to quantitative or mathematical formulations. To circumvent this problem, studies have investigated and reported options such as fuzzy logic [30] and image analysis [31]. Here we discuss a computerized vision system for tongue inspection.

In this study, we investigate a novel imaging system for visual inspection of the tongue [19]. The objectives are to use a digital camera to make an image of a patient's tongue, then use software to extract the features from the digital image created, and finally make a diagnosis based on quantitative models. *The goal is not to replace the conventional diagnostic methods but to give an early alert signal* that can lead to further diagnosis by other methods, such as MRI, CT, X-ray, etc. This novel approach has various significant advantages. First, it makes the inspection objective and repeatable so that it prevents human bias and errors. Second, it can be implemented on an inexpensive personal computer or laptop computer for clinic or family use. Third, it's a unique exploration to combine Traditional Chinese Medicine (TCM) with contemporary computer vision technologies. The results of this project may inspire future long-term development of bio-computing technologies and further the use of computers in the medical field.

Studies show that there are correlations between the digestic diseases and tongue feature changes. Here we focus on colon polyps that would likely become colon cancer. This pilot study phase focuses on a preliminary investigation of the computer-based tongue inspection technology. A set of computer vision models have been developed to simulate the TCM diagnosis, for example, images that showed detectable cancer signatures such as color and coating texture of the tongue. Those visual feature descriptions will eventually be integrated into a decision-making model that will help to generate the final diagnosis or conclusion: normal, abnormal, likelihood of cancer, etc. The software includes the following issues: 1) *Segmentation:* The raw images are preprocessed with color normalized so that they have better numerical representation. Then each image is segmented to remove the background. The Deformable Template algorithm is applied to generate an accurate outline of the tongue. After the initial image processing, the improvement of the color normalization and segmentation is investigated. 2) *Texture feature extraction:* The texture, which includes cracks and distributions of the tongue proper, is the most important feature. It is the most challenging task in the project because the texture is not uniformly distributed and the orientation and size varies from image to image. 3) *Visualization models:* With the color measurement and texture features, a set of visualization methods are explored. 4) *Diagnosis with Neural Computing:* Artificial neural networks are used to classify samples.

3   Tongue Imaging

We have explored two scientific methods for tongue imaging so that we can recover the realistic measurement of physical values. The first approach is to use a modified hand-held color scanner with a microscopy slide on top of the tongue. As the scanner is gently moved from the root of the tongue to the tip, a flat image can be obtained. Figure 1 shows a sample image. The advantage of this method is its simplicity; it can avoid major color calibration and the removal of artifacts. However, it is a contact measurement that we want to try to avoid in a clinical environment, and the hardware needs to be specially designed to fit the size of tongues. The second approach is to take a picture of the tongue with a commercial digital camera (640 x 480 pixels) plus a Munsell ColorChecker [27] embedded inside the image. Since we already know the color value of the test cells on ColorChecker, we can calibrate the color of the image computationally.

Because the color in an image varies with cameras, lighting and equipment settings, we had to calibrate the color for each image before the analysis. We used the Mansall color calibration board and the newly developed color calibration software. Before the camera took a tongue image, the operator took a

Fig. 1. First image from the tongue scanner.

picture of the calibration board and saved it along with the tongue image. Then the computer performed the color calibration for the data. At this phase, we developed and tested the color calibration software.

A semi-automatic color calibration tool was developed for the project. By manually clicking the four corners of the ColorChecker, the software can perform the transformation and find the points in each square. Then a linear color calibration model is used to recover the original color of the tongue under various lighting conditions [27].

Parallel to the data collection from cancerous patients, tongue images were also collected from healthy subjects for studying the range of the deviation and mean of the 'normal' tongue images, such as RGB color space, coating texture, etc. Over 17 'normal' tongue images were collected in the database. Those images helped to establish a baseline for a 'normal tongue.'

We tested 17 tongue images taken from a "healthy" individual with a digital camera under different combinations of illumination and lighting orientations. The illumination conditions were daylight and indoor lighting in an office. 160 points from each tongue image were sampled to generate the data as shown in Table 1.

4   Segmentation of Tongue Image

There are many ways to segment the tongue area from the background. Color-based segmentation is the least reliable way because of the variations of tongue color and shadows. Active Contour may overcome the color variation problems by tracking the gradient of the intensity along the tongue edge. The typical al-

Table 1. Color variations of a normal tongue under different conditions.

Color Space	Before Calibrated Mean	STD	After Calibrated Mean	STD
R	0.4604	0.0439	0.6135	0.0339
G	0.4141	0.0323	0.4940	0.0288
B	0.4632	0.0492	0.5066	0.0288

gorithm is so-called 'snake' [19, 29]. It is a general algorithm for matching a deformable model to an image by means of energy minimization. However, for this particular problem, the snake algorithm suffers from various local optimization problems associated with initialization, poor convergence to concave boundaries, vulnerability to image noise and has a high computational complexity. Since regular tongue shapes are known, it makes sense to apply a Deformable Template for segmentation [49, 34]. Deformable Template models have been successfully used in tracking objects, such as vehicles and human figures. It is found that they are more robust against noise and local shape distortions than snake algorithms. The tongue has a specific shape with "landmark points" lying within a certain variance of the trained set. The model allows deformation of the class of objects by learning patterns from the training set of correctly annotated images.

Models of more specific classes of shapes demand the use of some hard constraints and "default" shapes which are more interesting than a simple straight line. This can be achieved by using a parametric shape-model $s(\mathbf{X})$, with relatively few degrees of freedom, known as a "deformable template". The template is matched to an image, in a manner similar to the snake, by searching for the value of the parameter vector $\mathbf{X}$ that minimizes the energy $E(\mathbf{X})$. The goal of the algorithm is to minimize the energy function: $E = E_{int} + E_{im} + E_{con}$, where, E_{int} is internal energy of the contour due to bending or discontinuities, E_{im} is energy due to image forces and E_{con} is energy due to external constraints.

In our study, we created a deformable template as shown in Fig. 2 and fit these templates to the image of the tongue by adjusting the various parameters that create the template of the tongue.

As shown in Fig. 2, we have the following parameters: x_o: center x-coordinate of the parabolic region. y_o: center y-coordinate of the parabolic region. α: angle (in radians) between the x-axis where the parabola ends and the line joining OO' equal to the length of the radius of the circle. r: radius of the circular portion (determined by a and α). θ: Angle (in radians) spanned by the circular arcs. Equation of parabola: $X = aY^2$, where a is a parameter that adjusts

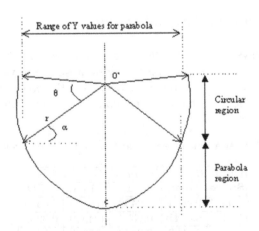

Fig. 2. Deformable Template.

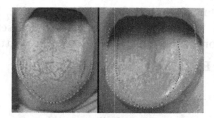

Fig. 3. Segmentation results (The black dots are the initial shape boundary and the white dots are the final shape boundary).

the thickness of the parabola. For the simplicity of the problem, we have not yet considered the axes rotation. Initially, we assumed symmetry in the tongue shape between the left and the right portions of the tongue. Then we accounted for more flexibility in the tongue shape by having different values of a, θ ($\theta_{1_{left}}$ and $\theta_{1_{right}}$), α ($\alpha_{1_{left}}$ and $\alpha_{1_{right}}$) and different parabola equations for the left and the right portions. Further, two additional circular portions were added to the left and the right portions giving different values for θ ($\theta_{2_{left}}$ and $\theta_{2_{right}}$), α ($\alpha_{2_{left}}$ and $\alpha_{2_{right}}$) and r. The template is given a good initial guess point (x_0, y_0). All the parameters are varied within a certain feasible limit (which defines the range of shapes the tongue template can take). The energy of the points (E) is calculated for all the possible templates. The average E is maximized and the resultant vector (or template corresponding to this maximum E) is the desired solution.

The algorithm was implemented in Matlab™. The black line indicates the initial starting template and the white line gives the final solution. Result samples are shown in Fig. 3.

Currently, we provide just a single point for the initial point (i.e. (x_0, y_0) or the lowest point of the tongue). It is desirable to provide more initial points that can be located visually. A total of 5 points on the tongue could fix the weakness mentioned above. Further, more constraints and finer step variations on the parameters can give more accurate results. Using an array of templates (instead of just a single template) can also give better results.

5   Feature Descriptions

Features on the tongue include color and texture. Most TCM practitioners do not have numerical descriptions of the color or texture features. Instead, they use analogies or qualitative descriptions, such as 'network-like cracks', or 'sandpaper-like surface'. It is possible to develop a scheme to map the qualitative descriptions to fuzzy sets of feature values.

However, in this chapter, we only discuss the numerical expressions of the features. In this study, we use CIE L*a*b* color space to represent the color features on the tongue. We also use several texture analysis methods that can correspond to human-descriptions of textures: 1) calculating fractal dimension

Db to represent roughness or smoothness of the tongue, 2) crack index CI to describe cracks on the tongue, 3) energy function for describing the roughness, and 4) entropy function to represent the order of the texture on the tongue:

$$\mathbf{F} = [a^*, b^*, Db, CI, energy, entropy] \tag{1}$$

5.1   Color Space Coordinates

The tongue project presents a unique challenge in the overall gross variance of the data set. There are tongues from different genders, ages and ethnic groups, which present unique difficulties in creating texture algorithms that are applicable to the entire data set. Minimal usage of parameters is key to developing a robust algorithm. A color space is a way of numerically describing a color. This almost always requires three numbers to accurately and succinctly describe all possible colors, as it is trivial to describe simple colors yet not so easy to describe colors like a faint red, in low-lighting. A simple example of a color space is that one may attempt to describe a color in terms of the actual color (red, orange, etc), its tint, or how deep the color is, and how much lighting there is on the color. Computer displays and televisions combine three primary colors (red, green and blue) in different proportions to form the different colors of the spectrum.

CIE 1976 L*a*b* is a color space that is an attempt to linearize the perceptibility of color differences. The non-linear relations for L*, a*, and b* are intended to mimic the logarithmic response of the eye, where L represents the lightness, a is the Redness/Greeness and b is the Yellowness/Blueness. However, the values from a digital camera are RBG-based. RGB values in a particular set of primaries can be transformed to and from CIE XYZ via a 3x3 matrix transform. To transform from RGB to XYZ (with D65 white point), the matrix transform used is [27, 39, 37]:

$$\begin{bmatrix} X \\ Y \\ Z \end{bmatrix} = \begin{bmatrix} 0.412453 & 0.357580 & 0.180423 \\ 0.212671 & 0.715160 & 0.072169 \\ 0.019334 & 0.119193 & 0.950227 \end{bmatrix} * \begin{bmatrix} R \\ G \\ B \end{bmatrix} \tag{2}$$

The L*, a*, and b* values can be converted from CIE XYZ, where coloring information is referred to the color of the white point of the system, subscript n. Here X_n, Y_n and Z_n are the tristimulus values of the reference white.

$$L^* = \begin{cases} 116 * (\frac{Y}{Y_n})^{\frac{1}{3}} - 16 & \text{for } \frac{Y}{Y_n} > 0.008856 \\ \\ 903.3 * \frac{Y}{Y_n} & \text{otherwise} \end{cases} \tag{3}$$

$$a^* = 500 * (f\left[\frac{X}{X_n}\right] - f\left[\frac{Y}{Y_n}\right]) \tag{4}$$

$$b^* = 200 * (f\left[\frac{Y}{Y_n}\right] - f\left[\frac{Z}{Z_n}\right]) \tag{5}$$

$$where \; f(t) = \begin{cases} t^{\frac{1}{3}} & \text{for } t > 0.008856 \\ 7.787 * t + \frac{16}{116} & \text{otherwise} \end{cases} \tag{6}$$

Since we tried to eliminate the lightness effect, we only used a* and b* as the color feature vector.

5.2 Fractal Dimensions

Fractal Dimension is another characterization of the texture on the tongue surface. Differential Box-Counting Dimension (DBCD) is an estimator of Hausdorff-Besicovitch dimension [8]. Like many other estimators of fractal dimension, DBCD is estimated by examining the relationship between a measure and the scale at which the measure was taken. DBCD is calculated on black and white images, where one value (for example, black) is taken to represent the object and the other value (white in this case) is taken to represent the background [28].

The image being measured was divided into equal sized squares. For a given size square (r x r pixels), the number of boxes containing any pixels belonging to the image, $N(r)$, is counted. This was done for several scales (several different r values), after which the relationship between $\log(N)$ and $\log(r)$ was calculated by finding the best-fit line between all r, $N(r)$ data points. The best-fit line corresponds to the relation:

$$N(r) = k \cdot r^{-Db} \tag{7}$$

The constant k is not important, but Db, the box dimension, is an estimator of fractal dimension. The implementation created for this project takes as a parameter an initial window size r to begin measuring. This window size was doubled repeatedly as long as the window size did not exceed the image size. Db was then calculated from the measurements taken at these scales. To adapt tongue images to be feasible for this algorithm, tongues were first converted to gray scale, using MatLab's rgb2gray function, and then from gray scale to black while running a Canny edge-detector on the gray scale image. The black and white image was analyzed using the DBCD algorithm described above.

5.3 Crack Detection

We also developed an algorithm to find and isolate cracks in the tongue. Cracks in the tongue can be an indicator of abnormality. Other crack detectors and classifiers [45, 46] have also been based on threshold and morphological operations in the primary stages. The system, outlined by Ukai [45], was used for detecting cracks in tunnel walls, and worked by using dynamic binarization (adaptive thresholding), dilation and erosion, eliminating particles, and analyzing the remaining particles. The interesting part of this system is its use of spatial frequency filters to distinguish between normal wall joints and cracks. It should be noted that this system appears to rely on hand-tuned parameters for each stage, which may be okay for its usage (provided that the equipment used to capture the input data, and the general properties of the walls do not change). A detector and classifier of cracks, described by Nieniewski et al [46], was used for analyzing cracked regions of ferrite. This system used morphological operations, bi-level thresholding, and a feature-based parallel K-nearest neighbor classifier [10]. This system was mainly intended for separating out cracks that are defects from grooves that occur from grinding. The morphological parts quickly generated all candidates for cracks, and the K-nearest neighbor classifier is used to reject those candidates who matched a training set of grooves. This system is interesting for its use of a K-nearest neighbor classifier, however it also relied on the grooves in the material to normally lie in a uniform direction. Also, the initial portion of the detector depends on hand-tuned parameters for the morphological operation and thresholding operations.

Crack detection is a multiple stage process that attempts to find places where there are cracks in the tongue. Each stage is essentially a filtering process to attempt to get rid of more unwanted information. The essential steps behind of the process are:

1. *Find all pixels that are bright in the S channel and dark in the V channel.*
2. *Remove pixels that fall on the edge of the tongue, as the edge area often has the most extreme illumination variances and causes difficulties for accurately finding cracks.*
3. *Remove all particles in the image except the largest ones.*

To convert color coordinates from RGB to HSV (Hue, Saturation, and Value), we used the following pseudo code:

```
max = largest RGB component
min = smallest RGB component
```

$$H = \begin{cases} 60*(G-B)/(max-min) & \text{if red is largest} \\ 180*(B-R)/(max-min) & \text{if green is largest} \\ 300*(R-G)/(max-min) & \text{if blue is largest} \end{cases}$$

```
S = (max-min)/max
```

```
V = max
```

Step 1 is based on the discovery that cracks appear bright in the S channel, and dark in the V channel. HSV color space is another way of representing color image. Computers typically use the RGB color space, which separates color into its red, green and blue components. In the RGB color space, white is represented by red, green and blue being at maximum intensity. Purple is represented by putting red and blue at half-intensity, and green at zero intensity. HSV represents colors in a method more understandable by humans: H represents the hue, or actual color, S represents the saturation, which is essentially how strong the hue appears, and V is the overall illumination present.

The HSV color space is used to accentuate cracks. As stated before, cracks appear bright in the S channel and dark in the V channel. "Appearing" bright and dark, is relative to other pixels in the same channel, as they are actually darker in the S channel, and only appear brighter because they are relatively bright compared to their surrounding pixels. Therefore, the algorithm enhances this contrast by thresholding local blocks relative to themselves. This is different than a normal threshold that simply compares each pixel to a number such as the mean of the entire image. The problem with the normal approach is that near the edges of the tongue, there is a very high variation, which can throw

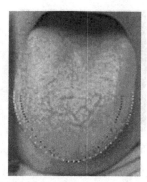

Fig. 4. Cracks on the Tongue.

off thresholding for the rest of the image. Since an adaptive threshold considers each block individually, this problem is avoided. For each window analyzed, the adaptive threshold sets its threshold first by finding the mean value and standard deviation of non-black pixels, and then setting a threshold based on these values. This allows the thresholder to provide consistent behavior for images with different illuminations, provided they fit a relatively normal lighting distribution, which was found to be typical for the tongues analyzed. For this project, the mean pixel value was used.

The next part of step one is to invert the V channel. This is done to reflect the fact that the cracks are dark in the V channel. By inverting it, the cracks (which would have been thresholded down to 0) are once again changed back to 1. The next step, essentially an "AND" operation on both images, chooses all pixels that appeared "bright" in the S channel and "dark" in the V channel.

At this stage, there is still a lot of noise. The main cracks, however, appear to be large, whereas the noise is limited down to small size pixels. To remove the noise in the image, the image is first eroded, then all remaining small pixels are removed. Eroding is a morphological operation that shrinks objects in an image, much like land erosion washes away dirt on hills, making the hills smaller. Erosion works by passing a structuring element over the image, and outputting a pixel only when the structuring element is completely covered by pixels in the original image [49].

Once the image has been eroded to enhance the separation of objects in the image, all objects belonging on the fringe edge of the image are removed. This is done to prevent erroneous detection of cracks that are really just places on the edge of the tongue where illumination falls off steeply. The first step in doing this is to calculate a mask that describes the edge of the tongue by thresholding the image. The mean pixel value of the non-black pixels in the image minus one-half of the standard deviation of the non-black pixel values is used as the threshold. Next, this mask is smoothed by performing a closing operation on it. Closing is simply dilating the image then eroding it, and has the effect of closing small gaps in the image. Just as dilating has its counterpart eroding, closing has a counterpart called opening which does the opposite by eroding then dilating.

Fig. 5. Cracks detected by the algorithm.

The previous result image is then masked with the inverse of the tongue-edge mask to retain only data that does not appear on the edge of the tongue.

After all objects in the image are shrunken with erosion, the pixel groupings are separated out into particles so that they can be analyzed individually. This is done by scanning the image and grouping pixels that are connected to each other. There are two typical definitions of pixels being "connected" to another. According to the 4-way definition, a pixel is connected to a group if the group appears to the right, left, bottom or top of the pixel. Under the 8-way definition, a pixel is connected to a group if any of the bordering pixels are in the group.

Once all pixel groupings are determined, then only the largest pixel groupings are chosen. This is done simply by comparing the area of the group to a threshold value. The area of a group is the number of pixels that form it. The threshold value is calculated by taking the mean plus one standard deviation of particle area values. This is done to keep only "large" particles and exclude smaller particles that result from noise in the image. Figure 5 shows the finished crack-detected image.

In order to summarize the crack information of an image, we have developed a simple numerical descriptor to describe cracks called "Crack Index". Crack Index (CI), is a number between 0 and 100 that describes the content of cracks in the image.

$$CI = 100 * \frac{A_{cracks}}{A_{total}} \tag{8}$$

A CI of 0 indicates no cracks were found, whereas increasing values indicate an increasing density of cracks. Crack Index is calculated by taking the area of cracks divided by the area of the total tongue and multiplying by 100.

5.4   Describers for Texture Homogeneous and Complexity

To give further descriptions of texture details such as homogeneous and complexity, we use energy and entropy functions that are based on the co-occurrence matrix. It describes the repeated occurrence of some gray-level configuration in the texture [36]. P is a 2-D n x n co-occurrence matrix, where n is the number of gray-levels within an image. The matrix acts as an accumulator so that $P[i, j]$ counts the number of pixel pairs having the intensities i and j. The idea is to scan the image and keep track of how often pixels that differ by Δz in value are separated by a particular distance d in position [49, 41]. Based on the co-occurrence matrix, we compute the energy function and entropy function for further texture descriptions. The energy function, or angular second moment, is an image homogeneity measure; the more homogeneous the image, the larger the value.

$$H_{entropy} = -\sum_{i,j} (P[i,j] \log_2(P[i,j])) \tag{9}$$

The entropy function, can also be used as a measure for "textureness or complexity."

$$H_{entropy} = -\sum_{i,j} \left(\frac{P[i,j]}{1 + |i - j|} \right) \tag{10}$$

where, P is a gray level co-occurrence matrix that contains information about the position of pixels having similar gray level values.

6 Visualization Techniques and Process

In this section, we show how visualization can provide insights and facilitate the analysis and clustering of tongues based on feature values. We have a feature vector: F=[a*,b*,Db,CI,energy,entropy]. Li & Cai extracted the values for these six features for a set of 34 tongues which belong to people of five different diagnostic categories: Healthy (H), History of Cancers (HC), History of Polyps (HP), Polyps (P), Colon Cancer (C) [50]. We used this data set to demonstrate the visualization techniques and process.

6.1 Cluster Plots

The goal of data exploration is to investigate if there are some obvious correlations between different features. This can be achieved by 2D and 3D cluster plots. We found that there are definite patterns for some categories as summarized in Table 2. Figure 6 shows a 2D cluster plot of Db-entropy which shows a clear pattern for Healthy (H) and Polyps (P) cases.

As a* and b* are two chromatic dimensions in the L*a*b* color space, observed definite ranges of values for these features for certain diagnostic conditions indicate that there is a strong correlation between the tongue color and these diagnostic conditions. We also observe two outliers with very high crack index, one with a Healthy condition and one with History of Polyps and History of Cancer. This suggests that these are special cases where these tongues normally have lots of cracks, and the amount of cracks therefore does not reflect on the disease condition.

For 3D cluster plots, we used different colors and glyphs for each category (see Fig. 7) and allowed users to rotate them around each axis to facilitate viewing. Rotating the plots increased the sense of depth and the perception of clusters and correlations. We also observed that the high precision of the raw data might

Table 2. Observed patterns obtained from 2D and 3D cluster plots.

category	Db	CI	a*	b*	Energy	Entropy
HP	medium	low medium	narrow mid-range	mid-range	low	
P	high			mid-range	high	
HC	low	low	narrow mid-range	narrow mid-range		
C			low	very high		high
H	low Db	or high CI				

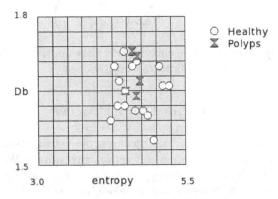

○ Healthy
✖ Polyps

Fig. 6. 2D cluster plot of Db-CI.

have adverse effects on the cluster viewing (in other words, the precision was higher than what was required). We therefore tried different quantization scales and finally chose a 10-interval scale which was the coarsest scale that could still distinguish each data point. The plots for each triplet of features (with a* and b* being always kept together) re-confirm the observations summarized in Table 2.

We also wished to determine from the 3D cluster plots which triplets of features give better discriminating power, in order to use these as a starting point to gradually explore rules for clustering in higher dimensions using parallel coordinates. Figure 7 shows a 3D cluster plot (Db, a*, b*) for Healthy and Polyps cases. However, we observed that although there appeared to be some groupings, these groupings were not separable and the rules underlying these groupings were not simple. We investigated this problem further using another visualization method based on parallel coordinates, which allowed the simultaneous viewing of multi (more than 3) dimensions.

6.2 Discovery of Rules Using Parallel Coordinates Plots

High dimensional data is often transformed or projected to 2D or 3D representations for visualization. However, this practice usually causes a loss of information. Parallel coordinates allow n-dimensional data to be displayed in 2D [51]. In this method, n Cartesian coordinates are mapped into n parallel coordinates, and an

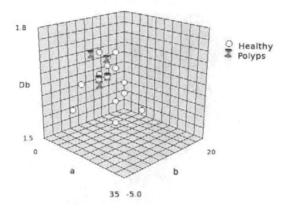

Fig. 7. 3D cluster plot for (Db,a*,b*) for H & P cases.

n-dimensional point becomes a series of $(n-1)$ lines connecting the values on n parallel axes. Berthold and Holve, [52] used this technique to visualize fuzzy rules underlying 3 classes of irises which resulted from a training set of 75 data samples with 4 features (petal length, petal width, sepal length, sepal width). Pham & Brown [54] extended this technique to 3D to provide better visualization of the membership function of the fuzzy sets and insight into the strength of the clustering. We now show how to apply these techniques to analyze the tongue data.

Since the set of data available at this stage only consisted of 34 tongues (6HP, 5P, 5HC, 2C, 16N), we attempted to cluster this data set through a display in six parallel coordinates: Db, CI, a*, b*, energy and entropy. Figure 8 shows the results for three categories: P, H and C. The shaded area representing each category is obtained by plotting the extent covered by the extreme values for each coordinate. It can be readily seen that these areas, though overlapped, are distinguishable from each other.

The order of the coordinates does not change the results, although it might affect the perceptibility. For example, a large number of intersections might cause confusion and make it difficult to discern the clusters. Thus, we provided tools to swap coordinates in order to choose the order with best perceptibility. We observed that the Cancer cases form a narrow band for all six coordinates as seen in Fig. 8.

We also observed that for Healthy cases, the variability in feature values is much greater than in the disease cases. However, this fact can only be confirmed when more data on disease cases is available. If a much larger set of data is available, it would also be possible to provide a more sophisticated visualization by integrating fuzzy sets and using 3D parallel coordinates. We discuss how this may be achieved in the next subsection.

6.3   Integration of Fuzzy Sets to Visualization

Fuzzy logic has been used extensively and successfully in many areas, especially in social sciences and engineering. While mathematical models are based on

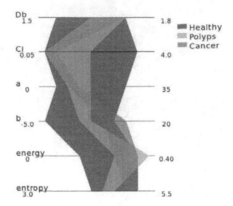

Fig. 8. Pattern of the cancer cases displayed in parallel coordinates.

algebraic operations (e.g. equations, integrals), logic models rely on logical connectives (and, or, if-then), often with linguistic parameters, which give rise to rule-based and knowledge-based systems. Fuzzy logic models can combine both of these types of modeling via the fuzzification of algebraic and logical operations. There are three common classes of fuzzy logic models: information processing model, which describes probabilistic relationships between sets of inputs and outputs; control models, which control the operations of systems governed by many fuzzy parameters; and decision models, which model human behavior incorporating subjective knowledge and needs, by using decision variables. For some applications, fuzzy systems often perform better than traditional systems because of their capability to deal with non-linearity and uncertainty. While traditional systems make precise decisions at every stage, fuzzy systems retain the information about uncertainty as long as possible and only draw a crisp decision at the last stage. Another advantage is that linguistic rules, when used in fuzzy systems, not only make tools more intuitive, but also provide better understanding and appreciation of the outcomes.

As more tongue data is available, it would be more appropriate to treat the extent of each feature value for each diagnostic category as a fuzzy set. The membership function for this fuzzy set can be computed from the frequency of each value. This membership value gives an indication of the confidence level that each value belongs to this set. Hence, the level of overall confidence that a given case belongs to a particular diagnostic category is the minimum of the membership values for all features. Since we have not yet obtained a large enough set of tongue data, we demonstrate this technique using the Iris data example. Figure 9 shows a 3D parallel coordinates display for this data set. The advantages of integrating fuzzy sets are two-fold. First, it provides an intuitive match with the way doctors fuzzily assess the condition of the tongues. Secondly, it is possible to select the tightness of clusters through the use of an alpha cut plane to discard those cases whose feature values have too low membership values (i.e. the level of confidence that a particular case belongs to a specific class is low).

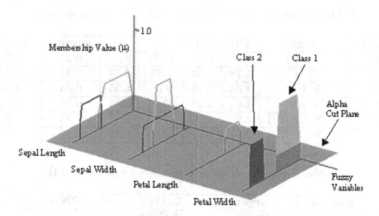

Fig. 9. A 3D parallel plot of Iris data example [Pham & Brown, 2003].

Another improvement can be made by asking doctors to provide the assessment of diagnostic categories with fuzzy grading. For example, instead of Healthy, three grades are introduced: Very Healthy, Moderately Healthy, and Slightly Healthy. Similarly, disease conditions can be expressed in three grades: Very Serious, Moderately Serious, Slightly Serious. Such fuzzy assessment would match more faithfully with real diagnosis practice. By linking fuzzy values for the color and texture features of the tongue with fuzzy diagnostic categories, it is envisaged that a more accurate classification of cases would result. However, in order to achieve this, we will need to collect more cases and more detailed diagnosis from doctors for each case.

7   Diagnosis with Neural Computing

Fuzzy visualization methods provide a promising interface for medical doctors to interact with the ambient diagnostic systems, especially at the early explorative stages. As we gain more insight about the data, it is time to build numerical models for diagnosis.

Ambient diagnostics is made largely by the interconnected elements. The metaphor can be simulated by artificial neural networks, which are composed of simple elements operating in parallel. We can train a neural network to perform a particular diagnostic function by adjusting the values of the connections (soup of weights) between elements. In the supervised learning process, many such input/target pairs are used to train a network [62].

Radial Basis Network is a feedforward backpropagation network. It is fast but needs more neurons so requires more memory [63]. It is also simple to be implemented on hardware, for example, a neural network on a chip, can perform 1 million recognitions per second. In a radial basis function network, each hidden unit produces a ball-shape 'pulse' driven by a Gaussian function. The output unit produces a linear combination of hidden unit pulses. In this case,

$$R(n) = e^{-n^2} \tag{11}$$

Table 3. Test samples (not included in the training dataset).

data set	target	Db	CI	a*	b*	energy	entropy
1	10 (P)	1.68	0.62	18.76	9.97	0.25	4.76
2	10 (P)	1.73	1.92	7.75	4.73	0.33	4.59
3	5 (HP)	1.64	0.55	9.98	5.35	0.33	4.66
4	5 (HP)	1.64	1.23	13.07	5.84	0.19	5.12
5	1 (NP/NHP)	1.63	0.1	11.55	8.77	0.33	4.91
6	1 (NP/NHP)	1.61	0.61	24.56	6.08	0.16	4.64

Table 4. Results for three types (spread factor = 0.4).

data set	target	GRNN	PNN
1	10 (P)	5 (HP)	5 (HP)
2	10 (P)	1 (NP/NHP)	1 (NP/NHP)
3	5 (HP)	4.56 (HP)	5 (HP)
4	5 (HP)	2.46 (NP/NHP)	1 (NP/NHP)
5	1 (NP/NHP)	1 (NP/NHP)	1 (NP/NHP)
6	1 (NP/NHP)	1 (NP/NHP)	1 (NP/NHP)

We test two variations of radial basis function: probabilistic neural network (PNN) and generalized regression neural networks (GRNN) provided by Mathworks [62]. Probabilistic neural networks (PNN) are suitable for classification problems. The PNN model $f(P, T, spread)$ takes three arguments: P is an R x Q matrix of Q input vectors; T is an S x Q matrix of Q target class vectors; and *spread* is the width of the radial basis function. To fit data very closely, we use a spread smaller than the typical distance between vectors. To fit the data more smoothly, we have to use a larger spread value. Generalized regression neural networks (GRNN) [61] are a radial basis network that is often used for function approximation. The GRNN model $f(P, T, spread)$ takes three inputs: P is an R x Q matrix of Q input vectors; T is an S x Q matrix of Q target class vectors; *spread* again is the width of the bottom of the radial basis function.

We used 28 samples to train the neural networks and another 6 samples to test the models. In our first case, we considered three types of targets: Polyps (P=10), History of Polyps (HP = 5), and the rest of the cases (NP/NHP = C = HC = H = 1). The test data set is listed in Table 3. We have the results in Table 4.

In the second test case, we only considered two types of targets: either Polyps (P = 10), or Non-Polyps (NP = 1). The input data set is listed in Table 5 and the results are in Table 6.

As the two test scenarios show, PNN performs the same as GRNN. Also we learned that neural networks work better when the target classes are fewer, e.g. in our cases, two targets are better than three targets. Although both GRNN and PNN can correctly identify 2 out of 3 Polyps cases, it just may be a result of the over-simplified process. It is not necessary to imply that these methods

Table 5. Test samples (not included in the training dataset).

data set	target	Db	CI	a*	b*	energy	entropy
1	10 (P)	1.68	0.62	18.76	9.97	0.25	4.76
2	10 (P)	1.64	0.55	9.98	5.35	0.33	4.66
3	10 (P)	1.73	1.92	7.75	4.73	0.33	4.59
4	1 (NP)	1.63	0.1	11.55	8.77	0.33	4.91
5	1 (NP)	1.61	0.61	24.56	6.08	0.16	4.64
6	1 (NP)	1.72	1.17	11.53	11.34	0.26	4.46

Table 6. Results for two types (spread factor = 0.4).

data set	target	GRNN	PNN
1	10 (P)	10 (P)	10 (P)
2	10 (P)	9.0049 (P)	10 (P)
3	10 (P)	1 (NP)	1 (NP)
4	1 (NP)	1 (NP)	1 (NP)
5	1 (NP)	1 (NP)	1 (NP)
6	1 (NP)	1 (NP)	1 (NP)

would work well with a larger sample size. There is still a long way to go before we can come up with a selective and robust classification method for the tongue inspection.

8 Conclusions

Ambient Diagnostics is a contemporary technology that is inspired by ancient medical practices. The goal is to detect abnormities from seemly disconnected ambient data. In this chapter, we focused on computerized tongue inspection. Our research started with collecting tongue samples at a clinical lab setting and building conceptual prototypes for scientific discovery along the way. The explorations include digital imaging, color calibration, feature descriptions, visualization and neural computing. From this preliminary study, we have learned the following lessons:

The portable tongue scanner is more reliable than the digital camera in terms of invariance of illumination, reflection and angles. However, its resolution is low and cost is rather high. We will do further investigation to reduce the cost and increase the resolution.

Previous TCM studies have shown strong correlations between the color of tongue coating and cancers. We found that the texture characteristics on the tongue surface is more sensitive to the colon polyps (pre-cancerous) or history of polyps than color characteristics. This discovery will lead us in a new direction toward effective tongue feature expressions, such as adding more texture describers in the feature vector. The more dimensions of the describers, the more accurate the classification and recognition of the model. We had four dimensions:

Energy, Entropy, Crack Index, and Fractal Dimension. We plan to add six more in the near future. In addition, we will add TCM expert's verbal descriptions into the model. We need to devise a scheme to map these qualitative descriptions into fuzzy sets of quantitative values so that computers can process them.

As comparing one patient's tongue to another patient's tongue is difficult in terms of shape, color and texture registration, we found that it is more accurate to compare the tongue images at a personal basis, e.g. the images of a cancer patient before and after chemo, etc. It could be used as a measurement of the effectiveness of a treatment. This is similar to the self-monitoring process that has been used in the head injury study with fMRI personal data. For each person, we can establish a base line and then use ubiquitous computing technologies to monitor the patient and compare the collected data to the base line at a predefined duration.

Neural computing is a promising method for generating diagnostic results and potentially can be hardened onto a chip that is less than one dollar. We use two neural networks for testing the concept: a general regression neural network (GRNN) and a probabilitistic neural network (PNN). As the two test scenarios show, both have virtually the same performance. Also we learned that neural networks work better when the target classes are fewer, e.g. in our cases, two targets are better than three targets. Although PNN and GRNN can correctly classify 2 Polyps test cases out of 3, it should not be implied that the methods would work well with a larger sample size. We still need more work to verify the selectivity and reliability of the models.

Visualization utilities are helpful in early stage data explorations. At this stage, the aim of visualization is to provide tools to aid the analysis, rather than to provide a precise proof of clustering decisions that can be provided by statistical and data mining techniques. We have not yet coupled visualization techniques with fuzzy algorithms. The 3D clustering figures were actually an animation that allows viewing from different angles with different triplets of variables. Clusters are observed in some cases, while in other cases, we could not see clusters. It is also not possible to see this effect when viewed as a figure on a flat piece of paper. The parallel coordinates approach provides multi-dimensional visualization. Although the variable values may overlap, as clusters, they do have distinct characteristics.

As more tongue data is available, we will be able to use more advanced techniques for visualization and classification of tongues to obtain better analysis and more accurate classification. We have received letters from a few colon cancer patients who have had 'geographical tongues'. Those feedbacks are significant resources for investigation. The combination of the tongue feature changes and other medical indications will increase the effectiveness of early diagnosis. We will continue to follow up the cases.

Affordable self-diagnostic kits are changing our lives. Decades ago, diabetes patients had to check their blood glucose in a lab or burn the sample with a candle. Today, they can buy a digital kit from a drugstore and test anywhere. Modern electronic technologies have been the building blocks for eDiagnostic kits. According to Gorden E. Moore's famous paper in 1965 [64], transistor density on integrated circuits doubles every couple of years. This exponential growth and ever-shrinking chip size results in more affordable Ambient Diagnostic devices.

Errors or mistakes are as inherent a possibility for ambient intelligence in scientific discovery as they are to any human activity. This initial study is no exception. Nevertheless, we hope that by presenting our findings we may inspire further explorations in this area of research.

Acknowledgements

We are deeply indebted to all of our supporters of this study, including the sponsor, Senior Project Officer Ms. Nancy Zionts from the Jewish Health Foundation. We are grateful for the clinical investigation and the IRB Process from Dr. Ron Herberman, Dr. Robert Schoen, Ms. Karen Foley and Ms. Betsy Hela from the University of Pittsburgh Medical Center, Pittsburgh Cancer Institute. The results and conclusions expressed by the authors in this chapter do not necessarily state or reflect those of their sponsors and supporters.

References

1. Spiteri, M.A., Cook, D.G., Clarke, S.W.: "Reliabilty of eliciting physical signs in examination of the chest." Lancet. 2:873-75. (1988)
2. Pasterkamp, H., Kraman, S.,S., Wodicka, G.R.: "Respiratory sounds: advances beyond the stethoscope." American Journal of Respiratory Critical Care Medicine. 156:974-87 (1997)
3. Anderson, K., Qiu, Y., Whittaker, A.R., Lucas, Margaret: "Breath sounds, asthma, and the mobile phone." Lancet. 358:1343-44. (2001)
4. Kaiser, R.: "Smart toilet a sure sign of future technology." Chicago Tribune. Saturday December 23. (2000)
5. Bodymedia: www.bodymedia.com
6. Givenimaging: www.givenimaging.com
7. McDermott, M.M. et al: "Functional Decline in Peripheral Arterial Disease: Associations With the Ankle Brachial Index and Leg Symptoms." JAMA, July. 292:453-461 (2004)
8. Yu, H., MacGregor, J., Haarsma, G., and Bourg, W.: "Digital Imaging for Online Monitoring and Control of Industrial Snack Food Processes." Ind. Eng. Chem. Res. 42. (2003) 3036-3044
9. Cai, Y.: "Trajectory Mapping for Landmine Detection." Lecture Notes in Computer Science, Edited by Peter M.A. Sloot et al, LNCS 2657, Computational Science, ICCS 2003, Part III, Springer-Verlag. (2003)
10. Hornbeckz, R. W.: Numerical Methods. Printice-Hall, Inc., Englewood Cliffs, New Jerscy. (1995)
11. Wu, H., Siegel, M., Stiefelhagen, R., and Yang, J.: "Sensor Fusion Using Dempster-Shafer Theory." The Proceedings of IMTC 2002. Anchorage, AK, USA, May 21-23. (2002)

12. Wu, H., Siegel,M. and Khosla,P.: "Vehicle Sound Signature Recognition by Frequency Principle Component Analysis." The Proceedings of IMTC 1998 , selected in the IEEE Transaction on Instrumentation and Measurement Vol. 48, No. 5, ISSN 0018-9456. October. (1999) 1005-1009
13. Feigenbaum, E.A. and Simon, H.A.: "EPAM-Like model of recognition and learning." Cognition Science. 8:305-360 (1984)
14. Zadeh, L.: "Fuzzy Sets." Journal of Information and Control, Vol.8. (1965) 338-353
15. Cai,Y., Hu, Y., Siegel, M., Gollapalli, S., Venugopal, A., Bardak, U.: "Onboard Feature Indexing from Satellite Lidar Images." IEEE IWADC, Perugia, Italy. (2003)
16. Post, Frits H., Nielson, Gregory M., Bonneau, Georges-Pierre (Eds.): Data Visualization: The State of the Art Series: The Kluwer International Series in Engineering and Computer Science. Vol. 713. (2002) http://www.springeronline.com/sgw/cda/frontpage/0,11855,5-149-69-33109107-0,00.html
17. Schroeder, W., Martin, K. and Lorensen, B.: The Visualization Toolkit. 2nd Edition, Prentice Hall, PTR. (1998)
18. Hraralick, R.M., Shanmugam, K., and Dinstein, I.: "Texture features for image classifaction." IEEE Transactions Systems, Man and Cybernetice, 3:610-621. (1973)
19. Cai, Y.: "A novel imaging system for tongue inspection." IEEE Instrumentation and Measurement Technology Conference, AK, USA, May. (2002)
20. Yao, P.: Comparison of TCM Tongue Images with Gastroscopy Images. Shangdong S&T Publisher, ISBN 7-5331-1849-9. in Chinese. (1996)
21. Li,N.M.: "130 cases of tongue analysis for liver patients." Journal of TCM & Western Medicine, Vol.6, No.3. in Chinese. (1986)
22. Chang,R. and Chen, R.S.: "Clinical studies for tongues of lung cancer patients." Journal of New TCM, No.7. in Chinese. (1987)
23. China Cancer Society & TCM Group.: "12448 clinical case studies of cancer patients' tongue images." Lung Cancer, Vol.7, No.3. in Chinese. (1987)
24. Chen, Z.L., et al.: "1046 case studies of cancer patients' tongues." Journal of TCM & Western Medicine, Vol.1, No.2. in Chinese. (1981)
25. Fang, D.R., Li,R.F., Li,X. and Fang, G.X.: "Stomach cancer patients' tongue images and analysis." Journal of TCM, No.10. in Chinese. (1991)
26. Zhang, E.: Diagnostics of Traditional Chinese Medicine. Publishing House of Shanghai University of Traditional Chinese Medicine, ISBN 7-81010-125-0. in both Chinese and English. (1990)
27. McCamy,C.S. et al: "A Color Rendition Chart." Journal of Applied Photographic Engineering, Summer Issue 1976, Vol.2, No.3. (1976) 95-99
28. Parker, J.R.: Algorithms for Image Processing and Computer Vision. Wiley Computer Publishing. (1976)
29. Akgul, Y.S., et at.: "Automatic Extraction and Tracking of the Tongue Contours." IEEE Trans. on Medical Imaging. Vol.18, No.10, October. (1999)
30. Watsuji, T., Arita,S., Shinohara,S., Kitade,T.: "Medical Application of Fuzzy Theory to the Diagnostic System of Tongue Inspection in Traditional Chinese Medicine." IEEE International Fuzzy Systems Conference Proceedings. (1999) 145-148
31. Jang,J.H., Kim,J.E., Park,K.M., Park,S.O., Chang,Y.S., Kim,B.Y.: "Development of the Digital Tongue Inspection System with Image Analysis." Proceedings of the Second Joint EMBS/BMES Conference. Houston, TX, USA. October 23-26. (2002)

32. Vico,P.G., Dequanter,D., Somerhausen,N., Andry,G., Cartilier,L.H.: "Fractal Dimension of the Deep Margin of Tongue Carcinoma: A Prognostic Tool." Microscopy and Analysis (The Americas). (2003) 19-21
33. Pang,B., Zhang,D.: Tongue Image Analysis for Appendicitis Diagnosis. (2002)
34. Xu,L., et al.: "Segmentation of skin cancer images." Image and Vision Computing 17. (1999) 65-74
35. Esgiar,A.N., Sharif,B.S., Naguib,R.N.G., Bennett,M.K., Murray,A.: "Texture Descriptions and Classification for Pathological Analysis of Cancerous Colonic Mucosa." IEEE Conference on Image Processing and Its Applications, No. 465. (1999) 335-338
36. Haralick, R.M.: "Statistical and structural approaches to texture." Proceedings of the IEEE, vol. 67, no. 5. (1979) 786-804
37. Amots, H.: "Machine vision monitoring of plant nutrition." Ph.D. Dissertation, Purdue University. (1994)
38. Backhaus,W.G.,Kliegl,R.,Werner,J.S.: Color vision. Walter de Gruyter. (1998)
39. McLaren, K.: "The development of the CIE 1976 (L*a*b*) uniform colour-space and colour-difference formula." Journal of the Society of Dyers and Colourists 92. (1976) 338-341
40. Agoston, G. A.: "Color Theory and Its Application in Art and Design." Heidelberg. (1979)
41. Gotleib, L.C., and Kreyszig, H.E.: "Texture descriptions based on co-occurrence matrices." Computer Vision, Graphics and Image Processing, vol. 51, no. 1. (1990) 70-86
42. Gose, E., Johnsonbaugh, R., and Jost, S.: Pattern Recognition and Image Analysis. Prentice-Hall PTR, Englewood Cliffs, NJ. (1996) 372-379
43. Kaplan,L.M.: "Extended Fractal Analysis for Texture Classification and Segmentation." IEEE Transactions on Image Processing, Vol. 8, No. 11. (1999) 1572-1584
44. Ait-Kheddache, A.: Classification of Textures Using Higher-Order Fractal Dimensions. NCSU Department of Electrical and Computer Engineering. (1998)
45. Ukai,M.: Developing an Image Processing Algorithm for Detection of Deformations of Tunnel Walls. http://www.rtri.or.jp/infoce/qr/1997/v38_3/news2.html
46. Nieniewski,M., Chmielewski,L., Jozwik,A., Sklodowski,M: "Morphological Detection and Feature-Based Classification of Cracked Regions in Ferrites." Proc. of IPMAM '99, Warsaw. (1999)
47. Reed, T. R., and DuBuff, J.M.H.: "A review of recent texture segmentation and feature extraction techniques." CVGIP: Image Understanding, vol. 57, no. 3. (1993) 359-372
48. Tamura, H., Mori, S., and Yamawaki, T.: "Texture features corresponding to visual perception." IEEE Transactions, SMC, vol. 8. (1978) 460-473
49. Sonka, M, et al.: Image Processing, Analysis and Machine Vision. PWS Publishing. (1999)
50. Li,G. and Cai, Y.: "Texture analysis for tongue analysis." Technical Report BV-2003-2, School of Computer Science, Carnegie Mellon University. May. (2003)
51. Inselberg, A and Dimsdale, B.: "Multidimensional lines i: representation." SIAM J. Applied Math, 54(2). (1994) 559-577
52. Hall, L. and Berthold, M.: "Fuzzy Parallel Coordinates." Fuzzy Information Processing Society, NAFIPS. 19th International Conference of the North American, Atlanta, GA, USA. (2000) 74-78
53. Mitchell, T.: Machine Learning. McGraw Hill. (1997)

54. Pham, B. and Brown, R.: "Multi-agent approach for visualisation of fuzzy systems." ICCS '03 International Conference on Computational Science, Melbourne, June. (2003) 995-1004

55. Bezdek, J.C.: Pattern Recognition with Fuzzy Objective Function Algorithms. Plenum Press, New York. (1981)

56. Kohonen, T.: Self-organization and Associative Memory. 2nd edition, Springer, Berlin. (1988)

57. Picton, P.: Neural Networks. 2nd edition, Palgrave, Basingstoke. (2000)

58. Spath, H.: Cluster analysis algorithms. Ellis Horwood Ltd., Chichester. (1980)

59. http://www.gretagmacbeth.com/

60. Chaney, G.R. Do you Snore?
    http://www.garnetchaney.com/help_for_snoring.shtml

61. Wasserman, P.D.: Advanced methods in neural computing. New York, Nostrand Reinhold. (1993)

62. Mathworks. Manual of the Neural Network Toolbox, MATHWORKS. (2004)

63. Chen, S., Cowan, C.F.N., and Grant, P.M.: "Orthogonal least squares learning algorithm for radial basis function networks." IEEE Transactions on Neural Networks, Vol.2, no.2, March. (1991) 302-309

64. Moore, G.: "Cramming more components onto integrated circuits." Electronics, Vol. 38, No. 8, April 19. (1965)

65. Gunarathne, G.P. Presmasiri, Gunarathne, Tharaka R.: "Arterial Blood-Volume Pulse Analyser." IEEE, Instrumentation and Measurement Technology Conference, AK, USA, May. (2002) 1249-1254

Wireless Local Area Network Positioning

Ophir Tanz and Jeremy Shaffer

Carnegie Mellon University, USA
ophir@halfbreath.com, jshaffer@ece.cmu.edu

1 Introduction

The ability to determine the location of a mobile device is a challenge that has persistently evaded technologists. Although solutions to this problem have been extensively developed, none provide the accuracy, range, or cost-effectiveness to serve as a solution over a large urban area. The Global Positioning System (GPS) does not work well indoors or in urban environments. Infrared based systems require line-of-site, are costly to install and do not perform well in direct sunlight [1]. Cellular network-based positioning systems are limited by cell size and also do not work well indoors [23]. The list goes on. With the rise of Wireless Internet, or WiFi as it is commonly dubbed, the best infrastructure for location awareness to date has been created. WiFi is standardized, inexpensive to deploy, easy to install and a default component in a wide-range of consumer devices. These characteristics are the drivers behind WiFi's most significant trait: increasing ubiquity. By developing within the existing 802.11 infrastructure, developers can leverage WiFi to create wide-spread context-aware services.

Location is significant because location suggests context. In addition to delivering information about a user's physical setting, a valuable piece of information in its own right, location implies an individual's current tasks and goals. We are living in a period of information overload where there is simply too much information to retrieve and intelligibly digest. Context-aware services address the problem of information overload for both information vendors and receivers by delivering content when it is most appropriate. Ambient intelligent applications are, in fact, considered intelligent precisely because they can respond to an individual in relation to his or her context. Examples of location-aware applications that have recently, or will soon merge include: tracking equipment, personnel and patients in hospitals, notifying friends when they are in close proximity to each other, providing on-the-fly directories and advertisements to mall visitors and providing guided tours of facilities such as a college campus [16] or museum.

The ability to locate a device in a wireless network was not inherently built into the 802.11 protocol. A real-time Wireless Local Area Network (WLAN) positioning system addresses this problem. A WLAN positioning system is a software system that aggregates the location data of all wireless devices within a network[1]. Through the clever utilization and processing of available information

---

[1] Often, to enhance and make better sense of the location data, statistical analysis is performed on it and a WLAN map is created that displays the data visually.

Y. Cai (Ed.): Ambient Intelligence for Scientific Discovery, LNAI 3345, pp. 248–262, 2005.
© Springer-Verlag Berlin Heidelberg 2005

and employment of a variety of methodologies and algorithms, location tracking can be performed to varying degrees of precision. Context-aware applications rely on swift and accurate location information to operate effectively and developers must put extensive emphasis on keeping location data private [6, 4, 22]. A WLAN positioning system, if properly constructed, creates a data layer that developers can interface with without the need for network-specific knowledge. This interface provides developers with the data they need to produce context-aware applications and provides users with security. This chapter will survey various models and implementations for generating location data and discuss related topics such as privacy, visualization and user movement and mobility.

2   Algorithms

2.1   Radio Waves

A basic understanding of the characteristics of a radio wave is quite helpful in understanding the challenges involved with WLAN positioning and making sense of the algorithms employed. A radio wave is an electromagnetic wave propagated by an antenna and travels at the speed of light. Radio waves have the ability to travel through obstructions such as people or walls, but this results in a loss of energy and interference, also known as attenuation and refraction. For example, lead walls dissipate signal strength rapidly while microwave ovens generate substantial interference when in use. Lastly, in free space, all electromagnetic waves obey the inverse-square law. This means that an electromagnetic wave's strength is proportional to $\frac{1}{d^2}$, where d represents the distance from the source, or access point in the case of wireless networks. Hence, doubling the distance from a transmitter reduces the strength to a quarter, and so on.

2.2   Association Method

The simplest and most straightforward means of determining a wireless device's position in a wireless network is the association method [10]. The association method simply entails associating a mobile device with the access point it is connected to. As each access point holds a unique identifier for every device that is connected to it, retrieving this information is simply a matter of querying the access points. This information places the mobile device's position within a certain radial distance of an access point.

While associating a device to an access point is rather easy to accomplish, it lacks granularity. Additionally, the area that a given access point covers varies [24]. The average area covered by an access point can be represented by a sphere that is 75 feet in diameter centered on the access point [19], limiting the use of the location data retrieved by this method for certain context-aware applications. Still, depending on the intended use, this method can prove sufficient.

2.3   Propagation Method

The propagation method involves using triangulation to calculate user locations. Recall that the strength of a wireless signal degrades as distance increases. This

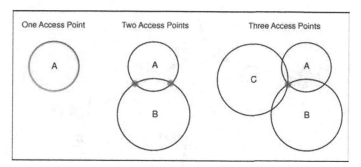

Fig. 1. Triangulation illustration with one, two, and three access points.

property enables us to infer the distance from an access point by considering the loss of signal strength. By calculating the distance to two or more access points triangulation can be used to determine user location [7]. This can be geometrically represented as rings centered at each access point (Fig. 1). Using the signal propagation model a device with a given signal strength can assume, under ideal conditions, that it is a proportional distance from the access point. This effectively places the device in a range of points formed by a circle centered on the access point as shown in Fig. 1. If the device can be detected by two access points then the possible locations can be reduced to the points at which the two circles centered on the access points intersect. With the addition of three access points the location can be determined to a single point, by calculating where the three circles intersect.

The propagation model can best be understood by assuming an ideal radio-frequency (RF) signal without any interference. Figure 2 represents a large open area with three fixed access points (A, B and C). This area is assumed to exist on a flat plane. The device shown in the figure is able to detect signals from all three of the access points. The signal strength[2] to access point A is 12mW, to access point B is 1mW, and to access point C is 0.05mW. Assuming all of the access points are sending a 100mW signal we can calculate the distance of the devices using the ideal propagation formula as shown.

$$AccessPoint_{distance} = \sqrt{\frac{sig_{orig}}{sig_{AP}}} \tag{1}$$

$$A_{distance} = \sqrt{\frac{100mW}{5mW}} = 4.47$$

$$B_{distance} = \sqrt{\frac{100mW}{1mW}} = 10$$

$$C_{distance} = \sqrt{\frac{100mW}{0.23mW}} = 20.58$$

---

[2] Signal strengths are traditionally represented in dBm a logarithmic value based on the mW. The following formula defines the relationship dBm = log(mW)*10.

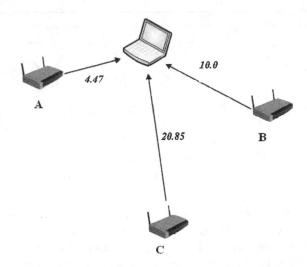

Fig. 2. Propagation Example.

Each of these distances represents the radius of a circle centered on the respective access point. There is only one possible location where these three distance lines can intersect at a single point. This point represents the device's location.

While a flat surface requires signals from three access points to pinpoint a location, to locate a point in three dimensional space, such as a multi-floored building, four access point signals are needed by the propagation model. Geometrically this can be viewed as the intersection of four spheres as opposed to the three circles described in the plane.

The Wall Attenuation Factor Model. In order to compensate for the effects of physical obstructions at a wirelessly networked site Microsoft Researchers working on the RADAR project [1] modified the Floor Attenuation Factor propagation model [17] in what they call the Wall Attenuation Factor model to account for obstacles (i.e.: walls) rather than floors.

The Wall Attenuation Factor (WAF) model [1]:

$$P(d)[dBm] = P(d_0)[dbm] - 10n \log\left(\frac{d}{d_0}\right) - \begin{cases} nW * WAF & nW < C \\ C * WAF & nW \geq C \end{cases} \quad (2)$$

- n is the rate at which the path loss increases with distance
- $P(d_0)$ represents the signal strength at some distance d_0
- d is the transmitter-receiver separation distance
- C is a constant that represents the number of obstructions that are factored into the model and the threshold above which nW makes no difference
- nW is the number of obstructions between the transmitter and receiver
- WAF is a constant that represents the wall attenuation factor
- The values n and WAF are derived empirically based on the building layout and construction material

The WAF factor is measured empirically by determining how much the signal drops as the number of walls increase. Researchers have tested this by measuring the signal strength when the wireless device and access point were in the same line of site. The signal strength was then measured with a various number of walls between the transmitter and receiver. The average of the difference between these signal strength values produced the Wall Attenuation Factor.

Accuracy of the Propagation Model. The propagation model offers accuracy as good as 4.3m at the 50th percentile and 1.86m at the 25th percentile [1], provided users are within a reasonable proximity to the access points. However, as the distance between the mobile device and access point increases, accuracy decreases [15]. In addition, radio signals in an indoor environment are victim to a barrage of obstacles causing reflection, diffraction and scattering, thereby significantly affecting signal propagation [1]. Environments with frequently changing interferences or significant obstacles can decrease accuracy. In general, the complexity of the model implemented is proportional to the accuracy achieved.

2.4   Empirical Method

The empirical method entails creating a radio frequency map by taking many measurements within a wireless network and recording Signal-To-Noise ratio (SNR) values from all access points within the range of each location. The SNR values at each location, also known as calibration nodes, are stored in a database with their associated location coordinates [2]. Subsequently, to find the position of a given mobile device its SNR values from all nearby access points are sent to the server which determines the closest match in the database by interpolating the probability distributions using the calibration nodes [18]. Two empirical model implementations, location fingerprinting and a k-nearest neighbor approach are discussed below. Algorithms used in the empirical model include Naïve Bayes, K-Nearest Neighbor, Neural Networks, Fuzzy Logic Subspace Techniques, Viterbi-like algorithms, and Hidden Markov Model based techniques.

Location Fingerprinting. Location fingerprinting, a positioning method researched at the University of Pittsburgh, is one method for implementing the empirical model [11]. This approach, like all empirical methods, requires a collection phase and a calculation phase. During the collection phase, a rectangular grid of points is collected by recording the received signal strength (RSS) from the access points on the site. Multiple measurements are taken from each point creating a vector of RSS values for a given coordinate (x,y). This vector of values is referred to as the location fingerprint of that point. During the calculation phase the Euclidean distance between the observed RSS vector and each fingerprint in the database is calculated. The fingerprint that returns the smallest Euclidean distance is returned as the user's position. The mathematical model for this method is represented as follows:

$$A_{sample} = [\rho_1, \rho_2, \rho_3, \ldots, \rho_N]$$
$$A_{fingerprint} = [r_1, r_2, r_3, \ldots, r_N]$$

The random variables ρ_i for all i are mutually independent and normally distributed. The true mean of the random variable ρ_i is denoted as r_i.

The Euclidean distance is calculated using the following equation:

$$Z = \left[\sum_{i-1}^{N} (\rho_i - r_i)^2 \right]^{\frac{1}{2}} = \left[\sum_{i-1}^{N} q^2 \right]^{\frac{1}{2}} \tag{3}$$

It is important to note that Euclidean distance does not imply physical distance. It is simply a means of selecting the best estimate from the average and sample RSS vectors.

In order to implement the location fingerprinting approach several parameters are needed, namely the number of access points in the network, the grid spacing, the path loss exponent (effects of obstacles and distance) and the standard deviation of the received signal strength.

Microsoft Research and the Empirical Method. Microsoft Research has performed extensive research on empirical positioning methodologies [1, 13]. Researchers tested their algorithms using the 802.11 network in the 10,500 square foot Microsoft Research building. They termed their methodology Nearest Neighbor(s) in Signal Space (NNSS).

The first stage involved collecting signal strengths at known locations throughout the experiment area. Microsoft researchers chose seventy points at which to record signal strength measurements. Given that signal strength can vary relative to orientation [1], measurements were taken from four different orientations at each point. At each position and orientation twenty different readings were recorded to average out any anomalies. All of this information was stored as tuples in the form $< x, y, d, ss, snr >$ where x, y represent position coordinates, d represents orientation, ss signal strength and snr signal-noise-ratio.

The location of a wireless device is determined by comparing the device's signal strengths to each access point to the database of signal strengths and orientations at the seventy different stored locations. The known tuple (nearest-neighbor) that best matches the device's signal strength returns its associated location. Using this method the mean error (50th percentile) was shown to be approximately 3m.

The k-nearest neighbor algorithm was applied to this model to improve accuracy. The algorithm involves defining a distance in radio space[3] [5] and selecting the k nearest neighbors from the training set to the unknown point. The positions of the k neighbors are then used to determine location. A user may be nearly an equal distance between two or more known locations, but in a nearest neighbor approach the location that is closer is chosen. With a k-nearest neighbor approach, the relative closeness to known signal strength positions is factored in. Using this additional logic, a slight improvement of 9% on the mean error was obtained. The improvement using the k-nearest neighbor approach is

---

[3] Radio space is defined to have 5 dimensions as it accounts for position in space and orientation.

dependent on the number of samples taken and average distance between them. In general, the fewer the number of samples (tuples) recorded the greater the improvement that is obtained using the k-nearest neighbor method.

Accuracy of the Empirical Model. The empirical model requires substantial time and effort to collect, organize, and employ the appropriate algorithms. The time of day that measurements are taken is of critical importance as the propagation of radio waves in an indoor environment varies greatly depending on changing obstacles in the building, most notably people. A solution to this problem is to create various maps and employ them at different times of the day. However, this further illustrates the inflexibility of the empirical model. The upkeep for this method must remain consistent, and evolve with architectural and usage changes. This being said, the empirical model is more accurate than the propagation model and is the most accurate model that exists to date, yielding an accuracy of under 2m [1]. The reason for this is because empirical measurements inherently take into account the obstacles and nuances of a building, such as doors, walls and building geometry [3] that the propagation model cannot account for.

3   Privacy Issues

Wireless LAN positioning introduces serious privacy issues. As mapping a wireless LAN involves associating connected users to real geographic locations it is possible to track the movement and location of a wireless device. This being the case, there is a responsibility among software developers and system administrators to keep users informed and their location data private. The good news is that the right tools, namely encryption and rule-based control systems, used appropriately, could eliminate many of the risks.

On a computer network users are identified by a hardware code called a Media Access Control (MAC) address. A MAC address is a code that identifies a particular network interface card, in this case a wireless card. MAC addresses are unique and never change. As such it is entirely possible to match a user to his or her MAC address. This makes determining a user's location possible whenever he or she is connected to the network and, depending on the nature of the positioning system, makes it possible to determine where the user has been throughout the course of his or her day. For this reason, strong encryption should be used in the handling of MAC addresses. MAC addresses should not be directly linked to identifying information about users and MAC address data should never be permanently stored or even kept lingering after it is no longer needed.

3.1   Rule-Based Control

Context-aware programs need to request information on users in order to operate properly. In order for users to maintain control over the distribution of their location information, there must be some control in place for approving or rejecting a location disclosure request. This control is typically achieved via a rule-based mechanism [19] where rules are set based on a variety of factors.

A common starting point is to allow or deny access by default to all users. Rules are then created that enable or restrict information distribution under a wide variety of criteria. As an example consider a rule that specifies a time-frame for when location information is made available, such as 9AM-5PM Monday through Friday. The common criteria on which rules are built include location (only show my location if I'm in certain areas and exclude all others), requestor relationship (allow friends, classmates and co-workers to locate me) and schedule (allow all people I will be meeting with today to see my location). Complex rules are subsequently created by combining simpler rules using boolean logic.

Many questions arise in dealing with location disclosure shedding light on just how complex the privacy issues associated with WLAN positioning can be. For example, how can we prevent someone who has authorization to acquire a user's location from passing it on to an unauthorized user? Should a person be notified every time their location is requested or does the requestor have some degree of privacy as well? Should a user have the ability to instruct the system to falsely report about his or her online status? Research is currently being done by a variety of groups[4] on this topic.

It is clear that users need a mechanism to control the availability of their location information, but the question of how to best implement this mechanism and what degree of control to afford users is not entirely clear. The availability of location data creates serious concerns over stalking, safety and big-brother applications. Many users will refuse to adopt context-aware applications if their concerns are not adequately addressed in a clear, concise, and reassuring manner.

4   Visualization

Geographic location information is easier to absorb and navigate when presented visually. In addition, visual representations of wireless LAN data are highly effective at supplying a great deal of information at short glance and are effective at making the information more accessible to non-technological people. From looking at a real-time map of a network one can easily discern where there are large concentrations of users, which access points are under-utilized and how usage changes throughout the day. cmuSKY is a near[5] real-time mapping system developed at Carnegie Mellon University (Fig. 3). cmuSKY performs positioning via a combination of the association and propagation methods, placing users a calculated distance away from the access point they are associated with. Each connected wireless device is represented as a yellow dot. The buildings on the map are clickable enabling users to examine each building on the campus at a finer granularity. cmuSKY also provides maps that show each active access point

---

[4] The Data Privacy Lab (http://privacy.cs.cmu.edu) at Carnegie Mellon University has explored these issues extensively.

[5] cmuSKY is defined as "near" real time because all the access points on the campus are queried about every two minutes.

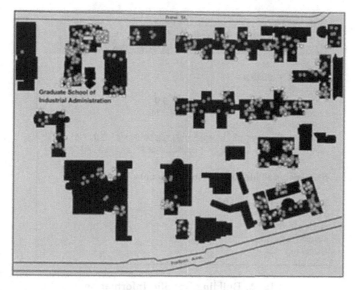

Fig. 3. User centric map of Wireless Andrew shows the locations of all mobile users connected to the network.

on campus, color-coded to represent the number of users connected to it, and a map that displays the location of every access point on campus. Figure 3 shows a screen shot of the user-centric map. A quick glance at the map shows the dispersion of students throughout the campus. Clicking on the Graduate School of Industrial Administration building tells us that there are 337 users connected to 18 access points with an average signal to noise ratio (SNR) of 18.72 (Fig. 4). Further, and significantly more detailed, comparative and historical statistical analysis on the network and its clients was performed as well and are featured on the cmuSKY web site.

4.1   Optimizing a Wireless LAN

The substitution of tangible cable with invisible radio wave has made the state and nature of wireless networks somewhat nebulous. Whereas the physicality of a wired network defines its bounds, wireless networks have indistinct boundaries which change from user to user, creating an array of logistic and security issues. Designing a wireless local area network is a highly empirical process requiring substantial testing and repositioning of access points and there are no rule-of-thumb heuristics that necessarily constitute good placement of wireless access points. This largely results from the fact that administrators do not know, up-front, the concentrations of wireless devices to expect in different areas of the network. As a result, administrators must carefully plan for both bandwidth capacity and RF coverage in what is generally an ad-hoc approach. To add to the challenge, administrators must account for the fact that they cannot contain the reach of their networks, thereby enhancing the possibility of unauthorized

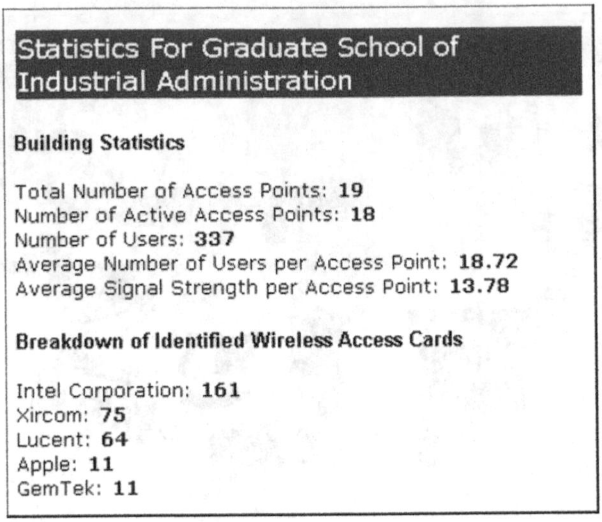

```
┌─────────────────────────────────────────────────────┐
│ ███████████████████████████████████████████████████ │
│ █ Statistics For Graduate School of               █ │
│ █ Industrial Administration                       █ │
│ ███████████████████████████████████████████████████ │
│                                                      │
│ Building Statistics                                  │
│                                                      │
│ Total Number of Access Points: 19                    │
│ Number of Active Access Points: 18                   │
│ Number of Users: 337                                 │
│ Average Number of Users per Access Point: 18.72      │
│ Average Signal Strength per Access Point: 13.78      │
│                                                      │
│ Breakdown of Identified Wireless Access Cards        │
│                                                      │
│ Intel Corporation: 161                               │
│ Xircom: 75                                           │
│ Lucent: 64                                           │
│ Apple: 11                                            │
│ GemTek: 11                                           │
└─────────────────────────────────────────────────────┘
```

Fig. 4. Building Specific Information.

access and eavesdropping of data. Using range-extending antennas and packet sniffing software a malicious user can capture data flowing across a network from a considerable, on the order of miles, distance away from the network. From an administrative point of view a wireless LAN map, in combination with statistical data, greatly aids network administrators in locating access points with high bandwidth requirements, pinpointing unused nodes, locating rogue access points and discerning network usage and trends over time.

5   User Movement and Mobility

Context-aware application developers should have a thorough understanding of their user communities. One common assumption is that the terms 'mobile' and 'wireless' are synonymous. By utilizing the data from wireless network mapping and location services this assumption has been put to the test by determining the mobility of users and basic information about their movement patterns.

A data set encompassing over 10,000 wireless devices was studied at Carnegie Mellon University on its Wireless Andrew network [9]. Using unique MAC addresses, wireless devices were tracked over the course of a four month period. This data allowed for a thorough study of mobility and movement patterns. Similar studies have been done at Dartmouth [12] and Stanford University [20, 21].

5.1   Two Distinct Communities

A quick analysis of the data set shows that there are two distinct user communities on campus. The first community is the Carnegie Mellon Tepper School of Business (GSIA) which represents slightly more than one thousand users. This community has institutionally embraced the use of wireless devices in course work, group meetings and other daily tasks, effectively providing a glimpse of what future user communities may look like. The second group represents the remainder of the campus community who use the wireless network to varying degrees and primarily for convenience.

5.2   Home-Node

The amount of time that a user spends at each location is an important measure of mobility. The home-node is defined as the network access point that the user is connected to for the greatest amount of time. Users who spend extensive time at a home-node tend to use their workstation or laptop in a single office or dormitory room. To determine the home-nodes, the time spent by unique each MAC address at each access point over the 4 month period was calculated.

Figure 5 shows that the most users spend a majority of their time at their home-node. Specifically, 62% of all wireless users spend 50% or more of their time at their home location and slightly over 8% of the wireless users never utilize more than a single access point. A significant number (23.4%) of users spend over 90% of their time on a single access point. As such, the performance of the home-node largely determines the online experience for users that do not exhibit extensive movement patterns.

The two distinct, GSIA and non-GSIA, communities on campus show significant differences in the percentage of time spent at their home-nodes. Non-GSIA users are over twice as likely to have a home-node where they spend over 90% of their time. The median time spent at the home-node for GSIA users is 46.7% while the median time for non-GSIA users is 63.9%. Measured by the home-node metric, GSIA users are considerably more mobile than their counterparts in other departments.

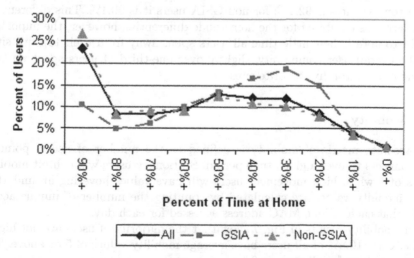

Fig. 5. Percent of Time at Home by user groups.

Fig. 6. GSIA Students actively using laptops.

5.3   Favorite Sites

In addition to a home-node, many users have a collection of favorite sites, defined as locations where they exhibit a high frequency of usage. Often, users follow set routines that take them to a handful of places throughout the day. For example, a student's class schedule can provide a predictable pattern of movement. Similarly, school faculty have a set schedule in which time is split between labs, class and an office.

To determine and rank the favorite sites, the time spent by each MAC address at each access point was calculated. We then took the top five access points, ranked by time, for each user; this includes the home-node discussed earlier. The results show an overall lack of mobility. Only 3% of users spent less than 50% of their time at their top 5 sites. This contrasts with the fact that 73% of users spent 90% or more of their time at their top 5 favorite locations. Consequently, the majority of users are mainly concerned about network performance in a handful of locations.

As with the home-node classification, the two user communities also exhibit different usage patterns. For GSIA users, the median percentage of time spent at the top five sites is 92.1%; for non-GSIA users it is 99.1%. This difference is not as great as exhibited for the home-node differential, however, the important feature to note is how little time all users spent away from their top five sites. For the overall user community, slightly over one-third of users spent no time outside of their top five favorite sites.

5.4   Mobility

The absolute metric of mobility is defined as the number of access points a user connects to over a given time period. Stationary users will exhibit mobility values of 1 while high movement users will have values hovering around 10+. These mobility values are calculated by counting the number of unique access points that each unique MAC address accessed for each day.

The mobility results in Fig. 7 show that the majority of users are not highly mobile. Only 10.5% of all users have average mobility values of 5 or above. The median mobility for all users is 2.1.

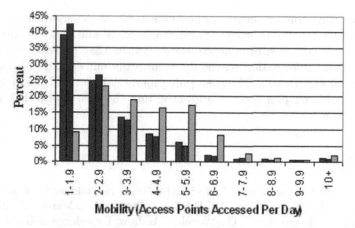

Fig. 7. Mobility Percentages. (First column for each group is for all users, the second for Non-GSIA users, and the third for GSIA users.)

Devices that would be considered highly mobile make up only a small minority of Wireless Andrew users. Specifically, only 1.9% of devices have mobility values of 10 or higher and 0.4% have values of 20 or higher. It is often this small fraction of users that context-aware application developers have in mind when developing their services, given that, by virtue of their mobility, these users stand to benefit the most from context-aware services.

Context-aware application developers should be aware that most users in a wireless network are not highly mobile. Often times, wireless users, especially those with laptops, will only utilize their devices in, at most, a handful of locations. While users may move around a great deal over the course of their day, their mobile devices are generally powered off while moving, limiting their potential ability to use context-aware applications. Context-aware developers will need to provide users with a compelling reason to leave their device on, or to obtain a device that is small enough to be conveniently left on, while moving.

6 Conclusion

As technology advances, novel tools are developed to help us manage growing complexity and take advantage of new opportunity. Wireless technology has opened the door to tremendous possibility, enabling us to roam untethered, while keeping data and communications within arm's reach. As wireless networks continue to blanket our homes, businesses, and rapidly, our cities, the ability to pinpoint a device's location in a wireless network becomes increasingly relevant to the vision of ambient intelligence.

Researchers have made great strides over the years in developing systems and methodologies to dynamically determine the position of wireless devices. The technology and associated infrastructure, however, need to be further developed before context-aware services can reach critical mass. Given that this is the case, existing context-aware applications have not yet scratched the surface of what is to come. As positioning systems improve and become standardized we will see an explosion of context-aware services that pervade our lives, delivering relevant information on-the-fly, facilitating our errands, and otherwise enhancing our experiences. The positioning methodologies and associated topics discussed in this chapter present a glimpse into the technology that will drive that revolution.

References

1. Bahl, P. and Padmanabhan, V. N.: "RADAR: An In-Building RF-based User Location and Tracking System." IEEE Infocom 2000, vol. 2. March. (2000) 775-784
2. Bennington, B. and Bartel, C.: "Wireless Andrew: Experience in Building a High Speed, Campus-Wide Wireless Data Network." In Mobicom 1997, ACM press, September. (1997) 55-65
3. Berna, Mary., Lisien, Brad., Sellner, Brennan., Gordon, Geoffrey., Pfenning, Frank., Thrun, Sebastian: "A Learning Algorithm for Localizing People Based On Wireless Signal Strength That Uses Labeled and Unlabeled Data." IJCAI, Pittsburgh, Pennsylvania. (2003) 1-6
4. Brown, P.J., Bovey, J.D., Chen, X.: "Context-Aware Applications: from the Laboratory to the Marketplace." IEEE Personal Communications 4(5). (1997) 58-64
5. Brunato, Muaro and Kiss Kallo, Csaba: "Trasparent Location Fingerprinting for Wireless Services." MED-HOC-NET. (2002)
6. Davies, N., Cheverst, K., Mitchel, A.: "Using and Determining Location in a Context-Sensitive Tour Guide." IEEE Computer 34(8). (2001) 35-41
7. Ferscha, Alois, Beer, Wolfgang and Narzt, Wolfgang: "Location Awareness in Community Wireless LANs." University of Linz.
8. Hackworth, Martin: "Waves - Transverse and Longitudinal Waves." (2002) 1-3
9. Hills, A. and Johnson, D.: "A Wireless Data Network Infrastructure at Carnegie Mellon University." IEEE Personal Communications 3(1). (1996) 56-63
10. Hightower, J., Boriello, G.: "Location Systems for Ubiquitous Computing." IEEE Computer 33(8), August. (2001)
11. Kaemarungsi, Kamot., Krishnamurthy, Prashant: "Modeling of Indoor Positioning Systems Based on Location Fingerprinting." IEEE INFOCOM 2004, Pittsburgh, Pennsylvania. (2004) 1-11
12. Kotz, D., and Essien, K.: "Analysis of a Campus-Wide Wireless Network." Proceedings of the Eighth Annual International Conference on Mobile Computing and Networking, Atlanta, Georgia. (2002) 107-118
13. Krumman, D., and Horviz, E: "Locadio: Inferring Motion and Location from WiFi Signal Strengths." Microsoft Research, Redmond Washington. (2004) 1-10
14. McLean, M.: "How to Design a Wireless Network." Communication News, September. (2003)
15. Nicola, Lenihan: "WLAN Positioning." University of Limerick. 2-14
16. Sadeh, Norman: MyCampus Project.
    http://www-2.cs.cmu.edu/ sadeh/mycampus.htm
17. Seidel, S. Y., and Rappaport, T. S.: "914 MHz Path Loss Prediction Models for Indoor Wireless Communications in Multifloored Buildings." IEEE Transactions on Antennas and Propagation, Vol. 40, No.2, February. (1992) 207-217

18. Small, J., Smailagic, A., and Siewiorek, D.P.: "Determining User Location for Context-Aware Computing through the Use of a Wireless LAN Infrastructure." ACM Mobile Networks and Applications, vol. 6. (2001)
19. Smailagic, A., Siewiorek, D. P., Anhalt, J., Kogan, D., Wang, Y.: "Location Sensing and Privacy in a Context Aware Computing Environment." Pervasive Computing. (2001)
20. Tang, D., and Baker, M.: "Analysis of a Local-Area Wireless Network." Proceedings of the 6th Annual ACM/IEEE International Conference on Mobile Computing and Networking, Boston, Massachusetts, August. (2000) 1-10
21. Tang, D., and Baker, M.: "Analysis of a Metropolitan-Area Wireless Network." Proceedings of the 5th Annual ACM/IEEE International Conference on Mobile Computing and Networking, Seattle, Washington, August. (1999) 13-23
22. Voida, S., Mynatt, E., MacIntyre, A.: "Supporting Collaboration in a Context-Aware Office Computing Environment." UbiComp 2002 Workshop. (2002)
23. Xiang, Z., Song, S., Chen, J., Wang, H., Huang, J., Gao, X.: "A Wireless LAN-Based Indoor Positioning Technology." IBM Research, September. (2004) 1-10
24. WaveLAN. http://www.wavelan.com. (now Agere)

Behavior-Based Indoor Navigation

Julio Abascal, Elena Lazkano, and Basilio Sierra

Euskal Herriko Unibertsitatea – The University of the Basque Country, Spain
julio.abascal@si.ehu.es, {ccplaore,ccpsiarb}@sc.ehu.es

1 Introduction

Ambience provides large amounts of heterogeneous data that can be used for diverse purposes, including indoor navigation in semi-structured environments. Indoor navigation is a very active research field due to its large number of possible applications: mobile guides for museums or other public buildings [36], office post delivering, assistance to people with disabilities and elderly people [34], etc.

The idea of using indoor navigation techniques to develop mobile guides is not new. Among the pioneers, Polly, a mobile robot acting as a guide for the MIT AI Lab [35], and Minerva, an autonomous guide developed for the National Museum of American History in Washington [69], are well known. A particular case are mobile guides for blind people which experienced a notable interest in the last years [40]. Another interesting application field is devoted to smart wheelchairs, which are provided with navigation aids for people with severe motor restrictions [64, 75]. All these applications share the need for a navigation system, even if its implementation may be different for each of them. For instance, the navigation system may act over the power stage of a smart wheelchair or may communicate with the user interface of a mobile navigation assistant in a museum. Evidently the implication of the user is different in each system, leading to diverse levels of human-system integration. Therefore, there are two key issues in the design of mobile guides: navigation strategy and user interface. Even if most of the mentioned systems use maps for navigation [36], there exist alternative, behavior-based systems, that use a procedural way to represent knowledge. Therefore, the selection of the approach not only conditions the navigational architecture but also the design of the human interface.

This chapter analyzes alternatives for navigation models and focuses on how properties of the environment can be intelligently exploited for indoor navigation tasks. In addition, it describes, in detail, an illustrative example based on behavior decomposition. Its navigational characteristics and influence upon the human interface design are also discussed.

1.1 Data for Navigation

All agent-environment interaction systems rely on the data obtained from sensors, and have to cope with their quantity and diversity. Sensors are needed to perceive the environment which is tightly coupled to the agent. In order to obtain

Y. Cai (Ed.): Ambient Intelligence for Scientific Discovery, LNAI 3345, pp. 263–285, 2005.

a detailed identification of the place where the mobile agent is localized or to recognize the several possible goals, indoor navigation requires managing different data provided by diverse sensors, and combining the type of information each sensor is able to give. In addition, the environment can provide complementary information for navigation by means of sensors that are usually devoted to other purposes (such as people location). In this way, the combination of the information obtained from the agent's own sensors and from the context may enhance navigational abilities. The data provided by a sensor can be scalars (such as the output of sonars, infrared, laser, ...), vectors (containing information about the position or the trajectory of the mobile agent provided by odometric sensors), booleans (provided by contact sensors or bumpers), waveform signals (such as pictures supplied by digital cameras or sounds from microphones), angles (from compasses), etc. [26, 11]. Proximity sensors are commonly used to handle geometrical concepts such as distances, position identification, etc. Among the vast diversity of sensors, vision systems are frequently used for indoor navigation to detect patterns in the environment, by means of artificial vision techniques. Images are potentially rich information sources [22] but computationally complex and expensive. Different information can be extracted from color images: shape of objects, color information, optical flow, etc. Textures and colors of the different environmental elements including people, walls, doors, floor, etc., can be used to navigate safely by avoiding obstacles or as natural landmarks that help the agent to locate itself globally in the environment.

2   Navigating Techniques from Mobile Robotics

Mobile Robotics has developed several methods for indoor navigation [42]. Many of them are based on centralized models of the environment: maps. Data provided by the robot's own sensors (frequently complemented by sensors located in the environment) are used to match the current state to the model in order to plan the path to the goal and perform related tasks. Alternatives to map-based navigation strategies are biologically inspired navigation methods (Behavior-based) that imitate navigational cues observed in animals [30]. This section reviews these two approaches starting with the later that is the approach taken in the example described in Section 3.

2.1   Behavior-Based Navigation

Behavior-based (BB) systems appeared in 1986, when R.A. Brooks proposed a bottom-up approach for robot control that imposed a new outlook for developing intelligent embodied agents capable of navigating in real environments and performing complex tasks. He introduced the Subsumption Architecture [13, 15] and developed multiple robotic creatures capable of showing different behaviors not seen before in real robots [21, 49, 16]. Behavior-based systems are originally inspired by biological systems. Even the most simple animals show navigation capabilities with a high degree of performance. For those systems, navigation consist of determining and maintaining a trajectory to the goal [47]. The main question to be answered for navigation is not *Where am I?* but *How do I reach the goal?* and the answer does not always require knowing the initial position. Therefore, the main abilities the agent needs in order to navigate are to move around and to identify goals. Neither a centralized world model nor the position of the robot with respect to this model needs to be maintained. Biorobotics, defined as the intersection between robotics and biology, is an emergent field whose aim is for biology to contribute to robotics and vice versa [72, 52, 10]. Different authors [71, 47] classify biomimetic navigation behaviors into two main groups:

1. *Local navigation* strategies are local control mechanisms that allow the agent to choose actions based only on its current sensory input. There are four strategies that fall in that group: search, path integration, taxis and goal orientation.
2. *Way-finding* methods are responsible for driving the agent to goals out of the agent's perceptual range that require recognition of different places and relations among them. They also rely on local strategies. Perception-triggered response, topological navigation and terrain inspection are the three main way-finding strategies mentioned in order of complexity.

The BB approach to robot navigation relies on the idea that the control problem is better assessed by bottom-up design and incremental addition of light-weight processes, called behaviors, where each one is responsible for reading its own inputs and sensors, and deciding the adequate motor actions. There is no centralized world model and data from multiple sensor do not need to be merged to match the current system state in the stored model. The motor responses of the several behavioral modules must be somehow coordinated in order to obtain valid intelligent behavior. As mentioned before, way-finding methods rely on local navigation strategies. How these local strategies are coordinated is a matter of study known as *motor fusion* in BB robotics, opposed to the well known *data fusion* process needed to model data information[1]. The aim is to match subsets of available data with motor decisions; outputs of all the active decisions somehow merge to obtain the final actions. In this case there is no semantic interpretation of the data if there is no behavior emergence.

Within this field, action coordination mechanisms can be classified into two main branches: competitive and cooperative [5]. In competitive or "winner takes all" strategies, active behaviors compete to reach the actuators and only the output of the winner has an effect on the robot's behavior. There are different

---

[1] Multi-sensor data fusion seeks to combine information from multiple sources to achieve inferences that are not feasible from a single sensor. This task is not trivial as sensor outputs often have overlaps and conflicts, their location is usually highly distributed, and their configuration very dynamic. In addition, their performance can vary with time. There are diverse techniques to implement data fusion models. Most of them are based on classical statistics and have a mathematical background which guarantee soundness. Hypothesis Tests, Principal Components Analysis and Transformation, Kalman Filtering, Particle Filtering, etc. are widely used data fusion methods. See [73, 63, 19] for good reviews of sensor data fusion.

methods to select the winner. Either a fixed prioritized scheme is defined as in the subsumption architecture; or a behavior activation level can also be used (action selection proposed by Maes [46]). An alternative is to use a voting mechanism [62] where behaviors give votes to a set of actions and the action which obtains the most votes wins.

An alternative to competitive methods are cooperative strategies, where the responses of the different behaviors all contribute to the overall response, generally by means of a weighted vectorial sum [6]. The final output is not the output of a single behavior but the combination of the outputs of the different active ones.

Pirjanian [60] makes a slightly different taxonomy. He also points out two main mechanisms: arbitration or action selection and command fusion. Arbitration mechanisms are "priority- or state-based" and "winner-takes all". Command fusion implies a cooperation among the behaviors in the selection or determination of the output, whether the final output is a single behavior output or a vector summation.

2.2 Probabilistic Map-Based Navigation

Among the different approaches to robot control, classical deliberative sense-plan-act (SPA) control is based on a sequential decomposition of the cognition process in three basic steps: sensing the environment and matching the sensed state in a stored centralized world model, planning according to the state, and acting [56]. In this decomposition of intelligence, the physical agent and the interaction with the environment were put aside. When BB approaches emerged, they opened the way for the development of the three-layered architectures [29] that look for the commitment between the two previous strategies. This hybrid approach incorporates a layer for basic interaction with the environment and, therefore, includes embodied and situated agents with interaction capabilities. Like the classical SPA strategy, it continues to rely on a centralized world model. It is exactly through the use of a centralized world model that the classical SPA nowadays evolved to the so-called hybrid and the behavior-based approach. Relying on this global world model, the robot navigation problem is mainly concerned with answering three questions [45]: *Where am I? Where are the other places regarding me? How can I reach them?* These questions give rise to the three main areas of robot navigation: environment mapping, localization and planning. Since the late eighties, the two main approaches to spatial models were metric and topological maps. Elfes [25] introduced *Occupancy grids*, nowadays known as probabilistic approaches, which are metric representations extended with a certain probabilistic belief of being in a cell [65, 67, 48, 23]. Although different techniques are constantly being developed to acquire the spatial model [68], they all must cope with incorrect odometry measurements and correspondence problems between data recorded at different time points. At present, there are robust methods for mapping static environments and those of limited size, however, mapping unstructured, dynamic or large-scale environments largely remains an open research problem.

Self-localization consists of determining the robot's position within the model starting from an initial unknown state. There are several approaches that try to solve the localization task. *Markov localization* is a method based on an extension of Hidden Markov models that maintain a belief over the robot global configuration space. It is based on the so named *Markov assumption* or static world assumption that presumes current robot sensor readings rely only on current position. Markov localization is a passive probabilistic process that calculates the probability the robot is at each state as a function of the acquired sensor model and the cinematic model [18, 27, 57]. Due to the high requirements of updating and maintaining the probability density function over the whole set of states, a number of authors proposed localization methods based on particle filters, where the *a posteriori* belief is represented by a set of particles together with an associated weighting factor of each particle, a discrete subset of the probability distribution [61, 28, 70].

A classic approach for generating maps is based on Kalman filters [37]. Kalman filter-based mapping algorithms are often referred to as SLAM algorithms. SLAM (Simultaneous Localization And Mapping) or CML (Concurrent Mapping and Localization) is not a solution itself, but a problem concerned with building the map while jointly computing the robot's localization [68]. The coupling of these two tasks should relieve the correspondence problem [44], which is hard to solve when mapping and localization are tackled separately. It is performed in two main steps: an exploration phase to reach different places and location revisiting for consistency that can also drive the robot to new unvisited locations [74, 33].

Planning is a traditional field of Artificial Intelligence (AI) and many algorithms and techniques that cope with problems as different in nature to robotics and manipulators as graphics animation or non-invasive surgery have been developed [41, 38, 42, 66]. However, planning in dynamic environments often requires re-planning due to changes in the robot-environment state [14].

2.3   Role of Machine Learning in Navigation

One of the characteristics of intelligent behavior is the capacity of adaptation. The ability to learn about the environment has long been considered an important characteristic of artificial intelligent systems. A number of mobile robots are able to learn from their navigational experience. Automatic learning paradigms are involved in the so called *Machine Learning* area, where a large number of models are defined. Mobile Robotics widely apply Machine Learning techniques for navigation [24]. Learning can be used for improving the interaction of the robot-environment system [12].

Over the last few years, many algorithms have been developed for very diverse problems, including natural language understanding, control, face recognition, etc. Learning may improve the whole system performance in different forms: concept generalization from multiple examples, past experience reuse, new concept discovering for environmental natural landmark learning and, of course, behavior implementation and coordination.

Machine Learning is usually divided into three subareas: supervised classification, unsupervised classification and searching methods, all three are useful for behavior and control developing purposes. An interesting survey on this topic can be found in [53].

3   Navigation Based on Environmental Cues: An Illustrative Example

Although the definition of control architecture lacks consensus in the context of robotics systems, here we refer to an architecture as a set of principles for control organization that, as Matarić [50] underlines, in addition to providing structure, it imposes constraints on the way control problems can be solved. In behavior-based strategy, the robot controller is organized as a collection of modules, called behaviors, that receive inputs from sensors and/or other behaviors, process the inputs and send outputs to actuators and/or other behaviors. All behaviors in a controller are executed in parallel, simultaneously receiving inputs and producing outputs. Behaviors are independently developed and tested, each one reading its particular sensors and generating the desired actions. More complex tasks involve incremental behavior addition and appropriate action fusion mechanisms.

Following this paradigm, the control architecture is being incrementally built, adding new modules as the task requires it. In this section we present a perception-triggered response based way of finding strategy that relies on two local strategies: free-space balancing and compass following.

The navigation behavior is combined with emergency exit panel recognition and door counting ability that supply the robot with the capability of identifying the different offices in a predefined route consisting of a sequence of landmarks. The robot's capabilities reflect the state of the behavior-based control architecture we are incrementally developing, describing the individual processes that are involved and how they communicate through the interaction with the environment according to the task. Therefore, it is the intelligent interaction between the robot and the environment through proper control that links perception and action, giving rise to the correct achievement of the task.

The robot platform used for the experiments is a small Pioneer 3 model from Activmedia Robots named Galtxagorri. It is provided with a front ring of eight sonar sensors, a Cannon VCC4 PTZ vision system and a TCM2 compass device mounted on a home-made wooden platform to avoid magnetic disturbances from the motors.

The Player-Stage [31] client/server library allows us to communicate with the different devices connected to the robot, all but the compass that is plugged to a serial port and accessed through an independent function set. This software, appropriately combined with the SORGIN software framework specifically developed to define and implement behavior-based control architectures [7] provide us with the adequate programming environment for robot control. Figure 1 shows how these two tools can be combined. For the experiment here described, only the internal host of the robot is used.

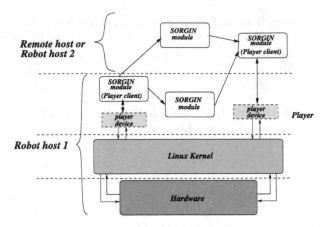

Fig. 1. SORGIN and Player combined software architecture.

The environment where the robot moves is a typical office-like semistructured environment, with rectangular halls connected by corridors, full of geometrical properties and natural landmarks that can be intelligently exploited (Fig. 7).

3.1 Wandering in a Preferred Compass Orientation

The robot needs to move around in order to interact with the environment. The basic movement behavior is obtained by combining two simple modules:

- Left and right free space balancing for corridor following that allows the robot to smoothly traverse corridors and halls. Here, rotational velocity is defined using the difference between left and right side sonar readings, and translation is dependent on the front sonars. This behavior acts also as an obstacle avoider when the obstacles are within the perceptual range of the sensors.
- Follow a desired compass orientation, a simple proportional control that directs the robot through the path defined by the compass orientation. In order to allow the robot to turn on the spot when it has free space around. The translational velocity is an inverse exponential function over the difference between the desired and the actual compass orientations.

Each module outputs translational and rotational velocity values and the final output motor command is simply the weighted sum of both modules. The behavior produced by the combination of these two modules is more than a simple wanderer as it directs the robot to the goal defined by the orientation avoiding collisions at the same time. The desired compass orientation acts as an attractor when there is sufficient space for the robot to move safely, thus adding persistence to the global behavior.

3.2 Landmark Identification Subsystems

For goal oriented navigation, the robot needs more knowledge that must be properly combined with the capability of wandering in a preferred compass orientation. More specifically, the robot needs to recognize several environmental properties that change the orientation to follow, according to the situation and the task. The environment can be provided with specific landmarks so that the robot can easily identify different locations. Instead, we chose to extract environmental characteristics that can be recognized by robot sensors. We think that it is necessary to assess the level of performance robotic intelligent systems can reach without limiting the properties of the environment to suit the robots' behavior. Therefore, our approach exploits natural landmarks, namely, corridors, emergency exit panels and doors.

Corridor Identification. Corridors present very strong properties that make them identifiable. Moreover, most of the office doors are located at the corridors. Thereby, corridor recognition is an interesting capability for the robot to consider. Equation (1) shows the single rule applied for corridor identification, where *dist* refers to the corridor width measured by left and right sonars.

$$corridor\_id(t) = \begin{cases} 1 \text{ if } dist \ < Threshold \\ 0 \text{ else} \end{cases} \tag{1}$$

To make the corridor identification more robust, instead of just trusting a single sonar and compass reading, we maintain a belief value of being in each corridor. For that we use a fixed sized FIFO (First In, First Out) buffer that contains the results of the corridor identification behavior for the last BSIZE (buffer size) readings:

$$Bel(corridor) = \sum_{k=(t-BSIZE)}^{t} corridor\_id(k) \times w_k$$

where w_k is an increasing weighting parameter that gives more importance to the recent values of *corridor_id*. The buffer size determines the delay with which the new location is identified and, together with the weights, the effect of disturbances on the confidence level.

The maintenance of a belief state of being in a corridor allows us to also detect transitions from corridors to non-corridor places. These transitions are used to change the desired compass orientation according to the state or location of where the robot is. Forcing the robot to enter narrow corridors becomes more difficult. Specific mechanisms are needed to detect crossroads and change the desired compass orientation to reach the next goal.

Emergency Exit Panel Identification. Emergency exit panels are international, natural landmarks mandatory in every public building that must follow some shape, color and location standards[2]. As natural landmarks in the environment, they can be used to implement navigation strategies such as recognition-triggered response. To extract the panel from the background in the image, a

---

[2] E.g., European "Council Directive 92/58/EEC of 24 June 1992 on the minimum requirements for the provision of safety and/or health signs at work". Official Journal L 245 , 26/08/1992 P. 0023–0042.

Fig. 2. Original and segmented images.

simple thresholding is enough to appropriately segment the green areas of the image. Once the image is segmented, we need a method to classify an image as containing, or not, a panel; instead of using image correlation functions we applied a Multi Layer Perceptron (MLP) neural network trained using as an input vector the quadratic weighted sums of 20×20 sized image blocks, resulting in 28 input neurons [43]. The training image set contained the inputs of 320 images, taken from the nominal trajectory maintaining constant pan, tilt and zoom values. The neural net has a single hidden layer of 3 neurons and the output is a binary vector that classifies the image as containing, or not, a panel. Applying a leaving-one-out (LOO) validation technique, and after a training period of 1000 epochs for each set, we obtained a validated performance of 96.25%. The MLP is improved by looking for appropriate input weights using a *Genetic Algorithm* [32] and associating to the individuals as a fitness function the LOO performance of the MLP itself, raising the accuracy up to 97.8%.

The emergency exit panel recognition module, based on the MLP, gives, as an output, the mean value of the last 10 images. This value is a measure of the confidence level (cl) of the recognition process. Therefore, it will send an output "1" indicating that a new landmark has been detected only after 10 positive identifications. When this occurs, the proper actions would be taken.

Identification of emergency exit panels is more difficult than of corridors due to their lack of duration in time. In spite of the defined confidence level, the positive identification relies on a few snapshots. To cope better with this problem, we made the confidence level affect the global translational velocity of the robot according to the following expression: $v' = (1 - cl) * v$. The aim of this velocity reduction is to slow down the robot when a panel is being recognized so that it maintains the panel in range of vision.

Wooden Doors Identification. Doors imply interesting locations in the environment. Anyone whose job is to dispatch the daily post, must be able to somehow identify the different offices that are accessed through doors. The doors in the robot's environment are made of wood. The objective of this module is to extract wooden door areas in images taken by the robot and to decide if the robot is, or not, in front of a door. To do so, the image must be first segmented by selecting the pixels belonging to a door.

The segmentation method should cope with noisy images; dynamic variations in the lighting conditions, due especially to the sunlight incoming through the windows, make the segmentation problem more difficult. We chose to apply the *Oc1* method [54], as implemented in the MLC++ library [39]. To learn the model, we built a database of 50,000 entries, each pixel being labeled as "wooden door" or "rest". No more precise division is needed, due to the fact that the only goal at this stage is to be able to distinguish the wooden door from the other surfaces in the robot's environment. To obtain this database, we processed sixty images taken by the robot, in which the relevant elements of its environment appeared. We cut these images into 395 slices, each representative of one and only one of the different surfaces, labeling these pixels manually. With this procedure, we obtained a large database of more than 4,000,000 labeled pixels. From this huge set, we randomly selected 50,000 to build a training set of 40,000, from which the model is learned, and a test set of 10,000, to test the accuracy of the model. This procedure was repeated ten times, obtaining a mean accuracy over 97%. Figure 3 shows an example of the result given by the segmentation process.

In order to decide whether the robot is in front of a door or not, we take into account that, when the camera's tilt angle is appropriately set, the door always fills the upper half of the image, so the floor may appear in the lower half. It is then enough to process only the rows in the upper half in order to make a decision. If the robot is in front of a door, the wood will fill the columns in the middle of the camera image, thereby our algorithm just processes the forty columns in the middle. Therefore, from an original image of 120 × 160, it only considers a block of 60 × 40 from the segmented image.

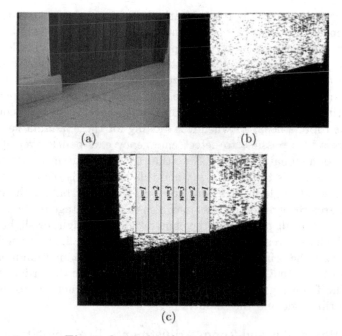

(a)   (b)

(c)

Fig. 3. Original and segmented images.

From this reduced image a number between 0 and 1 measuring the confidence level when in front of a door is obtained computing the percentage of pixels labeled as "wooden door" across each column, and calculating the weighted mean across all the columns, according to the following formula:

$$cl_{wood} = \frac{\sum_{i=1}^{n} w_i p_i}{\sum_{i=1}^{n} w_i} \tag{2}$$

p_i being the percentage of pixels labeled as "wooden door" in the i-th column and w_i the weight of the i-th column in the weighted mean. We implemented a schema in which there are three zones inside the middle columns, according to the distance from the center of the image. The weight of the columns (w_i) decreases according to the distance from the middle of the image. Columns near the outside borders have a weight one third of the columns in the inner zone and one half of the columns in the intermediate zone. When the confidence level obtained from an image raises over 0.5, a door has entered in the visual field of the robot. This number increases over 0.9 when the door fills the center of the image, and decreases smoothly when the robot surpasses the door. When the confidence level falls to 0.05 during a predefined number of consecutive images (to prevent noise effects), the robot has completely passed the door and the door counter is incremented.

3.3   Active Head Control System

Visual processes are directly related with the task to be performed by the observer. Animate or purposive vision mandates that perception is linked to action and that vision must be based on expectations [9, 4]. The knowledge on the environment may somehow condition the interpretation of what is being seen. Emergency exit panels are small in size and the robot may miss them if the camera is not adequately focused to the area where the panel is expected to be. Zoom and tilt values' adaptation, according to distance to the wall, could greatly improve the robot's behavior when it is looking for these landmarks. With such active process it is possible to detect emergency exit panels even if the robot turns aside its nominal trajectory. Note that the tilt adjustment is not desirable when the robot needs to find doors; when this behavior is required, it is preferable to fix the tilt angle so that door areas fill the upper half of the image. The wood color area recognition process may also take advantage of the reduced size of the robot if the tilt position of the camera points straight or slightly down to the floor; the lower areas of the walls are less sensitive to lighting conditions. All this emphasizes the principle that vision does not have to function in isolation, if not as part of a system that interacts with its environment in order to carry out its task. The following section describes the selected functions to dynamically modify the tilt angle and the zoom value.

Distance Based Tilt and Zoom Adjustment. To establish the relationship between the camera's tilt angle and the distance to the wall, measured by means of the robot's sonar sensors, instead of imposing a model to the system, we let the trained MLP network tell us the adequate parameter values for each distance. To do so, we placed the robot at different positions and considered a valid tilt angle if there existed a zoom range for which the MLP was able to robustly identify the panel. Although the collected data did not show a precise linear relationship among the parameters, we approximated the curve using a linear function with bounded minimum and maximum values. Figure 4 shows the ideal relationship between the distance to the wall and the tilt angle ($g(x)$), the collected data and the selected linear approximation ($f(x)$).

With the dynamic tilt adjustment behavior running on the robot, we collected data for the zoom values in a similar manner. Letting the robot select the tilt angle and changing the zoom value using uniform intervals, we captured the MLP results for each zoom value and the sonar measured distance to the wall.

Using, as centroid, the mean value of the acceptable zoom range for each measured distance, we interpolated the curve using a B-spline, a mathematical, parametric definition of a series of connected geometric curve segments, belonging to the spline curve family extensively used in the CAD industry and more widely in computing for 3D geometry generation and modeling [58]. Figure 5 shows the obtained curve. Moreover, the selection of middle points of valid zoom ranges makes final behavior more robust as it allows a confidence interval for noisy readings (see [8] for more details).

3.4   Behavior Coordination for Task Achievement

In previous sections we showed how the robot is able to perform collision-free navigation in a privileged compass orientation and dynamic landmark detection. In order to acquire favorable data from the environment (i.e detect emergency exit panels from different viewpoints) the dynamic landmark detection system was improved with an active camera head control.

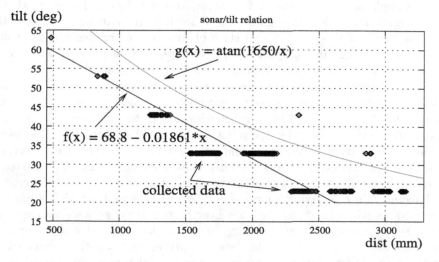

Fig. 4. Sonar measured distance versus tilt angle.

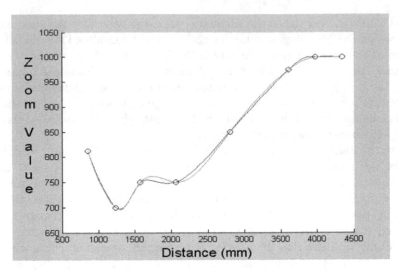

Fig. 5. B-spline for zoom adjustment.

Although low level navigational skills do not depend on the higher level landmark detector systems, each behavior was designed taking the robot's task into account. Through the user interface the robot receives the number of the office as input data and it looks for the office navigating through corridors and halls.

As Matarić says in [51], any solution superior to random walk needs internal information on the robot's current location, the desired goal location and the relationship between both of them. With our corridor identification behavior Galtxagorri has the ability to locate itself in the environment. The desired goal location is expressed in terms of the number of doors the robot has to find and accomplished by the *wooden door identification* behavior. However, what is the navigational method that guides the robot from its starting position to the goal location? At this development state of the control architecture, the robot performs the recognition-triggered response method, connecting different locations by means of local navigation algorithms. Thus, appropriately sequencing different recognition-triggered responses, the robot follows a pre-defined route. This navigational method has been implemented by means of small finite-state automata (FSA) integrated in each behavior, associating the sequence of landmarks with actions that guide the robot to the direction of the goal. Therefore, behaviors keep track of the state and subgoals to which they are concerned. The task is performed by means of inter-process communication while the robot interacts in a real environment. Figure 6 shows the overall view of the control architecture. Each behavior is represented by a circle and is a SORGIN process. The modules labeled as "manager" are directly related to hardware, and are only responsible for reading from or writing to this device. The video manager is an exception due to the nature of the data it captures, and it is the behavior that performs wood identification or emergency exit panel recognition depending on the state reflected by the corridor identification behavior. The link between the *door identification* behavior and the *motion coordinator* is meant to make the robot stop for a while when it reaches the goal door.

As offices are mainly located in corridors, while traversing them, the robot fixes the camera's parameters according to the office number it has to look for. On the other hand, when navigating in a hall, the emergency exit panel identification system is activated, actively adapting tilt and zoom values to better perceive them, and defining a new compass orientation to follow when a panel is identified. Each landmark identification process defines, through the confidence level, the activation function of the behavior itself.

3.5   Empirical Evaluation of the Architecture

Although all the modules developed were incrementally built and tested, the adequacy of the overall control architecture still needs to be measured. When a single behavior is to be evaluated, the most straightforward method is to run an experiment several times and give the overall performance. On the other hand,

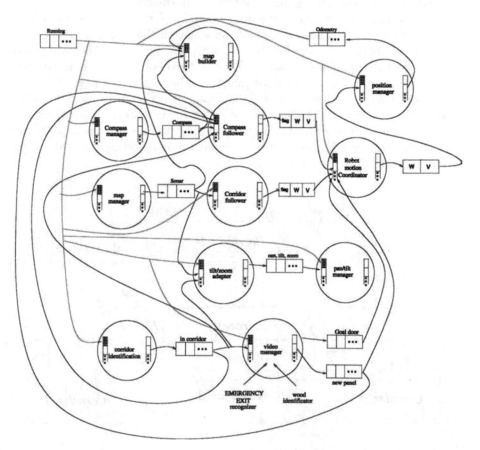

Fig. 6. Overall view of the control architecture.

to measure the appropriateness of the more complex emergent behavior is much more difficult. Robot behavior is encapsulated in its trajectory [55] and several numerical values can be defined to measure the properties of the trajectory [59]. However, as far as we know, there is not a standard quantitative way to measure the performance of the system by means of behavior assessment. This is probably the main weakness of the field of Intelligent Robotics and Autonomous Systems.

The approach taken in this paper has been to perform two sets of experiments. First, to evaluate the robustness of the landmark identification processes, the robot has been programmed to perform the route in Fig. 7; however before returning to corridor number one, three turns were to be made. Each trial then consisted of repeating the main loop in the center of the area three times before returning to the initial corridor, a path of about 300m. The experiment has been performed in both senses, clockwise (CW) and counter clockwise (CCW), four times each. This experimental bed sums a total of about 160 minutes for the robot to successfully identify the landmarks. Figure 8 shows the robot's viewpoint of the environment. Figures 8(a) and 8(b) were obtained in triple tours using the compass to build the maps, while Figs. 8(c) and 8(d) show the maps obtained in single tours, using pure odometric information.

Secondly, the performance of the door identification process had to be evaluated. We labeled doors on the right of the walls (in the direction of the tour) with even numbers and doors on the left with odd numbers. Then we placed the robot at the beginning of each corridor. The robot was, at each run, sent to each door number in the corridor and the robot signaled the goal door by going backwards for a short while when reaching it. Prior to sending the robot, the operator ensured all the doors in the corridor were closed. The experiment was repeated several times in each corridor without failure; more than 200 doors successfully identified. Figure 9 shows a typical plot reflecting the state of the landmark identification processes during a tour.

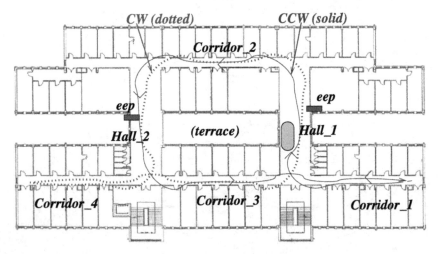

Fig. 7. Robot environment and the nominal trajectory for the task.

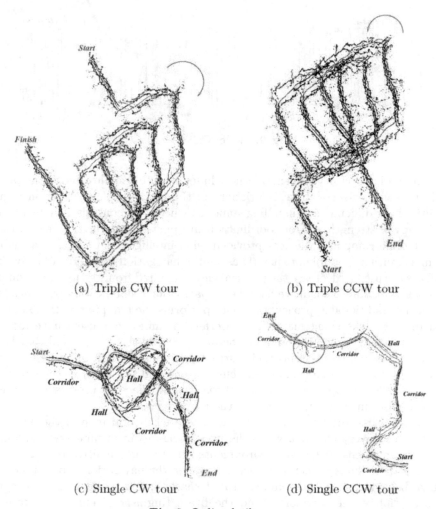

(a) Triple CW tour   (b) Triple CCW tour

(c) Single CW tour   (d) Single CCW tour

Fig. 8. Online built maps.

4   Behavior-Based Indoor Navigation for a Smart Wheelchair

Smart electrically powered wheelchairs are used by severely motor-impaired people that may experience difficulties when driving standard, manual or electrically powered wheelchairs. Smart wheelchairs are provided with computerized control units and simple interfaces that assist the users with driving tasks [20]. While the control stage is based on well-established Mobile Robotics and Automatic Guided Vehicles techniques, the design of the adequate navigation system requires significant research effort due to its crucial influence on the user interface [2]. Smart wheelchairs are provided with elements (such as sensors, controllers, processors) required to be considered as mobile robots. Therefore the previously mentioned navigation techniques are fully applicable to these kind of systems.

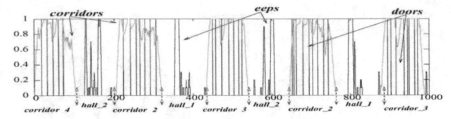

Fig. 9. Plot of CCW tour.

Human interaction with smart wheelchairs is quite complex due to the physical and sometimes cognitive, restrictions of the user. People with physical disabilities have difficulties in handling standard wheelchair controls, usually due to their lack of strength and/or coordination in upper limbs. For this reason they need mobile computing devices provided with intelligent interfaces that assist them as much as possible, frequently assuming navigation tasks [1]. Adaptive interfaces are used to decrease the physical effort required from the user and, simultaneously, maximize cognitive user participation for rehabilitation purposes [3].

In the traditional approach, the robot performs the mapping, path planning, and driving tasks using maps. The interface assumes that users have mental maps of the environment similar to the ones used by the system and that they know (or can ask the system) their current position. In addition users must be able to locate positions (mainly the current one and the goal) in their mental map [17]. The map-based approach allows the interface to process the orders from the user in terms of elements of the map.

Nevertheless, the user seldom has a structured mental map of the environment. This is very common when the user navigates in an unknown building. This also happens in known environments due to the cognitive difficulties in building these kinds of mental structures. When the navigation is based on biological behavior, the human and the robot share relative navigational concepts, such as "follow the corridor," "find the fire extinguisher," etc., that are easier to be mentally processed by the user. In this case, the interface can both, accept complex orders (such as "go to room number 5") that include many individual actions or partial and relative descriptions of the path, such as "go straight ahead," "find the window near the lift," "turn left," etc. The previously described biologically inspired model follows this procedure. In this way, it allows for "natural" human-robot interaction, similar to the interaction between humans.

The user-wheelchair interface designed for this system share, with other smart wheelchairs, (e.g. the one proposed by Yanco [75]) the physical structure (input and output devices, dialogue modes, etc.). However, the design of the cognitive interaction model is based on concepts, well understood at both sides of the interface, that allow for both complex commands coming from users with a clear mental map of the place and simple commands issued by users with a partial knowledge of the environment, which is not possible for wheelchairs based on classical navigation models.

4.1   TetraNauta Smart Wheelchair

The behavior-based indoor navigation techniques previously presented have been applied to our smart wheelchair, called TetraNauta (Fig. 10), which is able to navigate in semi-structured environments (such as hospitals). The TetraNauta's physical interface is supported by a mobile computer provided with input/output devices and procedures fitted to the user's specific features. Its main goal is to automate interaction tasks as much as possible in order to minimize user intervention. Therefore, the type of devices that may be handled by the user to communicate with the robot must be quite diverse. TetraNauta maintains the joystick (or a similar device, mouthstick, headstick, etc., handled with any part of the body with residual control) as the main input device. In addition one or more push-buttons are used for start-stop and similar functions. The system provides feedback to the user by means of a voice synthesizer and a graphical display. Synthetic voice is useful for short messages with location information or security warnings, however, when the information provided is more complex, a graphical display of the results is more convenient.

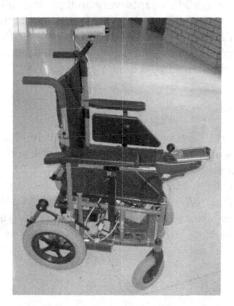

Fig. 10. A prototype of the TetraNauta System.

The physical interface supports a user-system dialogue model directly related to the world model of both agents. The interaction is based on a number of shared assumptions that configure a common vision of the world taking into account that, usually, humans have a multilevel abstract description of world. On the subject of spatial navigation, the user tends to think in terms of places described by attributes such as activity performed there, proximity, people occupying them, etc. Even if the physical interface is the same designed for a classical navigation model, the cognitive interface is not based on a shared centralized map of the environment, but rather on individual behaviors. In this way, the user interface allows user participation by means of the selection of simple behaviors, such as "go ahead". For more complex orders, a higher abstract level has been designed. At this level the possible destinations are matched with a set of complex behaviors, which can also be composed by sets of simpler behaviors because, frequently, sequential descriptions of the way reflect the mental path of the user better.

5   Conclusion

The behavior-based strategy presented in this chapter exploits properties of the environment in order to perform intelligent indoor navigation. The intelligence comes not only from the system processing and sensing capabilities; it mainly emerges from the adequate combination of behaviors. Moreover, due to the procedural nature of the approach, its intelligence, which is "stored" in the individual behaviors, depends on the capability of interacting with the environment.

Behavior-based navigation adapts very well to indoor semi-structured dynamic environments and facilitates human-system interaction in intelligent ambients, providing an adequate basis to design any kind of assistants for human autonomous navigation, such as guidance for the blind, indoor assistance for the elderly, smart wheelchair control, museum guides, etc.

Acknowledgments

This work was supported by the Gipuzkoako Foru Aldundia under grant OF761/2003 and by the Spanish Ministry of Science and Technology (MCYT) within the project DomoSilla (TIC2000-0087-P4).

Special thanks to Prof. Man Graña for the uninterested offer to use his Pioneer3 robot, and to Aitzol Astigarraga and José María Martínez-Otzeta, for their contribution to the implementation of the control architecture. The authors also wish to thank the book's editor and the anonymous reviewer for their valuable comments and suggestions.

References

1. Abascal, J., Cagigas, D., Garay, N., and Gardeazabal, L.: "Interfacing users with very severe mobility restrictions with a semi-automatically guided wheelchair." ACM SIGCAPH Newsletter, (63). (1999) 16–20
2. Abascal, J., Cagigas, D., Garay, N., and Gardeazabal, L.: "Mobile interface for a smart wheelchair." In F. Patern'o, editor, Human Computer Interaction with Mobile devices, Springer Verlag. LNCS 411. (2002) 373–377
3. Abascal, J., Cagigas, D., Garay, N., and Gardeazabal, L.: "Mobile interfaces for people with severe motor restrictions." In C. Stephanidis, editor, Universal Access in HCI. Inclusive Design in the Information Society. Vol. 4. Lawrence Erlbaum Associates. (2003) 289–293

4. Aloimonos, J.: Active Perception. Lawrence Erlbaum Assoc Inc. (1993)
5. Arkin, R. C.: Behavior-Based Robotics. MIT Press. (1998)
6. Arkin, R.C.: "Motor schema-based mobile robot navigation." International Journal of Robotics Research, 8(4). (1989) 92–112
7. Astigarraga, A., Lazkano, E., Rañó, I., Sierra, B., and Zarautz, I.: "SORGIN: a software framework for behavior control implementation." In CSCS14, volume 1. (2003) 243–248
8. Astigarraga, A., Lazkano, E., Sierra, B., and Rañó, I.: Active landmark perception. In MMAR-2004 (in press). (2004)
9. Ballard, D. H. and Brown, C. M.: "Principles of animate vision." Image Understanding, 56. (1992) 3–21
10. Bennett, A. T. D.: "Do animals have cognitive maps?" The journal of experimental biology. (1997) 219–224
11. Borenstein, J., Everett, B., and Feng, L.: "Navigating Mobile Robots: Systems and Techniques." A. K. Peters. (1996)
12. Brooks, R.: The role of learning in autonomous robots. In Proceedings of the Fourth Annual Workshop on Computational Learning Theory, San Mateo, CA. Morgan Kaufmann. (1991) 5–10
13. Brooks, R. A.: A robust layered control system for a mobile robot. IEEE Journal of robotics and automation, RA–26. (1986) 14–23
14. Brooks, R. A.: "Planning is just a way of avoiding figuring out what to do next." Technical report, MIT Artificial Intelligence Laboratory. (1987)
15. Brooks, R. A. and Connell, J. H.: "Asynchronous distributed control system for a mobile robot." In Proceedings of the SPIE's Cambridge Symposyum on Optical and Optoelectronic Engineering. (1986) 77–84
16. Brooks, Rodney A.: "A robot that walks: Emergent behaviors from a carefully evolved network." Technical Report AI MEMO 1091, MIT. (1989)
17. Cagigas, D. and Abascal, J.: "Hierarchical path search with partial materialization of costs for a smart wheelchair." Journal of Intelligent and Robotic Systems, 39(4). (2004) 409–431
18. Cassandra, A. R., Kaelbling, L. P., and Kurien, J. A: "Acting under uncertainty: discrete bayesian models for mobile-robot navigation." In Proceedings of the IEEE/RSJ International Conference on Intelligent Robot and Systems. (1996)
19. Chung, H., Ojeda, L., and Borenstein, J.: "Sensor fusion for mobile robot dead-reckoning with a precision-calibrated fiber optic gyroscope." In proceedings of the 2001 IEEE International Conference on Robotics and Automation, ICRA 2001, 3. (2001) 3588–359
20. Civit, A. and Abascal, J.: "Tetranauta: A weheelchair controller for users with very severe mobility restrictions." In I. Placencia and E. Ballabio, editors, Improving the quality of Life for the European Citizen, Technology for Inclusive Design and Equality. IOS Press. (1998)
21. Connell, J. H.: Minimalist Mobile Robotics. A Colony-Style Architecture for an Artificial Creature. Academic Press, inc. (1990)
22. DeSouza, G. N. and Kak, A. C.: "Vision for mobile robot navigation: A survey." IEEE Transactions on pattern analysis and Machine Intelligence, 24(2). (2002) 237–267
23. Duckett, T. and Nehmzow, U.: Performance comparison of landmark recognition systems for navigating mobile robots. In AAAI. (2000)
24. Sharkey, N. (Ed.): "Special issue: Robot learning: the new wave." Robotics and Autonomous Systems, 22(3–4). (1997)

25. Elfes, A.: Using occupancy grids for mobile robot perception and navigation. Computer, 22. (1989) 46–57

26. Everett, H. R.: Sensors for Mobile Robots. Theory and Applications. A. K. Peters, Ltd. (1995)

27. Fox, D., Burgard, W., and Thrun, S.: "Active markov localization for mobile robots." Robotics and Autonomous Systems, 25(1). (1998) 195–207

28. Fox, D., Thrun, S., Burgard, W., and Dellaert, F.: Sequential Monte Carlo methods in practice, chapter Particle filters for mobile robot localization. Springer Verlag. (2002) 470–498

29. Gat, E.: On three-layer architectures. In D. Kortenkamp and R. P. Bonasso, editors, Artificial Intelligence and Mobile Robots. Case Studies of Succesful Robot Systems, MIT Press. (1997) 195–210

30. (Ed.) Gelenbe, E.: "Special issue: Biologically inspired autonomous systems." Robotics and Autonomous Systems, 22(1). (1997)

31. Gerkey, B. P., Vaughan, R. T., and Howard, A.: "The Player/Stage project: tools for multi-robot and distributed sensor systems." In Proc. of the International Conference on Advanced Robotics (ICAR). (2003) 317–323

32. Goldberg, D. E.: Genetic Algorithms in Search, Optimization and Machine Learning. Addison–Wesley. (1989)

33. González-Baños, H. H. and Latombe, J. C.: "Navigation strategies for exploring indoor environments." International Journal of Robotics Research, 21(10–11). (2002) 829–848

34. Goodman, J., Gray, P., Khammampad, K., and Brewster, S.: "Using landmarks to support older people in navigation." In M. Dunlop S. Brewster, editor, Proceedings of Mobile HCI 2004, volume 3160 of LNCS. Springer-Verlag. (2004)

35. Horswill, I.: "Polly: A vision-based artificial agent." In Proceedings of the 11th Conference of the American Association for Artificial Intelligence (AAAI- 93). (1993)

36. Kray, C., Baus, J., Cheverst, K.: "A survey of map-based mobile guides." In A. Zipf L. Meng, T. Reichenbacher, editor, Map-based mobile services- Theories, Methods and Implementations. Springer Verlag. (2004)

37. Kalman, R. R.: A new approach to linear filtering and prediction problems. Transactions of the ASME journal of Basic Engineering, 82. (1960) 35–45

38. Khatib, O: Real-time obstacle avoidance for manipulators and mobile robots. International Journal of Robotics Research, 5(1). (1996) 90–98

39. Kohavi, R., Sommerfield, D., and Dougherty, J.: "Data mining using MLC++: A machine learning library in C++." In International Journal on Artificial Intelligence Tools, volume 6(4). http://www.sgi.com/Technology/mlc (1997) 537–566

40. Kulyukin, V., Gharpure, C.P., Sute, P., De Graw, N., and Nicholson, J.: "A robotic wayfinding system for the visually impaired." In Proceedings of the Sixteenth Innovative Applications of Artificial Intelligence Conference (IAAI-04). (2004)

41. Latombe, J. C.: "Motion planning: a journey of robots, molecules, digital actors and other artifacts." International Journal of Robotics Research, 18(11). (1999) 1119–1128

42. Latombe, Jean Claude: Robot Motion Planning. Kluwer Academic. (1991)

43. Lazkano, E., Astigarraga, A., Sierra, B., and Rañó, I.: "On the adequateness of emergency exit panel and corridor identification as pilot scheme for a mobile robot." In Intelligent Autonomous Systems 8, volume 1. (2004) 915–924

44. Leonard , J. J. and Durrant-Whyte, H. F: Directed sonar sensing for mobile robot navigation. Kluwer Academic Publishers, Cambrage, MA. (1992)

45. Levitt, T. S. and Lawton, D. T.: Qualitative navigation for mobile robots. Artificial Intelligence, 44(3). (1990) 305–360
46. Maes, P.: "The dynamic of action selection." In Proceedings of the 1989 International Joint Conference on Artificial Intelligence, Detroit. (1989) 991–997
47. Mallot, H. A. and Franz, M. A.: Biomimetic robot navigation. Robotics and Autonomous System, 30. (2000) 133–153
48. Martin, M. C. and Moravec, H.: Robot evidence grids. Technical Report CMU-RI-TR-96-06, Robotics Institute. Carnagie Mellon University. (1996)
49. Matarić, M.: "A distributed model for mobile robot environment-learning and navigation." Master's thesis, MIT Artificial Intelligence Laboratory. (1990)
50. Matarić, M.: "Behavior-based control: Main properties and implications." Proceedings of the IEEE International Conference on Robotics and Automation. Workshop on Architectures for Intelligent Control Systems. (1992) 46–54
51. Matarić, M.: "Integration of representation into goal-driven behavior-based robotics." IEEE transactions on robotics and automation, 8(3):2. (1992) 304–31
52. Meyer, Jean-Arcady: From natural to artificial life: Biomimetic mechanisms in animat design. Robotics and Autonomous Systems, 22:3–21. (1997)
53. Mitchell, T.: Machine Learning. McGraw-Hill. (1997)
54. Murthy, S. K., Kasif, S., and Salzberg, S.: "A system for induction of oblique decision trees." Journal of Artificial Intelligence Research, 2. ftp://blaze.cs.jhu.edu/pub/oc1 (1994) 1–33
55. Nehmzow, U. and Walker, K.: Is the behavior of a mobile robot chaotic? In Proceedings of the Artificial Intelligence and Simulated Behavior. (2003)
56. Nilsson, N.: Shakey the robot. Technical Report 323, SRI International. (1984)
57. Nourbakhsh, Illah: "Dervish: An office-navigating robot." In D. Kortenkamp, R. P. Bonassi, and R. Murphy, editors, Artificial Intelligence and Mobile Robots. Case Studies of Succeful Robot Systems. The AAAI Press. MIT Press. (1998) 73–90
58. Piegl, L. A. and Tiller, W.: The NURBS Book. Springer Verlag. (1997)
59. Pirjanian, P.: Multiple Objective Action Selection and Behavior Fusion using Voting. PhD thesis, Institute of Electronic Systems, Aalborg University, Denmark. (1998)
60. Pirjanian, P.: Behavior coordination mechanisms – state of the art. Technical Report iris-99-375, Institute of Robotics and Intelligent Systems, USC. (1999)
61. Rekleitis, Ioannis M.: A particle filter tutorial for mobile robot localization. Technical Report TR-CIM-04-02, Centre for Intelligent Machines, McGill University, 3480 University St., Montreal, Québec, CANADA H3A 2A7. (2004)
62. Rosenblatt, J. K.: "DAMN: A distributed architecture for mobile navigation." In Proc. of the AAAI Spring Symp. on Lessons Learned from Implememted Software Architectures for Physical Agents, Stanford, CA. (1995) 167–178
63. Rosencrantz, M., Gordon, G., and Thrun, S.: Decentralized sensor fusion with distributed particle filters. In Proceedings of the 19th Annual Conference on Uncertainty in Artificial Intelligence (UAI-03). San Francisco, CA. Morgan Kaufmann Publishers. (2003) 493–500
64. Longhi, S., Fioretti, S., Leo, T.: "A navigation system for increasing the autonomy and the security of powered wheelchairs." IEEE Transactions on Rehabilitation Engineering, 8(4). (2000) 490–498
65. Simmons, Reid and Koenig, Sven: "Probabilistic robot navigation in partially observable environments." In Proceedings of the International Joint Conference on Artificial Intelligence. (1995) 1080–1087
66. Thorpe, C. F.: "Path relaxation: Path planning for a mobile robot." Technical Report CMU-RI-TR-84-5, The Robotics Institute. Carnagie-Mellon University. (1984)

67. Thrun S.: Learning maps for indoor mobile robot navigation. Artificial Intelligence, 99(1). (1998) 21–71
68. Thrun, S.: "Robotic mapping: A survey." In G. Lakemeyer and B. Nebel, editors, Exploring Artificial Intelligence in the New Millennium, Morgan Kaufmann. (2003) 1–35
69. Thrun, S., Bennewitz, M., Burgard, W., Cremers, A. B., Dellaert, F., Fox, D., Hahnel, D., Rosenberg, C., Roby, N., Schutle, J., and Schultz, D.: "Minerva: A second generation mobile tour-guide robot." In Proceedings of the IEEE International Conference on Robotics and Automation(ICRA-99) (1999)
70. Thrun, S., Fox, D., Burgard, W., and Dellaert, F.: Robust monte carlo localization for mobile robots. Artificial Intelligence, 128(1–2). (2001) 99–141
71. Trullier, O., Wiener, S. I., Berthoz, A., and Meyer, J. A.: Biologically-based artificial navigation systems: Review and prospects. Progress in Neurobiology, 51. (1997) 483–544
72. Webb, B.: Can robots make good models of biological behavior? Behavioral and Brain Sciences, 24(6). (2001)
73. Wu, H., Siegel, M., Stiefelhagen, R., and Yang, J.: Sensor fusion using dempster-shafer theory. In proceedings of the IEEE Instrumentation and Measurement Technology Conference. (2002)
74. Yamauchi, B., Schultz, A., and Adams, W.: Mobile robot exploration and map-building with continuous localization. In Proceedings of the IEEE International Conference on Robotics and Automation (1998) 3715–3720
75. Yanco, H. A.: Wheelesley, a robotic wheelchair system: Indoor navigation and user interface. Lecture Notes in Artificial Intelligence: Assistive Technology and Artificial Intelligence (1998) 256–268

Ambient Intelligence Through Agile Agents

Gregory M.P. O'Hare, M.J. O'Grady, R. Collier,
S. Keegan, D. O'Kane, R. Tynan, and D. Marsh

University College Dublin (UCD), Ireland
Gregory.OHare@ucd.ie

1 Introduction

The vision of ambient intelligence is one where the populas is supported in the conductance of their everyday lives through the pro-active, opportunistic support of non-intrusive computing devices offering intuitive interaction modalities.

This chapter advocates the adoption of mobile intentional agents as a key enabler in the delivery of ambient intelligence. Ambient computing, as an ideal, demands levels of functional attainment that have hithertofar not been realized. Ambient applications demand that the computing application be subsumed into the everyday context in an unobtrusive manner with interaction modalities which are natural, simple and appropriate to both the individual user and their associated context.

Ambient systems need to address some key issues:

- Recognition and accommodation of the diversity of devices that contribute to the organic nature of the ambient and ubiquitous computing nervous system;
- The need for personalization and system adaptivity;
- An understanding of the dynamics of context;
- Provision of support for collaboration and cooperation between distributed ambient system components;
- Delivery of systems that exhibit autonomic characteristics, yielding self management and self healing capabilities;

In addressing these core issues we commission an intentional agent based approach. Specifically we adopt a Belief-Desire-Intention (BDI) agent model. In the delivery of such agents we utilize the Agent Factory system. The Agent Factory (AF) System is an environment developed in part by two of the authors, which supports the rapid fabrication of agent-based applications. Agent Factory provides an integrated environment for the development of agent based systems providing a methodological framework together with an accompanying software membrane which provides a cohesive and integrated tool set which supports the various stages in the design, specification, implementation, debugging and visualization of agent behavior. Detailed descriptions of Agent Factory are provided elsewhere in the literature [3, 4, 27, 28]. Agent Factory supports Weak Migration where only the agent's object state and code is captured. Upon migration the system calls a known entry-point in the code to restart the agent on the new machine.

Y. Cai (Ed.): Ambient Intelligence for Scientific Discovery, LNAI 3345, pp. 286–310, 2005.

Within this chapter we explore the delivery of ambient computing through the examination of three case studies, namely Gulliver's Genie, Easishop and Autonomic Wireless Sensor Networks (AWSN). We use these to illustrate how our agile intentional agents contribute to overcoming the key issues identified above. These applications are chosen as they represent three challenging though complimentary points within the ambient intelligence landscape. Gulliver's Genie necessitates the identification of individual tourist profiles. Easishop demands the examination and formulation of buyer and seller behavior and ultimately the understanding of the particular m-commerce macro economy. The AWSN scenario is more far reaching involving large scale sensor topologies of collaboration, self regulation and self management. Within this chapter we will consider each in turn and reflect on the deployment of agile agents.

2   Agent Factory

Agent Factory (AF) [3, 4, 27, 28] is a cohesive framework, (illustrated in Figs. 1 and 3), for the development and deployment of agent-oriented applications that has been developed by the authors. Central to this framework is the Agent Factory Agent Programming Language (AF-APL), an Agent-Oriented Programming (AOP) language that supports the fabrication of agents that are: autonomous, situated, socially able, intentional, rational, and mobile [3, 27]. However, Agent Factory differs from other AOP offerings in that AF-APL has been embedded within a distributed FIPA-compliant [9] Run-Time Environment, and supports the development and deployment of agents through an integrated development environment, and an associated software engineering methodology (see Fig. 1). Details of these layers are presented in the following sections.

A key concern in the design of AF has been to ensure that AF-APL agents can be deployed on Personal Digital Assistants (PDAs) and ultimately on more

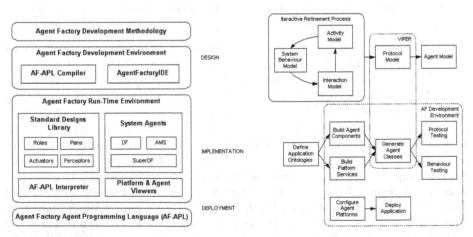

Fig. 1. The Agent Factory Framework (left) and its associated Development Methodology (right).

computationally challenged devices which will typify ambient scenarios. This has been achieved by ensuring that the Run-Time Environment, which includes the AF-APL Interpreter, is compliant with version 1.1.8 of the Java SDK (a.k.a. Personal Java for Mobile Devices). To check compatibility with future versions of Java, J2ME-compliant versions of the Run-Time Environment have also been developed. However, due to incompatibilities between Personal Java and J2ME, and as a result of our wish to ensure that AF can be deployed on the most prevalent operating system and JVM configuration for PDAs (e.g.. MS PocketPC and Jeode), AF is currently not J2ME-compliant.

2.1   AF-APL

AF-APL is a declarative Agent-Oriented Programming (AOP) language that supports the programming of agent behaviors. The basic premise behind AF-APL is the view that complex agent behaviors can be more naturally modeled by viewing agents to be mental entities that maintain an internal mental state which is comprised of mental attitudes, in this case: beliefs and commitments. Beliefs describe, using a first-order logic representation language, the current state of the agent and its environment, and commitments describe the current (and future) activities that the agent has decided to perform. Finally, decisions are modeled through a set of commitment rules that map situations (a conjunction of positive and negative beliefs) onto commitments. These rules are checked repeatedly within a sense-deliberate-act cycle.

Beliefs represent the current state of both the agent and its environment. In AF-APL, this state is realized as a set of facts that describe atomic information about the environment, and which are encoded as first-order structures wrapped within a belief operator (BELIEF). For example, in a mobile computing application an agent may be asked to monitor the users current position using a Global Positioning System (GPS) device. The agent may generate a belief about this position that takes the form: BELIEF(userPosition(Lat, Long)) where Lat and Long are replaced by values for the user's latitude and longitude respectively. In AF, the actual values for the latitude and longitude are retrieved directly from the GPS device by a perceptor unit, which converts the raw sensor data into corresponding beliefs. The triggering of this perceptor unit is part of a perception process, which is central to our strategy for updating the beliefs of agents and is realized by triggering a pre-selected set of perceptor units at regular intervals. The specific set of perceptor units to be used by an agent is specified as part of the agent program through the PERCEPTOR keyword.

Commitments represent the courses of action that the agent has chosen to perform. That is, they represent the results of some reasoning process in which the agent makes a decision about how best to act. From this perspective, commitment implicitly represents the intentions of the agent. This contrasts with more traditional BDI approaches [32, 37] in which intention is represented explicitly and commitment is an implicit feature of the agents' underlying reasoning process. This alternative treatment of commitment is motivated by our goal of explicitly representing the level of commitment the agent has to a chosen course of action. In AF-APL a commitment is comprised of: an agent identifier (the agent for whom the commitment has been made), a start time (before which the commitment should not be considered), a maintenance condition (which defines the conditions under which the commitment should not be dropped), and an activity (the course of action that the agent is committed to). Currently, an activity may take one of three forms: (1) an action identifier (i.e. some primitive action that the agent must perform), (2) a plan identifier (i.e. an identifier that can be used to retrieve a partial plan from the agents plan library), and (3) an explicit partial plan (i.e. partial plans can be directly encoded into a commitment).

Action identifiers are modeled as first-order structures where the parameters may be used to customize the action. For example, the activity of one agent informing another agent of something is realized through the inform(?agent, ?content) action. Here, the ?agent parameter refers to the agent to whom the message is to be sent (their identifier), and the ?content parameter refers to the content of the message. An example of an inform message can be seen in Fig. 2. Within AF-APL, actions are realized through the triggering of an associated *actuator unit*. As with perceptor units, actuator units are associated with specific agents as part of the agent program through the ACTUATOR keyword. Actions can be combined into plans that form more complex behaviors using one or more plan operators – currently there are four plan operators: sequence (SEQ), parallel (PAR), unordered choice (OR), and ordered choice (XOR). Plans can be stored within an agent's internal plan library, where they are distinguished from one another by a unique plan identifier.

Finally, commitment rules describe the situations, encoded as a conjunction of positive and negative belief literals, under which the agent should adopt a given commitment. An implication operator ($\Rightarrow$) delimits the situation and the commitment.

AF-APL agent programs (actuators + perceptors + plans + initial mental state + commitment rules) are executed upon a purpose-built agent interpreter. Specifically, the agent program is loaded into appropriate data structures inside the agent interpreter. The interpreter then manipulates these data structures through a simple control cycle that encapsulates various axioms defined in the associated logic of commitment. This cycle is comprised of three steps: (1) update the agents' beliefs, (2) manage the agents' commitments, and (3) check whether or not to migrate. It is invoked repeatedly for the lifetime of the agent (at least whenever the agent is active).

By way of illustration, Fig. 2 presents a fragment of AF-APL code from a WWW spider agent that provides a service in which it informs subscribed agents of any new documents it finds. This is realized through two commitment rules and one initial belief. The first commitment rule states that if the agent receives a request to subscribe to a service (identified by the variable ?svc), and the agent believes that it provides the service, then it should commit to performing two actions in parallel (specified by the PAR plan operator). The first action involves the agent informing the requester that they have successfully subscribed to the service, and the second action involves that adoption of a belief by the agent

```
// Perceptor & Actuator Configuration
PERCEPTOR ie.ucd.core.fipa.perceptor.MessagePerceptor;
ACTUATOR ie.ucd.core.fipa.actuator.InformActuator;
ACTUATOR ie.ucd.aflite.actuator.AdoptBeliefActuator;
// Initial Mental State
ALWAYS(BELIEF(providesService(docRelease)));
// Commitment Rules for DocService
BELIEF(fipaMessage(request, sender(?agt, ?addr),
 subscribe(?svc))) &
BELIEF(providesService(?svc)) =>
COMMIT(Self, Now, BELIEF(true),
 PAR(inform(?agt, subscribed(?svc)),
 adoptBelief(ALWAYS(BELIEF(subscribed(?svc, ?agt)))))));
BELIEF(newDocument(?doc)) &
 BELIEF(subscribed(docRelease, ?agt)) =>
COMMIT(Self, Now, BELIEF(true),
 inform(?agt, newDocument(?doc)));
```

Fig. 2. An Example AF-APL program for a World Wide Web (WWW) spider agent.

that the requester has been subscribed to the service. The second commitment rule states that if the agent believes that it has found a new document, and the agent believes that another agent (?agt) has subscribed to the docRelease service, then it should commit to informing that agent of the existence of the new document. Finally, the initial belief that the agent adopts on start up allows the agent to believe that it can provide the service docRelease.

As with other similar offerings, such as Goal-Directed 3APL [6], and AgentS-peak(L) [32], the syntax and semantics of AF-APL have been formally specified. In particular, AF-APL is based upon a logical model of reasoning that is centered about the notion of commitment. Further details of both the formal model and the syntax and semantics of AF-APL can be found in [3, 34].

2.2   The Run-Time Environment

The AF-APL interpreter is embedded within a distributed FIPA-compliant [9] Run-Time Environment. (RTE). Specifically, AF adheres to the following FIPA specifications:

- The FIPA Abstract Architecture Specification (0001)
- The FIPA Agent Management Specification (00023)
- The FIPA ACL Message Structure Specification (00061)
- The FIPA Agent Message Transport Service Specification (00067)
- The FIPA ACL Message Representation in String Specification (00070)
- The FIPA Message Transport Protocol for HTTP Specification (00084)
- The FIPA Agent Message Transport Envelope Representation in XML Spec-ification (00085).

Within the context of these specifications, the RTE is organized as a collection of *agent platforms*. An Agent Platform (AP) provides the basic infrastructure that is necessary to deploy agents. Specifically, each AP implements a number of *platform* services, which provide various mandatory and optional infrastructure services. One platform service is the Agent Management System (AMS) service. This service is mandatory and is responsible for the creation, termination, suspension, resumption, registration, deregistration, and execution of agents that are residing of the AP. A second service is the optional HTTP Message Transport Service, which provides an HTTP-based message-passing infrastructure for the Run-Time Environment. Other services include directory facilitator services (i.e. yellow pages services), persistence services, migration services, and cloning services. During the development of agent-oriented applications, developers are required to identify and implement an appropriate set of platform services.

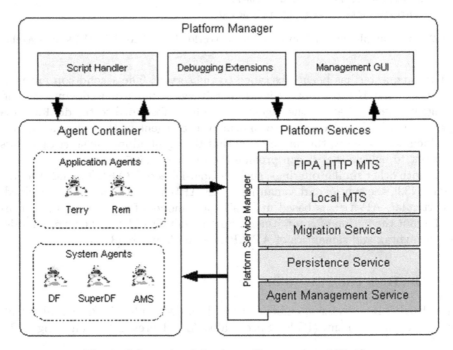

Fig. 3. Schematic of the Agent Factory Agent Platform.

In addition to the platform services, the RTE also implements a number of System Agents. Such System Agents implement a number of infrastructure services that are needed to support the inter-AP infrastructure. Specifically, AF currently implements three System Agents. The AMS and DF agents are, in effect, agent wrappers which envelop the associated AMS and DF platform services. Both agents control access to the relevant service on the AP. However, in the context of a multi-AP environment, which is expected for most agent-oriented applications, there is a need to support the federation of AMS and DF services. This federated service is realized by a third System Agent, entitled the Super DF. The Super DF provides a common point of interaction between the various AMS and DF agents. Within the configuration of individual APs, developers are able to specify the agent identifier of a Super DF agent that they would like the AMS and DF agents to connect to. Upon start-up, this agent identifier is passed to the AMS and DF agents who register themselves with the specified Super DF. Once registered, the AMS and DF agents are able to perform global (at least within the set of APs that are connected to the Super DF) white and yellow pages searches. Ongoing research is concerned with the development of a more robust infrastructure that exhibits autonomic properties such as self-organization and self-healing, and which contains no single point of failure.

2.3   The Development Methodology

Methodological support for the fabrication of agent-oriented applications using Agent Factory is provided through a UML-based software engineering process that supports the design, implementation, testing, and deployment phases of the software engineering lifecycle. A diagrammatical overview of this process, details of which can be found in [5], is presented in Fig. 1. In this diagram, it can be seen that the design stage of the process is focused around the development of five models:

- The *System Behavior Model (SBM)* identifies the main roles that agents will play within the system, and associates those roles with the key system behaviors. Visually, this model is formalized using a customized UML Use Case Diagrams where actors are stereotyped as roles, and use-cases are stereotyped as system behaviors. Some typical system behaviors that might apply to a mobile computing system include: user movement updates, hotspot activation, and map generation.
- The *Interaction Model (IM)* expands on the SBM through the modeling of the interactions that occur within each of the system behaviors. Visually, this model is formalized using a customized UML Collaboration Diagram. Specifically, objects are stereotyped as roles, and messages are restricted to valid FIPA ACL performatives via the "fipa-acl" stereotype.
- The *Activity Model (ActM)* complements the IM, in that it expands on the SBM through the modeling of the set of activities that occur within each of the system behaviors. Visually, this model is formalized using a customized UML Activity Diagram where swimlanes are employed to represent roles.
- The *Protocol Model (PM)* represents a demarcation point within the methodology, in that, it represents the transition point where the focus turns from understanding system behaviors to the formalization of those behaviors as a set of protocols and agent-classes. Specifically, the PM is derived from the IM with agent interactions formalized as protocols. Visually, these protocols are represented using Agent UML Sequence Diagrams.

– Finally, the *Agent Model (AgtM)* completes the design by switching the focus from roles, interactions, and activities to a more agent-centric view of the target system. Specifically, this model focuses upon two concepts: roles, and *agent classes*. The roles specify meaningful aggregations of protocols (e.g. in a mobile computing application, roles may include the Map Creator, the Interface Manager, and the PDA Cache Manager). These roles are then *implemented* through certain agent classes. As such, the agent classes combine one or more roles, with any additional protocols, and finally, a set of activities that are required to realize the protocols. These activities are derived from the ActM.

Further details of the visual notation employed within the AgtM and the implementation and deployment phases of the methodology can be found in [3].

2.4   The Development Environment

Agent development is realized through a federation of toolsets. The Agent Factory Integrated Development Environment (IDE), illustrated in Fig. 4, provides a standard programming environment in the vein of NetBeans and JBuilder. Specifically, the editor includes features such as syntax highlighting, code compilation, and application execution.

In addition, VIPER [33] is a graphical tool suite that allows the user to compose the Agent UML Sequence Diagrams that sit at the heart of the Protocol Model. VIPER is comprised of two tools: a Protocol Editor that provides a visual tool for generating Agent UML Sequence Diagrams, and a Rule Editor that further supports the user by guiding them through the step of implementing the protocols in AF-APL. Further tools that have been provided to support the development of AF-APL agents, the Agent Factory Development Environment also includes a suite of tools that facilitate the testing and debugging of agent-oriented applications. These tools are associated with the Agent Platform component of the Run-Time Environment. Debugging environment tools include:

– the *Agent Viewer Tool*, which allows the developer to monitor and modify the agents internal state;
– the *Message Sender*, which allows the developer to interact with other agents as if they were themselves an agent; and
– the *Community Monitor*, which allows the developer to monitor interactions between a specified set of agents.

Further details of these tools can be found in [3]. Having reviewed the design and fabrication environment by which we develop our agile agents we will now illustrate how such agents can be utilized in the realization of ambient intelligence systems.

3   Gulliver's Genie

At its simplest, Gulliver's Genie may be regarded as a mobile context-aware tourist guide. In many respects, it is a classic example of an mobile applica-

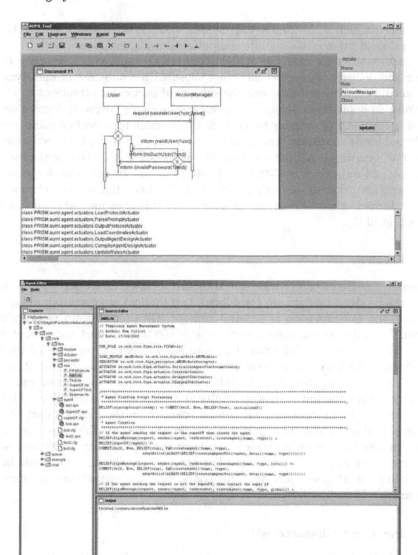

Fig. 4. The Agent Factory IDE (top) and the VIPER Protocol Editor (bottom).

tion or service that many people would anticipate being available in the coming years. In this it is not unique as the literature is sprinkled with prototypical systems for various application domains. Gulliver's Genie harvests concepts from a number of disciplines. It exhibits context-awareness, adaptivity and incorporates principles from user modelling. One of its distinguishing features is its proactive anticipation of user needs and the subsequent intelligent precaching of multimedia content on the tourist's host device thus achieving the distribution of content in a just-in-time basis [26].

Gulliver's Genie [23–26, 29] has investigated various issues relating to the practical realization of the mobile computing paradigm. More specifically, suitable architectures for realizing mobile computing applications, thereby facilitating the delivery of services including those with a substantial and dynamic multimedia component have been the subject of particular attention.

From an application domain perspective, the Genie currently focuses on addressing the needs of roaming tourists, as this domain represents a microcosm of the broad issues facing ambient intelligence. In this the Genie is not a unique endeavor as a cursory examination of the literature will testify. One project similar in scope and objectives is CRUMPET [30]. The indoor scenario, for example, museums, art galleries and exhibitions, has also been the subject of much research. Indeed, a useful overview of activity in this area may also be found in Bellotti et al [2].

3.1   Services

In theory, the Genie can provide any standard location-aware service. However, when the needs of tourists are considered, two services are essential: navigation support and the provision of cultural content. Given that tourists are almost inevitably exploring unknown territory, a navigation-support component is of practical importance. While roaming, tourists will encounter sites of cultural significance. Various aspects concerning such sites may be of interest to the tourist. In addition, there may be relationships between those sites and other attractions that the tourist has encountered during their travels. Such relationships may not be obvious without careful research on the visitor's part. As the tourist's spatial context and personal profile are known, there are significant opportunities for enhancing their experience through the proactive and selective delivery of appropriate content. The service is realized in the Genie in the form of rich multimedia presentations concerning the attractions encountered. An example of such a presentation may be seen in Fig. 5.

3.2   Pertinent Characteristics

Gulliver's Genie differs in a number of key aspects from other efforts in this area. However, two key differentiators are of special interest. The first is that, similar to CRUMPET, it adopts an approach based on intelligent agents. More specifically, however, it incorporates agents that conform to the strong notion of agency as articulated by Wooldridge & Jennings [38], and, in this case, such agents adopt a reasoning strategy based on the Belief-Desire-Intention (BDI) paradigm. Traditionally, the computational cost of deploying such agents on lightweight devices was prohibitively expensive. Recent developments in hardware and software have rendered such concerns obsolete, except of course in the case of the most basic devices.

A second feature of particular interest is the strategy the Genie adopts for disseminating content. Users have high expectations and seek immediate access to desired content at any time, in any place and, increasingly, on any device.

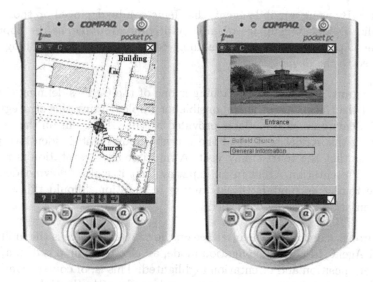

Fig. 5. Genie locates user adjacent to the church (left) and assembles and displays a Presentation for the Church on the Campus (right).

Meeting such expectations within the confines of limited devices and the limited bandwidth availability of wireless networks, particularly the cellular variety, is difficult. In an effort to address this, the Genie adopts a strategy that has been termed intelligent pre-caching [25]. In brief: a model of the tourist's environment is maintained which contains, amongst other things, specific details of the various tourist attractions within it. If this model is considered in light of the tourist's spatial context, that is, their position and orientation, as well as their personal interest profile, their likely future behavior can be estimated with a reasonably high degree of certainty. Therefore, the appropriate content can be downloaded to their device in just-in-time basis. As this content is inherently adapted to the tourist's context, as well as personalized to conform to their individual profiles, a satisfactory experience may be reasonably anticipated.

3.3 Architecture

In essence, Gulliver's Genie comprises a suite of agents residing both on the client and on the server. Currently some of these agents are mobile and based upon a given technological context they may autonomously decide where to reside. All these agents collaborate to deliver the necessary services to the tourist (Fig. 6). Each agent is now briefly described:

Spatial Agent. To determine a tourist's spatial context, this agent autonomously monitors the GPS signal and interprets it accordingly. This, it periodically broadcasts to other interested agents. This agent is unique in that it harnesses its capacity to migrate. Though GPS is the de facto standard for position determination at present, systems using cellular network techniques are envisaged in the future. By using a mobile agent, the Genie can be deployed on those devices that utilize cellular techniques when they become available, as the appropriate agent encompassing the logic for handling cellular network positioning may be dispatched to the device.

Cache Agent. Intelligent pre-caching is one of the Genie's defining characteristics and the Cache Agent is responsible for implementing this strategy on the client. An environmental model is provided by the GIS Agent on the server. By considering this model in light of the tourist's movement, it identifies possible attractions that the tourist may visit. A multimedia presentation is requested from the Presentation Agent in anticipation that it will be downloaded by the time the tourist encounters the attraction in question. Should this not occur, the presentation is simply discarded.

GUI Agent. Controlling the interface on the tourist's device is the main task of the GUI Agent. In normal navigation mode, an electronic map is displayed with the current position and orientation highlighted. This is, of course, continuously updated as the tourist moves, courtesy of updates from the Spatial Agent. Should the tourist encounter an attraction for which a presentation has been precached, the Cache Agent prompts the GUI Agent to display the presentation, monitor the tourist's interaction and provide feedback to the Profile Agent.

Profile Agent. User profiles are essential to realizing adaptivity and personalization. The Profile Agent is responsible for maintaining user profiles and updating them in light of ongoing tourist interactions with the Genie.

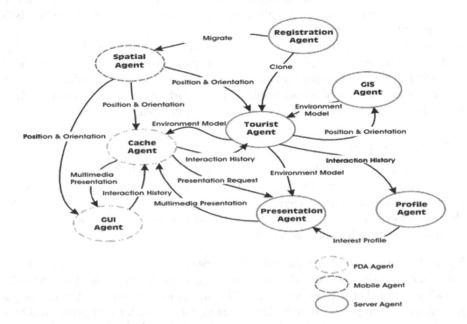

Fig. 6. Architecture of Gulliver's Genie.

Registration Agent. The tourist must first register for Genie services. The Registration Agent takes care of this process as well as assigning Tourist Agents to individual tourists in response to requests for Genie services.

Tourist Agent. All tourists registered for Genie services are assigned their own individual agent, termed Tourist Agents, on commencing a session. In agent parlance, such agents are cloned from the tourist agent template. Essentially, this agent is the tourist's interface to the services offered by the Genie. Acting on prompts from the Spatial Agent, it arranges the construction of environmental models in conjunction with the GIS Agent and prompts the Presentation Agent to maintain an updated list of presentations in anticipation of requests from the Cache Agent. Though there is some computational overhead in assigning an agent to each tourist, such an approach ensures the future scalability of the Genie as the number of concurrent tourists increase and a wider variety of services are offered.

GIS Agent. Accurate environmental models are necessary for the successful operation of the Genie. Such models are provided to the Cache Agent on the client as well as to the Presentation Agent for dynamic presentation pre-assembly on the server.

Presentation Agent. The provision of personalized multimedia presentations is a core tenet of the Genie's raison d'être. Such presentations are assembled in light of the tourist's profile and their current environmental model. This server-side presentation repository is continuously updated in light of tourist movement and changes to their individual profiles.

3.4   Implementation

At present, the Genie runs on a standard PDA, namely an iPAQ. GPS, which gives a position reading to within 20 metres on average, is used for determining location. Orientation can also be derived from GPS, albeit in an approximate manner. For data communications, the standard 2.5G technology, the General Packet Radio Service (GPRS) is used. In each case, a corresponding PCMCIA card was procured. Both cards were then incorporated into the IPAQ via a dual-slot expansion sleeve. From a software perspective, the client components are implemented in Java and a commercial JVM, namely Jeode, is used as the runtime environment on the IPAQ. All communication with the server takes place over a standard HTTP connection.

On the server side, the Agent Factory runtime environment is deployed. This is augmented with a sophisticated database that supports multiple data types including geospatial data and multimedia-related data. A toolkit for populating this database forms an indispensable component.

4   EasiShop

EasiShop [13–15] meanwhile is a pioneering m-commerce system that embraces a rich technological set. EasiShop distinguishes itself in various important respects.

Each shopper is provided with a shopping agent which is entrusted to assist with their personal shopping requirements. This is achieved through the profiling of users and the dynamic maintenance of user profiles. Agents are mobile in nature and migrate to a market place and participate in an auction adopting a Contact Net Protocol. Shops are also ascribed agents entrusted with the sale of their products. The purchase process is negotiative in nature with sellers and purchasers as active participants contributing to a true macro economy. Product acquisition is facilitated through the use of the UNSPSC product ontology [36] together with product description via XML. Agent migration and communication is supported over Bluetooth and using SMS over GSM. Scalability and stress testing have been conducted and performance results are promising, while user evaluations are currently on-going.

The EasiShop [13–15] project encapsulates efforts that have been made to deliver a practical and efficient mobile shopping system. To support this vision, research has been undertaken into the synthesis of wired and wireless infrastructure with smart portable devices and agent based user interfaces to enhance the shopping experience. Of particular focus has been the desire to develop the appropriate components to enable a scalable mobile multi-agent trading platform. The user interface of EasiShop is shown in Fig. 7.

The system is primarily targeted towards providing a convenient retail solution to the shopper and, to a lesser extent, enabling a new or enhanced revenue stream for retailers. Other efforts have endeavoured to address this application domain. Some, like Bargainfinder [18], are web-based auctioneering facilities while others, like My-Grocer [17], offer a similar type of mobile solution to that of EasiShop. A perspective on some of the issues inherent in this domain may be acquired upon consultation of the literature.

4.1 Services

EasiShop is primarily charged with the task of enabling cross-merchant comparison shopping. A user profile is maintained within the system. From this profile, a retailer may determine the extent of relevance that a particular user holds. When combined with the aspect of location determination, a powerful retailing channel can be realized. Retailers can automatically choose to focus efforts on users of interest.

4.2 Pertinent Characteristics

There are numerous characteristics which distinguish EasiShop from similar efforts. The first is that an approach based on intelligent agents is enlisted. More specifically, however, the system incorporates agents that conform to the notion of agency as formalized by Wooldridge & Jennings [38], and, in this case, such agents adopt a reasoning strategy based on the Belief-Desire-Intention (BDI) paradigm. In this regard, the system is similar to Gulliver's Genie. A second feature of particular distinction is the employment of a reverse-auction model to procure commercial transactions. In this model, an agent which embodies the

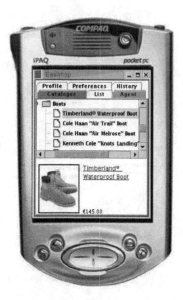

Fig. 7. EasiShop Graphical User Interface.

product requirements of the user, migrates to a centralized server where competing provider agents representing different retailers are invited to vie, using a predetermined auction protocol, for the custom of that user. The third distinguishing aspect of EasiShop is the utilization of user profile data which, together with a log of previous transactions, can be used to deliver appropriate product offerings to the mobile user. Finally, a product ontology is fundamental to the operation of EasiShop. The product ontology utilized is that of the UNSPSC product ontology [36] together with product descriptions provided via XML.

4.3   Architecture

The complete EasiShop architecture is comprised of a suite of agents residing both on three distinct nodes – the PDA, the Store Server and the Marketplace. All these agents collaborate to provide the required functionality (Fig. 8). Each agent is now briefly described.

PDA Agent. The tasks of the PDA Agent are twofold. First and foremost, it is concerned with controlling the onscreen components necessary to enable the user to create and maintain shopping lists and user profile. Secondly, the PDA Agent monitors the user's behavior and maintains records of this activity. From these records, the system attempts to more accurately predict which products will interest the user.

Shopper Agent. While ordinarily housed on the PDA, the Shopper Agent may decide to migrate to the Marketplace (via a conduit store – the active EasiShop HotSpot) to instigate the product auction process. The belief set of the Shopper

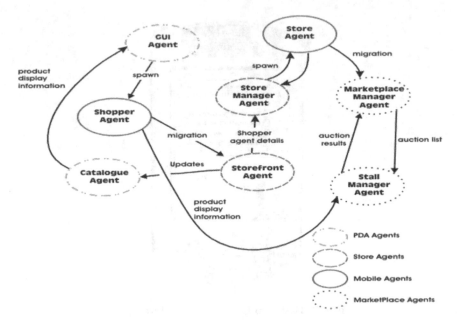

Fig. 8. Architecture of EasiShop.

Agent represents a data set, which is essentially the user's shopping list. At the marketplace the Shopper Agent is paired with interested Store Agents to procure those item(s) on the shopping list.

Catalouge Agent. The main duty of this agent is to ensure that all product catalogue information (price, new products, etc.) is kept up-to-date in the product list of the PDA. To accomplish this, it liaises with the Storefront Agent in the active EasiShop HotSpot, whenever one is in range. This means that the user, when viewing and selecting products via the PDA Agent, is accessing the up-to-date product data set.

Storefront Agent. When necessary, a certain proportion of communication is used to deliver product updates to the client (PDA) dataset. As previously mentioned, the Catalogue Agent interacts with the Store Agent to support this functionality.

Store Manager Agent. This agent monitors Shopper Agents which have migrated to the Store. From here, the Store Manager Agent contacts the Marketplace Manger to request further migration to the centralized Marketplace. Should migration ensue, the two agents (Store Agent and Shopper Agent) are transferred to the Marketplace where the auction will take place.

Store Agent. As previously outlined, the belief set of the Shopper Agent incorporates the shopping list of the user. Similarly, the belief set of the Store Agent is representative of the real world attributes of the store. This may include types of products on offer as well as stock and pricing information. The Store Agent is spawned and transferred by the Store Manager to the Marketplace to enter an auction as required.

Marketplace Manager Agent. Coordination of the centralized Marketplace is perhaps the most important factor in enabling the arena in which agents may buy and sell products. The Marketplace Manager Agent organizes and administers migration to the marketplace as well as allocating system resources required in the auctioning process. In practical terms, this means that a public market list, containing information on exactly what products are sought by whom, is maintained. This list is monitored by both the Stall Manager agents, which request to administer individual auctions and by the Store Agents who may request entrance to a particular auction, should an auction be of interest.

Stall Manager Agent. This agent is charged with the task of coordinating the auction process. After acquiring an auction from the market list, the auction is deemed to be open. A deadline for interested parties as well as opening and closing time values are set. At this point, the type of auction is also made known. This can be any one of a number of auction protocols – e.g. Dutch or Vickrey [22, 12]. It is important to note at this point that the Stall Manager is what is termed as an environmental agent. This means that the number of Stall Manager agents in the system is not fixed and may be adjusted by the Marketplace Manager agent as required. More Stall Manager Agents might be required at busy times, for example. The bid, accept and reject messaging of participating auctions is coordinated before the auction closes, at which point a winner is declared.

4.4 Implementation

The EasiShop (client-side) system is installed on a standard PDA – the iPAQ 3870. Bluetooth is used to determine the user's location. When the user is detected as being in the broadcast range of a particular EasiShop HotSpot (an area adjacent to a store within which agent communication may take place), the user's location may be determined to within an accuracy of approximately twenty meters. From a software perspective, the system components are implemented in Java. Kaffe, a free JVM licensed under the terms of the GNU General Public License, is used as the runtime environment. The operating system is Linux. Bluetooth functionality is implemented via a runtime interface to the Bluez [39] bluetooth protocol stack.

5   Toward Autonomic Wireless Sensor Networks (AWSNs)

Wireless sensor networks (WSN) are a relatively new concept in distributed computing and represent the third case study we will consider for ambient intelligence. Former distributed sensing systems were generally comprised of many dumb sensors wired directly to a centralized processing unit. WSNs differ in that the individual sensing nodes have the capacity to perform processing and sensing on the same device, as well as wirelessly communicating with other nodes [10]. Because of their ability to communicate, they can collectively monitor a much larger area with more accuracy than any one device alone could. Localization of environmental perception allows for much greater scalability and reduced deployment costs.

The primary issue at the heart of WSN research is that individual sensor nodes are resource constrained in all aspects of their operation. Currently the most commonly available sensor nodes use 8-bit processors, have 128 kilobytes of memory, use 10-100 kb/s radios and are approximately priced at €100 per unit, though there are more powerful (and hence expensive) devices available. Examples of these devices include Crossbow Motes, Ember Corporation, VTT Soapboxes, Modules and Sensoria's sGate and netGate products. All vendors are engaged in a race to produce devices with comparable specifications at less than €1 per unit, which would make wide-scale commercial deployment possible. Expected uses include environmental monitoring, provision of low-profile security systems, a broad spectrum of scientific data collection task and Ambient Intelligence applications.

Ordinarily the computation resources of a node would be sufficient to perform many of the tasks that WSN nodes would be expected to do, such as signal processing, in-network packet routing and collaborative calibration. However, a more fundamental problem exists in the form of power limitations. Thus far there have been no sensor devices created that can generate enough energy to run from ambient sources (e.g. vibrational energy [8]), and so they must all rely on capacitors or batteries. Thus there is a trade-off between any activities the node might wish to perform and the lifetime of the node. With anything other than radioisotope-based batteries [20], maximum expected lifetimes are a few years at best. In practical terms, this means that the nodes spend most of their time in a low-power sleep mode, which further reduces their computing capacity.

Much of the research into WSNs focuses upon power-efficient methods of running the network. In particular, efficient use of the radio is critical. Nodes usually transmit summary statistics of data rather than the raw data itself, and as the data packet is routed through the network its contents are often modified to include additional data from each relaying node. Algorithms that limit the scope of their input to nodes that are close neighbors of the node running the algorithm are particularly beneficial [31], since they limit the degree of relaying transmissions in the network.

There are a number of other critical areas that must be dealt with. One of the chief properties of WSNs is that they are often used where human supervision and maintenance is difficult or impossible. Even in cases where the network is easily accessible, the number of nodes deployed (which can run into the thousands) may prevent any practical degree of manual intervention. This means that an ability to auto-configure and autonomous maintenance is a definite advantage in a WSN. A network of nodes that can decide what their routing topology, sensor activation patterns, sleep cycles and communication frequencies should be, of their own accord, is a fundamental constituent of a real-world WSN.

5.1 Autonomic Computing

Autonomic computing has for many been thought of as synonymous with powerful systems running or resource rich hardware platforms, [7]. The concept of autonomic computing is based on the human autonomic nervous system, in which many functions of the human body happen without conscious guidance from the brain e.g. heartbeat, immune system and homeostasis.

Autonomic computing is essentially the imbuing of knowledge into future software systems and thus allowing these systems to utilize and employ this knowledge to maximize the potential for self-maintenance [11,1]. Several key principles of autonomic computing have emerged, the ability to self-heal, self-protect, self-configure and self-optimize. These principles provide autonomically infused systems with adaptability, flexibility and increased robustness, unfortunately this is achieved at a greater computational cost. Researchers at IBM, [16], have identified that one of the implicit underlying threads of autonomic computing is that of Multi-Agent Systems (MAS).

The autonomous and deliberative nature of agents is central to the notion of self-maintenance. An agent can use the fusion of its perceptions about its environment and its ability to act on the surrounding environment to form strategies to achieve specific goals. These perceptions and actions can be motivated by mentalistic notions such as self-protection and self-healing [7].

5.2 Autonomic Wireless Sensor Network

Autonomic Wireless Sensor Networks (AWSN) [21], constitute a new generation of ubiquitous sensing technology. Such systems are typified by their highly distributed, complex real-time nature together with responsiveness to a dynamic and ever changing environment. We discuss how the portfolio of autonomic characteristics may be achieved within wireless sensor networks, through the deployment of mobile and agile agent-based technologies. In this chapter we aim to show that autonomic properties can be incorporated into distributed, computationally challenged devices typified by processing, power and memory limitations. These hardware elements have varying degrees of memory, processing and energy capacity, as well as a variety of transmission ranges. Typical of the sensor hardware that we consider are the Berkley Motes (Fig. 9), which have extremely limited resources. While they can support simple agents, they are not capable of running fully deliberative autonomic agents.

We discuss how a portfolio of autonomic characteristics may be achieved within wireless sensor networks, through the deployment of mobile and agile agent-based technologies. Every node needs to both cooperate and coordinate with the system in order to function correctly and efficiently. Utilizing the distributed and intelligent nature of agents together with their mobility, autonomic properties can be brought to distributed devices such as wireless sensor networks.

Each node in a WSN has a need for discrete and unconscious maintenance. Failure in any part of the network should be dealt with without requiring the involvement of every node. It is the necessity for such system reactions to unexpected and unforeseen events such as failure that acts as the catalyst for autonomic wireless sensor networks.

It is thus clear that instilling a WSN and its nodes with autonomic properties is not only valuable but also vital in order to work with such large and dynamic systems. System self-management using an autonomic and multi-agent based approach is we believe the most appropriate means for administrating such large, complex,dynamic and distributed systems reliably and efficiently.

5.3 μAgentFactory

AgentFactory (AF) began its development journey as a SmallTalk implementation. Following this a Java-based version was developed. Since this was written in Java it was executable on any machine capable of running a JVM. Today we have devices so small, both physically and computationally that the mere thought of having a JVM hosted on them is ridiculous. Even Suns recent effort to shrink the JVM to a Micro Edition has proved ineffective for certain devices.

In order to port AF to a device incapable of hosting a JVM we began to look at various devices and possible ways of implementing AF on them. For our purposes we selected the Mica2 platform developed at University of California, Berkeley. See Fig. 9 for a picture of this platform.

These devices have both a wireless communication capability and the ability to execute user defined programs. The programs must fit into 128K of instruction memory and 4K of variable memory. Various sensor boards can be attached to this platform. They mate with it through the long white rectangular connector on the side of the board. Such boards can contain sensors for light, heat, sound, humidity and acceleration. There is also an expansion board that allows users to design their own sensors and attach them to the board. Indeed we have successfully created programs that use chemical sensors which are an extension to the basic sensor suite.

When endeavoring to port a large framework like AF it is important to adopt an incremental porting strategy. Embedded systems, like the Motes, are by their nature notoriously difficult to program and debug. With this in mind, we began

Fig. 9. Mica2 Mote Platform.

to look at the kernel functionality of AF and made an attempt at porting it. At the heart of each agent execution lies a central process called the Agent Deliberative Cycle, which is fundamental to the behavior of our agents and was the starting point for the porting of Agent Factory. The Agent Deliberative Cycle consists of 4 basic stages:

1. *Perceive* – All the agents preceptors sense their environment through their perceptors and the agents mental state is updated to reflect the new state of the agents environmental perception.
2. *Deliberate* – Based on the behavior of the agent and its new perception the deliberation involves identification of those actuators that will need to be activated in the next stage.
3. *Actuate* – All the actuators that need to be activated are now set in motion.
4. *Pause* – The thread of execution for the agent is paused for a predefined time and the whole cycle begins again.

This cycle has been implemented on the WSN nodes. In order to demonstrate this, we characterize the behavior through a small example illustrating what happens at each stage within the cycle.

1. *Perceive* – The temperature sensor is read
2. *Deliberate* – If (*temperature > threshold*) then commit to transmit value to base station
3. *Actuate* – Transmit *temperature* to base station[1]
4. *Pause* – The agent pauses for 2 seconds

In this case the AF-APL syntax for this behavior would be defined in the following Commitment Rules (Fig. 10). A detailed discussion of Agent Factory was provided earlier.

This small example details a program that will only transmit to the base station if the temperature exceeds a certain threshold. Thus the base station will not be flooded with many Motes reporting values when there is no significant change in the sensed value. To demonstrate a more complicated version of this, we developed an agent-based intrusion detection system on the Motes. This used a drop in light levels as an indication that a person had entered the room. Details of this experiment are presented elsewhere [21].

```
1. BELIEF(temp(?x)) ⇒
   COMMIT(Self, Now, BELIEF(true), thresholdExceeded(?x));
2. BELIEF(thresholdIsExceeded(?temp)) ⇒
   COMMIT(Self, Now, BELIEF(true), sendToBase(?temp));
```

Fig. 10. AF-APL syntax for simple agent.

---

[1] This will only be accomplished if the previous stage deems it necessary to transmit i.e. *temperature > threshold*.

So how could this be implemented on the Motes? The Mica Motes are programmed in nesC and use TinyOS [35] for their program execution model. The first step is the perception of the temperature sensor. A request is sent to the ADC to sample temperature. On return the ADC gives a value in the range 0 to 1023.[2] Using a predefined conversion formula, the temperature is given in degrees Celsius. This in effect causes the adoption of the following belief:

```
BELIEF(temp(25))
```

This is then matched to the left hand side of rule 1 in Fig. 10. Now in our deliberate cycle we call the actuator `temperatureExceeded`, which will cause the agent to adopt a belief that the threshold has been breached if in fact this is the case. This will happen at the end of this current cycle and the agent will pause. On the next cycle the agent will have:

```
BELIEF(thresholdIsExceeded(25))
```

So the agent will commit to calling the `sendToBase(25)` actuator, which will inform the base station of the temperature. The actual representation of the beliefs of the agent is represented in bytecodes for which we have implemented an interpreter. A bytecode interpreter already exists for the Motes [19] but we felt it would be more efficient to implement our own version tailored to our specific needs.

Using bytecodes has one great advantage that we are currently exploring, namely agent mobility. Bytecodes could encapsulate an agents mental state and be sent to a remote node for incarnation. An interesting corollary to this could be the investigation of the possibility of migrating an agent off the Mote network and into a Java environment.

Looking to the future we are keen to investigate the migration of a μAgent-Factory Agent across the whole sensor network for example to perform simple data aggregation. We are also currently experimenting with mechanisms to implement fully deliberative agents.

6   Conclusions

This chapter has advocated the adoption of agile mobile intentional agents as the instrument of choice for the effective delivery of ambient intelligence. Such systems by virtue of their complexity, dynamics, distribution and fault tolerance need to be empowered with intelligence and autonomic capabilities.

We have described the Agent Factory environment together with the nature of the agents fabricated and the tool and methodological support for this process. We have furthermore illustrated, through three case studies, how such a development metaphor can be used to deliver ambient intelligence systems.

Ambient intelligence systems of the future will exhibit all of the functional characteristics contained within these three case studies and more and will typi-

---

[2] It is a 10 bit ADC.

cally necessitate interoperable agents that can migrate from subsystem to subsystem. Agents provide the necessary apparatus to manage such system complexity. Our on-going research is seeking to install a myriad of challenged devices within the real-world environment, which can host agents of varying form and complexity in order to monitor and respond to the needs of the public moving through that environment.

Acknowledgements

This material is based, in part, upon works supported by Science Foundation Ireland (SFI) through Grant No. 03/IN.3/1361. We gratefully acknowledge this support. Michael O'Grady gratefully acknowledges the support of the Irish Research Council for Science, Engineering and Technology (IRCSET) through the Embark Post-Doctoral award.

References

1. Bantz, D. F., Bisdikian, C., Challener, D., Karidis, J. P., Mastrianni, S., Mohindra, A., Shea, D.G., Vanover, M.,. Autonomic Personal Computing. IBM Systems Journal, Volume 42, Issue 1. IBM Technical Journals, Yorktown Heights, NY, USA (2003).
2. Bellotti , F. Berta, R., De Gloria, A., Margarone, M.: User Testing a Hypermedia Tour Guide, Pervasive Computing, 1(2), pp 33-41, (2002).
3. Collier., R., Agent Factory: A Framework for the Engineering of Agent-Oriented Applications, PhD Thesis, Dept. Computer Science, University College Dublin, (2001).
4. Collier,R., O'Hare, G. M. P. Lowen, T. D., and Rooney, C. F. B., Beyond Prototyping in the Factory of Agents, In Proc. 3rd Int. Central and Eastern European Conference on Multi-Agent Systems (CEEMAS), Prague, Czech Republic, (2003).
5. Collier, R., O'Hare, G., Rooney, C.: A UML-based Software Engineering Methodology for Agent Factory. In: Proc. 16th Int. Conf. on Software Engineering and Knowledge Engineering (SEKE), Banff, Alberta, Canada, (2004).
6. Dastani, M., van Riensdijk, B., Dignum, F., Meyer, J.J., A programming language for cognitive agents: Goal directed 3APL, In: Proc. AAMAS2003, Melbourne, Australia, (2003).
7. Diao, Y., Hellerstein, J. L., Parekh, S., Bigus, J. P. Managing Web Server Performance with AutoTune Agents. IBM Systems Journal, Volume 42, Issue 1. IBM Technical Journals, Yorktown Heights, NY, USA, (2003).
8. http://www.ferrosi.com/products.htm – Ferro Solutions' Energy Harvester Product.
9. FIPA, The FIPA 2000 Specifications, FIPA Website URL: http://www.fipa.org, (2000)
10. Hill, J. System Architecture for Wireless Sensor Networks. PhD Thesis, University of California, Berkeley, (2003).
11. Horn, P., Autonomic Computing: IBM's Perspective on the State of Information Technology. IBM Corporation, (2001).
   http://www.research.ibm.com/autonomic/manifesto/autonomic_computing.pdf

12. Howard, J. A., Sheth, J. N..: The Theory of Buyer Behavior. New York, John Wiley & Sons, Inc., (1969).
13. Keegan, K. & O'Hare, G.M.P. EasiShop: Context sensitive Shopping for the Mobile User through Mobile Agent Technology, Proceedings of PIMRC 2002 13th IEEE International Symposium on Personal Indoor and Mobile Radio Communications, IEEE Press. Sept. 15th-18th, Lisbon, Portugal, (2002).
14. Keegan, S. and O'Hare, G.M.P., Easishop: Enabling uCommerce through Intelligent Mobile Agent Technologies, Proceedings of 5th International Workshop on Mobile Agents for Telecommunication Applications (MATA'03), Marrakesh, Morocco, October 8th-10th, 2003, Springer-Verlag LNCS, (2003).
15. Keegan, S, O'Hare, G.M.P.: EasiShop – Agent-Based Cross Merchant Product Comparison Shopping for the Mobile User. In: Proc. of 1st Int. Conf. on Information & Communication Technologies: From Theory to Applications (ICTTA '04), Damascus, Syria, (2004).
16. Kephart, J.O., Chess, D.M.,.The Vision of Autonomic Computing. IEEE Computer Magazine. Volume 36, Issue 1. Pages: 41-50. IEEE Computer Society Press Los Alamitos, CA, USA. (2003).
17. Kourouthanasis, P., Spinellis, D., Roussos, G., Giaglis, G.: Intelligent cokes and diapers: MyGrocer ubiquitous computing environment. In: Proc. 1st Int. Mobile Business Conf., 150-172, (2002).
18. Krulwich, B., The Bargainfinder Agent: Comparison Price Shopping On The Internet, in Bots, and other Internet Beasties, J. Williams, Ed., pp. 257-263. Macmillan Computer Publishing (1996).
19. Levis, P. & Culler, D., Architectural Support for Programming Languages and Operating Systems archive, Proceedings of the 10th International conference on Architectural support for programming languages and operating systems table of contents, San Jose, California pp: 85–95 ACM Press, (2002).
20. Li, H. & Lal, A., Blanchard J. & Henderson, D., Self-Reciprocating Radioisotope-Powered Cantilever, Journal of Applied Physics Vol. 92, No. 2, pp. 1122-1127, American Institute of Physics, (2002).
21. Marsh, D., Tynan, R., O'Kane, D. & O'Hare, G.M.P., Autonomic Wireless Sensor Networks, Engineering Applications of Artificial Intelligence Journal, Elsevier Science, (In Press), (2004).
22. Milgrom, P.R. and Weber, R.J., A Theory of Auctions and Competitive Bidding, Econometrica, Vol. 50 (5), pp. 1089-1122. Econometric Society (1982).
23. O'Grady, M.J., O'Hare, G.M.P.: Accessing Cultural Tourist Information via a Context Sensitive Tourist Guide, Information Technology and Tourism Journal, 5(1), 2002, 35-47. Cognizant Publishers, NY,(2002).
24. O'Grady, M.J. & O'Hare, G.M.P., Mobile Devices & Intelligent Agents-Towards a New Generation of Applications and Services, Special Issue on Intelligent Embedded Agents, Journal of Information Sciences, Elsevier Press, (2004).
25. O'Grady, M.J., & O'Hare G.M.P., Gullivers's Genie: Agency, Mobility & Adaptivity, Computers & Graphics Journal, Special Issue on Pervasive Computing and Ambient Intelligence – Mobility, Ubiquity and Wearables Get Together., Elsevier Science, Vol 28, No. 4, (2004).
26. O'Grady, M. J. and O'Hare, G. M. P. Just-In-Time Multimedia Distribution in a Mobile Computing Environment, IEEE Multimedia (forthcoming), (2004).
27. O'Hare G.M.P., Agent Factory: An Environment for the Fabrication of Multi-Agent Systems, in Foundations of Distributed Artificial Intelligence (G.M.P. O'Hare and N. Jennings eds) pp449-484, John Wiley and Sons, Inc., (1996).

28. O'Hare, G.M.P., Duffy, B.R., Collier, R.W, Rooney, C.F.B., O'Donoghue, R.P.S., Agent Factory: Towards Social Robots, Proc. First International Workshop of Central and Eastern Europe on Multi-Agent Systems (CEEMAS'99), St.Petersburg, Russia, (1999).

29. O'Hare, G. M. P., O'Grady, M. J.: Gulliver's Genie: A Multi-Agent System for Ubiquitous and Intelligent Content Delivery, Computer Communications, 26 (11), 1177-1187, (2003).

30. Poslad, S., Laamanen, H., Malaka, R. Nick, A., Buckle, P., Zipf, A.: CRUMPET: Creation of User-friendly Mobile Services Personalised For Tourism. Proceedings of the 2nd International Conference on 3G Mobile Communication Technologies, London, UK, (2001).

31. Qi, H.,Kuruganti P. T.& Yingyue Xu, Y.,: The Development of Localized Algorithms in Wireless Sensor Networks, Sensors, Vol. 2,, pp. 286-293, July (2002).

32. Rao, A., AgentSpeak(L): BDI Agents speak out in a logical computable language, in Proceeding of the 7th International Workshop on Modelling Autonomous Agents in a Multi-Agent World (de Velde, W. Va;Perram, J. W eds) , Eindhoven, The Netherlands, January 22-25 1996. LNAI 1038. Springer Verlag, (1996).

33. Rooney, C.F.B., Collier, R.W., O'Hare., G.M.P., VIPER: Visual protocol editor, in Proceedings of COORDINATION 2004, Pisa, Italy (2004)

34. Ross, R., Collier, R., O'Hare, G.M.P, AF-APL Bridging Principles & Practice in Agent-Oriented Languages, Proceedings of the 2nd International Workshop on Programming Multi-Agent Systems Languages and Tools (PROMAS-2004), New York, 19-20th July, Workshop at Third International Joint Conference on Autonomous Agents and Multi Agent Systems(AAMAS04), Columbia University, New York, 20th, July 2004. Lecture Notes in Computer Science (LNCS), Springer Verlag Publishers, (2004).

35. http://www.tinyos.net/support.html

36. United Nations Standard Products and Services Code: http://www.unspsc.org.

37. Wooldridge, M., Practical Reasoning with Procedural Knowledge: A Logic of BDI Agents with Know-How, in Proceedings of the International Conference on Formal and Applied Practical Reasoning, (D. M. Gabbay and H.-J. Ohlbach, eds), Springer-Verlag, (1996).

38. Wooldridge M. and Jennings N., Agent theories, architectures, and languages. In Wooldridge and Jennings, editors, Intelligent Agents, pages 1–22. Springer-Verlag, (1995).

39. http://www.bluez.org

Author Index

Lecture Notes in Artificial Intelligence (LNAI)

Vol. 3120: J. Shawe-Taylor, Y. Singer (Eds.), Learning Theory. X, 648 pages. 2004.

Vol. 3097: D. Basin, M. Rusinowitch (Eds.), Automated Reasoning. XII, 493 pages. 2004.

Vol. 3071: A. Omicini, P. Petta, J. Pitt (Eds.), Engineering Societies in the Agents World. XIII, 409 pages. 2004.

Vol. 3070: L. Rutkowski, J. Siekmann, R. Tadeusiewicz, L.A. Zadeh (Eds.), Artificial Intelligence and Soft Computing - ICAISC 2004. XXV, 1208 pages. 2004.

Vol. 3068: E. André, L. Dybkjær, W. Minker, P. Heisterkamp (Eds.), Affective Dialogue Systems. XII, 324 pages. 2004.

Vol. 3067: M. Dastani, J. Dix, A. El Fallah-Seghrouchni (Eds.), Programming Multi-Agent Systems. X, 221 pages. 2004.

Vol. 3066: S. Tsumoto, R. Słowiński, J. Komorowski, J.W. Grzymała-Busse (Eds.), Rough Sets and Current Trends in Computing. XX, 853 pages. 2004.

Vol. 3065: A. Lomuscio, D. Nute (Eds.), Deontic Logic in Computer Science. X, 275 pages. 2004.

Vol. 3060: A.Y. Tawfik, S.D. Goodwin (Eds.), Advances in Artificial Intelligence. XIII, 582 pages. 2004.

Vol. 3056: H. Dai, R. Srikant, C. Zhang (Eds.), Advances in Knowledge Discovery and Data Mining. XIX, 713 pages. 2004.

Vol. 3055: H. Christiansen, M.-S. Hacid, T. Andreasen, H.L. Larsen (Eds.), Flexible Query Answering Systems. X, 500 pages. 2004.

Vol. 3048: P. Faratin, D.C. Parkes, J.A. Rodríguez-Aguilar, W.E. Walsh (Eds.), Agent-Mediated Electronic Commerce V. XI, 155 pages. 2004.

Vol. 3040: R. Conejo, M. Urretavizcaya, J.-L. Pérez-de-la-Cruz (Eds.), Current Topics in Artificial Intelligence. XIV, 689 pages. 2004.

Vol. 3035: M.A. Wimmer (Ed.), Knowledge Management in Electronic Government. XII, 326 pages. 2004.

Vol. 3034: J. Favela, E. Menasalvas, E. Chávez (Eds.), Advances in Web Intelligence. XIII, 227 pages. 2004.

Vol. 3030: P. Giorgini, B. Henderson-Sellers, M. Winikoff (Eds.), Agent-Oriented Information Systems. XIV, 207 pages. 2004.

Vol. 3029: B. Orchard, C. Yang, M. Ali (Eds.), Innovations in Applied Artificial Intelligence. XXI, 1272 pages. 2004.

Vol. 3025: G.A. Vouros, T. Panayiotopoulos (Eds.), Methods and Applications of Artificial Intelligence. XV, 546 pages. 2004.

Vol. 3020: D. Polani, B. Browning, A. Bonarini, K. Yoshida (Eds.), RoboCup 2003: Robot Soccer World Cup VII. XVI, 767 pages. 2004.

Vol. 3012: K. Kurumatani, S.-H. Chen, A. Ohuchi (Eds.), Multi-Agents for Mass User Support. X, 217 pages. 2004.

Vol. 3010: K.R. Apt, F. Fages, F. Rossi, P. Szeredi, J. Váncza (Eds.), Recent Advances in Constraints. VIII, 285 pages. 2004.

Vol. 2990: J. Leite, A. Omicini, L. Sterling, P. Torroni (Eds.), Declarative Agent Languages and Technologies. XII, 281 pages. 2004.

Vol. 2980: A. Blackwell, K. Marriott, A. Shimojima (Eds.), Diagrammatic Representation and Inference. XV, 448 pages. 2004.

Vol. 2977: G. Di Marzo Serugendo, A. Karageorgos, O.F. Rana, F. Zambonelli (Eds.), Engineering Self-Organising Systems. X, 299 pages. 2004.

Vol. 2972: R. Monroy, G. Arroyo-Figueroa, L.E. Sucar, H. Sossa (Eds.), MICAI 2004: Advances in Artificial Intelligence. XVII, 923 pages. 2004.

Vol. 2969: M. Nickles, M. Rovatsos, G. Weiss (Eds.), Agents and Computational Autonomy. X, 275 pages. 2004.

Vol. 2961: P. Eklund (Ed.), Concept Lattices. IX, 411 pages. 2004.

Vol. 2953: K. Konrad, Model Generation for Natural Language Interpretation and Analysis. XIII, 166 pages. 2004.

Vol. 2934: G. Lindemann, D. Moldt, M. Paolucci (Eds.), Regulated Agent-Based Social Systems. X, 301 pages. 2004.

Vol. 2930: F. Winkler (Ed.), Automated Deduction in Geometry. VII, 231 pages. 2004.

Vol. 2926: L. van Elst, V. Dignum, A. Abecker (Eds.), Agent-Mediated Knowledge Management. XI, 428 pages. 2004.

Vol. 2923: V. Lifschitz, I. Niemelä (Eds.), Logic Programming and Nonmonotonic Reasoning. IX, 365 pages. 2003.

Vol. 2915: A. Camurri, G. Volpe (Eds.), Gesture-Based Communication in Human-Computer Interaction. XIII, 558 pages. 2004.

Vol. 2913: T.M. Pinkston, V.K. Prasanna (Eds.), High Performance Computing - HiPC 2003. XX, 512 pages. 2003.

Vol. 2903: T.D. Gedeon, L.C.C. Fung (Eds.), AI 2003: Advances in Artificial Intelligence. XVI, 1075 pages. 2003.

Vol. 2902: F.M. Pires, S.P. Abreu (Eds.), Progress in Artificial Intelligence. XV, 504 pages. 2003.

Vol. 2892: F. Dau, The Logic System of Concept Graphs with Negation. XI, 213 pages. 2003.

Vol. 2891: J. Lee, M. Barley (Eds.), Intelligent Agents and Multi-Agent Systems. X, 215 pages. 2003.

Vol. 2882: D. Veit, Matchmaking in Electronic Markets. XV, 180 pages. 2003.

Vol. 2872: G. Moro, C. Sartori, M.P. Singh (Eds.), Agents and Peer-to-Peer Computing. XII, 205 pages. 2004.

Vol. 2871: N. Zhong, Z.W. Raś, S. Tsumoto, E. Suzuki (Eds.), Foundations of Intelligent Systems. XV, 697 pages. 2003.

Vol. 2854: J. Hoffmann, Utilizing Problem Structure in Planing. XIII, 251 pages. 2003.

Vol. 2843: G. Grieser, Y. Tanaka, A. Yamamoto (Eds.), Discovery Science. XII, 504 pages. 2003.

Vol. 2842: R. Gavaldá, K.P. Jantke, E. Takimoto (Eds.), Algorithmic Learning Theory. XI, 313 pages. 2003.

Vol. 2838: N. Lavrač, D. Gamberger, L. Todorovski, H. Blockeel (Eds.), Knowledge Discovery in Databases: PKDD 2003. XVI, 508 pages. 2003.

Vol. 2837: N. Lavrač, D. Gamberger, L. Todorovski, H. Blockeel (Eds.), Machine Learning: ECML 2003. XVI, 504 pages. 2003.